Economic Development in the Soviet Union and Eastern Europe, Volume 2

edited by
Zbigniew M. Fallenbuchl

The third of eight volumes of papers from the first international conference sponsored by the American Association for the Advancement of Slavic Studies, British National Association for Soviet and East European Studies, British Universities Association of Slavists, and Canadian Association of Slavists.

General Editor: Roger E. Kanet

The Praeger Special Studies program—utilizing the most modern and efficient book production techniques and a selective worldwide distribution network—makes available to the academic, government, and business communities significant, timely research in U.S. and international economic, social, and political development.

Economic Development in the Soviet Union and Eastern Europe, Volume 2

Sectoral Analysis

PRAEGER SPECIAL STUDIES IN INTERNATIONAL POLITICS AND GOVERNMENT

Praeger Publishers   New York   Washington   London

330.947
I 6 1
v. 2

Library of Congress Cataloging in Publication Data

International Slavic Conference, 1st, Banff, Alta., 1974.
    Economic development in the Soviet Union and Eastern Europe.

    (Praeger special studies in international politics and government)
    Includes bibliographical references and indexes.
    CONTENTS: v. 1. Reforms, technology, and income distribu-
tion. —v. 2. Sectoral analysis.
    1. Europe, Eastern—Economic conditions—Congresses.
2. Russia—Economic conditions—1965-   —Congresses.
I. Fallenbuchl, Zbigniew M. II. American Association for the
Advancement of Slavic Studies. III. Title.
HC244.I5293 1974   330.9'47'085   75-19780
ISBN 0-275-56150-X (v. 1)
ISBN 0-275-56160-7 (v. 2)

PRAEGER PUBLISHERS
111 Fourth Avenue, New York, N.Y. 10003, U.S.A.

Published in the United States of America in 1976
by Praeger Publishers, Inc.

Printed in the United States of America

GENERAL EDITOR'S FOREWORD

Roger E. Kanet

The studies published in this volume are selected from among those presented at the First International Slavic Conference, held in Banff, Alberta, Canada, September 4-7, 1974. The conference, which was attended by approximately 1,500 persons, was sponsored by the American Association for the Advancement of Slavic Studies, the British Universities Association of Slavists, the British National Association for Soviet and East Europe Studies, and the Canadian Association of Slavists. Although the sponsorship of the conference was limited to the four major English-speaking Slavic associations, attendance and participation was much broader and included numerous scholars from continental Western Europe, Asia, Africa, Latin America, and Oceania. In addition, a substantial number of scholars from the Soviet Union and Eastern Europe participated in the deliberations of the conference.

Among the more than 250 papers presented at the international conference, a relatively large number have been selected for publication in two series of conference volumes. Papers in the social sciences are included in the series of volumes being published by Praeger Publishers of New York and those in the humanities are appearing in the series of books being published by Slavica Publishers of Cambridge, Massachusetts.

As general editor of both the Praeger and Slavica series of Banff publications, I wish to express my sincere appreciation to all of those individuals and institutions who made the conference possible. This includes the numerous government and private organizations that provided financial assistance, the members of the International Planning Committee who prepared the conference, and the participants themselves. Finally, I wish to thank the editors of the individual volumes in the two series and the authors of the papers for their major contributions to the preparation of these volumes.

CONTENTS

LIST OF TABLES AND FIGURES

INTRODUCTION
Zbigniew M. Fallenbuchl

The first of the two volumes of this collection of the Banff Conference economics papers deals with reforms, scientific and technological progress, and income distribution. This volume presents the analysis of recent developments in industry and foreign trade, agriculture, and in the sector that traditionally belongs to public finance. Some of the most currently important topics are covered and several contributions to this volume truly belong to the "frontier of knowledge" type of research.

The deceleration of industrial growth in the Soviet Union and Eastern Europe was, undoubtedly, an important factor behind the wave of economic reforms of the second half of the 1960s. Its explanation is one of the most controversial topics among Western specialists. The first chapter in Part I represents a new approach to the problem and arrives at some most interesting conclusions. Equally important is the problem of the industrial structure that has been created as the result of an investment policy based on some clearly defined priorities. Chapter 2 discusses the implications of the investment policy in the Soviet Union which, of course, has also been applied in Eastern Europe. Again, this topic is a subject of considerable controversy among Western specialists. Because of the pioneering nature of these two excellent studies, they are supplemented by critical comments of an economist who himself has worked in this field for some years. Chapter 3 deals with the location of industrial plants, a topic closely connected with the objectives of growth and efficiency, as well as with various, often conflicting, political, strategic, and social goals. The system of incentives, including greater utilization of profit, is one of the main pillars of the New Economic Mechanism in Hungary, which represents the boldest attempt to reorganize a Soviet-type economy in Eastern Europe. Certain problems that were created, among others in the field of income distribution and monopolistic or oligopolistic power, are discussed in Volume I. Here, in Chapter 4, a survey of policy changes since the introduction of the great experiment is presented in a concise manner. The last two chapters in Part I deal with growth and structural change in foreign trade with reference to the Soviet Union since the end of the postwar reconstruction and Hungary since the introduction of the reform. This is a topic closely connected with economic reforms, the quest for increased efficiency and attempts to accelerate technological progress.

Agriculture has been traditionally a weak spot of all Soviet-type economies. In the past this sector was seriously neglected, and during some periods even ruthlessly exploited, sacrificed in the name of doctrinal and political objectives and did not enjoy even a fraction of the prestige that was attached to the manufacturing industry, particularly heavy industry. Although discrimination against the rural population has not yet been completely removed, the importance of agriculture has now been rediscovered. Not only a considerable volume of resources is directed to this sector but also some interesting changes appear in its organizational structure. The first chapter in Part II (Chapter 7) provides a solid, detailed, and well-researched introduction to the analysis of recent development in Soviet agriculture. It is followed by the examination of the two currently most important problems: the development of the agrarian-industrial complexes and the expansion of the feed-livestock sector. Chapters 10 and 11 examine the performance of Soviet agriculture. Chapter 10 compares Soviet agricultural productivity with the performance of the U.S. agriculture, Chapter 11 compares one of the western Soviet republics, Belorussia, with two eastern wojewodztwa (provinces) in Poland. The analysis of developments in the Soviet Union is supplemented in Chapters 12 and 13 by a study of recent changes in the organizational structure in Bulgaria, Czechoslovakia, East Germany, Hungary, and Romania and an examination of the performance of Hungarian agriculture since the introduction of the New Economic Mechanism.

The discussion of topics in Soviet public finance is preceded by a brief introduction provided by the organizer and chairman of the session at which the papers of the third section were presented. The main theme of Part III is the conflict among various goals, the problem that has been at the center of the discussion presented in Volume I and in the other two sections of this volume. The studies deal with some important issues: the use of public land, recent financial reforms, and the production and consumption of alcohol and control of alcoholism. These are topics that are rarely discussed by Western scholars and the studies presented here represent a significant contribution to the study of the Soviet economy.

The editor wishes to express his thanks to the authors for their cooperation and to those colleagues who organized various sessions of the Banff Conference at which these studies were originally presented. They selected the authors and, in many cases, the topics. The contribution of the three secretaries of the Department of Economics at the University of Windsor—Mrs. Pat Dowling, Miss Maureen Meloche, and Mrs. Marilyn Stewart—to the editing of this volume is acknowledged with thanks.

I

INDUSTRY AND
FOREIGN TRADE

SOVIET POSTWAR INDUSTRIAL GROWTH, CAPITAL-LABOR SUBSTITUTION, AND TECHNICAL CHANGES: A REEXAMINATION

Stanislaw Gomulka

Over the recent years a broad concensus has been reached that whatever the origin of the data, Soviet or Western, the Soviet Union has experienced a major retardation in the postwar growth of its industrial output without a slowdown of the same magnitude in the growth of inputs. In the debate on the causes of slowdown several alternative interpretations have been offered. They could be classified into two groups, which are homogenous enough to be regarded as simply two alternative interpretations. One interpretation, which

---

An earlier draft of this chapter was presented to the Banff 1974 International Conference, September 1974, and to Professor Bergson's seminar at Harvard University. Extensive numerical experiments, which proved very helpful in the formulation of the final model of this study, were done by Jerzy Sylwestrowicz from the London School of Economics aided by Joanna Gomulka from the Numerical Optimization Centre (NOC) at the Hatfield Polytechnic. I owe a great deal to their patience and skill. The computer programs used at NOC have been developed by Michael Biggs and John J. McKeown. I am also indebted to Padma Desai for providing me with her man-hours estimate for 1966-71 as well as with her estimates of Soviet industrial data at the branch level. For suggestions, comments, and criticism my thanks are due to many readers of the earlier draft, but especially to Adam Bergson, Stanley Cohn, Philip Hanson, Raymond Hutchings, Oldrych Kyn, Judith Thornton, Martin Weitzman, Peter Wiles, and Alfred Zauberman. I am also indebted to Peter Wiles and Raymond Hutchings for their invitation to write this paper for the Banff conference and for subsequent encouragement.

I shall call the standard explanation (Balassa, Bergson, Brubaker, Kaplan, Moorsteen and Powell, Noren, and others), assumes that capital's (imputed) share in output was essentially constant over time and stresses the notion that except for the period 1954-58 the growth rate of technical progress, or the so-called productivity residual, was gradually declining.[1] In contrast, the other explanation (Weitzman, Desai, and others) suggests that the Soviet growth record is adequately accounted for by the productivity residual constant over time and the elasticity of capital-labor substitution significantly less than one, the combination implying a sharp decline in the (imputed) capital share.[2]

Within the standard approach the following are thought to be the primary reasons for decreased growth in the productivity residual: (1) diminishing decline in the average age of capital goods during the 1950s,[3] (2) decline in organizational efficiency, especially in the post-1958 period, because of increased complexity of resource allocation,[4] (3) postwar recovery from wartime disruption in the period 1947-55,[5] (4) change in the structure of production more favorable to growth in the 1950s,[6] (5) decline in the rate of increase in the educational attainment of the labor force,[7] (6) increased difficulty to allocate resources efficiently within almost unchanged institutional arrangements.[8]

However, with one exception the standard approach has largely failed to offer any quantitative estimate of the above-listed potentially contributing factors.[9] Consequently, it has failed to identify the relative importance of these factors and thereby the exact causes of growth retardation. Being a qualitative statement rather than a quantitative one, the standard explanation is also not very helpful in making judgments concerning future Soviet industrial growth performance.

In contrast, Weitzman's challenge offered not only an alternative, but also a more rigorous approach. His emphasis on low elasticity of substitution as the most likely factor contributing to slowdown generated a wide interest in estimating various CES (constant elasticity of substitution) and VES (variable elasticity of substitution) production functions for the Soviet industry as a whole as well as for its individual industrial branches. Although the results vary widely in terms of the estimated parameters, they largely tend to support Weitzman's major hypothesis that in Soviet industry of the post-1950 period the productivity residual was stable over time and that the (imputed) capital share was instead sharply declining.

Yet, I shall argue in this study that Weitzman's hypothesis is incorrect. But first an attempt will be made to show that in the debate on Soviet postwar industrial growth certain important properties of the labor productivity data have been overlooked and, consequently, the technical progress terms in the production functions estimated

were misspecified in a manner that crucially affected the estimation
results as well as the implied interpretations. And this applies
especially to the Weitzman-type interpretation. Second, a distinctly
new economic interpretation of slowdown will be developed. It will
be based on a new specification of the technical progress terms. This
new specification attempts to capture the growth effects of several
phenomena that were so far either ignored (Weitzman, Desai) or only
verbally mentioned as potentially relevant (the standard approach).
Two such phenomena appear to have been of critical importance:
(a) the postwar recovery trend in technical progress (also known as
the catch-up phenomenon) and (b) a 20 percent reduction in the annual
number of working hours per man in the period 1956-61. The growth
effects of these two phenomena are estimated and their prominent
role in the postwar industrial growth scenario discussed. Also
estimated are growth effects of changes in the branch composition
of production, in the age composition of fixed capital, and in the
"subvintage composition" of investments. All these three growth
effects are found to be comparatively much less significant than (a)
and (b).

The major findings of this study are as follows: (1) When the
growth effects (a) and (b) are taken into account, then the Soviet
industrial growth record is adequately explained by a CES production
function with technical progress of predominantly Harrod-neutral
type; (2) The growth rate of technical progress was a sum of three
components. Two of these components, associated with phenomena
(a) and (b) respectively, were variable over time and transitory.
They were superimposed on a third, constant term, equal to about
4.2 percent, which is associated with a long-run trend in technical
progress; (3) The error sum of squares is found to be almost insensitive to changes in the value of the elasticity of substitution. This
finding implies that even if the actual elasticity of substitution was
low it is not likely that it has been a cause, all the more a main
cause, of the Soviet growth slowdown.

Finding (2), in particular the fact that the assumption of constant
long-run term in the residual is found consistent with data, seems to
be in variance with the notion of long-run downward trend in Soviet
economic efficiency, although the latter might well have been low all
along. On the other hand, findings (1) and (3) are in variance with
Weitzman's hypothesis that serious difficulties in substituting capital
for labor have been the main cause of the Soviet growth slowdown.
Moreover, finding (1) combined with a moderate increase in the
Soviet industrial capital/output ratio implies the (imputed) capital
share to be almost constant over time, irrespective of the value of
the capital-labor elasticity of substitution. This result supports the
basic assumption of the traditional school. All the findings imply, and

this is the central hypothesis of this study, that instead of either low
magnitude of the elasticity of substitution or a decline in economic
efficiency, and apart from the effect of some decline in the growth
rate of labor and capital, the variable components of technical
progress associated with phenomena (a) and (b) have probably alone
been responsible for slowdown in the output growth.

Finally, it may be recalled that Weitzman's interpretation
implied that the Soviet growth slowdown would continue in the future
until the growth rate of output decreases to about 2 percent plus the
growth rate of employment (in man-hours). In contrast, our interpretation, which is based on the same data, implies that already
since about 1970 the growth rate of output has been close to its long-
run equilibrium level, and that this level is about 6 percent plus the
growth rate of employment (also in man-hours). The difference of
4 percent in the limit growth rate of output is so high that it should
soon become clear which of these two alternative interpretations
stands unmistakably better against the test of actual growth performance.

Concluding this introduction, it should be emphasized that
despite the fact that our interpretation appears to be both significantly
better in terms of the explanatory power and free of unreasonable
economic implications, this chapter is not an attempt to set forth
definitive conclusions about the factors underlying the retardation
in growth. The margin of error that still remains present, weak
theoretical underpinnings of the aggregate production function and
unavoidable pitfalls of the estimation techniques, cannot simply allow
for this. Therefore other interpretations, and in particular interpretations of the Weitzman-type, cannot as yet, and indeed may never,
be ruled out completely.

PRESENTATION OF BASIC DATA AND THEIR
PRELIMINARY INTERPRETATION

The basic facts of Soviet industrial growth are given in Table
1.1.[10] However, it will prove useful to present these facts also in
the form of several diagrams. The purpose of this presentation is to
see whether a search for a correct specification of the production
function can be helped by revealing the time trends that have under-
lined the growth of Soviet industry in the period 1928-73.

In Figure 1.1, a decline in the growth rate of output is seen to
be fairly systematic, though much more evident in the years 1948-52.
The growth rate of labor (in man-hours) is somewhat irregular, with
a downward trend relatively weak. The growth rate of labor

productivity was in the years 1947-51 extremely high, despite the fact that the capital/output ratio was at that time falling. One inevitably thinks that we see here, in the years 1947-51 at least, an imprint of the extraordinary opportunities for rapid growth operating during the postwar reconstruction period—the so-called catch-up phenomenon.

Figure 1.2 reveals an interesting regularity in the growth rate of output per man-hour. It is seen that rather than a slowdown in this rate there was in fact a jumpdown in 1962 from a high level of about 10 percent, prevailing until 1961, to a level of about 5 percent prevailing since 1962. A slowdown may however be detected in the growth rate of output per worker. The years of rapid growth of output per man-hour are seen more clearly in Figure 1.3. Two observations can be made: (1) the years 1947-61 are exceptional for both the prewar and the postwar growth experience; (2) they follow a six-year period (1941-46) of negative growth of output per man-hour. Also, there appear to be two distinct subperiods of the 1947-61 period—1957-53 and 1954-61. Just from inspection of Figure 1.3 one may be tempted to associate the catch-up effect only with the first of the two subperiods. One thus has to look for a separate explanation of the high growth record in the years 1954-61.

Let us now turn to Figure 1.4. The level of labor productivity, the index of working hours, and the capital/output ratio are all given on the logarithmic scale. The growth rate of these variables is thus given by the slope of the respective curves. The period 1947-73 may now be seen to fall into four separate subperiods: (A) 1947-55, (B) 1956-61, (C) 1962-68, and (D) 1969-73. In 1946 the level of output was equal to about .74 of the 1944 level. In that year the level of output per man-hour was also at the bottom, being just about 0.85 of the 1944 level and about 0.8 of the 1940 level, the latter being despite the fact that the 1946 capital/output ratio was at the level of about 1.25 of the 1940 capital/output ratio. Clearly two powerful phenomena were then operating: war destruction and the postwar major reduction in the production of arms. A switch from war to peace economy needed time, resulting in the fall of both output and labor productivity in 1946. But from 1947 the labor productivity was increasing rapidly, though with a gradually declining rate of growth as the distance to the long-run trend was diminishing. In period (B) there was, however, a significant increase in this growth rate. This is the same period of six years when the annual number of working hours per man was being reduced at the average annual rate of about 3.6 percent. My reading of Figure 1.4 is that the policy in period (B) was to keep the old tempo of gains in the productivity per man rather than per man-hour. An increased labor efficiency was needed

TABLE 1.1

Basic Facts of Soviet Industrial Growth, 1928-73

Year	Global Product (index) X	Growth of Global Product g_x^a	Value Added (index) Y(1)	Growth of Value Added $g_y^a(1)$	Value Added (billion 1955 rubles) Y(2)	Gross Investment (billion 1955 rubles) I	Capital Stock (billion 1955 rubles) K	Growth of Capital Stock g_k^a	Capital-Output Ratio (index) V	Employment (index) L
	1	2	3	4	5	6	7	8	9	10
1928	8.95				.93	.33				28.33
1929	10.72	19.8			1.12	.42				
1930	13.03	22.1			1.37	.58				
1931	15.81	20.8			1.65	.67				
1932	18.11	14.5			1.89	.75				61.20
1933	19.06	5.2			1.99	.92				
1934	22.73	19.3			2.37	1.00				
1935	27.88	22.7			2.91	1.24				
1936	35.89	28.7			3.74	1.4				
1937	39.90	11.2			4.16	1.6				76.00
1938	44.57	11.7			4.65	1.7				
1939	51.76	16.1			5.40	1.8				
1940	57.80	11.7			6.03	1.8	20.0		124.06	80.39
1941	56.65	- 2.0			5.91	1.1				
1942	44.51	-21.4			4.64	1.5				
1943	53.02	16.9			5.43	1.6				
1944	60.12	15.6			6.27	1.8				70.37
1945	53.18	-11.5			8.04	2.0				69.63
1946	44.51	-16.3			6.73	2.2	19.6b		155.0	71.55
1947	53.76	20.8			8.12	2.6	21.2b	8.2b	138.8	77.29
1948	68.21	26.9			10.31	3.1	23.9b	12.7b	123.3	85.71
1949	81.50	19.5			12.31	3.6	26.00	8.8b	114.16	90.76
1950	100.00	22.7	100.0		15.11	4.2	28.49	9.3	101.87	100.00

Year										
1951	116.76	16.8	115.24	15.2	17.64	5.0	31.62	11.3	98.40	105.96
1952	130.06	11.4	128.39	11.4	19.65	5.6	35.63	12.6	99.51	110.16
1953	145.67	12.0	142.84	11.3	22.01	6.2	39.51	10.9	99.48	115.02
1954	164.74	13.1	161.27	12.9	24.78	6.9	43.90	11.1	97.61	120.79
1955	184.97	12.3	182.03	12.9	27.95	7.7	49.33	12.4	97.18	123.49
1956		10.6	200.10	9.9	30.92	8.2	55.22	11.9	98.96	127.71
1957	225.43	10.2	220.25	10.1	34.06	8.7	60.99	10.5	99.30	131.82
1958	248.56	10.3	245.23	11.3	37.56	10.0	67.68	11.0	98.97	135.87
1959	276.88	11.4	273.20	11.4	41.84	11.8	75.44	11.5	99.02	139.72
1960	302.89	9.4	301.67	10.4	45.77	12.7	84.13	11.5	100.00	147.69
1961	330.62	5.2	330.36	9.6	49.96	13.1	93.88	11.6	101.85	153.30
1962	362.41	9.6	362.90	9.8	54.76	14.0	104.26	11.1	103.04	158.60
1963	391.88	8.1	395.80	9.1	59.21	14.9	116.18	11.4	105.25	163.62
1964	420.78	7.4	427.75	8.1	63.58	16.7	129.82	11.7	108.84	169.30
1965	457.20	8.7	462.75	8.2	69.08	17.7	143.37	10.4	111.09	179.22
1966	497.08	8.7	504.10	8.9	75.11	18.3	156.59	9.2	111.40	186.14
1967	546.79	10.0	553.85	9.9	82.62	19.5	169.72	8.4	109.85	192.28
1968	591.87	8.2	603.05	8.9	89.43	21.3	183.73	7.9	108.89	198.68
1969	634.07	7.1	645.87	7.1	95.81	22.0	197.79	8.0	109.81	203.44
1970	687.82	8.4	700.12	8.4	103.93	24.9	215.37	8.9	110.20	206.25
1971	741.57	7.8	754.73	7.8	112.0	25.9	234.72	9.0	111.20	209.12
1972	788.97	6.4	803.03	6.4	119.2	27.0	256.60[b]	9.3[b]	114.23[b]	211.87
1973	846.88	7.3	861.65	7.3	123.0		278.40[b]	8.5[b]	115.57[b]	214.61

(continued)

(Table 1.1, continued)

	11	12	13	14	15	16	17	18	19	20
Year	Working Hours Per Man (index) h	Labor (in man-hours) L*-hL	Growth of Labor (in man-hours) $g_{L*}^{(1)}$	Growth of Labor (in man-hours) $g_{L*}^{(2)}$	Investment in Industry as Percentage of Total State Investment I/Its	Total State Investment Rate in GNP (index) Its/GNP	Output per Man-hours (index) y*	Trend in Output per Man-hours (index) ytr*	(18)-(17) ytr*-y*	(19)/(18) (y*tr-y*)/y*tr
1928	87.2	24.70					36.25	34.34		
1929								36.40		
1930								38.58		
1931								40.88		
1932							34.41	43.34		
1933								45.94		
1934								48.70		
1935								51.62		
1936								54.72		
1937	84.7	64.37					61.95	58.00		
1938								61.48		
1939								65.97		
1940	92.4	78.90			38.0	100.0	73.26	69.08		
1941								73.23		
1942								77.62		
1943								82.28		
1944	122.0	85.85					70.03	87.22		
1945	112.0	78.04			47.5	107.2	68.18	92.45	24.27	.263
1946	105.0	75.93			43.7	136.7	59.24	98.00	38.76	.395
1947	100.0	77.29	2.9		47.5		69.56	103.88	34.32	.330
1948	100.0	85.71	10.9		46.8		79.58	110.11	30.53	.279
1949	100.0	90.76	5.9		44.4	126.1	89.80	116.72	26.92	.239
1950	100.00	100.00	11.0		44.7	121.2	100.00	123.72	23.72	.192

1951	99.98	105.96	6.0	5.8	47.2	121.8	108.97	131.14	22.17	.169
1952	99.66	109.52	3.4	3.7	47.0	123.3	117.12	139.01	21.89	.157
1953	99.57	114.26	4.3	4.3	49.6	118.0	124.88	147.35	22.47	.132
1954	99.34	119.83	4.9	4.8	47.3	123.0	134.52	156.19	21.67	.139
1955	99.12	122.01	1.8	1.9	47.8	121.1	148.99	165.56	16.57	.100
1956	94.24	120.40	– 1.3	–1.3	44.1	125.6	166.01	175.49	8.48	.059
1957	91.41	120.76	.3	.3	41.2	133.6	182.26	186.01	3.75	.020
1958	90.77	123.33	2.1	2.6	41.8	133.7	197.69	197.17	– .62	–.003
1959	89.27	124.73	1.1	1.5	44.2	139.7	218.90	209.00	– 7.30	–.038
1960	84.34	125.45	.6	– .7	42.3	145.8	241.08	221.54	–19.54	–.088
1961	80.29	123.08	– 1.9	– .5	41.1	145.0	265.4	234.83	–30.5	–.130
1962	80.06	126.98	3.2	3.3	41.2	146.4	282.0	248.32	–33.1	–.133
1963	80.38	131.52	3.6	3.5	41.3	149.4	297.2	263.86	–33.3	–.125
1964	81.02	137.17	4.3	4.2	42.4	143.0	308.9	279.69	–28.4	–.102
1965	81.02	145.20	5.9	4.3	41.5	151.2	319.8	296.47	–23.3	–.075
1966	79.97	148.82	2.5	2.6	40.0	150.1	339.5	314.26	–25.2	–.080
1967	82.62	158.9	6.8	6.8	39.5	149.4	349.4	333.16	–16.5	–.050
1968	85.28	169.4	6.6	6.6	39.8	149.0	355.8	353.15	– 3.7	–.010
1969	84.94	172.8	2.0	1.8	39.4	148.2	394.8	374.34	– .5	–.001
1970	85.28	175.9	1.8	2.0	40.0	155.9	399.5	396.80	– 2.7	–.007
1971	85.70	179.2	1.9	1.8			422.5	420.61	– 1.3	–.005
1972	85.70^b	181.6^b	1.3^b	1.3^b			443.6^b	445.85	2.3^b	.005^b
1973	85.70^b	183.9^b	1.3^b	1.3^b			470.2^b	472.60	2.2.4^b	.005^b

Notes:
Column

1: X global product (index), Soviet estimate.

2: g_X annual percentage rate of growth of global product.

3: Y(1) value added (index), Weitzman "hybrid" index 1950–68, global product index 1969–73.

4: $g_{Y(1)}$ annual percentage rate of growth of value added.

5: Y(2) value added, billion of the 1955 rubles; $Y_L^{(2)} = u \dfrac{X1958}{X1955} Xt$ where u = value added in 1955 (J. Thornton).

6: I gross investment in fixed capital, billion of the 1955 rubles, in industry, Soviet estimate, author's interpolations.

7: K gross fixed capital, billion of the 1955 rubles, Soviet estimate.

8: g_K annual percentage rate of growth of gross fixed capital

9: v capital–output ratio, (index), $v = K/Y^{(1)}$ for 1950–68: $v = K/X$ otherwise.

10: L total industrial employment (index), Soviet estimate.

11: h annual working hours per man (index), Bergson–Weitzman–Desai index.

12: $L^* = hL$ man-hours (index).

13: g(1) annual percentage growth rate of labor, L^* given in column 12.
L^*
(2)

14: g_{L^*} annual percentage rate of growth of labor (in man-hours), Weitzman estimate for 1951–66, Desai estimate for 1968–71.

15: u industrial gross investment in fixed capital as percentage of total state investment in fixed capital.

16: total state investment in fixed capital as proportion of gross national product (material) product (index).

17: y* output per man-hour (index), equal to $Y^{(1)}/L^*$ for 1950–73, and to X/L^* otherwise.

18: y^*_{tr} 6.0 percent growth trend in y*.

b = preliminary.

Sources: Columns 1, 2, 6, 10. Roger A. Clarke, Soviet Economic Facts (London: Macmillan, 1972). These data were compiled from Soviet official publications. They are, therefore, referred to as "Soviet estimates."

Columns 3, 4, 7, 8, 11, 12, 14. The basic source is M. L. Weitzman, "Soviet Postwar Economic Growth and Capital-Labor Substitution," American Economic Review 60, no. 4 (1970): 677, Table 1 for the years 1951–68. His output, capital, and employment data are extended by Soviet official data.

Column 5. J. Thornton, "Value-Added and Factor Productivity in Soviet Industry," American Economic Review 60, no. 5 (1970): 863–71.

Column 11. Sources for the Bergson-Weitzman-Desai index of economic working hours per man are A. Bergson, The Real National Income of Soviet Russia since 1928 (Cambridge, Mass.: Harvard University Press, 1961), p. 425, Table H-2, for years 1928, 1937, 1940, 1944, and 1948–50; M. Weitzman, op. cit., p. 687, Table 4, for the years 1950–56; and P. Desai, "The Production Function and Technical Change in Postwar Soviet Industry: A Reexamination," 1974, forthcoming, Table 1 for the years 1968–71. In her paper, Mrs. Desai notes a difficulty, "in deriving meaningful magnitudes of the index for the 'transition' years 1967 and 1968." She obtained a sharp rise of 20 percent in 1967 and a decline of 3 percent in 1968 in industrial man-hours. According to her, "one possible reason [for this] is that while the change to a five-day workweek (or 8.0 hours per day during the week) is announced on a given date in 1967, the change does not necessarily become effective on that date. The average length of the working day in 1967 is most likely to be somewhere between 6.67 hours (the figure for 1966) and 8 hours (as per the announcement)." I accepted this point and assumed, somewhat arbitrarily, that the average length of the working day in 1967 was 6.67 + 1/2 (8.0 − 6.67) = 7.34 hours. I also assumed that there was no change in the number of annual working hours per man in the years 1972–73.

FIGURE 1.1

Basic Facts of Soviet Postwar Industrial Growth:
Annual Percentage Growth Rates of Output,
Labor in Terms of Man-Hours, and
Capital Output Ratio

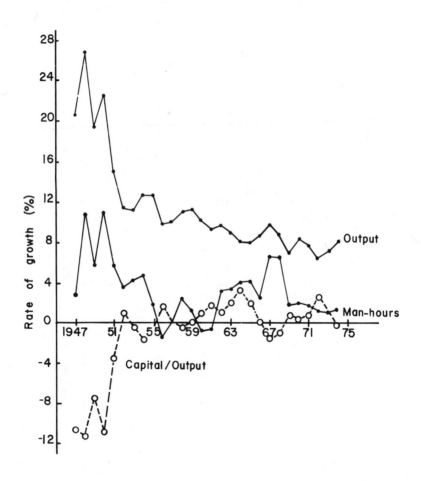

Source: Table 1.1.

14

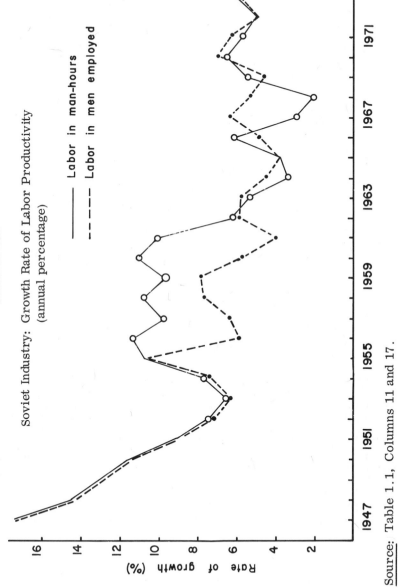

FIGURE 1.2

Soviet Industry: Growth Rate of Labor Productivity
(annual percentage)

—— Labor in man-hours
- - - - Labor in men employed

Source: Table 1.1, Columns 11 and 17.

FIGURE 1.3

Soviet Industry, 1928–73: Changes in the Growth Rate of Labor Productivity (labor in man–years)

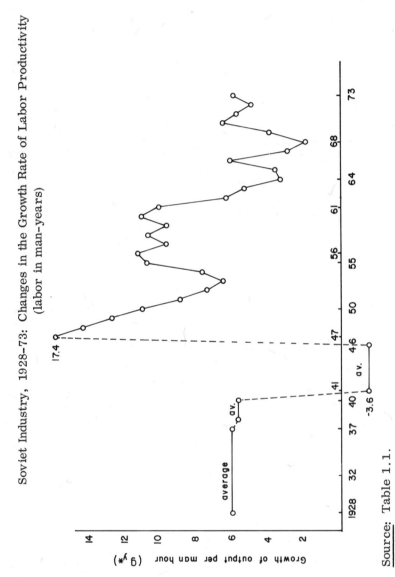

Source: Table 1.1.

FIGURE 1.4

Basic Facts of Soviet Industrial Growth: 1928–73

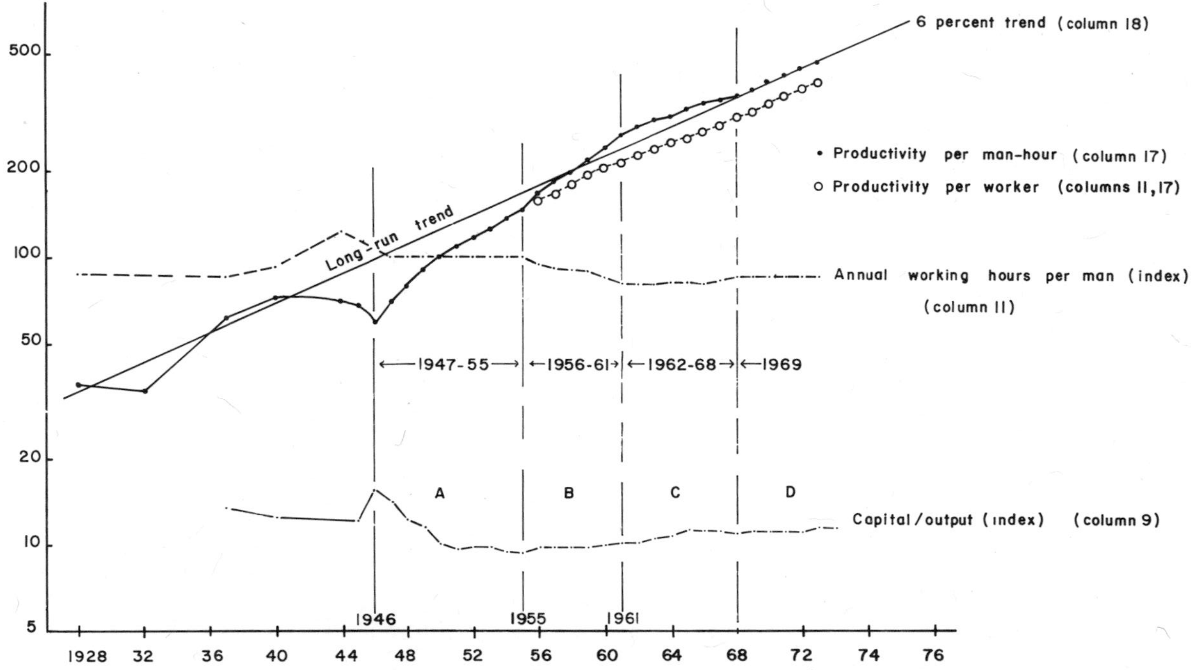

Source: Table 1.1.

for this policy to succeed. Several measures to this end must have been taken and the policy was apparently successful.[11] From this preliminary interpretation it would appear that (B) was a period when the economic efficiency was, over time, increasingly above its 1955 level. The extra pressure applied to keep the labor productivity high would then be expected to end by the end of 1961 when the reduction in working hours per man was completed. A sudden relaxation of tension in the following years should then result in at least partial, if not full, return of the overall efficiency to its "equilibrium" level. (C) would thus be a transitory period when the reduction in the number of annual working hours per man finally showed up in a decreased growth rate of labor productivity in terms of both per man and per man-hour.

From the above broad interpretation of data it would follow, first, that periods B and C are interlinked in the sense that period C absorbed a delayed effect of what happened in period B. This created a characteristic gap between above "normal" performance in the years 1956-61 and below "normal" performance in the following several years. Second, only from about 1970 the growth rate of labor productivity has been moving in the proximity of its long-run trend path of about 6.0 percent gain per annum. (See Figure 1.4)

Finally, let us turn to Figure 1.5 to see the trends in investments and capital. Since 1950 there has been a moderate decline both in the share u_t of the industrial investments in the total state investments and in the ratio s_t of the industrial gross investments to the industrial value added. But because the growth rate of the industrial value added declined quite rapidly, we have a definite downward trend in the growth rate of (gross) industrial investments. The latter was more or less the same as the growth rate of the total GNP, which was somewhat less than the growth rate of industrial output. Thus with u_t and s_t relatively stable, the growth rate of capital must imitate, though clearly with some delay, the growth rate of output. My preliminary interpretation of these data is, therefore, that the reason for the decreased growth rate of investment and (recently) capital is the slowdown in output, not the other way around.[12] Of course, a slowdown in the growth of capital stock is likely to contribute to a further slowdown in output; these two variables are closely interlinked. But my working hypothesis is, first, that the chain of events along a path down the hill toward a long-run growth equilibrium was set by an external factor, namely by an extraordinary starting point on this path in 1947. And second, that after 1955 this movement toward the equilibrium was seriously disturbed by another external factor, namely by the 20 percent reduction in the workyear introduced in the years 1956-61.

FIGURE 1.5

Soviet Industry: The Ratio of Gross Investments to the Value Added Originating in
Industry, and the Growth Rates of Capital and Investments

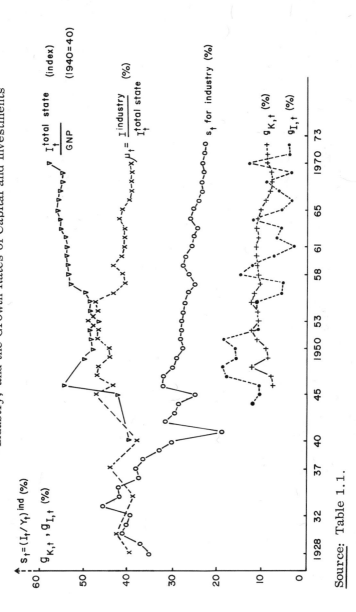

Source: Table 1.1.

PRELIMINARY TEST WITH A PRODUCTION FUNCTION: PERIOD 1951-73

Our preliminary interpretation of the data still has many loose ends, and the aim during the rest of the chapter will be to make this interpretation more precise. The first priority will be given to finding a good specification of the production function. Somewhat arbitrarily, I want this specification to satisfy the following three requirements: (1) to have high explanatory power in terms of the error sum of squares, with the essential parameters statistically significant, (2) to imply that the asymptotic growth rate of labor productivity is at a reasonable level, say in the range between 4 percent and 6 percent, (3) to take an account of both the postwar opportunities for rapid growth and the growth effect on the productivity per man-hour of the 20 percent reduction in working hours in the years 1956-61. A CES production function estimated by Weitzman satisfies (1), but it implies that the growth rate of labor productivity will continue to decline until it reaches a 2 percent level, which I regard as too low. Moreover, his interpretation ignores (3) completely.

Our tests cover data for the years 1951-73. These are Weitzman's data for the period 1951-68[13] extended by Soviet official data for the years 1969-73 (see Table 1.1, columns 4, 8 and 10). To reduce the influence of multicollinearity, a CES production function to be estimated is expressed directly in terms of growth rates, rather than in terms of levels or loglevels:

$$g_{(Y,t)} = \pi_t (g_{K,t} + \lambda_1) + (1 - \pi_t)(g_{L*,t} + \lambda_{2,t}) \tag{1}$$

where

$\pi_t \equiv \delta \gamma^{-\rho} e^{-\lambda_1 \rho t} v_t^{-\rho}$ = elasticity of output with respect to capital,

$v_t \equiv K_t / Y_t$ = capital/output ratio,

$\rho = (1 - \sigma)$, σ = elasticity of substitution,

$g_{Y,t}$ = output growth rate, $g_{K,t}$ = capital growth rate,

$g_{L*,t}$ = growth rate of labor in man-hours, $t = 1951, 1952, \ldots, 1973$.

Moreover, we shall assume that

$$\lambda_{2,t} = \begin{cases} \lambda_2 + \epsilon & \text{for } t = 1951, \ldots, 1961 \\ \lambda_2 & \text{for } t = 1962, \ldots, 1973 \end{cases} \qquad (2)$$

The terms λ_1 and $\lambda_{2,t}$ in equation 1 are the growth rates of, respectively, the capital-augmenting and the labor-augmenting components of (disembodied) technical changes. In contrast to Weitzman's specification, we not only allow these rates to differ but also permit the possibility that the growth rate of the labor-augmenting component of technical change was in the years 1951-61 (subperiods A and B) different by ϵ from that in the following years 1962-73 (subperiods C and D). Of course, we expect ϵ to be positive. In this admittedly crude manner we want to meet our requirement (3). Equation 1 is estimated directly, using an algorithm similar to that employed by Weitzman. The results are as follows:

$$\hat{\sigma} = .392, \hat{\lambda}_1 = .0077, \hat{\lambda}_2 = .0472, \hat{\epsilon} = .0402, \hat{\delta} = .463$$

$$\hat{\gamma} = .986, \text{ and ESS} = 2.34 \times 10^{-3}, \bar{R}^2 = .6823$$

For comparison, the more restricted hypothesis $\lambda_1 = \lambda_2, \epsilon = 0$, which reduces equation 1 to Weitzman's specification, gives these results:

$$\hat{\sigma} = .487, \hat{\lambda}_1 = \hat{\lambda}_2 = .0304, \hat{\delta} = .579, \hat{\gamma} = .741, \text{ ESS} = 3.06 \times 10^{-3},$$

$$\bar{R}^2 = .6292$$

It is seen here that the error sum of squares (ESS) is increased by 31 percent. Applying the F-test we find that at the 95 percent confidence level we would have to reject the hypothesis that the more restricted specification is the true functional form. Although the size of our sample of observations is such that we should not put too much confidence in the results of statistical tests designed for large samples, I am nevertheless inclined to interpret this particular result as an indication that equation 1 minus 2 offers a better explanation of the data than does the specification given by Weitzman. Moreover, we shall later be able to decrease the ESS considerably further.

The implied time series of imputed capital's share π_t is given in Table 1.2. Note a much slower decline in our π_t compared to that implied by Weitzman's hypothesis. This is despite the fact that our elasticity of substitution is also significantly less than one. This result is implied by the fact that the really essential variable affecting π is the type of technical change, not the elasticity of substitution. The

TABLE 1.2

Imputed Capital's Share Implied by
Preliminary Test Function

t	π_t	t	π_t
1951	0.479	1963	0.374
1952	0.466	1964	0.351
1953	0.462	1965	0.336
1954	0.468	1966	0.331
1955	0.466	1967	0.334
1956	0.448	1968	0.334
1957	0.440	1969	0.326
1958	0.437	1970	0.321
1959	0.432	1971	0.312
1960	0.420	1972	0.296
1961	0.403	1973	0.287
1962	0.391		

Source: Compiled by the author.

type of technical change implied by Weitzman's hypothesis is strongly
capital-saving in the Harrod sense, whereas under specification 1
it is almost neutral. We may note that when technical change is purely
Harrod-neutral and the capital/output ratio is constant, then the
magnitude of the elasticity of substitution is irrelevant. This is so
because then the capital/labor ratio, where both capital and labor are
expressed in efficiency units, is invariant over time. It therefore
follows that if technical changes in Soviet industry have actually been
predominantly Harrod-neutral, then in view of the relatively small
changes in the capital/output ratio (small especially in the 1950s) the
emphasis on difficulties in substituting capital for labor as a probable
cause of slowdown would be misdirected. The emphasis should instead
be on those factors that are likely to have contributed to a decline in
the growth rate of this (predominantly Harrod-neutral) technical
change. This decline in our preliminary test is represented by ϵ. It
is a decline between the 1951-61 period and the 1962-73 period. Its
magnitude is 4.0 percent. Another implication of our test production
function is that the asymptotic growth rate of labor productivity would
be 4.7 percent. Thus the function meets also our requirement (2).
We shall develop this test production function much further later. The
error and sensitivity analysis is postponed until then.

ESTIMATION OF THREE "EXTRA" GROWTH EFFECTS

Apart from the catch-up effect and the working hours effect there are at least three other factors that might have been captured by our ϵ. These are (1) a change in the branch composition of employment, (2) a change in the age composition of capital, and (3) a change in the rate of diffusion of the foreign-made technology. I call (1) the branch composition effect, (2) the age composition effect, and (3) the diffusional effect. Before proceeding with our search for a best specification of the production function, we shall attempt to obtain an approximate estimate of the magnitude of these three effects.

The Branch Composition Effect

The growth rate of aggregate labor productivity in industry as a whole could in the 1950s be relatively higher because labor employed in branches with a low level of labor productivity was then expanding relatively less rapidly than in the 1960s. My calculations show, however, that this branch composition effect was fairly minor. [14] It contributed only about -0.1 percent annually in the 1950s and about -0.3 percent annually in the 1960s. These calculations are based on Weitzman's value-added weights, [15] but the result does not change if Desai's weights are applied instead. The standard 11 industrial branches are distinguished. The relative difference of 0.2 percent in favor of the 1950s could perhaps be increased if the level of disaggregation was higher. I did not have enough data to pursue such an inquiry, but my feeling is that the result would not be much different.

The Age Composition Effect

Assuming that technical progress is partly of an embodied type, the average level of labor productivity would be a function of the age composition of the capital stock. A decrease (increase) in the average age of this capital is then an extra factor contributing positively (negatively) to the labor productivity growth rate. In my calculations of this contribution I assumed (1) the age composition of machines matters only, so that the stock of structures is ignored, (2) machines are a constant fraction of the total stock of the fixed capital, (3) all machines have the same service life, (4) one-third of each capital vintage added to the capital stock before 1942, was destroyed during the war, and

(5) there is a two-year delay before a newly produced machine is actually employed. Assumptions (4) and (5) are approximately consistent with the Soviet official investment and capital-stock data from 1940. On the basis of all assumptions I calculated the average life of machines:

$$u_i(t) = \sum_{\tau=t}^{t-n_i+1} (t - \tau) I_{\tau-2} \left/ \left(\sum_{\tau=t}^{t-n_i+1} I_{\tau-2} \right) \right. \tag{3}$$

where the time subscript is running from $t = 1947$ to $t = 1973$, and where n_i is the service life, the subscript i referring to the i's alternative. Eight alternatives were considered: $n_1 = 12$, $n_2 = 13$, . . . , $n_8 = 19$. The results are reported in Table 1.3. It is seen that for all these alternatives the average age was declining markedly from 1948, to reach a minimum sometime in the period 1954-58. Since then it has been increasing again. These findings indicate that for slowdown in the growth of output the age composition effect could have been a potentially contributing factor. The actual size of this contribution depends on the extent to which technical changes in Soviet industry have been of embodied type. It may be instructive to illustrate this point using Soviet investment data. Assume technical changes to be purely labor-augmenting and capital/output ratio the same for all vintages. Then we can find the labor productivity on vintage τ, expressed as a fraction of the labor productivity on vintage 1948,

$$y_\tau(t) = (1 + \alpha)^{\tau-1948} (1 + \beta)^{t-1948}, \quad \tau \leq t, \tag{4}$$
$$t = 1948, 1949, \ldots, 1973$$

where α is the rate of embodied technical change and β is the rate of disembodied technical change. We can also find the labor productivity for the industry as a whole:

$$y(t) = (I_{\tau-2}) \left/ \left\{ \sum_{\tau=t}^{t-n_i+1} [I_{\tau-2} / y_\tau(t)] \right\} \right. \tag{5}$$

When $\alpha = 0$, then $y(t) = y_\tau(t)$ for all τ, so that the age composition of machines is irrelevant. I computed the growth rate of $y(t)$, denoted by $g_y(t)$, for six pairs of α, β, from $\alpha = 1$ percent, $\beta = 5$ percent to $\alpha = 6$ percent, $\beta = $ zero percent. In Table 1.4 a sample of the results

TABLE 1.3

The Average Age u_i (t) of Soviet Industrial Machinery
and Equipment in the Period 1948-73

| | \multicolumn{8}{c}{Length of the Service Life n_i:} | | | | | | | |
Year	12 yrs. u_1	13 yrs. u_2	14 yrs. u_3	15 yrs. u_4	16 yrs. u_5	17 yrs. u_6	18 yrs. u_7	19 yrs. u_8
1948	4.47	4.78	5.06	5.31	5.53	5.75	5.93	6.05
1949	4.38	4.71	5.01	5.28	5.51	5.71	5.93	6.09
1950	4.25	4.59	4.89	5.18	5.43	5.66	5.85	6.04
1951	4.09	4.46	4.77	5.06	5.33	5.56	5.77	5.95
1952	3.96	4.29	4.63	4.93	5.20	5.45	5.67	5.87
1953	3.83	4.15	4.46	4.78	5.05	5.30	5.53	5.74
1954	3.78	4.06	4.36	4.64	4.94	5.19	5.42	5.64
1955	3.90	4.04	4.30	4.57	4.84	5.11	5.35	5.56
1956	3.91	4.17	4.30	4.54	4.80	5.04	5.29	5.51
1957	3.94	4.19	4.43	4.55	4.78	5.01	5.24	5.48
1958	4.01	4.25	4.48	4.71	4.83	5.04	5.26	5.47
1959	4.11	4.35	4.58	4.80	5.01	5.12	5.32	5.52
1960	4.19	4.42	4.65	4.86	5.07	5.27	5.37	5.55
1961	4.21	4.45	4.67	4.89	5.09	5.28	5.47	5.56
1962	4.25	4.51	4.73	4.94	5.14	5.33	5.51	5.69
1963	4.32	4.59	4.83	5.05	5.24	5.43	5.61	5.78
1964	4.39	4.67	4.92	5.15	5.36	5.55	5.73	5.90
1965	4.44	4.74	5.01	5.25	5.48	5.68	5.85	6.02
1966	4.46	4.77	5.06	5.32	5.55	5.77	5.96	6.12
1967	4.50	4.81	5.11	5.39	5.64	5.86	6.06	6.24
1968	4.55	4.87	5.18	5.46	5.73	5.97	6.18	6.38
1969	4.60	4.93	5.24	5.53	5.80	6.06	6.29	6.50
1970	4.64	4.96	5.28	5.58	5.86	6.12	6.37	6.59
1971	4.70	5.02	5.33	5.64	5.93	6.20	6.46	6.70
1972	4.71	5.05	5.35	5.66	5.96	6.23	6.50	6.74
1973	4.71	5.08	5.40	5.70	5.99	6.28	6.55	6.80

Source: Compiled by the author.

TABLE 1.4

The Age Composition Effect for Alternative Rates of
Embodied (α) and Disembodied (β) Technical
Change and the Service Life (n)

Year	$\alpha = 1.0$, n = 15	$\beta = 5.0$ n = 18	$\alpha = 3.0$, n = 15	$\beta = 3.0$ n = 18	$\alpha = 5.0$, n = 15	$\beta = 1.0$ n = 18
1949	6.1	6.0	6.2	6.1	6.2	6.0
1950	6.2	6.1	6.4	6.3	6.5	6.4
1951	6.2	6.1	6.5	6.3	6.7	6.3
1952	6.2	6.2	6.5	6.4	6.8	6.6
1953	6.2	6.2	6.6	6.5	6.9	6.8
1954	6.2	6.2	6.6	6.5	6.9	6.7
1955	6.1	6.1	6.3	6.4	6.5	6.5
1956	6.1	6.1	6.2	6.3	6.3	6.4
1957	5.9	7.1	6.1	6.3	6.0	6.5
1958	6.0	6.0	5.6	6.1	5.1	6.1
1959	6.0	6.0	5.8	5.9	5.7	5.8
1960	6.0	6.0	5.9	5.9	5.7	5.8
1961	6.0	5.9	6.0	5.7	5.9	5.4
1962	6.0	6.0	5.9	6.0	5.7	5.8
1963	5.9	5.9	5.7	5.8	5.5	5.5
1964	6.0	5.9	5.7	5.7	5.5	5.4
1965	6.0	5.9	5.8	5.7	5.5	5.4
1966	6.0	5.9	5.7	5.7	5.7	5.5
1967	6.0	5.9	5.9	5.7	5.7	5.4
1968	6.0	5.9	5.9	5.7	5.7	5.4
1969	6.0	5.9	5.9	5.7	5.7	5.4
1970	6.0	6.0	5.9	5.9	5.8	5.6
1971	6.0	6.0	5.9	5.8	5.7	5.6
1972	6.0	6.0	6.0	6.0	5.8	5.8
1973	6.0	6.0	6.0	5.9	5.8	5.7

Source: Compiled by the author.

is given. It is seen that g_y (t) is at the bottom in the early 1960s and, generally, it is higher during the 1950s than during the 1960s, the difference being in the range from about 0.1 percent ($\alpha = 1$, $\beta = 5$) to about 0.8 percent ($\alpha = 5$, $\beta = 1$). It would appear that this was the order of magnitude of the contribution of the age composition change to slowdown in the labor productivity growth. The contribution could actually be even smaller if in the 1960s the average service life of machines was reduced. An approximate rule is that such a reduction by k years, k = 1, 2, 3, 4, implies a reduction in the figures quoted above, 0.1 percent and 0.8 percent, by about 0.03 αk percent.

Diffusional Effect[16]

On the grounds of both theoretical arguments and empirical evidence it seems that for much of the world, with the notable exception of the United States, diffusion of foreign-made innovations is at present the single most important agent of technical change, and therefore also the key factor of the labor productivity growth. This "law" seems to apply for the market-oriented economies as well as for economies of the Soviet type, including the Soviet Union itself.[17] One thus has to explore a possibility that the collapse in the labor productivity growth in 1962 was a result of a sudden change in policy, or in socioeconomic environment, which has significantly reduced the growth rate of diffusion after 1961 compared to that prevailing until 1961. The growth rate of disembodied diffusion (licenses, patents, technological espionage, scientific journals, exchange of personnel) could well be declining in the 1950s as the more readily available Western advances in science and technology made during the war were gradually absorbed by Soviet research and development (R & D) sector. But there seems to be no evidence to indicate a sudden, large-scale decline in that rate by about 1960 or 1961.

There remains diffusion of the embodied type (import of investment goods incorporating new foreign-made technology). Elsewhere I made an attempt to compute the growth effect of Soviet imports of investment goods.[18] Table 1.5 gives six alternative sets of results, depending on the value of r and on the methodology adopted. The absolute values of these results vary considerably, especially for the 1950s. But their common characteristic feature is a gradual decline of the growth effect in the 1950s, rather than a sudden jumpdown at the beginning of the 1960s.

We therefore reject the hypothesis that our ϵ in Equation 2, estimated to be 4 percent, captures a change in the diffusional effect. There is however some evidence for a gradual decline in that effect.

TABLE 1.5

The (Indirect) Growth Effect of Embodied Diffusion in
Soviet Industry, 1951-72

Year	d_t^1 (r = 1.0)	d_t^2 (r = 1.0)	d_t^1 (r = 1.1)	d_t^2 (r = 1.1)	d_t^1 (r = 1.2)	d_t^2 (r = 1.2)
1951	0.74	0.35	1.24	0.45	1.49	0.65
1952	0.69	0.35	1.12	0.35	1.46	0.56
1953	0.26	0.26	0.68	0.26	1.14	0.32
1954	0.26	0.21	0.50	0.21	0.81	0.24
1955	0.27	0.23	0.50	0.23	0.61	0.26
1956	0.27	0.25	0.36	0.26	0.45	0.28
1957	0.12	0.11	0.14	0.18	0.25	0.13
1958	0.11	0.12	0.13	0.12	0.24	0.14
1959	0.13	0.13	0.16	0.14	0.26	0.16
1960	0.23	0.27	0.25	0.29	0.32	0.33
1961	0.15	0.16	0.15	0.18	0.19	0.21
1962	0.08	0.07	0.08	0.09	0.13	0.13
1963	0.06	0.07	0.06	0.08	0.10	0.11
1964	0.12	0.14	0.12	0.14	0.15	0.18
1965	0.06	0.07	0.06	0.08	0.10	0.09
1966	0.06	0.08	0.07	0.09	0.10	0.11
1967	0.05	0.05	0.06	0.07	0.11	0.10
1968	0.09	0.08	0.10	0.10	0.14	0.15
1969	0.14	0.16	0.16	0.18	0.20	0.22
1970	0.10	0.11	0.11	0.11	0.15	0.15
1971	0.09	0.11	0.10	0.11	0.13	0.13
1972	0.16	0.16	0.16	0.16	0.12	0.10

Notes: r is the parameter of "export specialization" and d_t is the growth contribution (in percent) of the machinery imports to the growth rate of labor productivity, when the level of technology is approximated by either labor productivity itself (d_t^1) or labor productivity adjusted for intercountry differences in the capital-output ratio (d_t^2). Parameter r is the technological level in the export sector in terms of the average industrial level of technology.

Source: S. Gomulka and J.D. Sylwestrowicz, "Import-led Growth: Theory and Estimation," in On the Measurement of Factor Productivities: Theoretical Problems and Empirical Results, Papers and Proceedings of the Second Reisenburg Symposium, ed. F.-L. Altmann, O. Kyn, H.-J. Wagener (Gotingen: Vandenhoeck and Ruprecht, forthcoming).

This will be used in the next section to support our interpretation
of the notion of "postwar recovery trend."

THE LONG-RUN TREND AND THE POSTWAR
RECOVERY TREND

      Let us come back again to the labor productivity data. These
data are very important for two reasons. First, the growth rate of
the labor/output ratio was in Soviet industry generally very high (in
absolute terms) and subject to major changes over time. In contrast,
the growth rate of the capital/output ratio was generally low and
subject to relatively minor changes over time. Second, at the Soviet
capital/output ratio changing slowly and at the technical changes
predominantly Harrod-neutral, the productivity residual in the Hicks
sense (respectively in the Harrod sense) is approximately proportional (equal) to the growth rate of labor productivity. Therefore a
careful study of the dynamics of the latter growth rate should help
greatly to specify more correctly the functional form of the technical
progress terms, the labor-augmenting term especially.
      The labor productivity per man-hour is denoted by y^*, and its
1937-73 long-run trend value by y^*_{tr}. The latter was already identified
in Figure 1.4. The values of both y^* and y^*_{tr} are given in Table 1.1.
Of particular interest is the difference $y^*_{tr} - y^*$, or rather the relative
difference $(y^*_{tr} - y^*)/y^*_{tr}$. Let us denote it by x. Clearly x measures
the relative distance of labor productivity from its long-run "trend"
path. The "normal" state of affairs is when x is equal or close to
zero. A significant deviation of x from the zero level is brought
about by factors which for a particular type of economy in a particular
technological epoch are "abnormal."
      The terms "normal" and "abnormal" should be used with care.
They are meaningful only if the notion of the labor productivity "trend"
is meaningful. The assumption implicitly made in Figure 1.6 is that
in the period 1937-73 the trend growth rate in labor productivity was
constant. This may be questioned on the grounds that throughout that
time the actual growth rate of capital, employment, and output were
highly unbalanced, and that, as a result of destructive war, their
trend growth paths must have changed permanently, as they no doubt
did. However, what applies to such economic variables as capital,
employment, and output does not necessarily apply to their ratios,
in particular to the capital/output ratios.
      The following three observations can in fact be made in defense
of the notion of the labor productivity constant trend.

1. Note that when technical changes are Harrod-neutral and when returns to scale are constant, then

$$Y_t = F (K_t, A_t L_t^*)$$

where A_t is the level of technical advance, L_t^* is employment in man-hours, K_t stands for capital, and Y_t is value added. On dividing this equation by AL^* and solving the resulting equation with respect to $\frac{Y}{AL^*}$, we have

$$y_t^* = h (v_t) . A_t$$

where $y_t^* = Y_t/L_t^*$ and $v_t = K_t/Y_t$. Thus when the capital-output v_t is relatively stable over time, the labor productivity is approximately proportional to the level of technical advance. From Figure 1.4 it is seen that in the period 1937-73 the Soviet industrial capital/output ratio was in fact fairly stable, though far from being exactly constant. In 1973 the value of v was only about 10 percent below its 1937 level, implying about (-.3) percent annual average growth rate. Hence it follows that in the long run y_t^* is nearly proportional to A_t, so that the trend growth rates in labor productivity and in technical progress are about the same.

2. Observation (1) switches attention from labor productivity changes to technical changes. During the war the growth rate of Soviet technical changes was probably significantly depressed, especially in those sectors that were not of immediate importance to the war effort. This proposition does not apply, however, to the world technological environment in which the Soviet economy operates. Indeed, the average annual growth rate of output per man-hour in the U.S. manufacturing sector was in the years 1930-50 about the same as it was in the following period, 1951-70 (2.1 percent and 2.35 percent, respectively).[19] This is despite the Great Depression in the 1930s and the fact that much of the world R & D sector was in the years 1940-45 at the service of the defense industries. Apparently most of the technical advances made then were later found useful also in civil industries. So it does not seem unreasonable to suppose that the trend growth rate of the U.S. (and possibly also West European) technological level was not affected much by the war. This war could still have changed the trend growth path of the Soviet R & D sector. Consequently, it could have changed the trend growth rate of the Soviet technical advances, since probably most of the foreign-made and home-made technology is, respectively, transmitted and produced by that sector. However, the average annual growth rate of the

Soviet R & D scientific personnel in the years 1914-50 was in fact
about the same as in the years 1951-71 (8.0 percent and 9.0 percent,
correspondingly).[20] The level of expenditure on R & D prior to 1941
is not available, but its growth rate in the years 1941-50 was not
much different than in the years 1951-71 (respectively 12 percent
and 13 percent).[21] We may thus conclude that there were present
both external and internal factors conducive to a sustained (constant)
trend in technological changes.

    3. Finally, the war represented a major organizational problem.
It forced the Soviet Union twice to make rapid and large-scale changes
in the composition of industrial output and in the skill composition of
the labor force, in 1941-42 and in 1945-46. These changes meant a
great organizational disruption in industrial production. But they
were mostly transitory and so resulted in something of a temporary
aberration from the underlying trend in technical and organizational
changes. After the 1946 switch from wartime to peacetime production,
the utilization of capital began to increase and the stock of innovations
accumulated at home and abroad during the war had started to be
gradually incorporated by civilian industries as new investment in
plant and equipment proceeded.

    Changes over time in x are given in Figure 1.6. It is seen that
in 1946 y^* was equal to $.6y^*_{tr}$, so that $x = .4$. In the years 1946-50
this distance was diminishing at the annual rate of about 20 percent.
The time path of y^*_t in those years traces out what we shall call the
postwar recovery trend path. However, after 1950 there seems to
have been two "shocks"—one relatively minor, the other relatively
major—that greatly disturbed the evolution of y^* along that postwar
recovery trend path. Disturbance No. 1 is located in the years 1951-
55. It looks significantly above normal in 1955. This minor growth
depression of 1951-53 may be interpreted as an imprint of increased
production of arms during the Korean War (1951-53) combined with a
crop failure in 1951. Both these factors had no doubt caused a degree
of transitional disruption in some industrial branches. Its subsequent
removal in the years 1954-55 could then produce a minor "growth
recovery." The big cycle (Disturbance No. 2 in Figure 1.6) begins
in 1956. It should in fact be called "anticycle," since its first (second)
part is marked with an above (below) normal expansion. Its start
coincides with the beginning of the program, adopted in March 1956
by the 20th Congress of the CPSU, to gradually reduce the standard
workweek from 48 hours to 41 hours. The first part of the cycle ends
in 1961, the year when the program was completed, with the average
annual number of working hours per man being actually reduced by
about 20 percent. During the years 1956-61 the distance x was increasing again to reach in 1961 its maximum of about .15. But in
the long run the labor productivity per man-hour may be expected to

FIGURE 1.6

Soviet Industry, 1946–73: Productivity Per Man–Hour

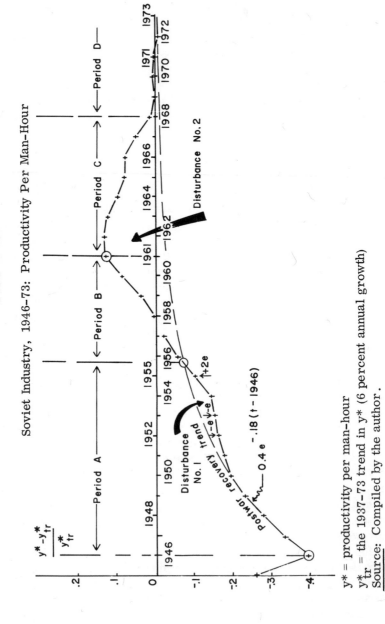

y^* = productivity per man–hour

y^*_{tr} = the 1937–73 trend in y^* (6 percent annual growth)

Source: Compiled by the author.

be largely independent of the number of hours worked per year. At
this point let us note that Weitzman admits that "in using hours worked
as an index of labor inputs, we are in effect operating with a hidden
assumption that labor efficiency per hour is unaffected by the reduction over time of total hours worked."[22] On the basis of Figure 1.6,
I adopt the same assumption for the long run, but in the short run
(periods B and C) the assumption appears to be unacceptable. Disturbances 1 and 2 are shown more clearly on the logarithmic scale
in Figure 1.7. On the basis of the 1946-50 data, the postwar recovery trend is estimated. The deviation from this trend for the years
1956-73 is presented in the bottom part of Figure 1.7. The type of
asymmetry seen in disturbance No. 2, fairly linear changes in x in
period B as opposed to bell-shaped or logistic-type changes in period
C, well corresponds to the nature of the different processes underlying these changes: a constant pressure applied in period B and a
gradual relaxation of tension enjoyed in period C.

VARIABLE TECHNICAL CHANGE VERSUS ELASTICITY OF SUBSTITUTION: A FURTHER TEST

The general form of a CES constant returns-to-scale production
function to be fitted in our second test is also a standard one:

$$Y = \gamma[\delta_1(BK)^{-\rho} + (1 - \delta_1)(AL)^{-\rho}]^{-1/\rho} \tag{6}$$

where parameters γ, ρ, and δ are constant, and where functions
$A = A(t)$ and $B = B(t)$ represent (disembodied) factor-augmenting
technical progress. The innovation in equation 6 is with a new specification of the technical progress terms, which are as follows:

$$B(t) = e^{\lambda_1 t} \tag{7}$$

$$A(t) = e^{\lambda_2 t}[1 - .4e^{-.18(t-1946)}][1 + .15\delta_{2t}e^{-.05(t-1962)^2}]e^{(\epsilon_t + \mu_t)t} \tag{8}$$

where time t runs from 1951 to 1973 and where δ_{2t}, ϵ_t, and μ_t are
dummy variables defined as follows:

FIGURE 1.7

The 1951–55 and the 1956–73 Deviations of the Actual Level of Productivity
(Per Man–Hour) from its Postwar Recovery Trend on the
Logarithmic Scale

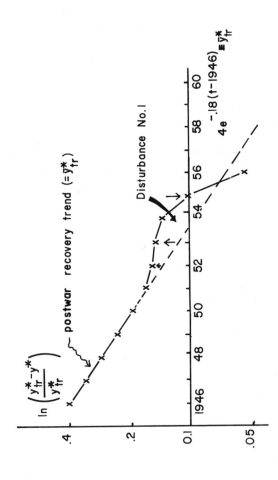

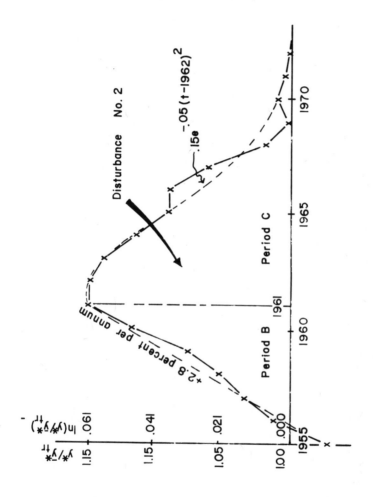

$$\delta_{2t} = \begin{array}{ll} \delta_2 & \text{for 1962-73} \\ 0 & \text{otherwise} \end{array} \quad, \quad \epsilon_t = \begin{array}{ll} -\epsilon & \text{for 1952-53} \\ +2\epsilon & \text{for 1955} \\ 0 & \text{otherwise} \end{array}, \quad \mu_t = \begin{array}{ll} \mu & \text{for 1956-61} \\ 0 & \text{otherwise} \end{array} \quad (9)$$

In specification 8 λ_2 is the trend growth rate of the labor-augmenting technical progress. Expression in the first square brackets in equation 8, increasing from .6 for 1946 to 1 for large t, represents the postwar correction of the long-run trend in that type of progress, as implied by the postwar recovery trend. Note that by definition of the postwar recovery trend, $\bar{y}_{tr}^*$ is an estimate of the ratio $(y_{tr}^* - y_t^*)/y_{tr}^* \equiv X_t$. Hence y_t^* is approximated by $(1 - \bar{y}_{tr}^*)y_{tr}^*$. As we noted in the previous section, if technical changes are predominantly neutral in the Harrod-Kalecki sense, then the index of the labor-augmenting component of technical advance A(t) is in the long run approximately proportional to y_t^*. Hence the trend term $e^{\lambda_2 t}$ in the level of technical advance A(t) is corrected to have the form $(1 - \bar{y}_{tr}^*) e^{\lambda_2 t}$. The expression for $\bar{y}_{tr}^*$ was estimated in the upper part of Figure 1.7. Expression in the second square brackets in equation 8, declining from 1.14 for 1962 to 1 for large t, represents the post-1961 gradual return of labor efficiency per hour to its long-run trend. Finally ϵ and μ are dummy variables covering, respectively, the 1952-55 cycle and the 1956-61 period of labor efficiency per hour being increasingly above its long-run trend corrected for the postwar recovery.

Equation 6 may be rewritten in terms of growth rates,

$$g_{Y,t} = \pi_t (g_{K,t} + \lambda_1) + (1 - \pi_t) \left[g_{L^*,t} + \lambda_2 + \epsilon_t + \mu_t \right.$$
$$\left. + \frac{.0288 e^{-.18(t-1951)}}{1 - .16 e^{-.18(t-1951)}} + \delta_{2t} \frac{.014(t-1962)e^{-.05(t-1962)^2}}{1 + .14 e^{-.05(t-1962)^2}} \right] \quad (10)$$

where, as before, $\pi_t = \delta_1^{\gamma - \rho} e^{-\lambda_1 \rho t} v_t^{-\rho}$ and $\rho = (1 - \sigma)/\sigma$.

Here eight parameters are to be estimated: λ_1, λ_2, δ_1, δ_2, γ, σ, μ, and ϵ. Data used for this estimation (as well as in the subsequent final test) are, with one exception, the same data as used in the first test. The exception is the man-hours data for 1967-71, which are now changed to comply with Desai's revised index of working hours per man (see Table 1.1, column 14). The estimation results are as follows:

$\hat{\lambda}_1 = -3 \times 10^{-6}$, $\hat{\lambda}_2 = .0597$, $\hat{\delta}_1 = .292$, $\delta_2 = -1.11$, $\hat{\gamma} = 1.00$, $\hat{\sigma} = 1.00$,

$\hat{\mu} = .0298$, $\hat{\epsilon} = .0167$, ESS $= 1.25 \times 10^{-3}$, $\bar{R}^2 = .8076$.

The technical change estimated is thus again predominantly Harrod-neutral. Compared to our previous test, the ESS is significantly reduced: from about 76 percent to about 41 percent of the ESS implied by the Weitzman-type specification. Also $\bar{R}^2$ is substantially increased: from .6823 to .8076. The elasticity of substitution estimated is almost exactly unity, and the (imputed) capital share almost exactly constant over time (equal to .292). However, only $\hat{\delta}_2$, $\hat{\mu}$, and $\hat{\epsilon}$ were found statistically significant. The sensitivity analysis revealed that there is a great deal of substitution between λ_1 and λ_2, as it in fact should be expected in the virtually Cobb-Douglas situation. The elasticity of substitution has a relatively large asymptotic standard error so that it could easily be anywhere in the range from .1 to 1.2. By fixing a few values of σ from this range and subminimizing the ESS it was found that the minimum was fairly flat, though σ's close to unity were giving the best fit. These results, however disappointing in terms of standard errors, are nevertheless instructive, since they indicate that there is likely to be no loss in the goodness of fit by directly fixing σ at one. The number of parameters would then be reduced from eight to five, and by reducing the substitution possibilities between the remaining parameters their statistical significance should significantly increase.

COBB-DOUGLAS FUNCTION WITH VARIABLE TECHNICAL CHANGES: THE FINAL SPECIFICATION

After this long journey of preliminary descriptive interpretation of data and two intermediate econometric tests with CES production functions we arrived at the point of formulating what will be our final specification of the production function for the Soviet industry. We shall fix σ at 1 so that $\pi = \delta_1$. Hence the form of the final specification:

$$g_{Y,t} = \delta_1 g_{K,t} + (1 - \delta_1) \left[g_{L*,t} + \frac{.0288e^{-.18(t-1951)}}{1 - .16e^{-.18(t-1951)}} \right]$$

$$+ \lambda + \epsilon_t + \mu_t + \delta_{2t} \frac{.015(t - 1962)e^{-.05(t-1962)^2}}{1 + .15e^{-.05(t-1962)^2}} \qquad (11)$$

The estimation results (standard errors in the parentheses) are now as follows:

$$\hat{\lambda} = .0423, \quad \hat{\delta}_1 = .292, \quad \hat{\delta}_2 = .788, \quad \hat{\mu} = .0211, \quad \hat{\epsilon} = .0118,$$
$$\quad (.0381) \qquad\; (.332) \qquad\; (.120) \qquad (.0086) \qquad (.0060)$$

$ESS = 1.25 \times 10^{-3}$, and $\bar{R}^2 = .8400$.

It may be seen that the ESS has remained at the previous very low level and, as a result of reducing the number of parameters, the value of $\bar{R}^2$ increased. The statistical significance of the estimated parameters is now also markedly improved.

Sensitivity analysis: It may be useful to find how sensitive the value of ESS is, in the neighborhood of the optimum point, to small changes in the parameter values. This may be established by computing the eigenvalues and the (normalized) eigenvectors of the Hessian of the objective function at the optimum point in the parameters space: $\lambda, \delta_1, \delta_2, \mu, \epsilon$.[23]

Eigenvalues: 25.0, 6.01, 4.09, .0092, and .0013.

Eigenvectors (in sequence):

1 (.95, .07, .00, .30, .00)
2 (.00, .01, .00, .00, 1.00)
3 (-.30, .02, -.01, .95, .00)
4 (-.03, .99, -.08, -.04, -.01)
5 (-.01, .08, 1.00, .00, .00)

Note that eigenvectors 2 and 5 are directed almost exactly along the δ_1 axis and the ϵ axis, respectively. Eigenvectors 1, 3, and 4 are mixed; 1 and 3 involve some combination of λ and μ, and 4 involves a combination of λ and δ_1. But the eigenvalues associated with vectors 1 and 3 are large, so that even a small change in λ and μ by .0003 increases the ESS by 25×10^{-3}, that is about twentyfold. However, along eigenvector 4 the ESS cannot be changed much by even a significant change in λ and δ_1; an increase by δ_1 by .01 and a decline in λ by .0006 imply an increase in the ESS by only $.1 \times 10^{-3}$. All this indicates, on the one hand, the absence of significant substitution possibilities between the parameters δ_1, δ_2, and ϵ, and, on the other hand, the existence of comparatively strong trade-off between λ and δ_1. This is probably the reason why these two parameters, the trend productivity residual λ and the capital share δ_1, have considerable standard errors.

At the conclusion of this section let it be emphasized that although our final specification is at $\sigma = 1$, this should not be taken to imply that the actual value of the elasticity of substitution is likely to be close to unity. After all, the ESS in the more general case (test No. 2) was found virtually insensitive to changes in σ. Therefore, rather than on a particular value of σ, the emphasis of this study is, instead, on the essentially Harrod-neutral type of technical changes in Soviet industry and on a rather complex dynamics of the growth rate of these technical changes during the postwar period. This study is thus also a rejection of the notion that in the context of slowdown in the Soviet industrial growth the basic parameter is the elasticity of (capital/labor) substitution and that therefore the basic choice is between the two production functions: (a) with σ close to unity and (b) with σ significantly less than unity.

SUMMARY

The summary of the estimation results is given in Figure 1.8. The explanatory power of three hypotheses—Weitzman's, our preliminary one (test No. 1), and the final one—is indicated by the values of ESS and $\bar{R}^2$. In terms of these two statistical indicators the final specification is seen to be significantly superior over the first two specifications. In particular, under this final specification the ESS equals about 41 percent of the ESS implied by Weitzman's specification. Moreover, out of 23 there are five years—1951, 1964, 1966, 1968, and 1972—that account for as much as 80 percent of the remaining ESS. If these five years are excluded, the average deviation of the estimated from the actual annual output growth rate would be .37 percent. As it is, the average deviation is .74. For comparison, under Weitzman's specification this deviation for the same 1951-73 period is 1.15 percent. To assess their relative weights all these deviations should be compared with the average annual growth rate of output, which was 9.85 percent.

Three major findings, together representing the main hypothesis of this chapter, may be summarized as follows:

1. Technical progress in Soviet industry was essentially neutral in the Harrod-Kalecki sense, that is to say, its labor-augmenting component was by far the dominant one.

2. The growth rate of this labor-augmenting component was a sum of three components. Two of these components were variable over time and transitory. One was produced by the postwar recovery in the level of technology (the catch-up phenomenon), while the other was associated with the 1956-61 changes in the workyear. Both these components were superimposed on a constant term associated with the long-run trend in technical change.

3. The error sum of squares was found almost insensitive to changes in the value of the elasticity of substitution from the range between .1 and 1.2. It is suggested therefore that the actual value of

FIGURE 1.8

Soviet Industry, 1951–74: Actual Versus Estimated Growth Rates of Output
(data for 1974 preliminary)

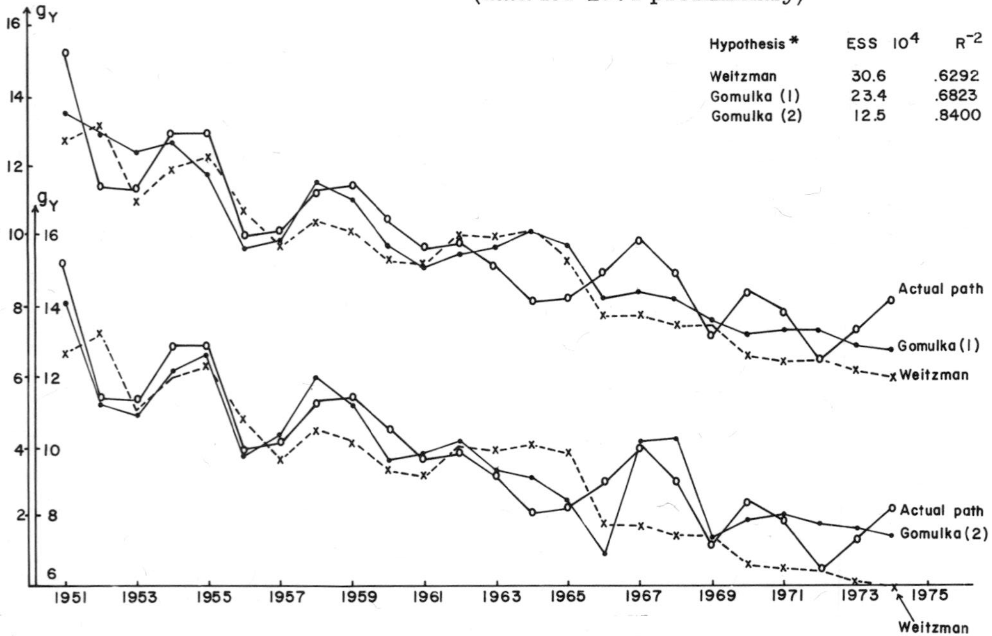

Hypothesis *	ESS 10^4	R^{-2}
Weitzman	30.6	.6292
Gomulka (1)	23.4	.6823
Gomulka (2)	12.5	.8400

* ESS and $\bar{R}^2$ given for the period 1951–73 for which the estimations were made.

Source: Compiled by the author.

40

TABLE 1.6

Sources of Soviet Industrial Growth, Estimated for 1951-73 and Implied for 1947-50, under the "Final" Specification

Year	Output Growth Rate	Capital's Contribution	Labor's Contribution	Components of the "Explained" Residual			Total Estimated Residual*	Unexplained Residual
				Postwar Recovery	Changes in the Workyear	Trend		
1951	15.2	3.3	4.1	2.4	.0	4.2	6.6	1.1
1952	11.4	3.7	2.6	2.0	.0	4.2	5.0	.1
1953	11.3	3.2	3.0	1.6	.0	4.2	4.7	.4
1954	12.3	3.2	3.4	1.3	.0	4.2	5.6	.7
1955	12.3	3.6	1.3	1.1	.0	4.2	7.6	.3
1956	9.9	3.5	-.9	.9	2.1	4.2	7.2	.1
1957	10.1	3.1	.2	.7	2.1	4.2	7.0	.2
1958	11.3	3.2	1.8	.6	2.1	4.2	6.9	-.7
1959	11.4	3.4	1.1	.5	2.1	4.2	6.8	.1
1960	10.4	3.4	-.5	.4	2.1	4.2	6.7	.8
1961	9.6	3.4	-.4	.3	2.4	4.2	6.6	-.1
1962	9.8	3.2	2.3	.3	.0	4.2	4.5	-.3
1963	9.1	3.3	2.5	.2	-.3	4.2	3.5	-.2
1964	8.1	3.4	3.0	.2	-1.7	4.2	2.7	-1.0
1965	8.2	3.0	3.0	.2	-2.1	4.2	2.3	-.2
1966	8.9	2.7	1.8	.2	-3.0	4.2	1.4	2.0
1967	9.9	2.5	4.8	.1	-1.6	4.2	2.7	-.1
1968	8.9	2.3	4.7	.1	-1.1	4.2	3.2	-1.3
1969	7.1	2.3	1.3	.1	-.7	4.2	3.8	-.1
1970	8.4	2.6	1.4	.1	-.4	4.2	3.9	.5
1971	7.8	2.6	1.3	.1	-.1	4.2	4.2	-.2
1972	6.4	2.7	.9	.1	-.1	4.2	4.2	-1.4
1973	7.3	2.5	.9	.0	.0	4.2	4.2	-.3

Sources of Growth Implied under the "Final" Specification

Year	Output Growth Rate	Capital's Contribution	Labor's Contribution	Postwar Recovery	Changes in the Workyear	Trend	Total Estimated Residual*	Unexplained Residual
1947	20.8	2.4	2.1	6.2		4.2	10.4	5.9
1948	26.9	3.7	7.7	4.8		4.2	9.0	5.5
1949	19.5	2.6	4.2	3.8		4.2	8.2	4.7
1950	22.7	2.7	7.8	3.0		4.2	7.2	5.0

*Includes the estimate of the Korean War Disturbance: -1.2 percent in both 1952 and 1953, and +2.4 percent in 1955.

Source: Compiled by the author.

41

FIGURE 1.9

Dynamics of the (Estimated) Productivity Residual and the Residual's Components

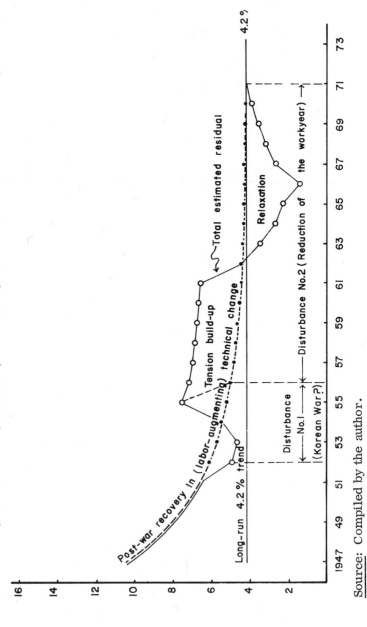

Source: Compiled by the author.

that parameter is largely irrelevant in the search to explain the Soviet growth slowdown.

Dynamics of the (estimated) productivity residual and the residual's three main components are given in Table 1.6 and in Figure 1.9. According to this estimate the catch-up phenomenon was quite important until about 1955, accounting in 1954 still for about one-tenth of the growth rate of output. The combined effect of the catch-up phenomenon and of the changes in the workyear increased the output growth rate by about 2.2 percent in the years 1951-61. However, this effect decreased this rate by (on average) about 1.4 percent in the years 1963-69, contributing thus greatly to the phenomenon of slowdown in the output growth and indeed producing the characteristic phenomenon of jumpdown in the labor productivity growth in 1962-63.

Our explanation of slowdown has two characteristics by which it may be viewed as an intermediate one between that of Weitzman and the traditional explanation. Common with the former but in variance with the latter is the notion of a constant trend component in the residual. On the other hand, the notion that the (imputed) capital share has been approximately constant is common with the traditional hypothesis, but in variance with that of Weitzman. Our computations of changes in the average age of machines are also in variance with Brubaker's findings.[24] Consequently, the age composition effect is in this study discounted as a major explanatory variable in the context of Soviet growth slowdown. Discounted are also both the effect of structural changes and the growth effect of embodied diffusion.

A DIGRESSION ON "UNEXPLAINED" RESIDUAL

The case of this study may be strengthened if a reasonable explanation could be offered for the "unexplained" residual in Table 1.6. As mentioned above, there are five years—1951, 1964, 1966, 1968, and 1972—when the unexplained term is particularly high. This term for 1951 may be explained if we note that the final specification of the production function assumes a constant level of capital utilization. However, a sharp decline in the capital/output ratio in the years 1947-51 is likely to indicate a more or less equally sharp increase in the utilization of capital stock (see Figure 1.4). Our disregard of the (growth) effect of this increase must have resulted in high unexplained positive terms for the years 1947-50 and, although only marginally, for the year 1951. An unexplained loss of 1.0 percent in the growth rate of output in 1964 might be partly associated with a major harvest failure in 1963. This view is supported by the fact that both the light industry and the food industry were in 1964 the only sectors where the labor productivity actually declined.[25] An unexplained gain of 2.0 percent in 1966 cannot be easily accounted for. The gain seems to be associated mainly with relatively high output and labor productivity increases in the following three sectors: machine-building and metal-working, construction materials, and light industry.[26] These increases resulted, perhaps, from the organizational and policy changes introduced in the first year of the first post-Khrushchev five-year plan.

In the years 1967-68 the Soviet industry changed from a six-day workweek to a five-day workweek. Although the number of hours worked per week was kept the same, this changeover resulted, nevertheless, in an increase in the number of hours worked per year from 1,755 in the year 1966 to about 1,870 in 1968 and thereafter, an increase by about 6.6 percent. Such an increase in the workyear may well account for much of the unexplained loss in residual in the year 1968.

Finally, the only plausible reason for unexplained loss of about 1.4 percent (6.4 percent growth rate instead of predicted 7.8 percent) in 1972 is, it seems, the 1972 large-scale decline in agricultural output, affecting adversely the supply of agricultural inputs for processed food and soft goods industries.

CONCLUSION

According to the (final) findings of this study the productivity residual is now close to its trend or equilibrium level of 4.2 percent, so that the growth rate of output g_Y is approaching the level $.3g_K + .7g_{L*} + 4.2$. Since $g_K = g_Y$ in a long-run growth equilibrium state, the growth rate of Soviet industrial output (as well as the growth rate of fixed capital) is therefore already now close to its equilibrium level of $g_{L*} + 6.0$. This prediction of the Soviet industrial growth potential may need to be corrected upward in case of large-scale imports of U.S. machinery and equipment, which should temporarily increase the residual above the 4.2 level. On the other hand, with the technological gap to the West gradually closing, diminishing returns to diffusion of the foreign-made technology should soon set in. But with this gap being as considerable as it still seems to be, especially vis-a-vis the United States, a noticeable decline in the trend growth rate of technical change may not yet begin before some 10 to 15 years. In the meantime the annual growth rate of industrial output (and capital) should be expected to stabilize around the level of some 7.3 percent, assuming that labor expressed in man-years will continue to grow at 1.3 percent.

NOTES

1. B. Balassa, "The Dynamic Efficiency of the Soviet Economy,"
American Economic Review 54, no. 3 (1964): 490-506; A.
Bergson, Prospects for Soviet Economic Growth in the 1970's (Brussels:
Symposium NATO, 1971), and "Comparative Productivity and Effi-
ciency in the Soviet Union and the United States," in Comparison of
Economic Systems: Theoretical and Methodological Approaches, ed.
A. Eckstein (Berkeley: University of California Press, 1973);
E. R. Brubaker, "Embodied Technology, the Asymptotic Behavior of
Capital's Age, the Soviet Growth," Review of Economics and Statistics
50, no. 3 (1968): 304-11, and "Soviet Postwar Economic Growth and
Capital-Labor Substitution: Comment," American Economic Review
62, no. 4 (1972): 675-78; N. M. Kaplan, "Retardation in Soviet
Growth," Review of Economics and Statistics 50, no. 3 (1968): 293-
303; R. H. Moorsteen and R. P. Powell, The Soviet Capital Stock
1928-1962 (Homewood, Ill.: Irwin, 1966), and Two Supplements to
the Soviet Capital Stock (New Haven, Conn.: The Economic Growth
Center of Yale University, 1968); J. H. Noren, "Soviet Industry
Trends in Output, Inputs and Productivity," in New Directions in the
Soviet Economy, U.S. Congress, Joint Economic Committee (Washington, D.C.: U.S. Government Printing Office, 1966), pp. 271-326.
2. M. L. Weitzman, "Soviet Postwar Economic Growth and
Capital-Labor Substitution," American Economic Review 60, no. 4
(1970): 676-92, and "Soviet Postwar Economic Growth and Capital-
Labor Substitution: Reply," American Economic Review 62, no. 4
(1972): 682-84; P. Desai, "The Production Function and Technical
Change in Postwar Soviet Industry: A Reexamination," forthcoming,
and "Technical Change, Factor Elasticity of Substitution and Returns
to Scale in Branches of Soviet Industry in the Postwar Period," in
On the Measurement of Factor Productivities: Theoretical Problems
and Empirical Results, Papers and Proceedings of the Second
Reisenburg Symposium, ed. F.-L. Altmann, O. Kyn, H.-J. Wagener
(Gottingen: Vanderhoeck and Ruprecht, forthcoming).
3. Brubaker, "Embodied Technology," op. cit.
4. Kaplan, op. cit., p. 302.
5. Noren, op. cit., p. 295; Bergson, Prospects, op. cit.,
p. 25.
6. Noren, op. cit., p. 298.
7. Ibid., pp. 296-97.
8. Moorsteen and Powell, Two Supplements, op. cit., p. 9.
9. The exception is Brubaker's attempt to estimate the effect
of change in the average age of capital goods on changes in the productivity residual. However, our recalculation of the effect, which will

be given in this chapter, largely discounts it as a main reason for the growth slowdown.

10. Most of the data in Table 1.1 are either based on or directly the Soviet official data. The problems with quality of any Soviet data, official or nonofficial, are well known. But to secure comparability with Weitzman's paper I use above all his data (Weitzman, "Soviet Postwar Economic Growth," op. cit., Table 1, period 1950-68). My econometric tests cover the period 1951-73. The base year is thus 1950. The data for the period 1928-50 are used to formulate their descriptive, preliminary interpretation. Only the data for the period 1947-50 are used more directly to estimate the so-called postwar recovery trend in the labor-augmenting component of technical change. To estimate changes in the workyear I used what I call the Bergson-Weitzman-Desai index of working hours per man-year. This index takes into account also the length of vacation time and the number of work holidays.

11. Recently also in Poland there has begun a reduction in the workyear. In 1974 six Saturdays were free, in 1975 their number will be increased to twelve. The principles upon which the reduction program is based are spelled out by the Directive No. 41 of the Polish Council of Ministers, dated February 7, 1974. Two of these principles, 4 and 7, make it clear (1) that the "introduction of additional free days is conditional upon an increase in labor productivity sufficient to fulfill the production targets without any additional increase in employment," and (2) that "workers are not to be paid for additional free days." The savings in the wage fund that result from the reduction in working days are to be used "to pay for increased labor norms." It seems thus that in Poland the additional free days are openly used as an instrument of pressure applied to decrease disguised unemployment below its long-run "trend" level. If my interpretation of the Soviet experience is correct and if it can be applied generally to any Soviet-type economy, then a period of increased pressure when the workyear is reduced, with a resulting increase in the growth of output per man-hour, will also in Poland be followed by a period of relaxation of tension, with a resulting collapse in the labor productivity growth. If the reduction in workyear continues at the present rate of 36 hours per year, the magnitude of the increase is about 1.8 percent annually, so that the magnitude of the collapse will be about 3.5 percent.

12. The relative stability of s_t also virtually eliminates the possible explanation of slowdown in the growth rate of labor productivity based on the notion of positive association of the growth rate of technical change and the investment ratio.

13. Weitzman (1970), op. cit., pp. 676-92. For the purpose of comparability with Weitzman's results I retain his assumption of no change in the workyear after 1966. Later in the paper this assumption will be relaxed and, instead, Desai's index of working hours adopted.

14. Let $Y_t = \sum_{i=1}^{n} Y_t$, $L_t = \sum_{i=1}^{n} L_{it}$, $y_t = Y_t/L_t$, $y_{it} = Y_{it}/L_{it}$, and $\rho_{it} = L_{it}/L_t$, where i numbers industrial branches. Note that $y_t = \sum_1 \rho_{it} y_{it}$. Therefore, $\dot{y}_t = \sum_i \dot{\rho}_{it} y_{it} + \sum_i \rho_{it} \dot{y}_{it}$. The term $\sum_i \dot{\rho}_{it} y_{it} \equiv \dot{y}_t^s$ represents a change in y_t brought about by a change in the branch composition of employment. By the branch composition (growth) effect, we mean the rate $\dot{y}_t^s/y_t$.

15. Weitzman (1970), op. cit., p. 689, Table 6.

16. This brief section is based mainly on my macromodels of intercountry technological diffusion developed in S. Gomulka, "Extensions of the Research of Phelps," Review of Economic Studies, No. 1, 1970, pp. 73-93 and S. Gomulka and J. D. Sylwestrowicz, "Import-led Growth: Theory and Estimation" in On the Measurement of Factor Productivities: Theoretical Problems and Empirical Results, Papers and Proceedings of the Second Reisenburg Symposium, ed. F.-L. Altmann, O. Kyn, H.-J. Wagener (Gottingen: Vandenhoeck and Ruprecht, forthcoming).

17. S. Gomulka, Inventive Activity, Diffusion and the Stages of Economic Growth (Aarhus, Denmark: Economic Institute, 1971), Chapters 3 and 4, in particular the "hat-shape relationship."

18. S. Gomulka and J. D. Sylwestrowicz, (forthcoming), op. cit.

19. Data from Historical Statistics of the United States, pp. 600, 601, and Economic Report of the President, 1972, p. 234.

20. Narkhoz, U.S.S.R. 1922-1972 (Moscow, 1972), p. 103, puts the number of "scientific workers" at 162,500 in 1950 and at 1.003 million in 1971. C. Freeman and A. Young, The Research and Development Effort in Western Europe, North America, and the Soviet Union (Paris: OECD, 1965), p. 140, give 10,200 as the number of "scientists" in Russia in 1914. If we assume that the same 10.2 thousand were active in the Soviet Union in 1926 and that the term "scientist" is fully equivalent to the term "scientific worker" then the annual rate of increase of the number of Soviet scientists for the period 1927-50 would be 12.5 percent.

21. Narkhoz, U.S.S.R., 1922-1972, op. cit., p. 483. These expenditures are put at .3 billion rubles in 1940, at 1.0 billion rubles in 1950, and at 13.0 billion rubles in 1971.

22. Weitzman (1970), op. cit., pp. 687-88.

23. Desai, "The Production Function," op. cit.

24. Brubaker, "Embodied Technology," op. cit.

25. Desai, "Technical Change," op. cit.

26. Ibid.

2

INDUSTRY ADJUSTMENT TO
INVESTMENT PRIORITIES
Judith A. Thornton

Until recently, Soviet planners used the allocation of investment as one of the main means of exercising influence over the structure of Soviet industrial output. Unfortunately, acting on the investment process was likely to affect not only the structure of output but also the mix of inputs used to produce each and every output.

The Standard Methodology for Determining the Economic Effectiveness of Capital Investments in use between 1959 and 1969 provided differentiated payback periods ranging from 3 to 20 years for different Soviet industries.[1] High-priority industries, facing long payback periods and implicitly low interest rates, were led to choose highly capital-intensive variants of technology and their output prices were set so as to provide below-average returns from profits into the government budget. Low-priority industries displayed low capital/labor ratios, and their output prices were set, even before turnover taxes, at levels that did, in fact, pay back high yields into the government budget as deductions from enterprise profits.[2]

Different Western economists interpreted the implications of Soviet capital allocation procedures and Soviet pricing policies in different ways. One approach that I explored in some earlier articles was to assume that the differentiated criteria applied to the allocation of capital in different industries would lead to an inefficient allocation of capital and labor among industries.[3] On the assumption that distortions in nominal returns and actual productivity of capital were

I owe thanks to Laurie Kurzweg and Potluri Rao for valuable advice and assistance. Andrew Ivancho contributed able research assistance. I, of course, am responsible for any errors.

proportional, I estimated the potential resource saving that could be enjoyed in Soviet industry by reallocation of capital and labor among industries so as to equalize nominal returns. Subsequently, John Whalley and Yasushi Toda have made further estimates of resource misallocation in Soviet industry. In a recent paper, "Thornton's Estimates of Efficiency Losses in Soviet Industry: Some Fixed Point Method Recalculations," Whalley applies a fixed-point procedure and an assumed planners' utility function to Soviet industry data to estimate the extent of loss due to allocative efficiency in Soviet industry.[4] His results are similar to mine, but both more general and more complete. They are very interesting. Yasushi Toda interprets the same price data in a different way and observes that there is resource misallocation in Soviet industrial investment, but in just the opposite direction to that estimated by Whalley and myself—he concludes that high-priority industries are, if anything, insufficiently capital intensive, and the reverse is true for low-priority industries.[5]

A second, quite different way of dealing with the structure of Soviet industrial capital stock and prices is to assume that the observed structure of industrial capital stock is an efficient structure and that at "true" marginal cost prices, capital would be earning everywhere the same, efficient rate of return. Using this approach, one could then estimate "true" industrial value added that would equal the observed wages bill in each industry plus an assumed rate of return to capital earned by the observed capital stock in the industry. This is the approach used by Rush Greenslade and Wade Robertson to derive their 1968 base-year weights for Soviet industry.[6]

A good case can be made for this approach. Since 1960, the share of nonlabor returns in Soviet industrial value added has crept steadily upward, implying that nominal enterprise prices include growing amounts of implicit tax or monopoly return. On the other hand, it goes without saying that if observed capital stock series are used to derive factor-cost estimates of value added, then the resulting estimates cannot be fit as a production function (since part of output is simply a constant times one input).[7]

There is still a third way of dealing with Soviet capital allocation procedures that would yield altogether different implications from the two approaches just summarized above. This is to consider the decentralized adjustment of production units to the differentiated terms on which they receive their capital. We would expect firms to respond in predictable ways to discriminatory access to capital. A low-priority sector to which capital was strictly rationed or available only on unfavorable terms would have incentives to acquire capital assets in alternative ways. Firms would find it profitable to trade labor for capital by arranging implicit exchanges with firms in high-priority sectors, to divert their labor force from the production of output to the construction of investment in their own plant. They would have an incentive to write up raw materials purchases and repair norms as a way of acquiring capital on raw materials account. Or they might implicitly use the capital of other firms by increasing the share of purchased inputs in their total output, thus reducing the share of own value added. If such adjustment possibilities existed, then low-priority industries would have relatively more effective capital stock than the amount credited to them in the official statistics.

This is not the only adjustment that one would expect. If sectors receive capital on different terms, then their incentives to become vertically and horizontally integrated become distinctly different. A sector with priority access to capital could produce its own supplies more cheaply than it could buy them from a sector that received its capital on less favorable terms. It could diversify more cheaply—to produce related consumer goods, for example—and have access to cost conditions that would be more favorable than the costs facing specialized but low-priority firms in light industry. So we would expect, other things being equal, that high-priority industries would show both more vertical integration and a larger share of out-of-industry output than low-priority industries.

The empirical problem is to test whether any systematic industry adjustments can be measured that might be interpreted as decentralized responses to differential investment criteria. I have done some preliminary empirical work that raises almost as many questions as it answers.

EMPIRICAL TESTS

The data for study were taken from Vladimir Treml et al., The Structure of the Soviet Economy, which presents an analysis and reconstruction of the 1966 Input-Output Table.[8] (In fact, I made use of an earlier computer printout of the data that was made available by the authors.) Cross-section data on industrial output, capital, and labor and the detailed structure of industrial purchases were provided for 64 (later 69) industrial sectors. This is industry data in much greater detail than has been available previously. Data on pre-1966 and post-1966 rates of growth of output and capital stock were provided by recent studies of Rush Greenslade and Wade Robertson and by James Noren and Douglas Whitehouse.[9]

I wanted to ask, first, whether there was any evidence that low-priority sectors might acquire capital goods through alternative channels and, second, whether high-priority sectors were observed to expand either vertically or horizontally into secondary lines of

activity to a greater extent than low-priority sectors. To study the
allocation of capital stock, I reasoned as follows: Consider two
sectors that receive allocations of capital on differential terms.
Assume that, in the absence of discriminatory priority policies on
the part of the planners, the two sectors would be expected to make
repair and replacement purchases on raw-materials account from the
investment supply sectors (those sectors that accounted for their
original allocations of machinery and equipment) at approximately
average rates. For all industries, "normal" investment-goods raw
materials purchases would be expected to be some constant percentage
of industry capital stock in machinery and equipment:

$$R_j = gK_j \tag{1}$$

where R refers to purchases of goods on raw materials account from
the investment supply sectors and K refers to industry capital stock
in machinery and equipment in the jth sector. Individual industry
purchase norms are assumed to be distributed around the all-industry
norm in a manner reflecting differences in the particular characteristics of industry capital stock, which we assume to be unrelated to
the level of priority of the industry.

Now, consider a sector that is either heavily rationed in its
allocation of capital or that can acquire capital only on highly unfavorable terms. One rational adjustment for such a sector to make
would be to attempt to acquire capital goods from the investment
supply sectors on raw materials account rather than on investment
account. If an industry facing unfavorable terms were able to adjust
in this manner, its individual purchase norm would be increased by
two effects. Its raw materials norm from the investment supply
sectors would be inflated directly to provide the hidden investment.
Its effective capital stock would be larger than the official value of
its capital stock on investment account, so the average amount of
raw materials purchases required to service true capital stock would
appear to be above-average when compared with the nominal capital
stock in the official accounts.

The predicted value of purchases from investment supply sectors
on raw materials account made by sector j may be specified as:

$$R_j = \beta_1 K_j + \beta_2 P_j + u_j \tag{2}$$

where P refers to an index of industry priority in the allocation of
capital. The index, P, in turn, might be specified as a weighted
index of a number of indicators or determinants of industry priority:

$$P_j = \Sigma \, \alpha_{ij} \, P_{ij} \tag{3}$$

The coefficient of capital should be positive and, in percentage terms, equal the average purchase norm for given values of the other variables. If there is effective decentralized evasion of government terms of allocation, then the coefficient between purchases and "priority" should be negative.

Estimation of the regression equation required identification of the investment supply sectors and some attempt at quantification of the notion of industry priority. Investment supply sectors were defined as sectors that supplied a major share of their output to nonconsumption final demand. Table 2.1 identifies the sectors and lists the share of output going to "other final demand" in the Soviet Union and also the share of the corresponding U.S. sector's gross output going to private fixed capital formation. (After the fact, agricultural machinery and equipment should have been excluded from the test of industry; its inclusion reduced the significance level of the estimates.)

The problem of defining an index of sectoral priority presented a much more difficult problem. The Standard Methodology for Determining the Economic Effectiveness of Capital Investments defines payback periods for a relatively few, highly aggregate sectors. In the past, I had used earned differential returns in industry as a surrogate for the terms on which capital was allocated. For the 1960 industrial data, there was a close rank order correlation between stated payback periods and earned capital charges in industry.[10] But for the 1966 input-output data, the relationship had disappeared—not a very promising development. The alternative measures that I tested as potential indices of sectoral priority were earned returns to capital, capital/labor (or capital/output) ratios, indices of industry growth between 1959-66, and a dummy variable, taking the value of either 1 or 0, that partitioned industry into investment and noninvestment sectors.

The regression estimates took the form:

$$R = b_0 + b_1 K + b_2 G + b_3 D + b_4 K/L + b_5 C + u \tag{4}$$

where the variables were identified as follows: R = purchases on raw materials account from investment supply sectors; K = industry capital stock in machinery and equipment in 1966; G = index of industry growth between 1959 and 1966; D = dummy variable designated 1 for investment sectors and 0 for noninvestment sectors; K/L = a single variable measuring capital intensity; C = capital charge measured as gross returns to capital.

TABLE 2.1

Investment-Supply Sectors for Soviet Industry, 1966

Sector	Soviet Union (ratio of "other final demand" to gross value of output)	United States (ratio of gross private capital formation to gross value of output)
15 Energy and power machinery and equipment	60.9	
18 Machine tools	91.7	50.2
19 Forge and press machinery and equipment	91.5	49.5
22 Precision instruments	65.2	
23 Mining and metals machinery and equipment	81.5	41.4
24 Pumps and compressors	59.0	
25 Logging and paper machinery and equipment	68.3	55.9
26 Light industry machinery and equipment	64.8	45.1
27 Food industry machinery and equipment	86.6	59.6
28 Printing machinery and equipment	99.0	61.2
29 Hoist and transport equipment	81.9	40.8
30 Construction machinery and equipment	76.9	43.9
32 Transportation machinery and equipment	89.0	34.7
34 Agricultural machinery and equipment	41.8	61.8
36 Other machinery and equipment	47.1	
40 Repair	81.6	

Sources: Soviet data from Vladimir Treml et al., The Structure of the Soviet Economy (New York: Praeger, 1972), computer printout of 1966, input-output table; U.S. data from U.S. Bureau of the Census, U.S. input-output table for 1963.

Table 2.2 summarizes the results. As expected, purchases from investment-supply sectors on raw materials account are closely associated with industry capital stock. Evaluated at the means of the two variables, a 10 percent increment in capital stock was associated with a 5.9 percent increase in purchases. (A 100,000-ruble increment in capital results in a 6,579-ruble rise in purchases.) Since the capital stock measure is functioning, in part, as a surrogate for industry size, I found that the introduction of a separate index of industry size was insignificant and did not affect the values of the coefficients in any significant way. Knowledge of two other variables, industry growth and the dummy variable for investment sectors, both had substantial effects on the expected value of purchases from investment supply sectors; a 1 percent increment in the observed growth index for the period was associated with a 125,801-ruble increment in expected purchases. Membership in the investment sector increased expected purchases by 201,154 rubles compared with noninvestment industries. These are large amounts when we consider that the mean amount of purchases was 149,199 rubles. Neither the capital/labor ratio nor returns to capital shed any additional light on purchases.

What can be concluded from these numbers? If we interpret the explanatory variables, other than capital, as indices of priority, then clearly we find no evidence that low-priority industries evade the official capital rationing norms through substitution of purchases on raw materials account. Quite the contrary, if we interpreted above-average growth or membership in the investment sector as indices of high priority, then the positive regression slopes would imply that high-priority industries were able to make above-average purchases of investment-type goods on raw materials account. The only variable with a negative (but insignificant) coefficient, consistent with the evasion hypothesis, is the capital/labor ratio; and that coefficient might be observed if industries with higher capital/labor ratios had a larger share of capital assets in long-lived assets that required little servicing.

I can come up with an equally plausible set of arguments for the signs of the growth and investment coefficients that would be unrelated to priority. Consider the growth coefficient—the input-output capital stock series are defined gross of depreciation. Since faster-growing industries have a newer capital stock, the ratio of their effective capital stock to their nominal capital stock is larger than for slow-growing industries. The positive slope of the growth coefficient might simply reflect a pattern of industry purchases that was a constant percentage of effective, rather than nominal, capital stock.

The effect of membership in the investment sector may be rationalized similarly in a manner unrelated to priorities. In

TABLE 2.2

Regression of Soviet Raw Materials Purchases from Investment Supply Sectors

Equation	Constant	K	G	D	C	K/L	R^2	$\bar{R}^2$
2.1	-158844	0.067	120983	195249		-2.84601	.5080	.4747
	(74887)	(0.011)	(44925)	(69495)		(2.5692)		
	[-2.1211]	[6.0456]	[2.6930]	[2.8095]		[-1.1077]		
2.2	-192067	0.066	125801	201154	13119		.4986	.4646
	(76818)	(0.011)	(46080)	(70652)	(41546)			
	[-2.5003]	[5.9159]	[2.7301]	[2.8471]	[.3158]			

Source: Compiled by the author.

statistical tests on the rest of the input-output table, I found that the coefficients for purchases from "own sector" tended to be higher than the coefficients for purchase by other sectors. So the dummy variable for investment sectors might simply be picking up this "own sector" effect and be unrelated to any priority for the investment sectors in the allocation plan.[11]

So, in sum, there is no evidence that firms are able to evade the planned allocations of capital through this channel. The results might be interpreted as indicating the workings of priority allocations, but the results also can be explained in other ways.

VERTICAL AND HORIZONTAL INTEGRATION

The second set of tests referred to evidence of horizontal or vertical integration of Soviet industries. We asked if there was evidence that high-priority industries would expand horizontally to produce additional out-of-sector outputs or vertically to supply more own value added.

Systematic evidence on horizontal integration is sparse. The best evidence for 1966 comes from estimates of the commodity-establishment ratios for several industries made by Fidler and cited in Treml's input-output study.[12] Table 2.3 lists the commodity-establishment ratios, net returns to capital, and growth indices for several sectors. A high commodity-establishment ratio implies that a relatively large amount of commodity output is produced outside of the parent sector by other sectors. A low commodity-establishment ratio is associated with industries that produce goods other than the primary commodities of their industry. If industries were observed to adjust to differential access to resources, we would expect high commodity-establishment ratios in low-priority industries, low commodity-establishment ratios in high-priority industries. The reader may form his own opinion as to whether he observes any systematic ranking between commodity-establishment ratios in Column 1 of Table 2.3 and what he thinks are "true" priorities. However, rank order correlation tests found no relationship between commodity-establishment ratios and the possible indices of priority in Columns 2, 4, and 3.

Evidence on vertical integration was tested using the 1966 input-output data described earlier. Our hypothesis was that, in the absence of adjustment to priority allocation, the extent of vertical integration in a sector might be predicted by the industry's stage in the production process or "nearness to final use" (estimated as the ratio of production for final demand to total output). If decentralized

TABLE 2.3

Commodity-Establishment Ratios for Selected
Soviet Industries, 1966

Industry	Commodity-Establishment Ratio	Industry Growth Index (1959–66)	Returns to Capital	Capital-Labor Ratio
Woodworking	119.8	120.4	.027	1784.7
Ferrous ores	105.8	130.0	.053	15813.4
Apparel	96.8	155.7	1.07	929.8
Ball bearings	95.8	141.2	.244	3495.8
Gas	93.1	138.2	.105	38426.7
Light industry machinery and equipment	89.9	139.0	.512	2853.0
Forge and press machinery and equipment	85.4	139.8	.333	5198.4

Sources: Data on commodity-establishment ratios from
M. Fidler, Vestnik statistiki, no. 9 (1969), p. 36, cited in
Vladimir Treml et al., The Structure of the Soviet Economy (New
York: Praeger, 1972), p. 566.

adjustment to priorities occurred, then the amount of vertical integration would also be related to indices of industry priority. As before,
possible indices of priority were growth, capital intensity, returns
to capital, and membership in the investment sector. The resulting
regression estimates took the form:

$$V = b_0 + b_1 F + b_2 C + b_3 K + b_4 G + b_5 D + u \qquad (5)$$

where the variables were identified as follows: V = ratio of own value
added to total sales; F = ratio of production for final demand to total
production; K = capital intensity; C = capital charges; G = growth
index; D = dummy variable for investment sectors. Table 2.4 gives
the regression results.

From Table 2.4 there appears to be a significant central
tendency in the value added/gross output ratio. However, variation
from the average ratio is, surprisingly enough, unrelated to the
nearness to final demand of the sector, once the effects of other
variables are included. The most obvious interpretation of the data

TABLE 2.4

Regression of Share of Output Supplied from Own Value Added

Equation	Constant	FD/GVO	C	K/X	G	R^2	$\bar{R}^2$
4.1	.2546	0.0165	.8932	0.0715		.52538	.50204
	(0.0458)	(0.0627)	(.1376)	(0.0250)			
	[5.5574]	[.2625]	[6.4917]	[2.8572]			
4.2	.3012		.9184	0.0680	-0.0257	.53075	.50767
	(0.0561)		(.1352)	(0.02332)	(0.0293)		
	[5.3704]		[6.7906]	[2.9177]	[-.8757]		

Source: Compiled by the author.

58

is simply that industries that are relatively capital intensive and industries that are earning relatively higher returns to capital tend to produce more of their output with own resources and to purchase less from other sectors. Measures of industry growth and membership in the investment sector were not significant.

So the data on vertical integration do lend tentative support to the notion that industries do adjust to the terms on which they are able to acquire resources, but we cannot say that high-priority industries tend to be more vertically integrated because the results of our regressions leave us with no very clear notion of what is meant by priority. Both the index of capital intensity and returns to capital have positive coefficients with the measure of vertical integration. Should higher returns to capital be interpreted as indicating higher priority?

CONCLUDING REMARKS

The results of the empirical work I have done so far do not support a single, clear-cut conclusion about industry adjustment to the terms of investment allocation. There was no statistical evidence that low-priority industries were acquiring capital goods on raw materials account; rather, there was evidence that rapidly growing industries and industries in the investment sector received larger allocations on raw-materials account from the investment-related sectors just as they received larger allocations on investment account. This could be interpreted as evidence of the successful working of the priority system. On the other hand, the regressions on vertical integration indicated that industries with lower capital-intensity and lower returns to capital tended to produce less of their output with their own resources and to purchase more of it from other sectors. This result suggested at least one avenue by which industries could evade relatively unfavorable terms of allocation facing them. But it did not seem to me that the responses that I measured could be interpreted in terms of any simple distinction between low- and high-priority sectors.

The independent variables introduced here—growth, profitability, capital-intensity, investment role—were intended to serve as partial proxies for the implicit priorities of the planners. But the results leave the investigator, and presumably the reader, quite uncertain as to how the concept of "priority" can be quantified.

First, the independent variables do not have any significant interrelationship. The correlation matrix of all variables for the regressions in Table 2.2 shows low correlations among the three variables, growth, returns to capital, and capital-intensity. The coefficients are the following: growth and returns to capital: -.11311; returns to capital and capital intensity: -.160934; capital-intensity and growth: -.11660. Their partial relationships are all low and negative. Which one, if any, should we expect to reflect planners' priorities?

Second, the variable, returns to capital, either has little effect on the dependent variables or it acts in the opposite direction than could be predicted. It is true that the sign of returns to capital is negative with respect to the other indicators of priority as we would expect, but the effect is quite weak. This leaves me with some question as to what implications I am justified in drawing from data on disequilibrium prices and differences in nominal returns to capital for the period of the late 1960s. Just as two separate models for estimating the efficiency loss from factor price distortion become available, the pattern of factor returns becomes less amenable to the efficiency loss interpretation. I think it would be worthwhile to explore some alternative explanations of Soviet value series based on either a tax model or a monopoly model.

We also need to do some more systematic statistical work on what is meant by priority. What is clear is that some of the conventional descriptive assumptions about the workings of a priority system in Soviet industry are out of date. It has been conventional to speak of high-priority industries as, roughly, heavy, investment-related, capital-intensive industries, growing rapidly with under-priced outputs; low-priority industries were light, consumer goods, labor-intensive, slower-growing industries whose prices were above marginal costs. Those descriptions are largely unsupported by the 1966 cross-section data. Has there been a substantial change in industry patterns between 1959 and 1966, or was the 1959 economy already contradicting our conventional wisdom about Soviet industry?

While the results of the regressions are ambivalent, it is obvious that there are substantial returns to further systematic statistical analysis of the input-output accounts.

NOTES

1. See L. Vagg, "When is Innovation Advantageous?" Pravda, September 24, 1969, p. 2; "Tipovaya metodika opredeleniya ekonomicheskoi effektivnosti kapital'nykh volzhenii i novoi tekhniki v narodnom khoziaistvo SSSR, " Planovoe khoziaistvo, no. 3 (1960); "Tipovaya metodika opredeleniya ekonomicheskoi effektivnosti kapital'nykh vlozhenii", Ekonomicheskaya gazeta, no. 39 (1969).

2. See Alan Abouchar, "The New Soviet Standard Methodology for Investment Allocation," Soviet Studies 24, no. 3 (1973): 402-10 for an excellent discussion of both the methodology and its economic content.

3. Judith Thornton, "The Estimation of Value–Added and average Returns to Capital in Soviet Industry from Cross-Section Data," Journal of Political Economy 73, no. 6 (1965): 620-35; and "Differential Capital Charges and Resource Allocation in Soviet Industry," Journal of Political Economy 79, no. 3 (1971): 545-61.

4. John Whalley, "Thornton's Estimates of Efficiency Losses in Soviet Industry: Some Fixed Point Method Recalculations," London School of Economics Working Paper, July 1974.

5. Yasushi Toda, "Estimation of a Cost Function in the State of Structural Disequilibrium: The Case of Soviet Manufacturing Industry, 1960-1969," in Planning in the Soviet Type System, ed. Judith Thornton (Cambridge: University Press, forthcoming).

6. Rush V. Greenslade and Wade Robertson, "Industrial Production in the USSR," in Soviet Economic Prospects for the Seventies, U.S. Congress, Joint Economic Committee, 93rd Cong., 1st Sess. (Washington, D.C.: U.S. Government Printing Office, 1973), pp. 270-82.

7. This is a problem associated with one set of estimates by M.L. Weitzman in "Soviet Postwar Economic Growth and Capital-Labor Substitution," American Economic Review 60, no. 4 (1970): 676-92.

8. Vladimir Treml, Dimitri Gallik, Barry Kostinsky, and Kurt Kruger, The Structure of the Soviet Economy (New York: Praeger, 1972).

9. Greenslade and Robertson, op. cit., and James Noren and Douglas Whitehouse, "Soviet Industry in the 1971-75 Plan," Soviet Economic Prospects for the Seventies, op. cit., pp. 206-45.

10. Thornton, "Differential Capital Charges," op. cit.

11. Laurie Kurzweg suggested this interpretation to me.

12. Treml et al., op. cit., p. 566.

3

AN INTRODUCTION TO THE SOCIALIST THEORY OF LOCATION
Paul Jonas

```
                    A
                 B     B
              R     R     R
           A     A     A     A
        C     C     C     C     C
     A     A     A     A     A     A
        D     D     D     D     D
           A     A     A     A
              B     B     B
                 R     R
                    A
```

The magic word "abracadabra," which in medieval times was engraved to protect the wearers from bad luck or disease, has fascinated many minds. Starting from the uppermost letter, how many paths can be located that yield the mysterious word? What are the shortest or the longest routes giving "abracadabra"?[1]

The letters, organized in a grid, remind us of a city consisting of perfectly square blocks, influencing not only mystics but also location theorists, who seek to establish specific zigzags in order to minimize or maximize various objectives.

Most cities, in reality, are multifunctional and include concentration points for specialized functions, such as industrial, manufacturing, trade, rural, or administrative activities to provide goods

---

I wish to thank my colleague Pham Chung for many helpful comments and suggestions.

and/or services for a surrounding tributary area.[2] Highly abstract
constructions have been proposed by location theorists to explain the
existing hierarchy among cities and the sites of the "economic land-
scape" within cities.[3] It is, however, interesting to note that a
comprehensive socialist theory of location is nonexistent and that
almost all works related to urbanization, industrial location, and
related issues are empirical and case oriented. In some exceptions,
broad sociological concepts are discussed with respect to urbanization,[4] and there are some sweeping statements, such as one of
Coloman Kadas which states that Western models of location theory
are inapplicable in a centrally planned system since in such a state
plant location is determined by "national economic, or, rather social
efficiency" rather than profit maximizing considerations.[5]

In the following, using the concepts of classical location theory,
we will make an attempt to construct a highly theoretical model to
solve the locational equilibrium of an industrial firm in the "abracadabra"-type plane lattice framework. The city grid, which could be
considered as a starting point for the development of more complex
and realistic models, will represent a locality in a centrally planned
system that is organized in accordance with the taste of a central
planning authority seeking to maximize "social efficiency."

Are the Thunenien-Weberian-Palanderian classical postulates
applicable in Soviet-type economies? We propose that with some
modifications they are; moreover, we argue that a transportation-
oriented model is perhaps more relevant in centrally planned systems
than in market-type economies. The reason for this is that recent
studies indicate that in developed capitalist countries the importance
of transportation costs is preceded by many factors, such as manpower characteristics, general legal aspects, corporate taxes that
may vary in different sites, the nature of local government, the
quality of industrial sites, and various recreational considerations
for the employees.[6] The majority of these factors can be considered
as constant in centrally planned systems or as receiving only marginal consideration from the decision-maker. Therefore, an aggregate
transportation cost minimization model to establish the optimum location for an industrial plant seems to be a fair assumption.

The characteristics in which a socialist location theory differs
from the general postulates relevant to a price-directed system is
that the planner determines the location of the firm by taking for
granted: (1) the ex ante determined quantity of goods to be produced;
(2) the marketplaces to which the goods should be delivered.

The quantity of goods to be produced in accordance with the
plan may approximate the existing demand or may partially disregard
it in accordance with national priorities. The established marketplaces
can play an important role in a planned urbanization process,

accelerating or slowing down urbanization in the city or in selected districts. When this conditions are given, it is proposed that the firm will be located in accordance with the main variable: minimum aggregate transportation costs resulting from the distance of the inputs necessary for the production and the routes to the markets where the goods are distributed to the households. While one should concede to Kadas[7] that a profit-maximization locational model of the Hotellingian type may be inapplicable to the decision-making process in a centrally planned economy, [8] we argue that the extensions and modifications of the Weberian Locational Triangle may lead to a theory of location that could explain the decision-making process in a centrally planned economy. This construction, in its basic form, deals with one product and two nonubiquitous inputs to solve one objective—the minimization of the isodapanes (equal aggregate transportation costs).

Before starting the analysis, one should, however, deal with a possible objection. Some critics would argue that a cost-minimization model would also be objectionable in Soviet-type economies since the latter have a systematic bias in pricing schemes and, therefore, costs do not represent actual scarcities.[9]

Current studies, based on empirical investigations using the input-output prices of production in various socialist East European countries conclude, however, that conventional prices calculated by the central planning bureaus are comparable, in toto, to those used by price-directed systems and that it is not possible to demonstrate in a comparative analysis any systematic bias by measuring the relative shares of national incomes.[10] Because of these unconventional findings, we are inclined to reject the familiar supposition held by most eminent Sovietologists[11] that there is a systematic relation originating from a "two-level pricing"—between the price ratios of capital and consumer goods in planned economies and the comparable relative prices in market-type systems.

The rejection of this widely accepted position should not imply that price schemes in the Soviet-bloc countries do not reflect various policy targets (going beyond the low price for books and high price for spirits) but should suggest that retail price distortions are not predictable ex ante and the variations, if the values of the goods are aggregated, may well cancel each other out. Moreover, and in our case this is the most important, it suggests that the real and actual costs of production and distribution do not differ significantly and that the actual costs play one of the most important roles in the decisions of the planner. We propose, therefore, that a Weberian type of locational model, which includes the enumerated prerequisites, could be relevant in a Soviet-type economy.

THE MODEL

To develop our model we make the following assumptions:

1. An $N \times N$ square-plane lattice is postulated to represent a city in a centrally planned economy and is placed in the first quadrant of a Cartesian system. N is even.

2. The area of the plane lattice is inhabited by a number of households equally distributed in the city. The planner prefers an even development and decides that each node in the plane lattice is a market.

3. It is estimated that a unit demand for each market exists and that the quantity produced exactly satisfies this demand.

4. One extracting site, with a place fixed, exists in a node. The planner searches for the best site for the industrial plant. It can be located at any node.

5. Transportation cannot go diagonally, and a movement from one adjacent point to another is to be considered as a one-distance movement.

6. The transportation cost per unit distance and unit quantity from the extracting place, with the "profit mark-up" given to the carriers, equals c_1, and the transportation cost for the same units from the plant to markets, assuming various modes of transportation, is equal to c_2. It is supposed that $c_2 > c_1$.

The planner takes these prerequisites as given and seeks for the optimum location for an industrial firm, which, in accordance with recent reforms in some Soviet-bloc countries, is an autonomous unit of socialist undertaking, operates with its own power, and aims for the maximization of its own interest within the limits of regulations.

To approach this problem, we construct a functional relationship, selecting the aggregate equal transportation costs, the Weberian isodapanes, as dependent variables and choosing, as explanatory variables, the envisioned location of the firm; the site of the raw material unit transportation costs to and from the firm, the diagonal elements, and the size of the city grid. Thus,

$$\text{isodapanes} = [(XF, YF), (X0, Y0), (XI, YI), c_1, c_2, N] \qquad (1)$$

where (XF, YF) are the coordinates of the firm; $(X0, Y0)$ are the coordinates of the extracting place; (XI, YI) are the coordinates of each point on the main diagonal connecting $(0, 0)$ and (N, N); c_1 and c_2 are the respective unit transportation costs; and N is the size of the city grid that is assumed to be an even integer.

To make the relationship expressed in equation 1 workable, several steps should be taken.

It can be seen intuitively that the distance from the resources to the firm is

$$D_A = ([XF - X0] + [YF - Y0]) ,\qquad(2)$$

and the distance from the firm to the markets is

$$D_B = (N + 1)[XF - 0] + \sum_{I=0}^{N} [YF - YI] + (N + 1)[XF - 1]$$

$$+ \sum_{I=0}^{N} [YF - YI] + (N + 1)[XF - 2] + \sum_{I=0}^{N} [YF - YI] + . . .$$

$$+ (N + 1)[XF - N] + \sum_{I=0}^{N} [YF - YI]$$

Combining and factoring this equation yields

$$D_B = (N + 1) \sum_{I=0}^{N} ([XF - XI] + [YF - YI]) .\qquad(3)$$

The multiplication of equation 2 by the unit cost of transportation c_1 and by the units of inputs required to supply markets in accordance with the plan yields the cost of transporting the raw material to the firm, the isovector A.[12]

$$I_A = c_1 (N + 1)^2 ([XF - X0] + [YF - Y0])\qquad(4)$$

Multiplying equation 3 by the unit cost of transportation c_2 yields the cost of transporting the finished products to the markets, the isovector B.

$$I_B = c_2 (N + 1) \sum_{I=0}^{N} ([XF - XI] + [YF - YI])\qquad(5)$$

Thus, the equal total costs of transportation are the sum of isovector A and isovector B.

$$\text{Isodapanes} = \text{Equal Total Costs (ETC)} = I_A + I_B$$

$$= c_1 (N + 1)^2 ([XF - X0] + [YF - Y0]) + c_2 (N + 1) \sum_{I=0}^{N} ([XF - XI]$$

$$+ [YF - YI])\qquad(6)$$

Dividing this equation by c_1, and using K for c_2/c_1, we receive the transportation costs in terms of the numeraire c_1.

$$\frac{ETC}{c_1} = ETC_{c_1} = (N + 1)^2 ([XF - X0] + [YF - Y0])$$

$$+ K(N + 1) \sum_{I=0}^{N} ([XF - XI] + [YF - YI]) \qquad (7)$$

For the main part of our analysis and conclusions, this latter equation will be used.

We previously assumed that $c_2 > c_1$. The reasons for this supposition should now be obvious, not only for empirical reasons but also for theoretical considerations. If $c_2 < c_1$, then the problem of searching for the best plant location becomes trivial since, in this case, the firm should always be located at the site of the raw materials. This can be shown heuristically.

It can be seen that the isovector A, (I_A), in equation 4 is zero if the factory is located at the site of the resources. Now, suppose that the factory is moved away from here, by one unit. The costs, in this case, will increase from zero to $c_1(N + 1)^2$ and, at the same time, isovector B, (I_B), in equation 5 will not decrease by a greater amount since c_1 is greater than c_2. Thus, this move can be considered irrational.

Using the concept of arithmetic progression,[13] we can translate equation 7 and locate the minimum values with respect to the coordinates of the firm by setting the first derivative of the equal total costs (ETC) expressed in units of c_1 with respect to the coordinates of the firm.

$$\frac{\partial ETC_{c_1}}{XF} = K(N + 1)(2XF - N) + (N + 1)^2 = 0 \qquad (8)$$

$$\frac{\partial ETC_{c_1}}{\partial XF} = K(N + 1)(2YF - N) + (N + 1)^2 = 0 \qquad (9)$$

These two equations give the solution for our problem.

THE HIDDEN PROPERTIES AND PATTERNS
OF THE DERIVED MODEL

Let us postulate first a 10×10 city grid; locate the raw material site at $(0, 1)$ and the plant site at $(5, 5)$; and leave c_1 and c_2 undetermined for the time being (Figure 3.1).

FIGURE 3.1

Isovector Construction and the Firm's Optimal Path
[Resources (0, 1); Firm (5, 5)]

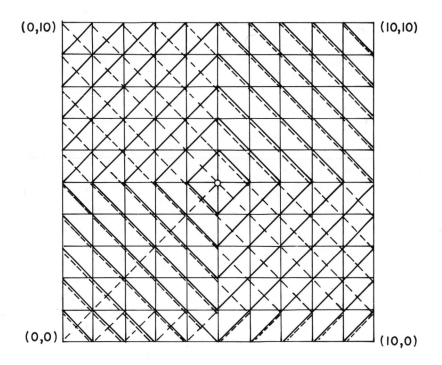

Source: Compiled by the author.

1. The Palanderian isovectors showing the loci of equal transportation costs from the fixed extracting place to the possible plant locations are the dotted lines, kinked at $y = 1$.

At $(0, 1)$ the transportation costs are zero; at the next isovector, one unit further, they are $2(N + 1)^2 c_1$; two units farther, $2(N + 1)^2 c_1$; five units further, where our plant site is now assumed, $5(N + 1)^2 c_1$; and the furthest possible site, $18(N + 1)^2 c_1$.

The dotted lines represent I_A, expressed in equation 4.

2. The Palanderian isovectors showing the loci of equal transportation costs from the plant site to the markets are drawn in solid lines around $(5, 5)$. Since all $(N + 1)^2$ markets should be supplied (markets are assumed to be at every node including the plant site and the node at the extracting place), the isovector is defined by summing up the costs at each node.

The solid lines represent I_B, expressed in equation 5.

3. The Weberian isodapanes are the points where $I_A + I_B$ yields an equal sum. The minimum values of these isodapanes determine the "optimum path." In our case, the loci of these points are determined by starting from the extracting place $(0, 1)$, going to $(1, 1)$, and following the diagonal to $(5, 5)$.

Our final equations 8 and 9 yield these ordinates. (One should remember that all these lines are, in fact, discontinuous and are relevant only at the nodes, since diagonal movements through the city blocks are not permitted.)

It should be obvious that the optimum location of the plant will be at some node crossed by the "optimum path." The exact point will be determined with ratio c_2/c_1, that is, the K value.

We can see heuristically that, the greater the K value, the greater are the pressures on the planner to locate the plant at the center. This optimum location moves in southwesterly direction as the value of K is diminished.

Tables 3.1 and 3.2 show the process of determining the relationship between K values and plant locations. Solving the values of K for Table 3.1 by equating the neighboring equation, we receive the results in Table 3.2.

Thus, for K values greater than 11.0 the planner should always locate the industrial plant in the middle of the city grid. If this rule is not observed, the values of both isovectors will increase. If the value of K equals 11.0, then the location is indifferent between A and B, and this condition remains valid until the value of K is reduced below 3.67, when it will shift to the indicated sites in accordance with Table 3.2. The problem of deciding about the location site, assuming pure transport orientation, is nontrivial for the planner if c_2/c_1 is between 1.22 and 11.0.[14]

TABLE 3.1

Equations to Determine the Critical Values of K

Plant Site	Isodapane
(0, 1)	111K
(1, 1)	121 + 1012K
(2, 2)	363 + 858K
(3, 3)	605 + 748K
(4, 4)	847 + 682K
(5, 5)	1089 + 660K

Source: Compiled by the author.

TABLE 3.2

K Values and Plant Locations

Plant Site	Range for K
A (5, 5)	11.00–
B (4, 4)	3.67–11.00
C (3, 3)	2.20– 3.67
D (2, 2)	1.57– 2.20
E (1, 1)	1.22– 1.57
F (0, 1)	0 – 1.22

Source: Compiled by the author.

The interrelationship among the respective isodapanes, keeping the K value constant in the critical range, is also interesting. A special case with K = 2.2 is tabulated in Table 3.3, and the aggregate transportation costs, with respect to the plant site, are plotted in Figure 3.2.

In Table 3.3 we can locate the minima minomorum of the isodapanes. The method is to select the minimum values in the first column (2637.80) and, similarly, the lowest figures in the first row (2395.60). The intersection of the selected column and row locates the plant sites where the aggregate transportation cost is minimum. For this given

TABLE 3.3

Aggregate Transportation Costs at Different Plant Sites
(K = 2.2, N = 10)

	0	1	2	3	4	5	6	7	8	9	10
0	2783.00	2444.20	2395.80	2395.80	2444.20	2541.00	2683.20	2879.80	3121.80	3412.20	3751.00
1	2686.20	2347.40	2299.00	2299.00	2347.40	2244.20	2589.40	2783.00	3025.00	3315.40	3654.20
2	2637.80	2299.00	2250.60	2250.60	2299.00	2395.80	2541.00	2734.60	2976.60	3267.00	3605.80
3	2637.80	2999.00	2250.60	2250.60	2299.00	2395.80	2541.00	2734.60	2976.60	3267.00	3605.80
4	2686.20	2347.40	2299.00	2299.00	2347.40	2444.20	2589.40	2783.00	3025.00	3315.40	3654.20
5	2783.00	2444.20	2385.80	2395.80	2444.20	2541.00	2686.20	2879.80	3121.80	2412.20	3751.00
6	2928.20	2589.40	2541.00	2541.00	2589.40	2686.20	2831.40	3025.00	3267.00	3557.40	3896.20
7	3121.80	2783.00	2734.60	2734.60	2783.00	2879.80	3025.00	3218.60	3460.60	3751.00	4089.80
8	3363.80	3025.00	2976.60	2976.60	3025.00	3121.80	3267.00	3460.60	3702.60	3993.00	4331.80
9	3654.20	3315.40	3267.00	3267.00	3315.40	3412.20	3557.40	3751.00	3993.00	4283.40	4662.20
10	3993.00	3654.20	3605.80	3605.80	3654.20	3751.00	3896.20	4089.80	4331.80	4622.20	4961.00

Min.

Source: Compiled by the author.

71

FIGURE 3.2

Aggregate Transportation Costs at Different Plant Sites

(K = 2.2; N = 10)

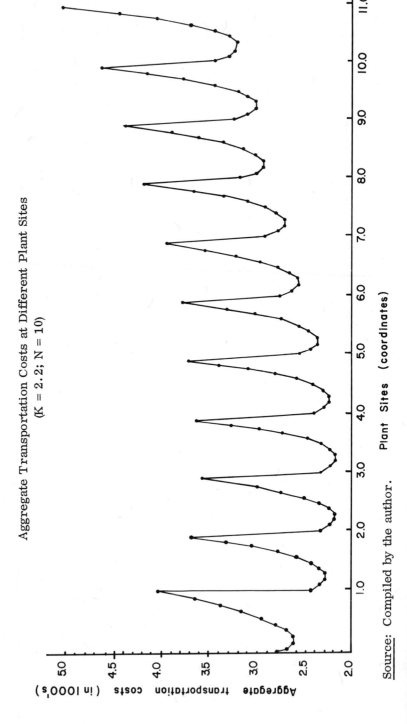

Source: Compiled by the author.

case, the planner may locate the industrial firm at nodes (2, 2), (2, 3), (3, 2) or (3, 3), since all these sites yield the lowest aggregate transportation cost (2250.60). The solution, therefore, yields a "critical square" which arises because of the discontinuity in the plane lattice. If this restriction were lifted, by assuming a more irrational uniform transport surface, then a unique solution would occur at the middle point of this area.

The selected numerical example is characteristic of the lower and higher limits of K ranges, with the exception that some selected K values can yield a unique minimum, or show an indifference situation between two sites instead of four.

In Figure 3.2, the aggregate transportation costs (representing the columns in Table 3.3) are plotted with respect to the plant sites. For the economist, the shape of the different cycles and the progression of the cycles is familiar. Let us imagine an envelope curve in Figure 3.2, supposing that each cycle touches this curve at one point and lies above it everywhere else. If the envelope curve decreases where it is tangent to the cycle, then the next cycle should yield a lower minimum point. However, when the tangent line to the envelope curve is parallel with the x-axis, this point gives the planner the most efficient location for the industrial plant. Thus, the concept is similar to the well-known relationship between short- and long-run average cost curves.

Another interesting characteristic of this construction is that if the values of K increase above the range given in Table 3.2, the minimum point jumps discontinuously to further and further cycles where the ordinates are equal, thus following the "critical path" depicted earlier. When K > 11.0, then the shape of Figure 3.2 will be symmetric, giving the optimum location at point (5, 5) as indicated earlier.

Table 3.4 gives the results of additional numerical examinations by postulating that resource sites also change. This, obviously, generates various critical paths that are recorded in given examples.

We would like to add a final note to our analysis. If the planner locates the industrial plant in accordance with objectives other than the minimization of the aggregate transportation cost, it is possible to calculate the optimal transportation cost ratio between material- and market-oriented goods.

Therefore, the model is not necessarily the solution for a locational equilibrium under pure transport orientation, but can also be considered as a tool for the determination of the optimum transportation costs if the plant site is given.

TABLE 3.4

Minimum Aggregate Transportation Costs
(N = 10)

Resource at	K =	Least Cost Coordinates				Minimum Costs
(0, 1)	.6000	(0, 1)				666.6
(0, 1)	.8000	(0, 1)				888.8
(0, 1)	1.2222	(0, 1)	(1, 1)			1357.9
(0, 1)	1.4000	(1, 1)				1537.8
(0, 1)	1.5714	(1, 2)	(2, 2)	(1, 1)	(2, 1)	1711.3
(0, 1)	1.6500	(2, 2)				1778.7
(0, 1)	1.9300	(2, 2)				2018.9
(0, 1)	2.2000	(2, 2)	(3, 2)	(2, 3)	(3, 3)	2250.6
(0, 1)	2.9000	(3, 3)				2774.2
(0, 1)	3.6667	(3, 3)	(4, 3)	(3, 4)	(4, 4)	3347.7
(0, 1)	6.0000	(4, 4)				4939.0
(0, 1)	11.0000	(4, 4)	(5, 4)	(4, 5)	(5, 5)	8349.0
(0, 1)	12.0000	(5, 5)				9009.0
(0, 1)	20.0000	(5, 5)				14289.0
(3, 3)	.6000	(3, 3)				448.0
(3, 3)	.8000	(3, 3)				598.4
(3, 3)	1.2222	(3, 3)				914.2
(3, 3)	1.4000	(3, 3)				1047.2
(3, 3)	1.5714	(3, 3)				1175.4
(3, 3)	1.6500	(3, 3)				1234.2
(3, 3)	1.9300	(3, 3)				1443.6
(3, 3)	2.2000	(3, 3)				1645.6
(3, 3)	2.9000	(3, 3)				2169.2
(3, 3)	3.6667	(3, 3)	(4, 3)	(3, 4)	(4, 4)	2742.7
(3, 3)	6.0000	(4, 4)				4334.0
(3, 3)	11.0000	(4, 4)	(5, 4)	(4, 5)	(5, 5)	7744.0
(3, 3)	12.0000	(5, 5)				8404.0
(3, 3)	20.0000	(5, 5)				13684.0
(0, 5)	.6000	(0, 5)				561.0
(0, 5)	.8000	(0, 5)				748.0
(0, 5)	1.2222	(0, 5)	(1, 5)			1142.8
(0, 5)	1.4000	(1, 5)				1291.4
(0, 5)	1.5714	(1, 5)	(2, 5)			1434.7
(0, 5)	1.6500	(2, 5)				1494.4
(0, 5)	1.9300	(2, 5)				1706.9
(0, 5)	2.2000	(2, 5)	(3, 5)			1911.8
(0, 5)	2.9000	(3, 5)				2404.6
(0, 5)	3.6667	(3, 5)	(4, 5)			2944.4
(0, 5)	6.0000	(4, 5)				4510.0
(0, 5)	11.0000	(4, 5)	(5, 5)			7865.0
(0, 5)	12.0000	(5, 5)				8525.0
(0, 5)	20.0000	(5, 5)				13805.0

Note: In cases where the critical values of K could not be expressed as exact decimals, we recorded the total costs obtained by rounding them to the nearest tenth. This attempts to compensate for the error in the thousands place which was incurred by using K values rounded to three decimals.

Source: Compiled by the author.

74

CONCLUSION AND NARRATIVE

The analysis presented was an attempt to solve the location of a socialist firm by postulating pure transport orientation in a plane lattice. This problem was solved theoretically, and various numerical solutions revealed some nontrivial solutions, when the firm, because of the decreasing ratio between material and market transportation costs, is drawn away from the center of the city grid. It was concluded that the solution should lie in the critical path, which is always the shortest route between the site of the resources and the center, and in the case of alternatives the shortest path should go in the direction of the grid's nearest diagonal.

An efficient algorithm for the generalization of this solution could ease the severe limitations of the model and would allow variations in the number of firms, market points, extracting places, nonuniform demand or supply, and some more realistic assumptions for the approximation of the centrally planned framework.

For the final evaluation, however, some remarks are necessary.

1. One can argue that the above analysis is nothing but an exercise, and with quantifications and abstractions the philosopher's stone cannot be found. "Mathematical functions are hardly able to capture reality and even less to suggest practical solutions or 'positive' advice to political leaders," said Lord Balogh.[15]

Such criticism could be valid for a segment of the overwhelming amount of theoretical studies dealing with price-directed systems, and is directed against these. Examination of the Soviet-type systems shows a serious shortcoming in the other side. In this subject, most of the studies are historical, political, or descriptive, and they shy away from application of theoretical tools. It is proposed that the study of centrally planned systems could benefit from a more theoretical approach.

2. The question could be also raised: "Is a socialist location theory relevant?" This view argues that the various centers of industrialization and infrastructure were established long before the socialist system was introduced; moreover, the settlement network in these countries represents ancient patterns.

This view disregards the increasingly dynamic transformation that takes place in centrally planned systems. The increments of the towns with "urban character" and the "abandonment" of villages with little potential occupy planning authorities more and more.[16] We suggest that a theoretical framework to at least clarify the relevant variables could not do any harm.

NOTES

1. See, for the history of this construction and the questions it poses, George Polya, Mathematical Discovery, Vol. I (New York: Wiley, 1962), pp. 68 et seq.

2. One of the best theoretical explanations of major settlement types is in Walter Christaller's "Rapports Fonctionnels Entre Les Agglomerations Urbaines et Campagnes," Comptes rendues du congres international de geographie Amsterdam, 2 (1938), pp. 123-37.

3. The literature that deals with the classic statements related to location and central place theory explaining the reasons for the site of the cities and the places for the urban trades and institutions within the city is too extensive to be quoted. Most of them are included in Brian J. L. Berry and Allen Pred, Central Place Studies a Bibliography of Theory and Applications (Philadelphia: Regional Science Research Institute, 1961).

4. Gyorgy Konrad and Ivan Szelenyi, "Social Conflicts in Delayed Urban Development," Valosag, December 1971; Gyorgy Enyedi, "Inquiry into Hungarian Urbanization," Valosag, March 1972.

5. Coloman Kadas, "Transportation Impact on Plant Size and Location," Regional Science Association Papers, Vol. XII (1964), p. 194.

6. See, for example, Paul E. Alyea, "Property Tax Inducements to Attract Industry," in Property Taxation—U.S.A., ed. R. W. Lindholm (Madison: University of Wisconsin Press, 1967), pp. 139-58, and also the remark of Edgar M. Hoover, "I have concluded that much of the geometrical analysis of transport orientation . . . is rather useless," in his classical study, Location Theory and Shoe and Leather Industries (Cambridge, Mass.: Harvard University Press, 1937), p. 57.

7. Kadas, op. cit.

8. In an earlier study, we extended this classical model (Harold Hotelling, "Stability in Competition," Economic Journal 39 [March 1929]: 41-57) to a two-dimensional market by using a uniform transport surface. See Paul Jonas, "Competition in a Two-Dimensional Market," Annals of Regional Science 2 (December 1968): 12-29.

9. See, among others, Paul Jonas, "The Nature of a Price Structure in a 'Classical' Soviet-type Economy," Jahrbuch der Wirtschaft Osteuropas (Munich: Gunter Olzog Verlag, 1972), pp. 115-35.

10. Jerzy Ostiatynski, "On the Price-Bias in Comparative Analysis of Planned and Market Economies," Forschungsberichte, 13 (Vienna: Wiener Institut fur Internationale Wirtschaftsvergleiche, March 1974).

11. A. Bergson, S. Kuznetz, A. Gerschenkron, N. Kaplan, N. Jasny, and others.

12. The isovectors are assumed to be Palanderian. See Tord Pallander, Beitrage zur Standortstheorie (Uppsala: Almquist & Wiksells, 1935), Stockholm dissertation, Chapters VII, IX.

13. See Mathematical Appendix to this chapter.

14. This range can be compared to Weber's problem, which, in effect, was to draw the firm away from the trivial site located in the interior of a convex hull at a point at which each side of the Locational Triangle subtends an angle of 120°.

15. Thomas Balogh's address delivered at Karl Marx University of Economics, Budapest, May 17, 1973. Reprinted as "Crisis of Capitalism," in The New Hungarian Quarterly 16 (Winter 1973): 40-61.

16. Romania is especially representative for a dynamic urban transformation. See Ilie Salapa, Director General of the Central Directorate of Statistics, "Rumania's Population in a Time of Major Socioeconomic Changes," Era Socialista 4 (February 1974).

MATHEMATICAL APPENDIX

Sum of an arithmetic progression is $S_a = \frac{n}{a}(a+1)$.

Thus, isovector B, equation 5, can be represented as

$$I_B = (XF + YF) + (XF + YF - 1) + (XF + YF - 2) + \ldots$$
$$+ (XF + YF - YF) + (XF + 1) + (XF + 2) + (XF + N - YF).$$

This procedure must be followed for each of the possible XF values. Hence,

$$(N+1)XF + \frac{(XF+1)}{2}(YF+0) + \frac{(N-YF)}{2}(1+N-YF),$$

or

$$(N+1)XF \qquad + \frac{(XF+1)(YF)}{2} + \frac{(N-YF)(1+N-YF)}{2} +$$

$$(N+1)(XF-1) \quad +$$

$$(N+1)(XF-2) \quad +$$

$(N + 1)(XF - XF) +$.   .

$\vdots$.   .

$(N + 1)\ 1$ +   .   .

$(N + 1)\ 2$ +   .   .

$(N + 1)(N - XF)$ +   .   .

Therefore, the entire equation 1 may be written as

$$Isodapanes = ETC_{c_1} = (N + 1)^2[(XF - X0) + (XF - Y0)]$$
$$+ \frac{K(N + 1)}{2}(2YF^2 + N^2 - 2NXF + N)$$
$$= (N + 1)^2[(XF - X0) + (YF - Y0)]$$
$$+ K(N + 1)(YF^2 - NYF + XF^2 + N^2 + N)$$

Taking the first partials with respect to the coordinates of the plant sites, we receive equations 8 and 9,

$$\frac{\partial ETC_{c_1}}{\partial XF} = K(N + 1)(2XF - N) + (N + 1)^2$$

$$\frac{\partial ETC_{c_1}}{\partial YF} = K(N + 1)(2YF - N) + (N + 1)^2$$

4

THE IMPACT ON THE HUNGARIAN MODEL OF POSTREFORM CHANGES IN REWARD, INCENTIVE, AND PROFIT POLICIES
Peter S. Elek

Much of the profit-oriented reward system contained in the original reform proposals has reverted to recentralization through planner-manipulated wage and reward codes. While acting reluctantly, the planning authorities felt it necessary to change the incentive methodology in certain selected areas. This was mainly caused by pressures of disequilibria, a not uncommon phenomena in any market system. While resources in markets indirectly absorb social costs and sacrifices, socialist ideology requires shifting the direct burden of such costs by underwriting these costs in the form of subsidies up to a predetermined social minima. This then compounds the disequilibria. The planners introduced corrective methodologies changing the incentive system. The result was sectorial adjustments, which eased the "short-run" disequilibria. However, the "long-run" effects of constant administrative interference reintroduced the well-documented pitfalls of the classical centrally planned model.

The blueprints and public-relations efforts of the economic reforms place profitability in the central stage of the reward system. In reality, planners since the reforms introduced a preponderance of coordinating regulations, whose impact neutralized the potency of most of the original propositions.

Therefore the question arises, to what extent has the economic behavior changed since abandoning direct centrally planned vertical controls for indirect horizontal controls? To what extent is the current system more flexible, if at all, and how much did it contribute to improvement of efficiency and productivity? Finally, what does the future hold, assuming the continuation of the current trend.

How do these changes affect the behavior of management, labor, the profit-seeking enterprise?

Because of the significance of the large foreign trade sector, the latter will be dealt with separately.

THE NEW SYSTEM

Incomes of enterprise and incentive premiums of employees are based predominantly on enterprise profits.[1] The base for profits is gross revenue minus cost. The latter includes materials, wages, depreciation allowances (minimum wages and depreciation allowances are still centrally determined), certain capital charges, payroll taxes, interest rates, and charges on credits. To offset loss subsidies, or excessive profits originating from heavily subsidized initial investment operations, an excess gross revenue tax is levied. Revenues remaining after all costs, taxes, and other charges enumerated above constitute taxable profits.

The core of the reward system is the division of enterprise profits into development (for capital), sharing (for labor), and reserve funds.[2] Historically, the decentralized planning system's first attempt to distribute labor's share of retained profits was developed through a three-level profit-sharing formula:

	Upper limit of the share of profits based on annual base wages
Workers	15%
Middle Management	50%
Top Management	80%

The formula led to highly emotional debates criticizing the grossly unequal distribution of income in a socialist state. While the authorities for a while held firm against pressures, this reward formula was abolished by the end of 1970.

Under new arrangements, each enterprise's top management share of the retained profit is determined by the supervising authorities, while all other employees' distribution of profit shares is determined by the enterprise. The practice of such distributions and the composition of distributing bodies within enterprises varies.

The paradox, whether managers in imperfectly competitive markets seek to maximize profits, material, or psychological self gains, is therefore duplicated in Hungary's decentralized economic system.

It weighs heavily on the postreform managerial decision-making process and both influences and is influenced by labor policies, which in turn affect economic performance.[3]

In line with changes, it was understandable that the major
managerial motivating force changed too. It moved from the concept
of public or individual gain to a complex multipurpose objective.
Within the framework, profit maximization still lurked in the background and acted as a good conversation piece. But satisfying superior
authorities moved high up on the scale of priorities. Carrying out
planners' directives or giving priorities to some insinuated objectives,
rather than self-interest, approximates the behavior of the classical
centrally planned model. On the other hand, the decentralized model
is characterized by planners' broad policies, which without interference from the center will be carried out, accomplishing the desired
task.

Whatever remained of the individual gain-induced managerial
incentive was further eroded by the specific conditions of the industry
or sector in which such a manager found himself operating. Lucrative
enterprises and sectors in addition to efficiency are functions of
productivity, which are functions of selective investment credit
policies, preplanned growth areas, favored accounting, profit, or
tax formulas. When a manager's enterprise is outside of these favored
areas, his effort and performance is not competitively comparable
with accomplishments performed and rewards received by the management of a favored sector.

Therefore, what today's successful manager seeks to maximize
is limited material self-gains, coupled with unlimited relative values
of public image, a micro- and macrostatus of both fellow workers
and peers.

This then unleashes the inner paradox of the postreform managerial functions. Was the managerial decision-making process of
"freedom of enterprise and choice" broadened or weakened? Authorities promoted a public image that declared it was broadened.[4] Further
investigation, however, reveals that such loosening up only applied
to the economic concept of the "short run" because in the "long run"
indirect fiscal and monetary policies, speckled with government fiat,
strongly limited the parametric behavior of the enterprise.

As the long run consists of cumulative phases of short runs,
the paradox is obvious. The daily gains in microdecision-making are
illusory when backing into such from the long run. The planners,
acting under the guise of coordinating general equilibrium conditions,
limit the enterprise's and market's behavior and this tightens the
freedom and choice of microdecision-making.

The contractionary trend is further visible when viewed through
the inner relationship and composition of the three labor-management
methodologies, operating side by side in the mid-1970s.

Certain sectors are under a centrally planned and directed
wage and reward structure (M_1 structure); other areas are controlled

by aggregate wage bill allocations (M2 structure); and the flexible wage rate structure made up profit shares above the social minima (M3 structure).

The latter methodology was the one synonomous with the reform proposals. It was changed so often and so much that its original form only survives as a theoretical model.

The planner's dilemma necessitating such changes stems from disequilibria, low productivity compounded by poor work discipline, and psychological spinbacks of unequal income distribution generated by like tasks in different industries, all within the framework of egalitarian social philosophy. Therefore, we note a shift from the third methodology (M3) to M2 and increasingly to M1, when approximately 100 key industries were added to a small, always centrally controlled sector.

INCENTIVE AND REWARD FORMULAS

We can observe seven steps changing and adjusting incentive and reward formulas through enterprises' retained profits or through centrally allocated credits, debits, or fiats.

1. Postreform base formula establishes a methodology of constructing enterprise retention funds that is based on the capital/labor ratio that produced the taxable profits.[5] Such profits are divided into sharing funds for labor and development funds for capital.

Hence Y = Income from retained pretax profits
TP = Wage bill (this is supposedly a measure of the value of labor)
K = Value of capital assets

Labor's $Y = TP \cdot \dfrac{W}{W + K}$ = Sharing fund

Hence
Capital's $Y = TP \cdot \dfrac{K}{W + K}$ = Development

2. As labor's share of profit did not add adequate funds to act as incentive, nor did added productivity improve pressures, the application of a wage multiplier was established to increase labor's share of profit (adjusting low productivity, which causes low income, by accounting methodology).

The formula for certain selected sectors reads

$$\text{Labor's } Y = TP \cdot \frac{2W}{2W = K}$$

Hence
$$\text{Capital's } Y = TP \cdot \frac{k}{2W = K}$$

To create better incentives, average industrial enterprises were instructed to multiply the wage bill with a weighting coefficient of 2, which changes retained profit's income distribution.[6] This procedure increases labor's share of retained profits at the expense of capital's share.

    3. There was a sectorial adjustment of a uniform loading coefficient.[7] The coefficient preceding W (wage share of profit) is now annually adjusted for each industry, but remains uniform within each industry. Coefficient wage multipliers varied between 0 and 9. (Some weighting coefficients in 1969: average sector 2, machine industry 2, metallurgy 4, heavy industry 2-3, engineering and drafting enterprises 1.)

    4. The formula M_3 contributed to labor unrest caused by unequal productivity within industries.[8] Therefore, additional outside controls were initiated to equalize incomes in the form of graduated enterprise taxes together with the tax breaks and more liberal depreciation allowances in bottleneck enterprises. Tax rates are to range from 40 to 70 percent, replacing the former 0 to 70 percent scale.

    5. There were additional fiscal controls, granting extra-favored status to sectors whose expansion was in keeping with the directives of the national five year plan.[9] They operated through interest-free or low-interest loans,[10] tax exemptions in the form of investment credit.[11]

    6. There also were sectorially allocated wage bill parameters. Sector chiefs within the government juggled funds allocating to the more productive industries larger allotments, choking off the poor performers.[12] This procedure would be in keeping with some sort of socialist marginal cost pricing. However, because of egalitarian considerations, the central planners changed this subsidizing minimum operations to poor performers, at least until such plants could be liquidated. Meanwhile, because of the relatively low wages guaranteed to management and labor of poor performers, employees fled these enterprises.[13] This process was facilitated by the well-codified industrial relations system (IRS), and by labor shortage, all precipitating the folding of these enterprises. Nevertheless, in poorly performing core sectors such as agriculture, which by nature and size could not be liquidated, the subsidies granted for minimal standards increased the disequilibria.[14]

7. And there was direct control of profits, wages, and incentives by central planners.[15] A core of utility and basic raw material producing industries remained originally in this group, which even through the reform remained under central control.[16] There is a marked growth in this area.

In technical language the broad structure in which the labor market institutions, with their regulatory functions (including wage fixing) operate is referred to as the industrial relations system.[17] It may be defined as the organizational and legal framework of a country in which rights and responsibilities of the parties to industrial relations are established, and the terms of employment and rewards are regulated.[18]

It is interesting to note that the trend toward more control is further stimulated by the liberal set up of labor relations and their role in the changing economy. This of course is a paradox. The IRS in Hungary has power and a strong clout. When negotiated contracts do not match productivity it contributes to the disequilibrium. Therefore, a close relationship is observable between a strong IRS and the planners' desire to counterbalance such gains by additional controls and recentralization.[19]

The management of state enterprises represents the employer side, the labor unions represent the employee side of the IRS. (The 19 unions represent 90 percent of wage earners and salaried employees.) The basic labor code was enacted in 1967 (and has been revised several times), and it contains procedural rules and provisions for regulations of substantive issues. Procedural rules are determined either directly or in broad terms by the code. Substantive issues of employment not determined by the labor code are determined by governmental decrees.[20] There are three levels of decrees issued by different authorities; the Council of Ministers, Ministerial Labor, or Economic Affairs.

The strong labor code renders inflexible elements in downward movements of costs.[21]

THE FOREIGN TRADE SECTOR

To improve profitability of the substantial foreign trade sector, additional incentives were created through preferential taxation and through subsidies granted to adjust to world market prices. In some recent changes disincentives too were introduced, by making the enterprise share in losses created by changes in world market prices or in downward changes of the relative values of foreign currencies.

Enterprise profits generated by price manipulation are threatened to be dealt with by administrative measures. Profits must arise from cost reduction, division of labor, or productivity.

The growing inflation in foreign countries has made its influence felt through domestic price pressure. To choke off the importation of inflation, unfavorable changes of world market prices are balanced by budget subsidies. When imported resource prices rise over an extended period of time, centrally set prices of domestic finished goods are likely to follow, to allow for other domestic price adjustments. Also, to offset world market price fluctuation, foreign trade enterprises are instructed to set up import and export reserve funds. Recommendations are now being considered to have foreign trade enterprises allocate 70-80 percent of their profits to their export or import reserve funds, using these funds to isolate fixed domestic prices from international price fluctuations. The remaining 20-30 percent of profit accruing to such enterprises is considered an adequate cushion for other aspects of risk-taking. Should such reserve funds become excessive, they could be utilized to lower fixed domestic prices. Enterprises producing goods whose prices fluctuate freely on the domestic market are encouraged to set aside 0.5-1.0 percent of their profits for an export-import foreign risk reserve fund. Certain frozen enterprise funds may also be channeled into such reserves.

Unprofitable foreign trade operations are to be liquidated by draining them of credit instruments and sheltered subsidies

As export amounts to about 40 percent of the national income, the economic effectiveness of foreign trade greatly influences the growth of the entire economy.[22]

Under the former system of economic management (until the end of 1967), foreign trade was organizationally divorced from other economic activities (that is, production and consumption); at the same time, the economic interaction of foreign and domestic markets—of production import and export prices and domestic consumer prices—was lacking.

The major share of export-import transactions was handled by foreign trading companies that specialized in foreign trading activity—which exclusively dealt with foreign sales and purchases—and paid the producing enterprise a fixed amount in forints, that is to say, a sum independent of the actual foreign currency price and the income from the export products. As the forint price of materials and industrial products purchased from abroad was not determined by the actual foreign currency outlay, but by the domestic price structure, world market prices were not permitted to sufficiently influence production and the domestic price structure, regardless of whether it was a matter of imports or exports. The principal characteristics of this domestic price structure were stability, fixed and unchanging prices.

Under the new system of economic management, the clearing procedures between productive and foreign trading companies have also altered. In the past the commercial activity of the foreign trading companies was actually more or less fictive. They purchased goods at officially fixed prices from the producers and then sold them abroad; or in the case of imports, they delivered products to consumers at authorized prices that had been bought at market prices abroad. Under such conditions there were no real merchants or enterprisers, for the risk was entirely borne by the state, and there were provisions in the budget to make up for the differences between domestic and foreign prices. Since 1968, the specialized foreign trading companies have generally acted as the agents of the producer and the consumer, concluding export and import deals assigned to them and receiving commission for this work. In this type of relationship, the commissioner fixes the price limits, and if the foreign trading company obtains a higher price, either its commission increases or it receives a share of the surplus.

On January 1, 1968, a new price structure came into effect in Hungarian foreign trade, which gave full play to the value assessment of external markets. Through the application of the standard foreign exchange conversion coefficients, industrial companies receive amounts in forints for their export products corresponding to the actual price in foreign currency. Further, tax refunds have been initiated to stimulate and improve the structure of foreign trade. Central authorities determined an export profit tax refund key for each separate branch of the economy. While this key is uniform within each branch, selective controls are exercised by stimulating or retarding export profits within branches by changing the size of the key.

The more profitable branches of the economy accrue larger profits, larger profit taxes, and larger refunds. These refunds are channeled into the exporting enterprises' retained profits.

Profit tax refund on exports is broken down according to the principles described between labor's and capital's share of profit (labor's sharing fund and capital's development fund), through the following formula:

Sharing fund (Labor's Y) = $ET_s C$

Development fund (Capital's Y) = $ET_d C$

where E = the total volume of export product (stimulated by tax refund) a constant foreign exchange rate's forint equivalent divided by the enterprise's net total revenue,

where T_s = Tax on profit accruing to the sharing fund

where T_d = Tax on profit accruing to the development fund

where C = A centrally planned constant (generally applying to one
specific branch of the economy), which expresses the
coefficient of the stimulated export volumes profit tax,
which may be refunded to the enterprise's share or
development fund.

The system has further built in incentives through the graduated use
of the C constant. In certain instances to reward for greater profits
a higher C applies.

THE FUTURE OF THE NEW SYSTEM

The maze of regulations introduced to control the decentralized
Hungarian economy seriously endangers the success of the reform,
and moves it back to recentralization. Aristotle maintained, "Many
small exceptions do not add up to one small thing, but to a big thing"
(Politics 11). The short-run adjustments to stem disequilibria have
become a complex long-run administrative mechanism. Preestab-
lished profit shares, incentives, and IRS codes have little to offer to
future improvement of real incomes, whether national or individual,
if not matched by gains of productivity and efficiency. Administrative
accounting mechanisms hold no answer for the long run.

The root of the problem lies in the price system. If prices in the
long run are free to operate through uninhibited markets, wages, profit
shares, and incomes are automatically established without the need of
fancy formulas. To what extent this can be achieved is a function of
the political superstructure—on the trade-offs between the technicians
and the politicians. The proliferation of further administrative controls will neutralize most of the high hopes of the reform.

NOTES

1. Gabor Revesz, "Osztonzes munka szerinti elosztas
keresetszabalyozas" (Stimulation, Distribution According to the
Work Done, Regulation of Earnings) Kozgazdasagi Szemle 20, no. 11
(1973), p. 1253.

2. Jeno Wilcsek, "Berszabalyozas es nyereseg," (Wage Regulation and Profits) Kozgazdasagi Szemle 19, no. 1 (1972), p. 17.

3. Magyar Statisztikai Zsebkonyv; (Hungarian Statistical Pocket
Book) (Budapest: Kozponti Statisztikai Hivatal, 1970), p. 85.

4. Nepszabadsag; A Round Table Conference Sponsored by the Semi-official Party Daily Nepszabadsag, April 4, 1968. Participants: Deputy Premier Timar, Deputy Minister of Labor Buda, Secretary Beckl of the National Council of Trade Unions.

5. Gabor Havas, Beruhazas Vallalati Forrasbol, (Investments from the Enterprises Retained Profits) (Budapest: Kozgazdasagi es Jogi Konyvkiado, 1968), p. 55-58.

6. Janos Bokor, A Vallalatok Nyeresegerdekeltsege Es a Vallati Alapok (Profit Shares and Internal Funds of the Enterprise) (Budapest: Kozgazdasagi es Jogi Konyvkiado, 1969), pp. 79-90.

7. Ibid.

8. Ibid., p. 79.

9. Ibid.

10. Janos Kadar, Address at the 10th Conference of the Hungarian People's Party (November 23, 1970); Report to the 10th Party Congress, as reviewed in the article by Nyers Rezso, Kozgazdasagi Szemle 18, no. 1 (1971), p. 16.

11. Bela Sulyok, "Review of Financial Mechanism," in Penzugyi Szemle 12 (1970), p. 320.

12. Department of Public Information, Republic of Hungary, Reform, Foreign Trade and the New Price Structure (Budapest: Pannonia Press, 1969), p. 142.

13. Julia M. Venyige, "A Munkaero Fluktuacio nehany problemaja", (Some Problems of Labor Fluctuation) Kozgazdasagi Szemle 20, no. 9 (1973).

14. Laszlo Nagy, "Gazdasagi epitomunkank eredmenyei" (National Economic Performance), Kozgazdasagi Szemle 18, no. 1 (1971), p. 1.

15. Hegedus Zsuzsa-Tardos Marton, "A Vallalati vezetek motivaciojanak Nehany Problemaja" (Position and Motivation of Enterprise Managers) Kozgazdasagi Szemle 21, no. 3 (1974), pp. 162-73.

16. Janos Bokor, "Jovedelem szabalyozas az iparban", (Revenue Control in the Industrial Sector) Penzugyi Szemle 17, no. 12 (1973), pp. 971-77.

17. Laszlo Popper, "A kereseti aranyok es a berpolitika", (Wage Policy and Relative Incomes) Kozgazdasagi Szemle 20, no. 4 (1973), pp. 242-60.

18. Imre Pozsgay, "A part es az osztarsadalmi erdek", (The Party and Public Interest) Tarsadalmi Szemle, no. 1 (1972), p. 110.

19. Julius Rezler, The Industrial Relation System in Hungary After the Economic Reform, (Chicago: Institute of Industrial Relations, Loyola University, 1973) pp. 125-50.

20. Imre Gerebenics, "Jovedelemszabalyozasi es anyagi erdekeltsegi rendszer a forgalmi es szolgaltatas agazataiban",

(Ground Rules of Income Control and Shared Financial Interest in the Service Sectors) Penzugyi Szemle 17, no. 1 (1973), pp. 978-80.

21. Jozsef Rozsa, "Foglalkoztatottsag es munkahelyzet", (Employment Conditions, Levels and Demands) Kozgazdasagi Szemle 17, no. 1 (1970), pp. 640-48.

22. Department of Public Information, Republic of Hungary, Reform, Foreign Trade and the New Price Structure (Budapest: Pannonia Press, 1969), p. 142.

5

FOREIGN TRADE SPECIALIZATION
AND ITS DETERMINANTS IN THE
POSTWAR SOVIET ECONOMY, 1950-70
Michael R. Dohan

> Thanks to the advantages of international division
> of labor, Soviet foreign trade has served to promote
> the country's technological progress and economic
> growth and improve the people's living standard.
>
> Nikolai Patolichev
> Soviet Minister of Foreign Trade[1]

Foreign trade has been among the most rapidly growing sectors of the Soviet economy during 1950-70. In this study we consider two interrelated questions about foreign trade's changing relationship to the Soviet economy. First, in what areas and why have different sectors of the economy been specialized for the expansion of exports and imports? And second, to what extent has the rapid growth of trade increased the economic dependence of the Soviet economy on the world economy?

There are differing hypotheses concerning Soviet foreign trade and its relationship to the domestic economy.[2] For many years the principle of autarky or trade avoidance was thought to thwart the development of foreign trade.[3] In this traditional Western interpretation, the level of exports was determined by the need for imports. These in turn seemed to be restricted by the principle of "economic independence" to providing only high technology machinery, noncompeting imports, commodities in temporary deficit, and politically opportune imports. The principle of economic independence was seen to preclude both systematic reliance on imports and systematic development of export sectors (relying instead on ad hoc export of surpluses). Planners were seen as avoiding trade because of its uncertainty and their lack of control. Finally, "irrational domestic prices" made rational trade decisions difficult and there was an apparent bias against imports of consumer goods. Thus, trade was depressed.

Soviet policy statements, on the other hand, repeatedly stressed both the goal of "economic independence" from the world capitalist economies and also the expansion of trade when beneficial to the Soviet economy and consistent with its economic independence.[4] In fact, Soviet foreign trade has expanded rapidly since World War II, so rapidly that the question of hyperpoly (excessive trade) has been raised by both Western and, in a different way, Soviet economists.[5] And, as shown in this chapter, considerable export specialization has occurred along with a marked shift from agricultural exports to exports of "heavy industry" products. While less specialization appears to have occurred in imports, the structure of imports has shifted toward consumer goods and away from raw industrial materials. Why?

Recent studies by Steven Rosefielde and Carl MacMillan show that this structural development of Soviet foreign trade in the postwar period is not inconsistent with the Hecksher-Ohlin theory of relative factor endowment.[6] These changes in factor endowment however may not be the "causal factor." Here we suggest that institutional characteristics, historic domestic priorities, natural resources, and "exogenously determined" trade partners may have had a greater effect on comparative costs, trade, and trade specialization than changes in relative factor endowments. Furthermore, an analysis of the trade structure and the import-utilization ratios suggests that the rapid growth of Soviet trade has not significantly compromised the principle of economic independence (as understood by Soviet economists). But in view of the qualitative nature of some of my data, these ideas are offered more as conjectures to be explored by others than proven conclusions.

STRUCTURE, METHODOLOGY, AND QUALIFICATIONS

This study approaches these questions at several levels. After estimating aggregate measure of trade specialization, we analyze changes in the structure of exports and imports in relation to changes in the domestic economy. Then trade, output, and consumption trends are compared both at a sectoral level and for specific commodity items in physical terms (by means of modified trade-output ratios). Finally we examine our results in light of productivity trends and selected technological, historical, and other qualitative characteristics of the major commodities.

TABLE 5.1

Aggregate Trends and Trade Participation Ratios in
Soviet Foreign Trade, Selected Years, 1913–70
(billions of rubles)

Year	Exports (billions of rubles, current prices) (1)	Imports (2)	Balance of Trade (3)	Volume Indices (1959 = 100) Export (4)	Import (5)	Terms of Trade (6)	USSR GNP 1959 Factor Cost (7)	Exports in 1959 Domestic Rubles (8)	Imports (9)	Export Participation Ratio percent (10)	Import Participation percent (11)
1913	1,192	1,078	113.8	[35.1]	[37.6]	[111]					
1926/27	633	560	73.2	[11.9]	[14.3]	[120]					
1931	636	867	- 230.4	[24.2]	[32.0]	[93]					
1938	230	245	115.5	[10.7]	[12.0]	[98]					
1950	1,615	1,310	305	33.1	30.5	106	77.5	1.74	2.15	2.2	2.8
1955	3,084	2,755	329	58.5	55.3	99	102.7	3.08	3.91	3.0	3.8
1956	3,253	3,251	2	62	64.5	97	[111.4]	3.26	4.55		
1957	3,943	3,544	399	73.7	69.2	97	[118.5]	3.89	4.89		
1958	3,869	3,915	- 46	75.6	83.1	101	127.5	3.98	5.87	3.1	4.6
1959	4,905	4,566	339	100.0	100.0	100	133.7	5.26	7.06	3.9	5.3
1960	5,007	5,066	- 59	98.8	107.7	99	140.4	5.25	7.60	3.7	5.4
1961	5,398	5,245	153	109.4	111.2	97	149.2	5.76	7.85	3.9	5.3
1962	6,328	5,810	518	128.2	124.1	98	154.3	6.75	8.76	4.4	5.7
1963	6,545	6,353	192	132.3	135.3	98	158.2	6.96	9.55	4.4	6.0
1964	6,915	6,963	- 48	138.8	140.5	94	170.9	7.31	9.92	4.3	5.8
1965	7,357	7,253	104	156.8	148.9	90	181.2	8.25	10.51	4.6	5.8
1966	7,957	7,122	835	174.1	147.6	88	192.8	9.16	10.42	4.8	5.4
1967	8,687	7,683	1,004	188.4	100.3	90	202.3	9.92	11.32	4.9	5.6
1968	9,571	8,489	1,082	208.2	174.4	90	211.4	10.96	12.67	5.2	6.0
1969	10,490	9,294	1,196	230.3	192.4	88	216.2	12.13	13.58	5.6	6.3
1970	11,520	10,565	955	245.4	207.6	85	[234.7]	12.94	14.61	5.5	6.2

Brackets indicate estimates differing from original series.

Notes and Sources: General note re sources to tables in this chapter. Trade data from Ministerstvo vneshnei torgovli SSSR, Vneshniaia Torgovlia SSSR Statisticheskii Obzor (Moscow: Izdatel'stvo "Mezhdunarodnye otnosheniia, various years); Vneshniaia torgovlia SSSR za 1918–1940 g.g. (Moscow: Vneshtorgizdat, 1960); and Vneshniaia Torgovlia SSSR Statisticheskii bornki, 1918–1966 (Moscow: Izdatel'stvo "Mezhdunarodnye otnosh-eniia," 1967). Output data from Tsentral'noe statisticheskoe upravlenie SSSR, Narodnoe khoziakstvo SSSR v 1970 g Statisticheskii ezhegodnik (Moscow: Izd. "Statistika," 1971); Warren Nutter, The Growth of Industrial Production in the Soviet Union (Princeton, N.J.: Princeton University Press, 1962); James Noren and Douglas Whitehouse, "Soviet Industry in the 1971–75 Plan" in Soviet Economic Prospects for the Seventies, U.S. Congress, Joint Economic Committee, 93d Cong., 1st Sess. (Washington, D.C.: U.S. Government Printing Office, 1973), pp. 206–45; and Douglas Diamond, "Developments in Soviet Agriculture," in Soviet Economic Prospects for the Seventies, pp. 337–39. All values converted to post-1961 rubles. Data for 1913 refer to Russia excluding Finland (for foreign trade) and to current Soviet boundaries (for output). Data for 1931 refer to pre–1939 borders. Volume and price indices of Soviet trade for 1913–38 are from Michael Dohan, Two Studies in Soviet Terms of Trade (Bloomington: International Development Center of Indiana University, 1973). The specific commodity items and groups are identified by their "ETN" numbers of the Soviet United Commodity Classification of Foreign Trade (Edinaia Tovarnaia Nomenklatura Vneshei Torgovli, Moscow: Vneshtorgizdat introduced in 1962).

Notation. To simplify the tables some notation has been developed. See Tables 5.5, 5.6, 5.7, and 5.8. Exports are usually compared to output, imports to supply (output plus gross imports), or net imports to consumption (output plus net imports).

Notes to Table 5.1. Volume indices for 1938–70 are from the above–cited Soviet sources and are linked indices with fixed price weights; estimates for 1913, 1926/27, and 1931 are volume indices with 1937 price weights linked with Soviet data for 1938. The terms of trade are calculated from the volume indices and value and are "variable weighted"; for 1913, 1926/27, and 1931 estimates of the Soviet commodity terms–of–trade with 1927/28 price weights are linked with estimates for 1938. Estimates of Soviet GNP in 1959 factor costs for 1950, 1955, and 1958–69 are from Stanley Cohn, "General Growth Performance of the Soviet Economy" in

(continued)

93

(Table 5.1 continued)

Economic Performance and the Military Burden in the Soviet Union, U.S. Congress, Joint Economic Committee, 91st Cong., 2d Sess., (Washington, D.C.: U.S. Government Printing Office, 1970), p. 17, based on 1968-weighted estimates cited in John Hardt, "Summary", in Soviet Economic Prospects for the Seventies, op. cit., p. xi; 1957 and 1958 are based on Moorsteen's 1937 estimates in Richard Moorsteen and Raymond Powell, The Soviet Capital Stock 1928–1962 (Homewood, Ill.: Irwin, 1966), pp. 622–23. Exports valued in 1959 domestic ruble prices (net of turnover taxes) are based on an estimate of exports in 1959 prices (Steven Rosefielde, Soviet International Trade in Heckscher–Ohlin Perspective [Lexington, Mass.: D.C. Heath, 1973], pp. 21, 36) and the export volume indices. The changing composition of exports makes these procedures less valid over time. Estimating the import–GNP ratio is complicated by the absence of a similar estimate of imports in domestic prices, which is net of turnover taxes. We compute such an estimate by reducing Efimov's pppr's (purchasing power parity ratios) of domestic–import ruble prices (cited in footnote 26) (which include turnover taxes) by rough estimates of the turnover tax for these three categories (nil for producer goods, 30 percent for consumer goods, and 40 percent for agricultural goods) based on Marshall Goldman, Soviet Marketing (London: Collier–Macmillan, 1963), p. 86 and Narodnoe Khoziakstvo . . 1970, op. cit. These adjusted pppr's times the values of producer, consumer, and agricultural imports in 1959 (distributed 2.8, 1.06, and 0.6 billion foreign trade rubles respectively) obtains a rough estimate of imports of 7.1 billion rubles in 1959 domestic prices net of turnover tax. We then proceed as with exports to estimate import–GNP ratios. The valve of imports in 1959 domestic prices exceeds that of exports because of the higher pppr. for domestic–import ruble prices. Export-participation ratios are column 8 divided by column 7. Import-participation ratios are column 9 divided by column 7.

The nature of Soviet foreign trade and output statistics introduces considerable uncertainty in any analysis.[7] Several problems
are particularly troublesome: inconsistent prices, a large unspecified
component of exports, unspecified components of machinery exports,
omission of traded items (platinum) from commodity totals, re-export
of purchases on Soviet accounts but delivered to a third country, and
the incompleteness of domestic output and price data.[8] In particular,
the different prices used for identical products in trade with socialist
and market economies distorts the value structure of exports and
imports,[9] and the separation of the domestic price structure from
foreign prices introduces problems in comparing foreign trade values
with domestic values.[10] Only limited account has been taken of these
factors.

COMPARATIVE TRENDS IN FOREIGN TRADE
AND AGGREGATE OUTPUT

The postwar growth of Soviet foreign trade is remarkable. In
1938 Soviet exports were only 65 percent of 1929 levels, 31 percent
of 1913 levels (Table 5.1), and accounted for about 0.5 percent of
GNP.[11]

But after World War II, exports grew rapidly and surpassed
1938 levels by 1946, the prewar 1931 peak by 1950, and 1913 levels
by 1951. Between 1950 and 1960 export volume grew 11.5 percent
per year, and import volume 13.7 percent per year, or almost double
the 6.1 percent growth rate of GNP. Exports ranked among the fastest
growing uses of output and imports among the fastest growing sources
of goods in the Soviet economy. Between 1960 and 1970 there was a
distinct slowdown in both output and foreign trade. Nevertheless,
exports grew at 9.4 percent per year and imports grew at 6.7 percent
per year, still faster than the 5.3 percent per year growth of GNP
(Table 5.1).

The role of foreign trade in the economy grew rapidly as measured by trade participation ratios.[12] Based on estimates of GNP
and exports in 1959 domestic ruble factor prices (shown in Table 5.1)
the share of exports in GNP rose from 2.2 percent in 1950 to 3.7
percent in 1960 to about 5.5 percent in 1970. The share of imports
in GNP rose from about 2.8 percent in 1950, to 5.4 percent in 1960,
to 6.2 percent of GNP by 1970—approximately the same as the United
States in the 1970s. These aggregate measures of trade participation
indicate a normalization of the role of foreign trade in the Soviet
economy since World War II and contrast sharply with the Soviet
position at the end of the 1930s.

What has been the basis for such trade expansion and what has been its impact on domestic economic policy? Does the growth reflect a fundamental shift in Soviet policy with respect to adapting its economy to world trade and economic independence?

EXPORTS AND INDUSTRIAL GROWTH

The most notable change in Soviet exports has been the shift from the largely agrarian structure in 1913 Russia to a structure best characterized as "heavy industrial" (Table 5.2).[13] Why? The hypothesis developed in this study is that domestic priorities toward heavy industry, light industry, and agriculture, and the strengths and weaknesses of Soviet economic institutions (collectivized agriculture, centralized planning, incentives, CMEA, etc.) have led to systematic changes in export capacity and comparative costs, and have been important determinants in the growth and structure of Soviet exports in this period. (One might wish to call it an "institutional theory of comparative advantage.") Some evidence to support this conjecture is found in comparing the growth of exports and output by sector.

GROWTH OF EXPORT

Machinery has become the major Soviet export in the postwar period (22 percent in 1970) and has grown faster than civilian machinery output, which in turn was among the most favored domestic sectors (Table 5.2). For reasons discussed below, the Soviet Union has remained a large net importer of machinery throughout the period (Table 5.3).

The other sources of export expansion during 1950-70 are primarily fuels, mineral ores, ferrous and nonferrous metals, timber products, and many lesser items such as synthetic rubber, construction materials, sulfur, electricity, natural gas, fertilizers, small consumer durables (watches, cameras, radios, bicycles, and sewing machines). Current exports of most of these products far exceed their prewar and 1913 volume (Table 5.4), and their share in total exports has expanded greatly. Significantly most of these growing exports also are closely related to heavy industry or the exploitation of natural resources.

Agricultural exports, on the other hand, grew slowly and their share in exports fell from about 30 percent in the early 1950s to about 13-15 percent in the late 1960s. (This is to be compared with

TABLE 5.2

Soviet Exports by Commodity Group, 1913–70
(million of rubles, current prices)

Year	1 Machinery	2 Fuels, Minerals, Metals	3 Chemicals, Fertilizers, Rubber	4 Building Material	5 Forest Products, Raw Material	7 Agricultural Foodstuffs, Raw	8 Agricultural Food, Processed	9 Manufacturing Consumer Goods	Unspecified; Not Classified	Total Exports
1913	3	76	14	1	372	426	226	56	—	1,192
1926/27	1	127	3	1	203	156	115	26	—	633
1931	4	125	9	1	204	123	107	63	—	636
1938	12	38	9	1	91	49	19	18	—	230
1950	191	247	67	3	300	212	103	61	431	1,615
1951	306	360	75	4	421	322	116	76	383	2,062
1952	408	455	74	5	410	425	119	61	557	2,511
1953	471	578	72	9	432	288	186	64	554	2,653
1954	479	774	91	15	523	280	143	74	524	2,901
1955	539	811	92	15	538	271	99	93	627	3,084
1956	562	1,019	108	13	513	220	133	91	596	3,253
1957	587	1,354	124	9	558	523	191	128	474	3,943
1958	717	1,410	132	8	560	333	140	138	433	3,869
1959	1,060	1,614	144	10	624	469	267	139	578	4,905
1960	1,029	1,821	167	13	713	453	197	142	474	5,007
1961	868	2,041	199	14	766	458	277	155	624	5,398
1962	1,052	2,240	196	16	801	510	324	162	1,030	6,328
1963	1,292	2,384	216	20	795	421	420	169	832	6,545
1964	1,455	2,702	216	26	892	254	276	165	937	6,915
1965	1,472	2,794	247	35	1,012	284	325	170	1,023	7,357
1966	1,654	2,845	292	43	1,113	255	472	180	1,108	7,957
1967	1,832	2,966	338	45	1,110	466	552	215	1,169	8,687
1968	2,072	3,236	374	57	1,177	415	562	232	1,453	9,571
1969	2,361	3,622	394	63	1,117	521	573	245	1,601	10,490
1970	2,482	4,026	464	74	1,269	416	517	282	1,991	11,520

Sources: 1913–38 from Vneshniaia torgovlia SSSR za 1918–1940 g.g. (Moscow: Vneshtorgizdat, 1960), p. 38; 1950–69 from Paul Marer, Soviet and East European Foreign Trade, 1946–1969 (Bloomington: Indiana University Press, 1972), pp. 44, 53; 1970 from Vneshniaia Torgovlia SSSR Statisticheskii Obzor (Moscow: Izdatel'stvo "Mezhdunarodnye otnosheniia," 1970), ETN 6 is included in "Unspecified." See also Table 5.1, "General notes re. sources to tables in this chapter."

TABLE 5.3

Soviet Imports by Commodity Group, 1913-70
(millions of rubles, current prices)

Year	1 Machinery	2 Fuels, Minerals, Metals	3 Chemicals, Fertilizers, Rubber	4 Building Material	5 Forest Products, Raw Material	7 Agricultural Foodstuffs, Raw	8 Agricultural Food, Processed	9 Manufacturing Consumer Goods	Unspecified; Not Classified	Total Imports
1913	197	155	85	11	306	123	105	112	—	108
1926/27	123	75	51	3	242	68	16	10	—	560
1931	467	193	28	11	102	37	20	8	—	867
1938	85	76	13	0	38	22	9	3	—	425
1950	282	334	76	18	202	119	100	86	94	1,310
1951	372	451	214	17	210	154	133	131	106	1,792
1952	486	603	194	25	362	186	188	157	91	2,256
1953	685	699	99	24	322	156	258	164	93	2,492
1954	875	655	84	17	390	169	383	111	111	2,864
1955	833	678	93	18	348	182	399	132	101	2,755
1956	806	891	188	29	422	204	323	307	80	2,352
1957	846	925	186	35	560	179	327	403	83	3,544
1958	958	906	252	44	537	201	368	556	94	3,915
1959	1,217	971	273	41	568	219	355	821	101	4,566
1960	1,507	1,061	304	41	584	190	417	866	96	5,066
1961	1,561	978	370	49	533	169	565	900	119	5,245
1962	2,021	1,029	383	50	526	125	539	1,024	111	5,810
1963	2,219	944	397	53	619	325	484	1,160	151	6,354
1964	2,399	846	383	30	638	608	773	1,069	209	6,964
1965	2,423	900	450	43	713	558	896	1,028	241	7,253
1966	2,308	797	457	46	742	590	800	1,163	217	7,122
1967	2,625	582	469	56	753	287	921	1,498	492	7,684
1968	3,127	671	498	65	719	282	865	1,659	583	8,470
1969	3,485	798	557	69	814	262	1,930	1,724	654	9,296
1970	3,706	1,206	1,794	76	1,041	333	1,273	1,921	445	11,795

Sources: 1913-38 from Vneshniaia torgovlia SSSR za 1918-1940 g.g. (Moscow: Vneshtorgizdat, 1960), p. 38; 1950-69 from Paul Marer, Soviet and East European Foreign Trade, 1946-1969 (Bloomington: Indiana University Press, 1972), pp. 44, 53; 1970 from Vneshniaia Torgovlia SSSR Statisticheskii Obzor (Moscow: Izdatel'stvo "Mezhdunarodnye otnosheniia," 1970), ETN 6 is included in "Unspecified." See also Table 5.1, "General notes re. sources to tables in this chapter."

TABLE 5.4

Export, Import, and Output of Industrial Products
in the Soviet Union, 1913-70, Selected Years

Q = domestic output in units
X = simple exports
XX = "embodied" in related X
M = simple imports
MM = "embodied" in related M
net X = X - M (net exports)
net XX = XX - MM (net embodied exports)
net M = M - X (net imports)
net MM = MM - XX (net embodied imports)

S = total supply = Q + M or Q + MM
C = consumption = Q + net M or Q = net MM
. = not estimated
- = no trade
0 = less than 1/2 unit shown
[ ] = different data sources or assumptions
~ = very approximate magnitude
n.a. = no data
e = small exports
m = small imports

EQ indicates series that include commodity "embodied" in related exports or imports.

Year	Coal + EQ million metric tons (standard units)					Crude Oil + EQm million metric tons		
	Q	X	XX	net XX	net XX/Q	Q	net XX	net XX/Q
1913	36	- 7.6	.	- 1.3	-21 %	9	1.1	12 %
1931	56	1.6	.	- 1.5	2.6	22	5.8	26
1950	205	1.1	3.8	- 6.3	- 2.4	38	- 1.6	- 4.3
1955	311	4.3	11.2	0.8	0.3	71	3.7	5.3
1960	373	12.3	23.9	14.8	4.0	148	30.0	20.3
1965	413	22.1	37.1	26.1	6.3	243	64.4	26.5
1966	420	21.7	38.4	27.6	6.6	265	74.1	27.9
1967	429	21.2	43.4	31.4	7.3	288	80.0	27.8
1968	429	21.1	44.4	32.1	7.5	309	87.6	28.3
1969	440	23.2	50.3	36.5	8.3	328	85.8	26.1
1970	451	24.3	53.2	39.1	8.7	353	94.0	27.7

Year	Iron Ore + EQ million metric tons				Manganese Orem + EQ million metric tons		
	Q	X	net XX	net XX/Q	Q	XX	XX/Q
1913	9.2	.48	.26	0.3%	1.25	1.2	95%
1931	10.6	11.1	- 1.3	[10.9]	.88	.7	84
1950	40	3.2	4.2	10.6	3.4	[0.3]	8
1955	82	8.8	11.6	16.1	4.7	0.9	19
1960	106	15.2	20.6	19.5	5.9	1.1	18
1965	153	24.1	32.1	20.9	7.6	1.1	15
1966	160	26.1	39.0	22.8	7.7	1.4	18
1967	168	28.7	46.8	26.0	7.2	1.4	20
1968	177	32.2	51.1	26.6	6.6	1.3	21
1969	186	33.1	54.3	26.4	6.6	1.4	22
1970	195	36.1	58.4	27.1	6.8	1.4	21

(continued)

(Table 5.4 continued)

	Chromite Orem + EQ 1,000 metric tons			Semiprocessed Ferrous Metals million metric tons				Pipe %
Year	Q	XX	XX/Q	[Q]	XX	net XX	net XX/Q	net M/Q
1913	26	n.1.	n.1.	3.4	.1	- .1	[- 3%]	17%
1931	94	29%	31%	4.1	.0	-1.6	[-38]	40
1950	n.a.	[96]	n.a.	18.1	0.7	0.3	1.7	4
1955	n.a.	[158]	[24]	30.5	1.8	1.5	4.9	-1.8
1960	918	477	52	43.7	3.0	1.4	3.2	6.4
1965	1,424	804	57	61.7	2.5	0.9	1.5	2.9
1966	1,503	987	66	66.2	2.8	2.5	3.8	3.0
1967	1,574	1,099	70	70.6	5.7	4.1	5.8	2.8
1968	1,655	1,123	68	74.1	6.0	3.8	5.1	4.2
1969	1,704	1,228	72	76.3	7.1	4.3	5.6	6.2
1970	1,755	1,300	74	80.6	7.6	4.6	5.7	7.7

	New Ferrous Metals million metric tons			Copper + EQ 1,000 metric tons		Lead 1,000 metric tons	
Year	Q	net XX	net XX/Q	net XX	net XX/Q	net X	net X/Q
1913	4.2	- .1	[- 3%]	[- 7.2]	[-18]%	[-58]	[-97]
1931	4.8	-1.6	[-25]	[-26.5]	[-37]	[42]	[-73]
1950	19.2	.6	3	18.7	~8	n.a.	.
1955	33.3	2.1	6.2	3.5	~1	18	~3
1960	46.8	3.0	6.5	26.8	~5	60	~19
1965	66.2	4.5	6.7	46.3	~6	89	~21
1966	70.3	5.8	8.3	28.3	~6	79	~17
1967	74.8	8.4	11.2	37.5	~3	79	~16
1968	78.8	8.2	10.5	40.2	~4	81	~15
1969	81.6	8.9	10.9	43.7	~4	91	~16
1970	85.9	9.4	10.9	43.5	~4	82	~14

	Zinc & EQ 1,000 metric tons		Tin 1,000 metric tons		Aluminum 1,000 metric tons			Bauxite & EQ
Year	net XX	net XX/Q	net M	net M/S	Q	net X	net X/Q	M/S
1913	[25.7]	[-57]%	6.0	100%	0	- 1.8	[-100]%	0
1931	[23.7]	[73]	4.5	100	0	- 20.3	[100]	0
1950	-16.3	[-12]	[5.2]	[~30]	[~200]	9.5	~5	[-]
1955	-10.9	[4]	14.8	[~60]	[~435]	38	~8	[-]
1960	18.2	~5	3.6	18	~640	73	~11	~9%
1965	63.8	~13	5.8	~23	~840	266	~32	10
1966	59.4	~11	4.8	~18	~890	312	~35	~12
1967	38.3	~6	5.7	~20	~965	313	~32	~22
1968	35.8	~5	7.1	~22	~1,000	367	~37	~32
1969	38.4	~5	6.8	~20	~1,100	423	~38	~40
1970	37.5	n.a.	8.3	~24	[~1,120]	499	~44	~40

Year	Magnesium[m] 1,000 metric tons		Asbestos[m] 1,000 metric tons			Apatite Concentrate 1,000 metric tons 38% P_2O_5		
	X	X/Q	Q	X	X/Q	Q	XX	XX/Q
1913	.	.	25	12	48%		0	0%
1931	.	.	65	13	20	[280]	3	~1
1950	n.a.	.	n.a.	39	.	[1,000]	410	~41
1955	1.7	[11%]	~400	67	17	[1,500]	670	~44
1960	1.3	5	~600	146	24	[3,800]	1,690	~52
1965	3.5	11	~745	248	33	7,550	3,636	48
1966	8.1	22	~755	256	34	8,000	4,480	56
1967	8.6	21	~770	285	37	8,800	4,730	54
1968	14.5	35	800	304	38	9,700	5,350	55
1969	15.0	33	~1,000	347	36	10,500	5,850	55
1970	16.8	34	~1,050	385	36	11,300	5,950	53

Year	Potash 1,000 metric tons K_2O content			Caustic Soda 1,000 metric tons		Soda Ash 1,000 metric tons		Rubber 1,000 metric tons
	Q	XX[a]	XX/Q	net M	net M/Q	net M	M/Q	M
1913	0	0	0	0.4	0 %	1.7	1.1%	13
1931	0	0	0	0	0	0	0	28
1950	312	290?	93%?	14	4.0	23	5.6	87
1955	790	20	2	24	4.2	80	5.2	35
1960	1,084	260	24	90	10.5	165	8.1	191
1965	2,370	340	14	186	12.5	180	5.9	271
1966	2,630	450	17	271	16.3	349	10.5	311
1967	2,870	570	20	275	15.3	315	9.1	278
1968	3,120	720	23	186	10.1	430	11.5	325
1969	3,180	700	22	214	10.6	500	12.6	295
1970	4,090	1,290	32	147	7.0	503	12.1	316

Year	Artificial Fiber 1,000 metric tons			Synthetic Fiber 1,000 metric tons			Cement million metric tons	
	Q	MM	MM/S	Q	M	M/S	Q	X/Q
1913	.2	.2	50%	0	—	—	1.5	-10%
1931	2.8	0	0	0	—	—	3.3	1.4
1950	23	6.7	23	1.3	0?	0%	10.2	1.0
1955	102	29	22	8.9	0	0	22.5	1.2
1960	196	68	26	15.0	.7	5	45.5	0.8
1965	330	59	15	78	7.3	9	72.4	2.8
1966	362	43	11	.	.	.	80.0	2.7
1967	395	58	13	.	.	.	84.8	2.7
1968	424	54	11	.	.	.	87.5	3.0
1969	441	57	11	.	.	.	89.8	3.3
1970	623	72	10	167	30	15	95.2	3.4

(continued)

(Table 5.4 continued)

Year	Commercial Timber % Equivalents million solid cubic meters				Sawn Lumber million cubic meters		
	Q	X	net XX	XX/Q	Q	net X	X/Q
1913	74	6.3	14.6	19.5%	14.2	5.9	41.5%
1931	104	4.9	11.6	11.2	23.4	4.6	19.3
1950	161	.7	1.6	0.6	20.0	[-0.1]	[- 0.5]
1955	212	1.6	4.6	2.2	76.0	1.7	3.0
1960	262	4.4	12.3	4.7	106.0	4.6	4.7
1965	274	11.1	23.6	8.6	111.0	7.7	7.2
1966	272	12.4	25.4	9.4	107.0	7.7	7.5
1967	287	12.4	24.6	8.6	109.0	7.1	6.8
1968	290	12.8	26.2	9.0	110.0	7.6	7.2
1969	286	13.6	27.2	9.5	112.0	7.6	7.0
1970	299	15.3	28.9	9.7	116.0	7.7	6.9

Year	Pulp & Equivalents 1,000 metric tons					Plywood million cubic meters		
	Q	X	M	net XX	net XX/Q	Q	net X	X/Q
1913	216	13	26	-127	[-37%]	203	n.1.	
1931	410	0	68	- 91	[-22]	[420]	87%	20.7
1950	1,500	68	3	69	4.6	657	[48]	7.2
1955	[2,440]	146	37	68	2.7	1,049	[89]	8.5
1960	3,213	244	83	169	5.2	1,354	109	8.1
1965	4,252	262	197	230	5.4	1,756	137	7.8
1966	4,768	296	164	136	2.8	1,830	137	7.5
1967	5,211	370	261	116	2.2	1,878	149	7.9
1968	5,527	390	220	54	1.0	1,899	188	9.9
1969	5,798	426	275	172	3.0	1,946	188	9.7
1970	6,657	448	287	157	2.3	2,045	226	11.0

Year	Paper (excl. carton) 1,000 metric tons				Carton 1,000 metric tons	Pesticides, 1,000 metric tons, standard units		
	Q	X	M	net X/Q	X/Q	Q	M	M/S
1913	269	0	126	[-34.%]	[-34]%	n.a.	1.2	.
1931	505	0	29	[- 5.4]	- 0.5	n.a.	1.5	.
1950	1,180	30	18	1.0	- 2.2	n.a.	0	0%
1955	1,848	63	76	- 0.7	- 4.4	30	[10]	25
1960	2,334	123	70	2.3	- 4.6	63	19	24
1965	3,231	204	145	1.8	- 3.8	198	271	58
1966	3,568	272	155	3.3	0.4	207	180	46
1967	3,800	293	218	2.0	2.8	222	102	30
1968	3,955	367	284	2.1	2.0	244	79	23
1969	4,046	429	336	2.3	4.7	277	88	23
1970	4,185	475	417	1.4	9.3	292	42	9

Notes and Sources: Quality of "domestic item" and "trade item" assumed to be approximately identical.

Coal and equivalent (standard 7,000 kilocalorie units). XX in coal equivalents refers to direct exports plus coal embodied in exports of coke (201) converted to equivalents by "1.4," pig iron by "1.0," and steel by "2.0" (based on Gardner Clark, The Economics of Soviet Steel [Cambridge, Mass.: Harvard University Press, 1965], pp. 114-15) and electricity assuming 1 billion kwh requires one-third million tons of coal.

Oil and equivalents. XX is crude oil (21) plus refined products (22) adjusted for refining losses of 8 percent.

Iron ore and equivalents. Net XX include net exports of iron ore (24001) plus pig iron and semiprocessed ferrous metals converted to ore equivalents by coefficient of 1.8 (based on Clark, Economics of Soviet Steel, op. cit., pp. 114-15). Soviet machinery trade is not taken into account.

Manganese ore and equivalents. Gross XX is manganese (tovarnii) ore (24002) plus 3 times ferromanganese (26101) (based on Clark, Economics of Soviet Steel, op. cit., p. 105).

Chromite ore. Gross XX includes chromite ore (24005) plus 2.2 times ferrochrome (26103) based on relative chromium content of ferrochrome (78 percent) and chromite ore.

Semiprocessed ferrous metals. Q equals total rolled metals, X and M are ferrous rolled products, rolled steel, tubing, and pipe (264-267).

Pipe. Q refers to steel pipe, M to pipe (266).

New ferrous metals. Subtraction by exports from new metal from ore. Q refers to pig iron output. Net XX is total exports minus imports in ferrous products (26).

Nonferrous metals. Q estimates refer to newly refined metals and are rough approximations (especially for aluminum).

Copper. XX and MM include copper ingots (27001), 88 percent of bronze (27002 and 27202), rolled copper (27201) and 70 percent of brass (27203).

Zinc. XX and MM include zinc (27004) and 30 percent of brass.

Aluminum. XX and MM include ingots (27008), rolled aluminum (27205), and 15 percent of ferroaluminum wire (2910102).

Bauxite. M in 1961-69 based on changes in value from 1969. One ton of alumina (24216) assumed to equal 2.45 tons of bauxite.

Apatite concentrate. (36 percent P_2O_5) XX includes ore (25012), concentrate (34001) and superphosphate (34005). Pre-1965 data differs from 1965-70.

Potash. (41.6 percent K_2O).

Synthetic fiber. XX and MM include synthetic fiber and yarn (51302, 51402).

Artificial fiber. XX and MM include fiber and yarn (51301, 02).

Pesticides. Identical to the Soviet "standard unit."

Commercial timber. Solid cubic meters, Q refers to "commercial timber hauled" (delovaia drevcina). X is round timber (500). Net XX is round wood equivalents: (a) round timber (500), (b) sawn timber and plywood (501 and 502) multiplied by 1.55, (c) pulp (505) multiplied by 5, and (d) paper and paperboard (505-6) multiplied by 4. Conversion coefficients are approximate.

Pulp. Q, X, M include tselliuloza and drevesnaia massa. Net XX included the pulp content embodied in paper (506) and paperboard (507) multiplied by 0.8.

See also Table 5.1, "General notes re sources to tables in this chapter."

103

74 percent of exports in 1913, 52 percent in the NEP [New Economic Policy, 1926/27], and 37 percent as late as 1938.) Individual products reflect this trend. In the postwar period net grain exports have fluctuated widely and never reached the volume of 1913. By the late 1960s gross grain exports made up a small diminishing portion of total exports (4 percent in 1970 compared to 33 percent in 1913). Many other major 1913 export products such as flax, hemp, oil cake, bran, eggs, and bacon are now exported in relatively small amounts (Table 5.5). Even though gross exports of butter, wool, and hides grew considerably during 1950-70, they now are barely above the 1913 levels and the Soviet Union remains a large net importer of wool and hides. Although gross sugar exports far exceed the substantial 1913 levels, they are a re-export of raw sugar imported for refining. In the postwar period the Soviet Union has become a large net importer of sugar! Thus, of the five principal agricultural exports in recent years—grain, butter, cotton, sunflower seed and oil, and sugar—only the export of cotton and sunflower seed and oil are significantly higher than in 1913 when examined on a net export basis. The Soviet Union has been unable to restore its traditional agricultural exports.

EXPORTS AND OUTPUT TRENDS COMPARED

The immediate explanation of these differing export trends is found in the comparatively slow growth rate of agriculture versus the high growth rates of ferrous metals and other industrial branches (Table 5.6). Net agricultural crop output grew only 2 percent per year during 1950-60 and 4.3 percent per year during 1960-70. Growth rates for industrial output during comparable periods are 11.5 and 8.7 percent for machinery, 13.4 and 8.8 percent for oil, 9.8 and 5.8 percent for ferrous metals, and 9.9 and 14.1 percent for nonferrous metals. (Data for selected individual products are in Table 5.4). Similarly the output of consumer soft goods and processed foods, of which the Soviet Union is a large net importer, grew more slowly than small consumer durables of which it is a growing net exporter.

The direction of causality, however, depends on whether or not export and import opportunities influenced the growth of the different sectors. Historically, these comparative trends in output in the postwar period have their origins in the domestic policies, priorities, and institutions of the prewar five-year plans—indeed they are the hallmarks of Soviet development during its so-called autarkic stage in the 1930s with its priorities of heavy industry over light industry

TABLE 5.5

Export, Import, and Output of Agricultural Commodities in the Soviet Union, 1913-70, Selected Years

Q = domestic output in units
X = simple exports
XX = "embodied" in related X
M = simple imports
MM = "embodied" in related M
net X = X - M (net exports)
net XX = XX - MM (net embodied exports)
net M = M - X (net imports)
net MM = MM - XX (net embodied imports)
EQ indicates series that include commodity "embodied" in related exports or imports

S = total supply = Q + M or Q + MM
C. = consumption = Q + net M or Q + net MM
. = not estimated
- = no trade
0 = less than 1/2 unit shown
[ ] = datum based on different source or assumptions
~ = very approximate magnitude
n.a. = no data

| | Grain + EQ | | | | Cotton Fiber + EQ | | | |
| | million metric tons | | | | 1,000 metric tons (ginned) | | | |
	Q	XX	MM	net XX/Q	Q	XX	MM	net XX/Q
1913	[81-93]	9.54	.46	10-11%	n.a.	0	197	[-45%]
1926/27	71.7	2.03	.04	2.7	[230]	0	138	[-45]
1931	66.0	4.78	.04	7.2	[420]	33	48	[-4]
1938	70.7	.57	.13	0.8	[855]	30	17	1.5
1950	81.2	2.95	0.21	3.3	1,204	227	56	14.2
1955	103.7	3.80	0.37	3.3	1,319	359	22	25.2
1960	93.0	6.84	0.27	7.1	1,459	421	214	14.2
1961	110.0	7.80	0.07	6.4	1,462	411	149	17.9
1962	109.0	8.10	3.13	7.4	1,771	375	165	11.8
1963	92.0	6.73	8.43	3.5	1,795	357	247	6.2
1964	120.0	3.88	6.72	-3.7	1,924	431	168	13.7
1965	100.0	4.81	6.72	-2.1	2,033	496	211	14.0
1966	140.0	4.00	8.13	-2.9	2,029	538	202	16.5
1967	122.0	6.64	2.43	3.5	2,023	574	177	19.6
1968	135.0	6.06	2.87	3.1	2,023	598	169	21.2
1969	128.0	7.90	.96	5.4	1,941	496	205	14.9
1970	150.0	6.61	2.46	2.8	2,129	561	293	12.6

(continued)

(Table 5.5 continued)

Year	Flax (1,000 metric tons)			Hemp (1,000 metric tons)	Wool (1,000 metric tons)				Butter (1,000 metric tons)		Jute[e] (1,000 metric tons)
	Q	net XX	XX/Q	X	Q	XX	MM	net M/C	net X	X/Q	M
1913	347	304	~88%	53.6	184	[17.4]	63	25%	78.1	[60%]	44.7
1931	443	65	15	5.9	94	[7.5]	33	[32]	30.9	[37]	23.4
1950	255	[7]	[2.7]	n.1.	173	12	35	11.8	28.9	8.6	13.2
1955	381	[6]	[1.5]	1.4	246	15	48	11.8	- .5	- 0.1	20.6
1960	425	43	10.3	10.3	343	18	64	11.9	33.2	4.5	16.9
1965	480	15	2.3	2.3	343	26	54	7.4	37.2	3.5	22.9
1966	461	19	3.9	3.9	356	28	62	8.8	51.8	5.0	33.5
1967	485	16	3.7	3.7	379	20	51	7.5	61.2	5.8	33.0
1968	402	18	3.7	3.7	398	26	72	10.3	73.2	7.0	27.0
1969	487	15	3.7	3.7	374	24	77	12.4	72.3	7.6	25.7
1970	456	20	3.9	3.9	402	18	84	14.1	70.8	7.4	42.0

Year	Hides Net M (million pieces)	Skins net M (million pieces)	Leather M (million pieces)	Hides, Skins Q	Sunflower Seed & Oil (million metric tons)			Sugar, granulated (1,000 metric tons)			
					Q	XX	XX/Q	Q	X	M	net M/
1913	[large]	[small]	[large]	n.a.	n.a.	(0)[a]	(0)%	1,363	147	0	-10.7%
1931	[1/2 1913]	[small]	[small]	n.a.	2.40	.02	0.1	1,486	320	0	-21.5
1950	.1	2.6	15	15	1.80	n.a.	n.a.	2,523	97	358	9.4
1955	1.3	10.2	16	16	3.80	.08	1.9	3,419	210	919	18.0
1960	2.7	18.2	48	18.3	3.65	.16	4.3	5,266	243	1,594	21.3
1965	2.7	16.5	60	25.3	5.01	.30	6.0	8,924	604	2,171	15.0
1966	2.9	20.9	22	24.0	5.65	.57	10.1	n.a.	993	1,715	8.2
1967	3.6	23.8	116	39.7	6.08	.97	16.0	n.a.	1,032	2,309	14.3
1968	2.2	20.1	182	40.7	6.15	.94	15.3	n.a.	1,300	1,632	3.5
1969	1.8	22.6	268	41.0	5.85	1.00	17.3	9,272	1,080	1,242	1.7
1970	2.4	25.6	425	41.4	5.65	.49	8.7	8,139	1,106	2,790	18.5

Notes and Sources: Grain. "Extended grain exports" include grain (70) and 1.18 times flour exports (84001) (assumed an 85 percent extraction rate for flour).

Cotton fiber. Ginned cotton. XX and MM include cotton fiber (51001), cotton thread (5140104), and cotton cloth (900).

Flax. (scutched basis) XX includes fiber, combings, thread, and cloth (51004, 005, 1301, and 903). Million meters fabric equals 127 metric tons.

Hemp. 5107.

Wool. Washed equivalent. XX and MM include wool fiber (511), wool yarn (5140105), tops (51401).

Butter. Q refers to "factory production" which was much less than total Q in 1913 and 1931.

Hides and skins. Cattle hides and calf skins.

Sunflower seed. XX is seed (72005) plus sunflower seed oil (84109).

Sugar. Output of granulated sugar refined from domestic sugar beets and imported raw sugar. Raw sugar is converted to granulated sugar by .93. Consumption equals Q plus net imports of refined sugar (assuming the raw sugar was used for Q). The net M/C ratio is net imports of raw and refined sugar divided by C.

See also Table 5.1, "General notes re sources to tables in this chapter."

107

TABLE 5.6

Soviet Union: Indexes of Output and Productivity for Selected Sectors, 1950-70
(1959 = 100)

Year	Machinery Producer Durables 1968 wt.	Ferrous Metals 1968 wt.	Non-Ferrous Metals 1968 wt.	Durables 1968 wt.	Consumer Goods: Soft Goods 1968 wt.	Processed Food 1968 wt.	Net Agricultural: Crop 1960 wt.	Animal Products 1960 wt.	Aggregate Factor Productivity: Industry	Aggregate Factor Productivity: Agriculture 1965 wt.
1950	39.5	42.2	64.7	27.6	44.5	47.6	83.5	50.0	67-71	80
1955	65.5	73.1	76.3	77.8	75.7	75.2	94.1	69.3		87
1956	75.2	79.0	81.7	81.8	81.7	81.4	109.4	75.0		
1957	87.7	84.3	86.4	87.0	85.6	83.4	101.2	86.4		
1958	94.4	90.2	91.6	90.2	92.8	92.2	112.9	90.9		
1959	100.0	100.0	100.0	100.0	100.0	100.0	100.0	100.0		
1960	113.4	107.8	109.3	112.5	106.3	105.1	101.2	106.0	100	100
1961	130.1	117.2	119.2	122.5	110.8	112.7	110.6	106.8		100
1962	146.2	126.5	130.0	130.4	115.4	120.8	103.5	108.0		94
1963	160.5	135.0	140.0	144.2	116.1	125.7	95.3	88.6		94
1964	169.9	146.8	150.6	159.1	118.3	131.8	127.1	101.2		95
1965	178.3	157.4	163.3	173.2	119.7	147.1	117.6	113.6	100	100
1966	193.3	169.1	178.7	199.7	129.3	151.5	136.5	117.0	103-104	102
1967	206.7	181.2	196.3	231.4	141.3	162.0	137.6	114.8		106
1968	223.2	189.4	215.5	271.0	153.6	168.9	148.2	119.3		106
1969	240.8	194.1	231.5	315.2	164.8	174.2	134.1	121.6		106
1970	260.5	205.7	246.3	348.8	175.9	185.3	154.1	137.5	109-112	111

Sources: Manufacturing sector indices are from Rush Greenslade, "Industrial Production in the USSR" in Soviet Economic Prospects for the Seventies, U.S. Congress, Joint Economic Committee, 93d Cong., 1st Sess. (Washington, D.C.: U.S. Government Printing Office, 1973), p. 280. Agricultural indices from Douglas Diamond, "Developments in Soviet Agriculture" in Soviet Economic Prospects for the Seventies, U.S. Congress, Joint Economic Committee, 93d Cong., 1st Sess. (Washington, D.C.: U.S. Government Printing Office, 1973), p. 336 and shifted to a 1959 base. The aggregate factor productivity for industry is derived from James Noren, "Soviet Industry in the 1971-75 Plan," in Soviet Economic Prospects for the Seventies, U.S. Congress, Joint Economic Committee, 93d Cong., 1st Sess. (Washington, D.C.: U.S. Government Printing Office, 1973), pp. 206-45, and Greenslade, Industrial Production, op. cit., p. 275 (using indices of man-hours, and capital in Cobb-Douglas production function), for agriculture from Diamond, Developments in Soviet Agriculture, op. cit., p. 318, shifted to a 1960 base. See also Table 5.1 for "General notes re. sources to tables in this chapter."

over agriculture. The "grain problem" is also not new to the 1970s—
stimulating agricultural output has been the continuing concern of
Soviet leadership. [14] That is, these relative trends in output were
well established before export development became a possible factor
in their overall growth.

EXPORT SPECIALIZATION IN THE SOVIET ECONOMY

It has been argued that in the past Soviet exports were based
on the principle of "exports of surpluses" rather than a systematic
development of export sectors. In the postwar period the Soviet
Union has increasingly stated that the principles of the "international
division of labor" are an important criteria for national economic
development and the expansion of trade. [15] To what extent and in what
sectors has such export specialization occurred during 1950-70?

The conventional measure of export specialization for a given
industry—the ratio of gross exports to output—overstates export
specialization when there are imports of identical or similar products
and understates export specialization when export product is used in
the production of other exports. To correct for these weaknesses,
we computed "extended" export-output ratios that include net direct
exports plus net indirect exports of the commodity embodied as a
major component of "other exports." (The export components of these
other products are essentially a physical input coefficient times the
quantity of "other exports.") Similar measures are computed for
import-consumption ratios (output plus net imports). [16] These extended export-output ratios for several major export products are
presented in Tables 5.4 and 5.5 along with time series of output,
direct exports, and total direct and indirect exports. We briefly
describe our results and rely on the reader to refer to the tables.

EXPORT SPECIALIZATION IN INDUSTRIES

The extended export/output ratios shown in Tables 5.4 and 5.5
indicate that export specialization has increased in the mining,
metallurgy, and energy sectors and that a large share of recent
increases of output in these sectors has been exported. [17]

Consider several major branches of heavy industry—coal, iron
ore, pig iron, and oil. Net exports of coal and coal-related products
rose rapidly from 4 percent of output in 1960 to almost 9 percent of
output in 1970; and exports absorbed 30 percent of the added output

during 1960-70. Iron ore exports comprised 10 percent of output in 1950, about 15 percent in the early 1960s, and 18 percent by 1970. If to this we add net exports of ferrous metals converted to iron ore equivalents, the extended export/output ratios for iron ore rises from 11 percent in 1950 to 27 percent in 1970. About 41 percent of the added ore output between 1959 and 1967 ended up embodied in exports.

Net exports of oil products grew from net imports in the early 1950s to 20 percent of crude oil output in 1960 and 28 percent in 1968. About 40 percent of the added output was exported between 1960 and 1968.

Similar trends in export specialization occurred for many other minerals and metals (including nonferrous metals) in the postwar period. The (extended) net export/output ratios in 1970 were about 21 percent for manganese ore, 74 percent for aluminium, 34 percent for magnesium, 36 percent for asbestos, about 33 percent of potash output and 50 percent of apatite ore output. Looking at Table 5.4 we conclude that (1) large shares of added output of many minerals, fuels, and metals were exported during the 1960s, so that most export/output ratios (except copper) rose, and (2) export/output ratios for mining and metallurgy products are often high. This suggests that in the postwar period the expansion of mining and metallurgy has been closely related to the expansion of exports.

The degree of export specialization is less extensive in other industrial sectors, but the pattern is interesting. For example, the extended export/output ratio for raw industrial timber hauled rose almost uninterruptedly from less than 1 percent in 1950 to about 10 percent in 1970 and to 7 percent for processed timber products and about 11 percent for plywood. Gross exports of paper and cellulose grew steadily and together were about 16 percent of cellulose output and 11 percent of paper output in 1970. But imports also grew rapidly so that the overall net expansion of the Soviet paper industry for exports turns out to be very slight.

Cotton cloth exports grew steadily, but because of large imports, net cotton cloth exports were only about 2 percent of output in 1970—the Soviet Union has lost its inherited export specialization in cotton cloth (Table 5.7). In contrast, the export of small consumer durables (which are produced by the machinery industry) expanded rapidly in 1950-70 and large portions of recent increments in output have been exported. In 1970 net export/output ratios are 12 percent for bicycles, 25 percent for watches and clocks, 30 percent for cameras, and 15 percent for radios. How do we explain this shift of export specialization to the technologically advanced precision and electronics industries (Table 5.7)?

TABLE 5.7

Export, Import, and Production of Consumer Products in the Soviet Union, 1913-70, Selected Years

Q = domestic output in units
X = simple exports
XX = "embodied" in related M
M = simple imports
MM = "embodied" in related M
net X = X - M (net exports)
net XX = XX - MM (net embodied exports)
net M = M - X (net imports)
net MM = MM - XX (net embodied imports)
a = large exports of related products in 1913
EQ = shows series that adjusts for "embodied" or related items

S = total supply = Q + M or Q + MM
C = consumption = Q + net M or Q + net MM
. = not estimated
- = no trade
0 = less than 1/2 unit shown
[ ] = datum based on different sources or assumptions
~ = very approximate magnitude
n.d. = no data
e = small exports
m = small imports
dr = approximate domestic value = foreign trade rubles times 3.4 for consumer manufactured goods

ETN	900 Cotton Cloth million meters length				901 Woolen Cloth million meters length		903 Silk-type Cloth million meters length		910, 913 Sewn Clothing million domestic rubles (1968)		
Year	Q	X	M	net X/Q	M	M/Q	Q	M	C	Mdr	Mdr/C
1913	2670	~172	37	5.1%	[~6.0]	[6%]	[43?]	[1]	n.a.	8	.
1931	2240	159	1	7.1	0.4	[0]	n.a.	0	n.a.	0	0%
1950	3900	80	81	0	5.5	3.5	130	.	2,970	0	0
1955	5900	139	16	2.1	10.7	4.2	526	33	5,580	8	0.1
1960	6390	195	143	0.8	26.5	7.7	810	61	8,080	710	8.8
1965	7080	272	95	2.5	9.0	2.5	937	.	8,590	830	9.6
1970	7480	307	155	2.0	12.0	2.4	1,241	57	15,200	1,490	9.8

(continued)

111

(Table 5.7 continued)

ETN	904 Rugs (million square meters)		914 Knitted Wear (million domestic 1968 rubles)				930 Leather Shoes (millions of pairs)			950 Furniture (million domestic 1968 rubles)	
Year	Mdr	Q	M	C	M*	M*/C	Q	M	M/Q	V	Mdr
1913	~5	n.a.	624 tons	n.a.	2.4	.	68.0	0.1	0%	n.a.	17.0
1931	0	n.a.	220 "	n.a.	0.0	.	~100.0	0.0	0	n.a.	.5
1950	~2	n.a.	0	985	0.0	~0	203.0	6.6	3.2	224	~1.0
1955	~70	n.a.	0.9	2,100	~13.0	0.6	271.2	0.9	0	685	~20.0
1960	~75	10.9	1.6	2,824	~290.0	10.3	419.3	29.7	7.1	1,590	~200.0
1965	~145	19.6	4.2	4,440	~350.0	7.9	486.0	27.9	5.7	2,600	~480.0
1970	~300	30.3	5.2	6,534	~700.0	10.7	675.7	60.7	9.0	3,460	~716.0

ETN	97001 Machines (1,000's)				97006 Bicycles (1,000's)		97011 Watches & Clocks (millions)		97013 Cameras (1,000's)		97017 TV's (1,000's)
Year	Q	X	M	net X/Q	Q	X	Q	X	Q	X	Q
1913	[272]	-	20.1	[-7]%	[5]	-20		-381	[0]	[-]	.
1931	501	-	-	0	[81]	-4		-11	23	[-]	.
1950	502	2.5	1.1	0	649	19	n.a.	[0]	261	17	12
1955	1,610	10.6	66.3	.	2,884	14	n.a.	.3		27	495
1960	3,096	18.5	314.8	-10	2,783	196	26.0	4.0	1,764	76	1,726
1965	800	52.2	63.5	-2	3,873	155	30.6	5.1	1,053	305	3,595
1970	1,400	117.3	63.1	4	4,443	510	40.2	10.7	2,045	622	6,682

ETN	97015 Radios 1,000's		965 Cosmetics million domestic rubles	960–2 Medicine million domestic rubles	83002 Canned Vegetables million standard cans			548846 Tobacco & EQ 1,000 metric tons			722 Spices 1,000 metric tons
Year	Q	X	M	M	Q	M	M/Q	Q	net MM	net M/Q	M
1913	·	·	7	9	n.a.	0	·	·	[– 13]	·	6.3
1931	n.a.	·	0	4	n.a.	n.a.	·				0.4
1950	1,072	8	n.a.	5	163	0.7	0.4	157	30	16%	3.1
1955	n.a.	46	2	8	n.a.	6.0		194	49	20	3.9
1960	4,165	19	8	80	1,055	40.0	3.8	178	76	30	8.4
1965	5,160	364	61	273	1,484	319.0	21.0	217	125	37	11.8
1970	7,815	1,200	230	571	2,611	623.0	24.0	263	106	29	11.7

ETN	72101 Coffee 1,000 metric tons	72102 Cocoa Beans 1,000 metric tons	72104 Tea 1,000 metric tons	84405 Wine million decalites		830 Vegetables 1,000 metric tons	832 Fruit million 1968 domestic rubles		1,000 metric tons	833 Fruit, Dried 1,000 metric tons	803 Eggs million
Year	M	M	M	Q	M	M	C	Mdr	M	M	M
1913	12.6	6	75.8	n.a.	0.9	60.9	n.a.	n.a.	133	53	−3,660
1931	1.2	4	20.7	n.a.	0.0	0.5	n.a.	n.a.	3	5	− 293
1950	1.2	12	5.7	24	0.0	48.0	1,020	0	3	6	36
1955	1.5	14	10.2	·	2.2	70.0	9,370	~89	133	28	231
1960	19.1	58	22.6	78	57.6	215	9,240	~180	335	77	113
1965	30.9	89	36.3	134	12.2	350	9,270	~291	501	85	706
1970	41.5	100	29.2	268	71.9	482	9,900	~402	680	128	662

(continued)

113

Notes and Sources: <u>General</u>. The values of imported nonfood consumer goods (denoted by *) were adjusted to the approximate level of domestic retail prices by coefficient 3.44, of imported food items by coefficient 4.17. (See footnote 28.) Value of consumption in 1968 retail prices from David W. Bronsen and Barbara S. Severin, "Soviet Consumer Welfare: The Brezhnev Era" in Soviet Economic Prospects for the Seventies, U.S. Congress, Joint Economic Committee, 93d Cong., 1st Sess. (Washington, D.C.: U.S. Government Printing Office, 1973), Sov. Con. Welfare, pp. 395-403.

<u>Silk-type cloth</u> (903) includes cloth of nonnatural fibers.

<u>Tobacco and equivalents</u>: Q includes high-grade tobacco and makhorka; net M includes raw tobacco (54), cigarettes (84603) converted to tobacco equivalents by 1 metric ton tobacco per 1 million cigarettes and "Dunza" (8460104).

See also Table 5.1, "General notes re sources to tables in this chapter."

DECLINE OF EXPORT SPECIALIZATION
IN AGRICULTURE

Export specialization of Soviet agriculture has declined continuously. In 1913 large shares of output were exported including 13
percent of grain, 68 percent of flax, 38 percent of butter, 31 percent
of eggs, 10 percent of sugar, and 44 percent of oilseed.[18]

The Soviet Union is still a large exporter of many important
agricultural products, but after adjusting for imports it is a net
exporter of only five major products—grain (usually), cotton, flax,
sunflower seed, and butter—plus a few lesser products, and it now is
a net importer of raw sugar and eggs (Table 5.5).

After World War II, the Soviet Union made an effort to reestab-
lish (net) grain exports; these rose from about 3 million tons in the
early 1950s to a peak of 7.7 million tons in 1962, or about 7 percent
of a record 1961 grain crop. Just two years later however net grain
imports rose to 3.8 million tons after a poor harvest. During 1968-
70 net exports averaged 4.6 million tons or only about 3 percent of the
harvest. Gross cotton fiber exports rose steadily; the gross export/
output ratio of 28 percent in 1970 suggests that cotton output had been
greatly expanded for export, but adjustment for the large (fluctuating)
imports reduces this only 12 percent (still quite substantial). Flax
exports declined during the 1960s and export/crop ratios declined
from 12 percent in 1959 to 4 percent in 1970. Net butter exports are
erratic but higher toward the end of the 1960s when they averaged
about 7 percent of output. Only exports of sunflower seed and oil
grew continually and extended export/crop ratios rose from 2-3 percent in 1955 to about 17 percent in 1967. The steady expansion of
gross sugar exports to about 9 percent of granulated sugar production
turns out to be "export specialization" in the sugar refining industry
rather than in sugar beet production.

SUMMARY OF EXPORT SPECIALIZATION

The basic findings shown in Tables 5.4, 5.5, 5.7 are that
(1) a number of major Soviet industries directly or indirectly exported an increasingly large share of their output during 1950-70,
(2) the trend seemed to accelerate in the 1960s, and (3) export
specialization has occurred largely in traditional priority branches
of heavy industry and relied heavily on natural resources. Relatively
little export specialization has occurred in light industry and by
1970 there was little evidence of the once-extensive export specialization in agriculture of 1913.

TRADE SPECIALIZATION MACHINERY
EXPORTS AND IMPORTS

Both exports and imports of machinery grew rapidly during 1950-70, but the Soviet Union remains a large net importer of machinery. In 1970 the gross export/output ratio for "producers' durables" (estimated in terms of 1959 domestic prices) was probably about 8 percent, the gross import/domestic deliveries ratio for "producers' durables" was about 9 percent; according to these measures the overall net import/domestic deliveries ratio is a rather low 1 or 2 percent in 1970 and has not been higher than 5 percent in the postwar period (Table 5.7).[19] That is, the large gross machinery imports are not indicative of extensive "import dependence" for the overall supply of machinery (especially when compared to the situation in 1913 or the NEP). Such ratios, of course, fail to measure the value of imported machinery in terms of "domestic opportunity cost" of domestically produced <u>identical</u> items principally because "technological transfer" and other qualitative characteristics are not taken into account. These qualitative benefits are often thought to be the principal gains from the large export and import of machinery.[20] The differences in structure of machinery imports and exports supports this conjecture.

COMPOSITION OF MACHINERY TRADE

A comparison of machinery imports and exports for selected subbranches in 1970 would reveal relatively little simultaneous export and import of machinery of the same subbranch or similar type items despite the large volume of trade. This suggests considerable intrabranch specialization in which some subbranches export a significant portion of their output and some subbranches rely to a significant degree on imports. What factors seem to determine the direction of foreign trade specialization of the Soviet machinery industry? (Such specialization has been a principal objective of CMEA!)

Certain "qualitative characteristics" are repeatedly found in Soviet intrabranch specialization in machinery trade. Soviet machinery exports (primarily to the less-developed economies in the Bloc and elsewhere) are concentrated in products that, in the history of the Soviet economy, have been high-priority products, are used in historically high-growth heavy industries, are mass-produced serial standardized products, or are military-related. Such characteristics would favor the export of these products because of 1) their favorable effect on reducing costs and 2) the "planners' inertia" in continuing to expand the output of mature products—but this anticipates our conclusions.

Machinery imports, primarily from Czechoslovakia, East Germany, Poland, and the Western industrialized countries, are more diversified and in 1970 tended to supply 1) machinery in which the Soviet machine-building industry lacks modern designing and manufacturing experience, 2) new technologies, 3) complex equipment required in relatively low volume, 4) machinery from traditional Bloc producers and intra-Bloc specialization agreements.[21] Machinery imports also reflect sudden shifts in investment priorities (chemicals, automobile manufacturing). In these qualitative aspects the Soviet economy seems to be comparatively disadvantaged. These sets of characteristics are reflected in the specialization ratios.

SOME SPECIALIZATION RATIOS FOR MACHINERY

Trade-specialization ratios for 32 selected machinery items are shown in Table 5.8. The estimation of such ratios for machinery is plagued by problems of aggregation, noncomparability of data for trade and domestic output, and bias in the nonrandom selection of items.[22] Some important items likely to have high export/output ratios, for example, aircraft are omitted because of insufficient data. Items are omitted because little trade occurred—yet this fact in itself is significant. Thus these estimates are offered only as rough indications of specialization. Keeping with this spirit, the ratios based on ruble values are not adjusted for the different purchasing power of domestic and foreign rubles or changes in domestic or foreign trade prices. The ratios are reported on a gross basis and are based on output or output plus imports.

Value-based ratios differ significantly from quantity-based ratios. They reflect (1) the downward bias imparted by the larger share of simple items in the domestic "mix" than in the traded "mix" of a given product; (2) the well-known Soviet preference to import technologically advanced and more complex models of given items; and (3) an apparent bias in machinery prices in CMEA trade.[23] Thus, in 1970 the export-output ratio for metal-cutting equipment is 6 percent based on quantity but 8 percent based on value, while the import-deliveries ratio is 5 percent based on quantity and 14 percent based on value (Table 5.8).

Of the items examined, machinery with gross export-output ratios greater than 10 percent in 1970 are automobiles (25 percent), graders (14 percent), tractors and parts (11 percent), equipment for

TABLE 5.8

Trade Specialization Ratios for Selected Machinery Products in the Soviet Union,
1950, 1960, 1965, 1970
(ratios listed in percent)

Q = domestic output in physical units (1,000)
V = domestic output current ruble prices (millions)
X = exports in appropriate units
M = imports in appropriate units
S = output plus imports
* = excludes items in "complete plants"

n.l. = "not listed"
(0) = "probably small"
n.a. = "data not available"
x = exports relatively small or zero
m = imports relatively small or zero
ETN = Soviet commodity number

| ETN | 100 | | | | | | 103-105 | | |
| | Metal Cutting Equipment | | | | | | Forges & Presses | | |
Item	Q	X/Q	M/Q	V	X/V	M/V	V	M/V	M/S
1950	71	*5%	2%	n.a.	n.a.	n.a.	16	6%	6%
1960	156	*1	5	419	*3%	13%	129	26	20
1965	192	*3	3	638	*6	13	161	22	18
1970	202	6	5	979	8	14	246	30	23

118

ETN Item	11101-02 Electric motors to 100 kw			11129 Power Transformers			140 Equipment for Food Processing		151 Equipment for Paper & Pulp[X]	
	Q	X/Q	M/Q	Q	X/Q	M/S	V	M/S	V	M/S
1950	4.2	1%	4%	10.2	9.8%	5.5%	n.l.	n.a.	n.l.	n.a.
1960	13.5	1	2	49.4	7.3	2.4	185	38%	19.7	60%
1965	21.6	0	8	95.3	3.0	4.5	249	24	40.1	47
1970	27.8	10	8	105.9	1.7	1.3	337	27	84	52

ETN Item	150 Equipment for Chemical Industry			15501 Pumps			13007 Cranes-Truck[m]		13009 Cranes-Railroad[x]	
	X	X/V	M/S	Q	X/Q	M/Q	Q	X/Q	Q	M/S
1950	24	n.a.	8%	92.6	1.6%	.6%	4,152	0%	478	0%
1960	223	*(0)	75	390.9	.8	1.2	6,692	4.1	444	4.7
1965	383	*(0)	49	774.3	.5	1.3	14,062	3.1	463	10.3
1970	464	11	41	1,161.0	4.1	.1	15,149	5.9	493	15.4

ETN Item	17301 Ball Bearings		13304 Lifts		15408 Bulldozers		15407 Graders		15401 Excavators	
	Q	X/Q	Q	M/S	Q	X/Q	Q	X/Q	X/Q	M/Q
1950	93	n.l.	466	n.l.	3,788	4.0%	33	n.l.	4.5	8.8%
1960	370	3.2%	3,365	19.4%	12,850	5.8	3,135	6.4	5.7	.1
1965	524	3.0	8,639	11.5	20,103	8.1	4,178	10.7	5.8	3.1
1970	673	5.2	18,107	4.3	33,499	5.4	4,590	13.5	7.4	4.5

(continued)

(Table 5.8 continued)

ETN Item	18001, 05 Tractors & Parts^m			181 Agricultural Machines			18101 Plows	18103 Harrows	18122 Mowers	18111 Seeders
	Q	X/Q	X'/Q	V	X/V	M/V	X/Q	X/Q	M/S	M/S
1950	117	7%	n.a.	286	2%	2	n.l.	n.1	3.2%	(0)%
1960	239	8	11%	759	5	1	5.0%	17.1%	9.0	(0)
1965	355	6	11	1,462	5	4	3.3	3.3	14.8	(0)
1970	459	6	11	2,115	3	10	1.7	8.3	18.2	15.4

ETN Item	18116 Combines		18138 Grain Cleaners^e		18157 Oil Cake Mills		19035 Trolleys^e	19103 Buses^e	19025 Metro^m
	X/Q	M/S	Q	M/S	Q	M/S	M/S	M/Q	X/Q
1950	0.8%	(0)%	6.4	n.1	2.3%	n.1.	n.1.	0%	n.1.
1960	7.4	(0)	17.0	n.1.	15.2	0%	18.3%	0	(0)
1965	6.1	10.0	24.1	6.9	17.6	44.7	19.9	2	(0)
1970	3.1	16.4	22.0	13.4	12.7	56.7	38.6	10	10.4

ETN Item	19124 Automobiles		19101 Trucks[m]		19007 Electric Locomotives[e]		19015–21 Railroad Freight Cars[e]		19024 Railroad Passenger Cars	
	Q	X/Q	Q	X/Q	Q	M/S	Q	M/S	Q	M/S
1950	65	8%	294	4%	102	(0)%	50.8	6%	912	10%
1960	139	22	362	7	396	22	36.4	8	1,656	47
1965	201	24	379	4	641	22	39.6	13	1,991	35
1970	344	25	524	7	323	26	58.7	7	1,791	30

Notes and Sources: General. Ratios are rough approximations. Domestic ruble value of imported equipment is assumed similar to value in foreign trade rubles (See "pppr" in footnote 26). No adjustment for price changes.

Graders. Autograders.

Tractors. X is complete tractors (18001–93) plus "complete tractor equivalents" of tractor parts (18091, 98) based on quantity/value ratio for complete tractors.

Combines. All types.

Oil Cake Mills. Hammer mills for grain and oil cake.

Metro. Refers to subway cars.

Electric Locomotives. Mainline locomotives.

See also Table 5.1, "General notes re. sources to tables in this chapter."

chemical industry (14 percent) (of which the Soviet Union is a large net importer), electric motors to 100 kw, subway cars, and quite likely metallurgical equipment, power station equipment, and aircraft.[24] A more complete sample would certainly reveal other items. Products with modest export/output ratios (5-10 percent) in 1970 are metal-cutting equipment, truck-mounted cranes, ball bearings, bulldozers, excavators, harrows, and trucks.

Products with relatively high import/gross supply ratios in 1970 were more numerous and included equipment for metal-cutting (8-14 percent), metal-forming (23 percent), paper and pulp industries (52 percent), the chemical industry (41 percent), the food-processing industry (27 percent), buses (10 percent), trolleys (39 percent), combines (16 percent), grain cleaners (13 percent), mowers (18 percent), oilseed presses (57 percent), electric locomotives (26 percent), and railroad passenger cars (30 percent). Other products likely to have high ratios are ships, industrial electric trucks, and equipment for the automobile industry and for other branches of light industry.[25] Products with modest import/gross supply ratios (5-10 percent) were excavators, lifts, and railroad freight cars. There are, of course, many products with low import/supply ratios. The large number of rather high ratios is surprising, however, especially for agricultural and railroad equipment and for equipment for the previously low priority sectors. Compared with 1913 or the NEP, the degree of import dependence still remains relatively low and is more widely diversified among the subbranches of the machinery industry. The pattern corresponds more or less to that suggested at the beginning of this section.

IMPORT GROWTH AND IMPORT DEPENDENCE

Despite the rapid expansion of imports in the postwar period, Soviet industry and probably the economy in general is less dependent on imports in 1970 than in 1950. Trends in imports and import/supply ratios support this.

As seen in Table 5.3, postwar imports have been characterized by a large but stable share of machinery (30-35 percent of total imports), a relative and absolute decline of fuel and raw materials in the 1960s (47 percent in 1950, 23 percent in 1970), a proportional increase in chemicals, and the rapid increase in consumer soft goods, nonbasic foodstuffs, and on occasion basic foodstuffs (from 23.4 percent in 1950 to 31 percent in 1970). This structure can be contrasted with Russia of 1913 (16 percent machinery, 50 percent industrial raw materials, and 31 percent consumer goods and foodstuffs) and with the Soviet Union of 1931 at the peak of its big push (54 percent machinery, 37 percent industrial raw materials, and only 7 percent of foodstuffs and consumer durables). That is, from a structural viewpoint, Soviet industry now relies relatively little on imports for raw materials and fuel.

RAW AND SEMIPROCESSED MATERIALS

At the heart of Russia's import dependence in 1913 was its reliance on imported raw materials. In 1913 (net) imports accounted for the following shares in consumption: 17 percent of coal, 45 percent of cotton fiber, 17 percent of wool, 20 percent of copper, 97 percent of lead, 59 percent of zinc, 100 percent of nickel, tin, aluminium, and rubber (but only 2 percent of rolled ferrous metals), 9 percent of pipe, 60 percent of paper products, 21 percent of pulp, and a large share of its hides, dyes, tanning materials, chemicals, and fertilizers.[26] By 1935 the Soviet Union had by necessity become almost independent of imported raw materials (except for small portions of its tin and rubber needs). Has the growth of postwar imports made the Soviet Union again dependent on imported raw materials?

This might appear so, for the gross import of many raw materials have a distinct upward trend. But after adjustment for exports the Soviet Union in 1970 is in fact a net exporter of most and a net importer of only a few important materials: rubber, tin, jute, wool, hides, several chemicals, large-diameter pipe, pesticides, and several lesser products. The Soviet Union has actually become less dependent on imports during the postwar period as the net imports of oil, coal, zinc, lead, copper, paper, cartons, and cloth in the earlier 1950s became important net exports in the 1960s. For only a few major materials have net imports grown during the postwar period (Tables 5.4 and 5.5); these include caustic soda and soda ash, artificial and synthetic fibers, several other chemicals, specialized paper, and large-diameter steel pipe (perhaps the most publicized example). In contrast, net tin imports peaked in the late 1950s, rubber and hide imports showed little trend in the 1960s, and net imports of wool showed little overall trend over the 20-year period. In sum, long-term Soviet industrial growth apparently has had a relatively low elasticity of demand for imports of raw and semiprocessed materials when considered on a net-import basis!

An examination of the import/supply ratios over the period confirms this impression of import independence with respect to major raw materials and fuels (Tables 5.4 and 5.5). Some net import/utilization ratios of 1950 have been transformed into net

exports. For the few other net import/utilization ratios are modest
and show little trend in the 1960s. In 1970 these ratios were 24
percent for tin, 14 percent for wool, 19 percent for artificial fiber,
15 percent for synthetic fiber, and perhaps 20-40 percent for hides.
They were somewhat higher for some less important minerals,
metals, chemicals, and "noncompeting" tropical products. Dependence
on imported natural rubber, however, is partly offset by large synthetic rubber production. The few exceptions to declining import-
utilization ratios of "competing" products are alumina, caustic soda,
soda ash, pesticides, and steel pipe. Alumina imports are interesting.
By 1970 40 percent of Soviet alumina requirements were supplied by
imports. However, since 30-40 percent of its aluminium output is
exported, the Soviet Union still meets most of its own aluminium
requirements from domestic ores. Here, as with sugar refining, the
Soviet Union has utilized its energy resources to establish large-
scale processing of imported raw materials for re-export. In sum,
we conclude that the rising volume of imports has not significantly
increased the overall dependence of the Soviet economy either on
machinery or on imports. Imports are relatively diversified and
often partially offset by exports of similar commodities; net import/
supply ratios remain relatively low, especially when compared to
1913 ratios.

CONSUMER GOODS IMPORTS

The fast growth of "consumer-oriented imports"—especially
manufactured goods, processed foods, and luxury goods—since 1953
contrasts dramatically with the Spartan days of the 1930s and late
Stalinism, and reflects the basic shift in Soviet policy toward improving living standards.[27]
    In the prewar period, consumer-oriented imports consisted
mainly of raw materials for light industry. In contrast, imports of
consumer-oriented goods during 1953-70 increasingly emphasized
semiprocessed goods, luxury foodstuffs (for example, cocoa and
fruit), basic foodstuffs (for example, grain and sugar) and a widening
range of manufactured consumer goods. The share of manufactured
consumer goods alone rises from 7 percent of total imports in the
early 1950s to 19-20 percent in the late 1960s. (For reasons discussed below, however, such imports do not include small consumer
durables and automobiles, of which the Soviet Union is a net exporter.)
    If any area of the Soviet economy has benefited from growing
imports it may well be the luxury aspects of consumption. The retail

value of imported foodstuffs and manufactured consumer goods was
probably about 4 percent of disposable income in 1950, 7 percent in
1960, and 7 percent in 1970.[28] Some imported consumer goods are
"noncompeting" tropical products with naturally high import consumption ratios, but many consumer imports are "competing" and
are reported to be preferred for their quality and design over similar
domestically produced goods.[29] Over the period, imports and import-
consumption ratios for such items have increased considerably, so
that by 1970 imports supplied 16 percent of sugar, 29 percent of
tobacco items, 8 percent of shoes, as much as 10 percent of furniture,
15 percent of rugs, 5 percent of sewn clothing, knit wear, haber-
dashery, and significant portions of canned goods, fruits, and
vegetables (Tables 5.5 and 5.7). The diversity of imported goods
has become almost bourgeois (rum, wine, cosmetics, pianos, baby
carriages, etc.). Import-dependence on such luxury items, however,
could easily be foregone compared to the consumers' dependence on
imported raw materials to produce essential consumer goods in
1913 and the 1920s.

    These dramatic changes in Soviet policy toward the consumer
imports are not without irony. Only now, 40 years after the First
Five-Year Plan, a major goal of its foreign trade plan is being
realized on a large scale—namely, to raise exports enough to permit
great increases in consumer goods imports. And the policy of
temporarily importing grain to offset the economic effects of a poor
harvest in 1960 and 1972 was last publicly advocated by Bukharin
and the Right in 1928 for virtually identical reasons, and was last
undertaken (albeit on a much smaller scale) in 1928.[30] In change,
unawaited continuity.

IDENTICAL IMPORTS AND EXPORTS IN
SOVIET FOREIGN TRADE

    An unusually large number of identical or similar items are
simultaneously imported and exported by the Soviet Union. The
traditional economic reason for such trade in a geographically large
nation is savings in transportation costs (for example, coal from
Poland). In the Soviet case, other factors seem to increase this
simultaneous trade including (1) bilaterality and long-term commitments with the socialist economies and developing countries; (2)
negotiated intrabranch specialization with CMEA; (3) improvement of
raw material quality; (4) the desire to increase the diversity and
quality of domestically consumed goods; (5) processing and re-export
(for example, sugar); and (6) different technological levels of domestic
and foreign equipment.[31]

For cotton, hides, tobacco, wool, and paper such trade reflects a desire to improve the quality of their raw materials. (A similar effect is also seen for consumer soft goods and several machinery items.) For products such as grain, metals, and crude oil, such simultaneous trade often results from long-term export commitments (with its socialist and developing country trading partners) in the absence of which imports of such goods probably would not occur at all. (Soviet grain imports from Canada have been delivered to Eastern Europe to fulfill Soviet export commitments.)[32] Goods imported in payment for credits are occasionally re-exported to get hard currency or other more desired goods. Such attempts to multilateralize other- wise bilateral trade through its own import and re-export operations tend to increase the overall volume of trade above that which would prevail with multilateral free trade and may account for a substantial share of the trade growth in the 1960s—a question for further study.

Finally, it should be noted that extensive simultaneous exports and imports further reduce the economic dependence of the Soviet economy on foreign trade.

QUALITATIVE FACTORS IN TRADE SPECIALIZATION

What explains the emergence of these distinct patterns of trade and trade-specialization in the postwar Soviet economy? The long-run determinants of the export and import structure in a free-trade mar- ket economy are usually thought to be comparative costs, which in turn depend on comparative factor endowments. And Rosefielde shows that this explanation may also be valid for the Soviet economy, for in terms of factor content the postwar development of Soviet foreign trade has been by and large consistent with the shift in factor proportions in the Soviet economy over the same period.[33] The change in factor proportions however may not be responsible for a shift in comparative costs toward heavy and extractive industries and away from agriculture and light industry. The development of export capacity, import needs, and comparative costs can also be explained in part by reference to its natural resource endowment but also by a set of "qualitative" institutional and historical factors peculiar to the Soviet economy: historical priority of sector, comparative technological levels, the complexity of the product in terms of assortment, "finish," and quality control (not technological complexity), the probability of plan fulfillment, the institution of "Soviet agriculture," and the trade pattern of bilateralized trading partners. The lack of quantitative measures and tests for such qualitative factors, however, should not prevent us from outlining tentatively their impact on Soviet trade.

First, the past domestic priority seems to be a major determinant in the postwar development of Soviet exports. "High priority"
has resulted in large exports, "low priority" in low exports or even
imports. There are several explanations for this. Expansion of a
priority sector becomes "built in" and can continue through "planners'
inertia," annual increments in the plan, and application of a well-
mastered (if outmoded) technology. Second, high-priority industries
may have favorable productivity and cost experiences due to greater
attention paid to developing and importing technology, greater investment in modernizing the plant and equipment, and wage preference
and status of labor skills. "High priority" often implies preferential
access to capital investment; which in turn leads to higher capital
intensiveness simultaneous with export expansions. (This would
explain Rosefielde's finding.) Export expansion provides the economic
justification for ideologically motivated growth of traditional "success
indicator" sectors beyond domestic requirements. Our examples are
coal, iron ore, metals, metallurgical equipment, tractors, and
mineral products as compared with agriculture, cloth, clothing, and
textile equipment.

Second, the composition of exports and imports also seems to
be influenced by the oft-described inability of the Soviet planning and
incentive systems to produce the "qualitative aspects" of output. Thus,
for commodities for which the assortment, quality, and design are
easily quantifiable and monitored or are subject to long serial production runs, Soviet industry does comparatively well. But when
design, assortment, and "finishing" are an essential aspect of a
product's utility to the users, Soviet industry seems less able to
produce these aspects of the good (although they might well be able
to produce the basic good itself).[34] Hence, clothing, shoes, fine
paper, furniture, and finer-quality raw materials are imported; while
raw materials, semiprocessed goods, newsprint, and mass produced
small consumer durables are exported.

The expression "Soviet agriculture" refers to the peculiar con-
figuration of institutions, organizations, and operations of Soviet
agriculture, its labor force, and the climate—all which seem to have
resulted in relatively slow growth and poor productivity experience
in agriculture compared to industry.[35] Over the 20 years, aggregate
factor productivity has grown at 1.6 percent per year compared to
2.2 percent in industry, thereby shifting comparative costs against
agriculture (Table 5.6).

A final factor that plays a role in the structural development
of Soviet exports and imports is trade preferences expressed by
"bilateralized preferred trading partners," namely the socialist
economies of CMEA and friendly developing countries—a topic beyond
the limited scope of this study.[36]

The changes in Soviet trade resulting from such qualitative factors are not necessarily incompatible with the observed increase in capital/labor ratios of exports compared to imports; the observed increase in the relative capital-intensity may well be the result of having a tradition of being a priority sector. An increase in the overall abundance of capital would, in fact, make such development or tendencies all the more easy to indulge in—even though it might be economically inefficient. Thus in the case of the Soviet Union it is very possible that a trade structure moving in the direction predicted on the basis of changing factor endowments may well turn out to be inefficient. Indeed such questions have recently been raised by Soviet economists.

EPILOGUE

An analysis of Soviet trade and output data in the postwar period suggests that systematic export specialization has in fact occurred in the Soviet Union, but that the accompanying increase in imports has not significantly increased its import dependence. The changing pattern of import and export development can be explained in terms of institutional and other qualitative factors as well as by factor endowments.

At this point it seems fitting to quote Kuibyshev speaking in 1932 about the future of Soviet foreign trade.

> We shall undertake a very large task—the task of making our socialist economy completely independent economically from the capitalist world. . . . so that we need fear neither threats nor blockades. But of course, this does not mean that our ideal is a shut-door economy. We shall extend our foreign trade connections, . . . but only such as help to strengthen socialist construction and are in consonance with the complete economic independence of the U.S.S.R.
>
> V. Kuibyshev[37]

NOTES

1. N. Patolichev, Foreign Trade (New York: Four Continent Book Corp., 1971).

2. P.J.D. Wiles, Communist International Economics (New York: Praeger, 1968); Alan A. Brown and Egon Neuberger, International Trade and Central Planning (Berkeley: University of California, 1968); Franklyn Holzman, "Foreign Trade" in Economic Trends in the Soviet Union, ed. Abram Bergson and Simon Kuznets (Cambridge, Mass.: Harvard University Press, 1963). A Soviet view is reflected by V. Kasyanenko, How Soviet Economy Won Technical Independence (Moscow: Progress Pub., 1966).

3. Leon M. Herman, "The Promise of Economic Self-Sufficiency under Soviet Socialism" in The Development of the Soviet Economy: Plan and Performance, ed. Vladimir G. Treml and Robert Farrell (New York: Praeger, 1968), pp. 213-48.

4. A. Frumkin, Modern Theories of International Economic Relations (New York: Four Continent Book Corp., 1969), pp. 470-84.

5. Wiles, op. cit., pp. 248, 427.

6. Steven Rosefielde, Soviet International Trade in Hecksher-Ohlin Perspective (Lexington, Mass.: D.C. Heath, 1973); C.H. MacMillan, "Factor Proportions and the Structure of Soviet Foreign Trade", ACES Bulletin 15, no. 1 (Spring 1973): 57-81.

7. Data sources are described in Notes to Tables.

8. Barry L. Kostinsky, Description and Analysis of Soviet Foreign Trade Statistics (Washington, D.C.: U.S. Department of Commerce, Bureau of Economic Analysis, FER-No. 5, 1974). Valentine Zabijaka, "The Soviet Grain Trade 1961-1970: A Decade of Change", ACES Bulletin 16, no. 1 (Spring 1974): 3-16.

9. Paul Marer, Postwar Pricing and Price Patterns in Socialist Foreign Trade (1946-1971) (Bloomington: International Research and Development Center of Indiana University, 1972).

10. Rosefielde, op. cit., pp. 25-39 and Vladimir G. Treml et al., "Inter-industry Structure of the Soviet Economy: 1959 and 1966" in Soviet Economic Prospects for the Seventies, U.S. Congress, Joint Economic Committee, 93rd Cong., 1st Sess. (Washington, D.C.: U.S. Government Printing Office, 1973), pp. 246-69.

11. Michael R. Dohan, "Volume, Price, and Terms of Trade Indices of Soviet Foreign Trade 1913-1938" in Two Studies in Soviet Terms of Trade, Michael R. Dohan and Edward Hewitt (Bloomington: International Development and Research Center of Indiana University, 1973); Holzman, "Foreign Trade," op. cit., p. 292.

12. See Notes to Table 5.1, U.S. data from Anne Bennett, "The Relative Role of U.S. Merchandise Trade," The Conference Board, no. 1734 (March 1974).

13. For a detailed discussion of 1913 and interwar trade see Michael R. Dohan, "Soviet Foreign Trade in the NEP Economy and Soviet Industrialization Strategy," Ph.D. thesis, MIT, 1969.

14. Douglas Whitehouse and Joseph F. Havelka, "Comparisons of Farm Output in the U.S. and U.S.S.R., 1950-1971" in Soviet Economic Prospects for the Seventies, op. cit., pp. 340-75. Douglas B. Diamond and Constance B. Krueger, "Recent Developments in Output in Productivity in Soviet Agriculture", in Soviet Economic Prospects for the Seventies, op. cit., pp. 316-39. Gale D. Johnson and Arcadius Kahan, "Soviet Agriculture: Structure and Growth," Comparisons of the United States and Soviet Economics, U.S. Congress, Joint Economic Committee, 86th Cong., 1st Sess. (Washington, D.C.: U.S. Government Printing Office, 1960), part I, pp. 201-37.

15. Michael Kaser, Comecon: Integration Problems of the Planned Economics (London: Oxford University Press, 1967).

16. For example, the total quantity of coal used directly or indirectly for export is calculated as net coal exports plus 1.4 times the net coke exports, 1.0 times pig iron plus .33 times the electricity exports in billion kwh plus 2 times net other ferrous metal exports. Notes to Table 5.4 describe coefficients and data.

17. These ratios are usually extended ratios, for example, manganese ore plus ferromanganese. These must be interpreted only as approximations because of the aggregate nature of export-input coefficients for related exports and the accuracy of the output data (especially for nonferrous metals).

18. Dohan, "Soviet Foreign Trade," op. cit., pp. 649-52.

19. The export-output ratio for producer durables is estimated from the domestic machinery output (net of consumer durables) delivered to final demand in 1959, derived from data in Rosefielde, op. cit., p. 21. These are multiplied by volume indices of producers' machinery output, (Rush Greenslade and Wade Robertson, "Industrial Production in the USSR," Soviet Economic Prospects for the Seventies, op. cit., p. 280) and machinery exports (derived using price indices of machinery export from Edward Hewett, "Estimating Price Indices from Unit Values: A New Technique and Its Application to Soviet Trade with the World, 1955-70" in Dohan and Hewett, Two Studies, op. cit.) to get comparable values in other years. The ratio of gross machinery imports to total deliveries of producer durables to the domestic economy was calculated in a similar manner using the same data sources. In 1959 the share of exports in domestically produced producer durables was about 9.1 percent, of gross imports in final deliveries about 9.0 percent, and of net imports in final deliveries only 0.7 percent!

20. Stanislaw Wasowski, East-West Trade and the Technology Gap (New York: Praeger, 1970).

21. Kaser, op. cit.

22. The sample was determined principally by availability of data. Furthermore before 1970, significant amounts of Soviet machinery exports were included in ETN 16 "Complete Plants" rather than in the proper classification. These are denoted by * in Table 5.8. This biases Soviet export/output ratios downward. Kostinsky, op. cit., pp. 15-38 analyses this problem. Comparisons of the value of imported and exported equipment with domestic values are also sources of difficulty but the order of magnitude is correct.

23. Marer, Postwar Pricing, op. cit., and Wasowski, op. cit.

24. See subbranch data in Treml, "Inter-industry Structure," op. cit., pp. 246-69 and Kostinsky, op. cit.

25. Compare 1970 output and import data for machinery for these industries in Narodnoe Khoziaistvo SSSR v 1970g Statisricheskii exhegodnik, (Moscow: Ied Statistika, 1971), pp. 211-16 and Vneshniaia Torgovlia SSSR za 1971 god Statisticheski obzor, (Moscow: Izd. Mezhdunarodnye otnosheniia, 1972), pp. 37-41.

26. Dohan, "Soviet Foreign Trade," op. cit., p. 121.

27. David W. Bronsen and Barbara S. Severin, "Soviet Consumer Welfare: The Brezhnev Era," in Soviet Economic Prospects for the Seventies, op. cit., pp. 367-403.

28. Disposable income from Bronsen and Severin, op. cit., p. 363. Purchasing power ratio (pppr) using domestic-foreign trade ruble prices (presumably in 1959) are for imports of producer goods 1.07 and of consumer goods 3.44, and of agricultural goods 4.17, for exports of producers' goods 1.12, of consumer goods 1.67, and of agricultural goods 1.32. (A. Efimov and L. Berri, eds. Metody Planerovaniia Mezhotraslevyikh Prosportsii [Moscow, 1966], cited in Rosefielde, op. cit., p. 36). Value of imports of ETN 7 times 4.17 (pppr includes tax) times 1.09 (retail markup) times volume index of ETN 7 on 1960 base (derived from Hewett, "Estimating Price Indices," op. cit; assumed average price change from 1950-55). Similarly with ETN 8 and 9, but with a pppr of 3.4. The results are the following (billions of rubles):

	1950	1960	1970
ETN 7 + 8 + 9 in "constant 1960 domestic prices"	1.24	5.75	11.82
Disposable income in constant prices	30.4	80.5	167.0

29. Bronsen and Severin, op. cit., p. 384.

30. Dohan, "Soviet Foreign Trade," op. cit., p. 554.

31. Kaser, op. cit., and Wasowski, op. cit.

32. Zabijaka, op. cit.

33. Rosenfielde, op. cit.

34. TV's, though technologically sophisticated, have 10, maybe 15, models and planning and control of production is simple compared to shoes, where 20 styles in 12 men's sizes and 2 colors gives 480 items—and shoe quality is very subtle with many parameters (leather, finish, last). Marshall Goldman, Soviet Marketing (London: Collier-Macmillan, 1963).

35. Diamond and Krueger, op. cit.

36. See discussion in Wiles, op. cit., p. 248.

37. V. Kuibyshev, Industrial Development Under the Second Five Year Plan, (Moscow: Cooperative Publishing Society of Foreign Workers in the U.S.S.R., 1932), p. 21.

6

THE VOLUME, STRUCTURE, AND DIRECTION OF THE POSTREFORM TRADE IN HUNGARY

Laszlo Zsoldos

In 1968 the Hungarian reforms introduced the New Economic Mechanism (NEM), which was a significant change in the laws and represented a break with earlier measures in the management of the economy. It was designed to improve the efficiency of the macro- and micromanagement by moving toward economic rationality in planning, particularly in the planning of foreign trade.

The broad purpose of this chapter is to appraise the influence of the 1968 reform upon the plans, practices, and performance of the foreign trade sector. More narrowly, I intend to review the background and the content of the reforms affecting foreign trade, and then turn to the question of how well did the NEM work in the foreign trade sector in terms of the theoretical implications of growing economic rationality in planning.

In this chapter "economic rationality in planning" will always mean the choice of "free trade norms corresponding to comparative advantage," a notion used by Abram Bergson.[1] In regard to the question of how well did the NEM work in the foreign trade sector, I will rely on a few broad criteria for improved performance, suggested again by Bergson, notably changes in the volume, structure, and direction of trade.[2] Bergson contends that if trade participation in the planned economies has tended to be below that of "comparable" capitalist economies, and if capitalist economies in general tended to be below levels corresponding to free trade norms, then "by implication . . . this would in itself indicate a . . . tendency under communism for trade to be below the free trade level."[3]

He continues to say that if there is a trend toward economic rationality, then this ought to show up in (1) growing relative volumes of trade, (2) changes in the structure of exports and imports reflecting the shifts in resource allocation, and (3) changes in the direction of trade, "often in favor of trade with the capitalist West."[4]

At the outset it will have to be established whether or not the NEM represents a de jure shift toward economic rationality in planning. Since the answer is in the affirmative, next to be considered is the question of a de facto shift toward rationality. That these questions must be given separate consideration needs no lengthy argument in light of the general proclivity of bureaucracies (regardless of the economic system in which they operate) for delay, inertia, and obfuscation. It is here that the commentary of Hungarian observers will be widely employed. Finally such data that is available on the Hungarian trade sector will be appraised using the Bergson criteria.

The first and the third of these criteria are perfectly straightforward. If one were to find that during the years following the introduction and continuing implementation of the NEM the relative trade volume, particularly with Western countries, was growing, then one may be permitted to attribute this (in the absence of evidence to the contrary) to increased economic rationality in Hungarian planning.

The matter is quite a bit more complicated in regard to changes in the structure of trade. Can any change, as compared to no change at all, be accepted as an evidence of increased economic rationality at work? What should no change in the structure of trade mean? The clarification depends, of course, on prior knowledge of the presumed distortions in the trade structure of the planned economy; but since there have been many studies over the decades regarding the nature and the extent of these distortions, it should not be difficult to define this criterion. In the case of Hungary, falling agricultural and food exports and corresponding rises in the importation of the same goods have been considered by some as developments running counter to comparative advantage. Again, Bergson, referring in particular to work done by Pryor and others, suspected that "the distortions must often have been of a very gross sort."[5] However, instead of accepting, without further questions, the existence of distortions in the structure of Hungarian trade, I will use more recent evidence presented, or cited, by Hungarian sources in this regard. Therefore, the definition of what constitutes an acceptable structural change indicating a shift toward increased economic rationality must be delayed and will be taken up after the review of Hungarian comments on the NEM.

THE BACKGROUND OF THE REFORM OF 1968

For years, indeed for decades, prior to the reform of 1968, volumes of critical commentary were written on the planned economies, what goes wrong with them, and what ought to be done to remedy the wrongs. Not the least of critics' concern was directed at the question

of how a system of highly centralized decisions would move toward
decentralization unless the alternatives to it were quite costly. What
would be these costs, specifically what would prompt internal reforms? The reasons, for the Hungarian reform at any rate, turned
out to be straightforward outgrowths of experiences with three suc-
cessive five-year plans. According to J. Bognar, from the early
1960s on it has become evident that economic growth under the prevailing system consumed too much energy, and that as a result there
was a need for change. He submits that centrally planned economic
activity opened up many new opportunities for success, but that the
economy's reserves for new growth were nearing exhaustion. As
more and more of the unfavorable developments began to occur, it
became clear, says Bognar, that "the alleviation or elimination of
these difficulties was unimaginable under a system of centralized
directives."[6] He cites five particular examples of the many reasons
that prompted the change in Hungary. (1) The economy was relatively
insensitive to changes in the rest of the world and furthermore its
capacity to adapt to changes was very low. For this reason the
economy's growth, in spite of efforts of the central planners and an
adequate scientific technical background, deteriorated. (2) The central planning system was not able to provide solutions for the internal
selection and differentiation of enterprises, even though it would have
been desirable to have a program of selective development and differentiation within the larger goal of full employment. (3) The internal
renewal of the economy as evidenced by the introduction of new products, new production methods, new management techniques, and new
marketing methods proceeded at a rate slower than desirable. (4)
Prior to the reform of 1968 substantial excess demand developed in
the household sector in part because of excessive efforts in the direction of economic growth and development and in part because of the
weak or unresponsive nature of the enterprises. (5) And finally, year
after year the losses of poorly organized enterprises increased, as
did the inventory of unsalable goods, and, also, considerable losses
were simultaneously suffered in the foreign trade sector.[7]
       There is widespread agreement on this appraisal in the Hun-
garian literature. No others need to be cited here knowing the standing
and the reputation of Bognar in Hungary and in the rest of the world.

SOME OUTSTANDING FEATURES OF THE REFORM

       With this background of events leading up to the drafting and the
adoption of the reform of 1968, it is not surprising that the principal
thrust of the measures was aimed at the price structure, the pricing
rules, and the weak market mechanism of the Hungarian economy.[8]

The reform, "in one sudden move," introduced several new characteristics into the macro- and micromanagement of the economy. It provided for new dependency relationships between the central planning office and the ministries on the one hand, and the enterprises, incentives, wages, prices, and credit, on the other hand. As told by J. Kornai:

> The reform was planned and prepared—under a mandate
> from the party and the cabinet—by theoretical and
> applied economists. Their recommendations were
> summed up in a document of several hundred pages,
> and were submitted to discussion in the party and
> the cabinet. Subsequently, it was "translated" into
> the language of state regulations and the laws. Finally,
> all regulations took force simultaneously. We are
> faced here with a new and very significant phenomenon.
> Planning has always been practiced in Hungary: plans
> have been used in setting the real activity of economy
> . . . and the related financial norms. The preparation
> of this reform involved "planning" in quite a different
> context: we have here planned a whole system.[9]

This appraisal of the origins was made a little over two years after the commencement of the NEM, at a time when preliminary estimates kept on turning up somewhat conflicting evidence on the probable success of the reforms. It was really not essential to receive empirical confirmation of unqualified success, the more so since that was not expected anyway. What mattered was that a new and definitive step was taken toward more economic rationality in planning.

Was the NEM a step toward more rationality? There should be no doubt about it. In its wording, as well as intent, the reform not only modified existing arrangements but provided for a new set of rules having a tendency to promote quicker and more accurate adjustment to change. Writing in early 1968 B. Csikos-Nagy characterized the reform as one that would bring the economy "closer to a system in which prices will be formed under the market mechanism,"[10] replacing an arrangement in which it was impossible to make the required adjustments with sufficient accuracy in regard to timing and detail.[11] Finally, he emphasized throughout the role of a more rational system of prices in the economy, replacing a public administration in which "the information system is tendentious and [the] methods bureaucratic."[12]

In the new price system four types of prices were created: (1) prices fixed by authorities; (2) prices fixed and "maximized" [the meaning of "maximized prices" is not too clear; in any case they seem to be a variant of fixed prices with a prescribed direction of permissible movement and one prescribed limit]; (3) prices with limited flexibility; and finally (4) prices with full flexibility.

According to Csikos-Nagy prices with full flexibility (that is free of direct, official controls) characterize 28 percent of output in the basic industries (energy, mining, textile fiber), 78 percent in the processing industries (chemicals, machinery, textiles and apparel, paper and wood products), 12 percent in agriculture, and 23 percent in the service industries.[13] It has been estimated that about half of all prices under the NEM fell into category 4 in 1971.[14]

What were the implications for foreign trade? Bognar has already been cited earlier as having expressed concern with the economy's lack of response to changes in the rest of the world. This was a very widespread view at the time of the reform that resulted in the creation of a set of rules and principles governing the relationship between domestic and foreign prices. (1) The autarkic character of home prices must gradually be eliminated, (2) changes in foreign prices must be allowed to reflect themselves in domestic costs and prices, (3) these changes must be filtered through the given system of financial instruments (exchange rates, tariffs, turnover tax on imports, rebates and subsidies), (4) domestic buyers (enterprises and cooperatives) should be granted the choice between domestic and foreign sources of supply. The increased competition between the domestic production of import substitutes and imports must be permitted to exert its influence on domestic costs of production and relative prices, (5) under the reform, "foreign prices" were defined as prices prevailing in capitalist markets, and not the Bloc prices, because even though Bloc prices reflect capitalist prices, they do so with a lag.[15]

It was recognized from the beginning that it might not be possible to achieve a uniform and simultaneous adjustment in domestic costs and prices according to the above principles and rules because of the differences in the reaction and lag patterns of the effected industries and enterprises.

In summary, it is safe to conclude that the reforms did represent a de jure move toward greater economic rationality in planning.

IS THE NEM A SUCCESS?

Since the potential effects of the reform are widespread and long lasting, any appraisal of its success or failure must be tentative and incomplete. Furthermore, published data, while presumably reliable (or certainly no less so than some published in the West), are not available in an integrated and comprehensive form beyond 1972. As a result of this unusually long lag, an "appraisal lag" also develops, putting impediments in the way of whatever conclusion may otherwise be drawn from the evidence available. Finally, perhaps more elaborate statistical procedures should have been used in the processing of the data, but that would have deprived the critics of their role, frequently a useful one.

With these caveats out of the way, the question may now be raised again: How well did the NEM work in the foreign trade sector, that is, in terms of the criteria set out earlier, has there been a de facto increase in economic rationality in planning?

The average annual rate of growth in national income increased, although only slightly, (Figure 6.1) during the period of the NEM, as compared to the years 1961-67, a comforting development to growth-oriented planners who have always been concerned with the relatively low Hungarian growth rate as compared to other Bloc economies. The slight increase from 5.7 percent in the pre-NEM period to 6 percent for the first five years of the NEM does not seem significant, and any attribution is rather hard to make, certainly within the confines of this study.

By contrast, developments in the foreign trade sector are a great deal more forceful. The jump in the growth rate of trade with the West from the annual average of 11 percent in the pre-NEM period to nearly 17 percent in the NEM period can hardly be attributed to chance. Certainly the increased rate of trade participation (trade as a percentage of national income, the first of Bergson's indicators) implied by these growth rates must be accepted as contraautarkic, hence as evidence of increasing economic rationality in planning. While the growth of the Bloc trade is below the growth of trade with the West, the sudden change in the period averages is similarly pronounced.

Changes in the direction of trade (the third of Bergson's indicators) are strongly implied by these growth rates and are readily reflected in the relative shift of trade from the Bloc to the West. The annual average level of pre-NEM (1961-67) imports from the West rose from 34.3 percent to 36.5 percent in the postreform period (1968-72), while the share of exports to the West increased from 33.6 percent to 35.4 percent. These are additional developments reinforcing previous indications of increasing rationality in planning (Table 6.1). The shares of the regions have, however, been affected by more rapid increases in prices in trade with non-CMEA countries than in the Bloc trade (see Table 6.2).

There is an observable shift in the commodity composition of trade, (the second of Bergson's indicators) corresponding to the NEM

FIGURE 6.1

Hungary: The Growth of Exports and National Income, 1961–72
(1961 = 100)

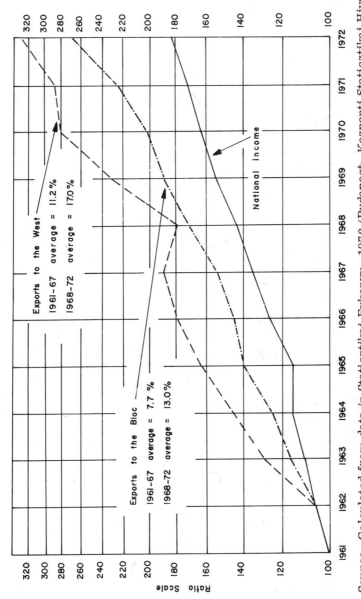

Source: Calculated from data in Statisztikai Evkonyv, 1972 (Budapest: Kozponti Statisztikai Hivatal), pp. 69, 308–09.

TABLE 6.1

Hungary: The Direction of Trade by Major Regions,
1961-72
(percentages)

	Export		Import	
Year	CMEA	Other Countries	CMEA	Other Countries
1961	69.0	31.0	66.7	33.3
1962	69.2	30.8	69.3	30.7
1963	65.9	34.1	67.5	32.5
1964	66.0	34.0	64.8	35.2
1965	65.6	34.4	65.0	35.0
1966	64.3	35.7	62.6	37.4
1967	64.9	35.1	64.1	35.9
1968	68.1	31.9	66.4	33.6
1969	64.2	35.8	64.6	35.4
1970	61.4	38.6	61.7	38.3
1971	64.0	36.0	62.2	37.8
1972	65.3	34.7	62.6	37.4

Source: Statisztikai Evkonyv, 1972 (Budapest: Kozponti
Statisztikai Hivatal), pp. 308-09.

and pre-NEM periods (Tables 6.3 and 6.4). The reasons for these
changes are not entirely clear, however, and interpretations differ.
Some contend that the rapid growth of imports in the NEM period is·
an unwanted obligation inherited from the Third Five-Year Plan,
which abounded in investment projects favoring the development of
import substitutes.[16] These projects did not develop as planned,
therefore, the output of import substitutes fell short of the targets.
The fact that all Bloc countries are committed to intensive growth
programs added to these problems, since these growth programs
have generated a high demand for investment goods without the capacity
to satisfy this demand. As a consequence, sudden and simultaneous
Blocwide shortages in machinery, supplies, semifinished goods, and
raw materials developed, forcing these countries to look to the world
markets for these commodities. Lastly, shifts in the consumption/
investment ratio, in favor of consumption, added to the demand for
more imports (Figure 6.2), since domestic capacity to meet the increased demand for consumer goods was lagging, given the structure
of relative prices. At the same time exports failed to increase as
fast as favorable cyclical developments in the West would have permitted them to do, because of the unusually slow growth of export

TABLE 6.2

Hungary: Export and Import Price Indexes, and the Terms of Trade, 1966-72

(1965 = 100)

	1966	1967	1968	1969	1970	1971	1972
Import price indexes							
Bloc trade	96.0	93.7	93.7	94.1	95.0	96.4	97.1
Others (mostly the West)	101.1	95.9	94.3	97.2	102.7	104.8	105.4
Total	97.5	94.3	93.8	94.8	97.1	98.7	99.3
Export price indexes							
Bloc trade	97.0	94.6	95.0	95.4	96.1	95.9	96.5
Others (mostly the West)	97.3	95.6	92.9	99.6	108.8	110.3	113.8
Total.	97.0	94.9	94.4	96.5	99.6	99.9	101.2
The Term of trade							
Bloc trade	101.0	101.0	101.4	101.4	101.2	99.5	99.3
Others	96.2	99.7	98.5	102.5	105.9	105.2	107.9
Total	99.5	100.6	100.6	101.8	102.6	101.2	101.8

Source: Statisztikai Evkonyv, vol. 1971, p. 322; vol. 1972, p. 344 (Budapest: Kozponti Statisztikai Hivatal).

TABLE 6.3

Hungary: The Commodity Composition of Exports, 1960–72

(percentages)

Commodity Groups	1960	1965	1966	1967	1968	1969	1970	1971	1972
					To the Bloc				
Fuels, electricity	1	1	1	1	1	1	1	1	1
Raw materials, semifinished goods, parts	22	25	25	24	22	23	24	23	23
Machinery, transport equipment, investment goods	44	36	34	34	36	34	35	33	35
Consumer goods (except food)	18	22	24	25	25	25	23	25	24
Raw materials of food processing industries, livestock, food	15	16	16	16	16	17	17	18	17
	100	100	100	100	100	100	100	100	100
					To Others				
Fuels, electricity	2	2	2	3	3	2	2	1	2
Raw materials, semifinished goods, parts	30	33	34	33	35	38	42	37	34
Machinery, transport equipment, investment goods	8	6	6	5	5	6	7	8	8
Consumer goods (except food)	20	20	20	21	23	18	16	18	18
Raw materials of food processing industries, livestock, food	40	39	38	38	34	36	33	36	37

Source: Statisztikai Evkonyv, vol. 1971, p. 291; vol. 1972, pp. 312–13 (Budapest: Kozponti Statisztikai Hivatal).

TABLE 6.4

Hungary: The Commodity Composition of Imports, 1960–72

(Percentages)

Commodity Group	1960	1965	1966	1967	1968	1969	1970	1971	1972
					From the Bloc				
Fuels, electricity	12	14	14	11	11	12	12	10	11
Raw materials, semifinished goods, parts	46	48	49	46	49	48	45	43	47
Machinery, transport equipment, investment goods	26	25	24	27	23	23	27	30	27
Consumer goods (except food)	7	7	8	9	10	9	12	10	10
Raw materials of food processing industries, livestock, food	9	6	5	7	7	8	5	7	5
Total	100	100	100	100	100	100	100	100	100
					From Others				
Fuel, electricity	0	0	1	0	0	0	1	1	2
Raw materials, semifinished goods, parts	74	61	60	59	65	64	60	57	55
Machinery, transport equipment, investment goods	11	12	13	16	12	13	12	16	18
Consumer goods (except food)	3	3	3	5	4	5	6	6	5
Raw materials of food processing industries, livestock, food	12	25	23	20	19	18	21	20	20
Total	100	100	100	100	100	100	100	100	100

Source: Statisztika: Evkonyv, vol. 1971, p. 291; vol. 1972, pp. 312–13 (Budapest: Kozponti Statisztikai Hivatal).

FIGURE 6.2

Hungary: The Growth of Imports and National Income, 1961–72
(1961 = 100)

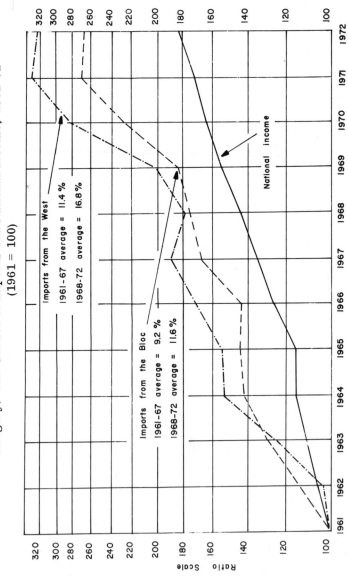

Source: Calculated from data in Statisztikai Evkonyv, 1972 (Budapest: Kozponti Statisztikai Hivatal).

144

capacities. For these reasons it is difficult to associate the observable structural changes with more rational planning.

As in the Western economies, quotas, tariffs, and other regulations of imports and exports continue to prevail, but at least prices since the 1968 reforms are free to respond to the influence of these restrictions in an enlarged domain of goods and services. The question of the economic consequences of continuing inconvertibility of Bloc currencies keeps on receiving closer attention in continuing debates about the further modification of economic controls. Also, since convertibility and the choice of the appropriate exchange rate mechanism are closely related, proposals are being advanced about some techniques that would permit a simulation of the exchange rate movements in freely floating rate systems, which obviously cannot occur under conditions of inconvertibility.

Taken together, the foregoing would seem to indicate that changes in the foreign trade sector and the foreign trade policy after the 1968 reform represent an improvement over the earlier, highly centralized and bureaucratized mode of macroeconomic management. The NEM is perhaps not an unqualified success; much remains in the system from the old regime that retards the pace of adjustment to new ways, but the capacity for greater flexibility is present now, and is likely to increase in the future.

NOTES

1. A. Bergson, "On Prospects for Communist Foreign Trade" in International Trade and Central Planning, ed. A.A. Brown and E. Neuberger (Berkeley: University of California Press, 1968), p. 384.

2. Ibid.

3. Ibid., pp. 384-88.

4. Ibid., p. 398.

5. Ibid., p. 387.

6. J. Bognar, "A magyar mechanizmusreform ket eve" (Two Years of the Hungarian Mechanism Reform), Kozgazdosagi Szemle 17, no. 1 (January 1970): 1.

7. Ibid., pp. 1-2.

8. J. Kornai, "Gozdasagi rendszerelmelet es altalanos egyensulyelmelet" (The Theory of Economic Systems and the General Equilibrium Theory), Kozgazdasagi Szemle 17, no. 9 (September 1970): 1057.

9. Ibid.

10. B. Csikos-Nagy, "Azuj magyar arrendszer", (The New Hungarian Price System), Kozgazdasagi Szemle 15, no. 3 (March 1968): 275.

11. Ibid.

12. Ibid., emphasis in the original.

13. Ibid., pp. 276-77.

14. J. Deak, "A kulkereskedelmi forgalom es a kozgazdasagi szabalyozok" (Foreign Trade and the Economic Regulations), Kozgazdasagi Szemle 18, no. 11 (November 1971): 1371.

15. I. Vincze, "A nemzetkozi es belfoldi arak kozotti kapcsolat kozgazdasagiszabalyozasi problemai" (The Economic-Regulatory Problems of the Interactions Between Foreign and Domestic Prices), Kozgazdasagi Szemle 18, no. 10 (October 1971): 1141.

16. Deak, op. cit., p. 1364.

COMMENTS ON SLOWDOWN IN THE
SOVIET POSTWAR INDUSTRIAL GROWTH
AND INDUSTRY ADJUSTMENTS TO
INVESTMENT PRIORITIES

Stanley H. Cohn

Stanislaw Gomulka has sought a new explanation of the deceleration in Soviet industrial growth in the postwar period by reexamining
and extracting the best features of earlier analysis offered by two
schools of scholars. To these he adds an innovative explanation of
his own. In essence he searches for a synthesis between the con-
tending theses of relatively constant capital-labor factor input shares
and declining residual joint factor productivity (technical progress)
and relatively constant residual factor productivity accompanied by
a sharp decline in the share of capital. The first approach uses the
traditional Cobb-Douglass production function, while the latter relies
on the standard CES form.

Gomulka's basic conclusion is that the first school is correct
in asserting that the share of capital has been relatively constant
(unit elasticity of substitution), but that the second approach is correct in its contention that there has been a nearly level secular trend
in technical progress (joint residual factor productivity). He arrives
at this optimistic (from the Soviet standpoint) conclusion by both
adjustment of underlying data and selection of a modified form of the
production function. Instead of the usual base year of 1950 that has
been used by most researchers, he extends his time series back
selectively to 1940, 1947, and 1928. He introduces a basic modification in labor input estimates by using a man-year instead of a
numbers-employed concept. These two data modifications comprise
the data essence of his reinterpretation. He has also decomposed his
CES production function in order to separate the impact of technical
progress between labor and capital. With fuller explanation this
innovation could be promising.

Instead of a falling trend of residual joint factor productivity,
Gomulka emphasizes that the trend has been flat with an immediate
postwar period far below the secular trend and the period 1955-61
considerably above the secular slope. Rather than attempt to measure
joint factor productivity, he uses the proxy of man-hour labor productivity. Central productivity is assumed to grow at a constant rate.

Those of us who have labored for many years in the Soviet
economic statistical jungle have been obliged to consume a considerable

part of our energies in recalculation of aggregate official industrial production and national product indexes in accordance with methodologies used in most market economies. In addition, it has been necessary to eliminate the inflationary impact of new product pricing on the industrial production indexes. By his uncritical acceptance of the official Soviet industrial gross industrial output index, Gomulka has built into his analysis overstatement of Soviet output accomplishments and, even more sensitively, exaggeration of productivity trends. Since, even by official admission, the degree of overstatement was greatest when 1926-27 base years weights were still in use, prior to 1951, the distortion has been modified over the years of his investigation. The effect of disregarding this declining degree of output and productivity overstatement has been to impart a spurious constancy to the capital-output ratio and too high a level and flat a trend to factor (labor) productivity.

Gomulka also overstates the technical progress trend by his selection of a base year. The choice of 1950 by most empirical researchers is partially determined by the improved availability of Soviet statistics after that date, but more importantly by the generally accepted premise that the period of the Fourth Five-Year Plan (1946-50) was preoccupied with recovery and reconstruction. Renewed expansion of the economy beyond levels obtained at the onset of the Nazi invasion did not commence until around 1950. Furthermore, any attempt to measure technical progress that incorporated the years prior to 1950 would have to recognize that there was extensive underutilization of capital until the reconstruction process was completed. Therefore, the extremely rapid increases in labor productivity that Gomulka records for this period reflects a mixture of recovery and true net growth and, thereby, should not be included in any attempt to measure long-run productivity trends. Of course, if Gomulka's base were shifted to 1950 a significantly different secular trend would emerge. His introduction of cyclical disturbances in longer-run trends represents a useful innovation to previous analyses, but they should be independent of such severely distorting exogenous circumstances as devastating wartime destruction and recovery.[1]

Gomulka introduces the effect of reductions in the length of the workweek into his measurement of labor input. Although other analysts have attempted to incorporate a man-hour instead of an employment numbers concept of labor input, Gomulka has accomplished this innovation in thoroughgoing fashion. However, he has not carried this essential modification far enough. The length of a man-year is the function of two variables—the average length of the workweek and average length of vacation time and the number of work holidays. Gomulka has adjusted for the former, but not the latter, variables. If the latter variables were introduced, he would discover that the average number of annual man-hours worked in Soviet industry continued to decline after 1961, even though the workweek was unchanged.[2] Inclusion of these factors would considerably dampen the productivity bulge on his long-run productivity trend. It would also contribute to a more rapidly rising capital/labor ratio.

Gomulka skillfully disposes of the effects of changes in industrial structure and of the age composition of capital stock as being minor influences on technical progress. Marginal changes in both phenomena are so gradual as to preclude important effects. He also mentions and minimizes the diffusion effect of changes in the rate of importation and assimilation of foreign technology. As a by-product, he demonstrates that the age of the capital stock was approaching an asymptotic minimum by the early 1960s.

The modified CES production function that Gomulka introduces appears to be technically superior to the one pioneered by Weitzman in having a smaller error sum. He also asserts that the important coefficients are statistically significant, but does not provide the pertinent statistical terms, such as "t" statistics or Durbin-Watson estimates. As for economic analytical content, he introduces the intriguing decomposition of technical progress into specific effects on capital and labor without indicating the derivation of these crucial estimates or their economic significance. In particular, it would be useful if he compared this division of technical progress with the more conventional one of embodied and disembodied advance. His innovation is an intriguing one.

His final production function, which decomposes the long-run production function so as to reflect the two major periods of productivity disturbance, should be more deliberately interpreted if the nontechnical reader is to comprehend its significance. This observation is equally applicable with respect to identification of the relevant coefficients and estimation of their statistical significance.

Gomulka's conclusions are unusually sanguine. Technological change has been Harrod-neutral (constant capital/output ratio), the capital factor input share has been nearly constant, the elasticity of substitution has been close to unity, and residual factor productivity has been approaching a respectable growth asymptote of 4.2 percent per annum. Given recent increases in manpower and capital stock inputs, such a productivity prospect would imply an annual industrial output growth rate of 7.3 percent. This favorable prognosis belies recent deteriorating growth performance[3] and the desperate fixation of the leadership and planners on technical progress as the latest panacea for rising dissatisfaction with the course of industrial development. Certainly the behavior of the Soviet leadership does not suggest the inevitability of a high acceptable rate of industrial productivity advance. On the contrary, the Ninth Five-Year Plan assumes an accelerated rate of technological progress in the face of a rising capital/labor ratio. Historical evidence, contrary to Gomulka's findings, is not at all hopeful on this score.

Gomulka, by combining the skills of an accomplished econometrician with those of a native student of a Soviet-type of economic organization, has provided deeper analytical understanding of the nature of Soviet industrial progress. In particular, his decomposition of a long time period into distinct shorter periods that reflect fundamental factor input availability and productivity changes and his innovative respecification of the CES production function into separate capital and labor technical augmentation terms represent worthwhile analytical advances. However, the effects of these analytical improvements have been vitiated by data overstatements and inconsistencies and inappropriate choices of a base period. These shortcomings in data specifications, if appropriately corrected, should considerably modify his basic conclusions, which appear to be at sharp variance with recent events and official policies. His exposition would be considerably strengthened also by more deliberate economic explanation of his empirical tests.

INDUSTRY ADJUSTMENTS TO INVESTMENT PRIORITIES

The present study represents a further extension of Judith Thornton's innovative studies in the field of Soviet industrial development. Her unique contribution has been in the decentralized analysis of the rationality of such developmental policies. She has succeeded in deflating the theory that Soviet industrial priorities have been rational in the sense of seeking equal return on capital investment. Such an assumption has formed the basis for calculation of value-added weights in the efforts of myself and others to construct industrial output and national product indexes. We have yet to incorporate her findings on differential industrial sector capital returns into our value-added weights to ascertain the effects on our aggregative indicators of Soviet economic performance.

Her newest study extends her previous analysis a step further and, necessarily more speculatively, tries to determine if and how priority industrial sectors manage to compensate for their inferior access to investment resources. Her central proposition is that low-priority sectors may offset their capital access disadvantages by obtaining such resources surreptitiously through ostensible raw materials purchases or, more overtly, by purchasing a larger portion of their material inputs from other sectors in lieu of producing them within their own sector. Her empirical tests correlate degrees of horizontal and vertical integration with such key indicators of priority status as growth, capitalization, and returns on investment. In the process of empirical testing she makes imaginative use of reconstructed Soviet input-output matrixes.

However, her empirical efforts are fraught with the introduction of heroic assumptions in the form of statistical proxies and, to some extent, data misspecifications, which largely stem from the limitations of available official data. Since she has openly expressed doubt as to the validity of many of her key assumptions and data series, my comments are intended to help resolve some of the questions she poses with the ultimate aim of strengthening demonstration of the interesting hypotheses she has so imaginatively voiced.

She hypothesizes that low-priority sectors purchase capital goods on material account from investment supplying sectors. The definition of investment supplying sectors—ratio of sales to nonconsumption final demand as a share of total sales—is oversimplified. Many capital goods sectors produce intermediate products. A typical example would be the production of electric motors, which are mainly purchased by machinery sectors rather than by final consumers. On the other hand, the final demand sales of a nonconsumption nature of some sectors may not be to investment, but to defense or for export. In addition, her comparison of the ratios as between the Soviet and U.S. input-output tables must be adjusted for the different degrees of "grossness" (fineness of industrial classification) in the two countries' tables.

The ideal table for her purpose would be one of capital flows, which shows the distribution of capital goods by both producing and consuming industries. Such a table was published by the Bureau of Labor Statistics for the U.S. economy in 1958.[4] Perhaps the 1966 official Soviet matrix of fixed capital assets, published in the 1968 economic handbook, might provide a point of departure. In Table 2.2 the high correlation between purchases from investment-supplying sectors and capitalization would be expected for the simple reason that such supplying sectors are the source of capital inputs.

In the test for the determinants of vertical integration, a propensity exhibited by high-priority sectors, the independent variable or "nearness of production to final use" (ratio of final demand sales to total sales) is not a valid indicator of degree of vertical integration as it is biased against those sectors that primarily supply raw materials. Their sales are largely intermediate in nature.

As in the horizontal integration test, the one for vertical integration may also be influenced by the industrial classification employed. Perhaps this limitation might be surmounted by defining vertical integration in Equation 5 as the ratio of value added plus intrasectoral purchases (values along mina diagonal) to total sales. Size as an independent variable should not be excluded since those sectors with a greater volume of output, presumably those that have been more favored, will also be more likely to be supplied from sources internal to those sectors.

Let me say a word about purely technical features of the empirical tests. The definitions of equations have not been specified clearly. Although what appear to be statistical levels of significance have been attached to the computed coefficients, no comment has appeared with regard to their values. The reader cannot readily appraise the significance of the tests.

The study concludes with some interesting speculative observations. Thornton notes the low and negative intercorrelations between capital intensity and both growth and capital returns. Since capital intensity is determined as much or more by technological than economic factors, such a relationship is not too surprising. As for the low correlation between capital returns and growth, it only serves to further substantiate earlier findings of the author.

The chapter concludes by posing to the reader suggestions for improved indicators of priority status. In addition to growth and capitalization, I would suggest manpower allocation, particularly in the skilled categories. Statistics on matriculations of engineers, scientists, and technicians by specialty may be of some value in this respect.

Lastly, it might be worthwhile to look beyond industrial sectors to the priorities structure for the entire economy. In the directives for the Ninth Five-Year Plan, the bulk of increments of employment have been reserved for the service sectors, while industrial sectors claim larger shares of investment resources than was the case in the two preceding plans.

While many admitted gaps still remain in her analysis, the Thornton study makes an imaginative incursion into a new area of understanding and should stimulate further investigation along a promising research path.

NOTES

1. Even the decision to reduce working hours after 1955 may be regarded by some analysts as an exogenous decision not motivated by mainly economic considerations. If so, the hours reduction should be excluded as an explicit economic variable and treated as a dummy variable.

2. The average number of days worked per wage worker in industry decline from 266.4 in 1965 to 232.6 in 1969 although rising again to 235.1 in 1971, according to the official Soviet economic handbook.

3. According to estimates of U.S. experts, the industrial growth rate has averaged only 6.3 percent since 1970.

4. U.S. Bureau of Labor Statistics, Capital Flow Matrix, 1958 (Bulletin 1601), 1968.

CHAPTER

7

SOVIET AGRICULTURE: TEN YEARS UNDER NEW MANAGEMENT
Keith Bush

Employing one-third of the work force, absorbing one-quarter of total investment, and generating one-fifth of the GNP, the agricultural sector still plays a decisive role in the Soviet economy. To facilitate an appraisal of the performance of Soviet agriculture since the retirement of Khrushchev, this chapter assembles materials from a variety of sources—primarily Soviet—on inputs supplied, on policy and organization, and on output levels attained. Official Soviet data are utilized, despite their known shortcomings.

The overall picture that emerges is one of a rather consistent policy consistently implemented. For political, strategic, and economic reasons, the present Soviet leadership is emulating its predecessors in striving for autarky in staple foodstuffs and in agricultural raw materials. Unlike its predecessors, it has tacitly acknowledged that the world's second economic power cannot indefinitely progress on the foundation of a cowed and sullen peasantry, nor can its modern industrial work force be nourished largely on carbohydrates. It has therefore sought to correct a third of the century's exploitation and neglect of the farm sector with a massive transfer of resources from the rest of the economy. Thus an intensified program of mechanization, chemicalization, land improvement, price support, material incentives, and industrialization of agriculture was launched at the March 1965 plenum and has been carried out with relatively little slippage. This priority accorded to inputs and a new sobriety in setting output targets has wrought a most creditable transformation: Whereas previously the agricultural sector met hardly any of its targets hardly any of the time, it now meets most of its targets most of the time. That the increases in output so far achieved and to be expected during the rest of the 1970s are incommensurately modest when set against the very substantial increases in inputs is due not only to an unfavorable natural

157

endowment but also in large part to a continuing penchant for the overcentralization of decision-making and for gigantic production units, to an ideological bias against the farmer, and to the inability to attract and retain the younger, skilled, and flexible cadres needed to man a modern industrialized agriculture.

AGRICULTURAL INPUTS AND OUTPUT, 1961-75

The major inputs into agriculture under the present administration are contrasted in Table 7.1 with the levels attained in the period 1961-65 (Khrushchev was removed from office in October 1964).

None of the principal material input targets during the Eighth Five-Year Plan period (1966-70) were met in full: Indeed, the shortfalls were large, for example, roughly 15 percent in productive investment, an average of 20 percent in the deliveries of agricultural machinery and fertilizer, and around 40 percent in new irrigation and drainage.[1] Some of the slippage resulted from a conscious decision by the Soviet leadership to switch funds from agriculture to other sectors and notably to defense,[2] while the inability to absorb funds allocated, delay in project completions, and the lack of trained cadres also played a role. Nevertheless, as Table 7.1 shows, very substantial gains were recorded, with new irrigation and drainage increased by a factor of three and supplies of fertilizer doubled.

The current (Ninth) Five-Year Plan period (1971-75) constitutes a landmark for Soviet agriculture in that the plan targets for the main material inputs will probably be met in full, with the notable exception of the very expensive program of land improvement. Mirabile dictu, as at mid-1974, some of the original Ninth Five-Year Plan targets for these indicators were reportedly being overfulfilled.[3]

The agricultural work force, as measured by average annual employment in the public sector, continues to decline gradually, primarily through wastage, although it still represents nearly 33 percent of the total Soviet work force against some 4 percent in the United States. The cultivated area also declined slightly in 1966-70, with the gains in reclaimed land being more than offset by losses due to abandoned marginal land, erosion, urban sprawl, and industrial development. But this trend was reversed after the shock of 1972 and the area under cultivation at mid-1974 was reported at 216 million hectares.[4]

Two further features of Table 7.1 appear to be worthy of comment. The first is that the quantitative 1971-75 targets for the deliveries of tractors and grain combines are actually smaller than those set for 1966-70, while the truck delivery plan is identical; yet

TABLE 7.1

Soviet Agricultural Input, 1961–65, 1966–70, and
1971–75 (Plan)

Indicator	Units	1961–65	1966–70	Percent Growth	1971–75 (Plan)	Percent Growth
Investment in agriculture						
Total productive	billion rubles[a]	38.0	59.9	58	95.2[b]	59
State	billion rubles[a]	21.4	36.3	70	63.9[b]	76
Kolkhoz	billion rubles[a]	16.6	23.6	42	31.4[b]	33
Manpower[c]						
Work force[d]	millions	28.7	27.4	- 5	26.4	- 4
Labor productivity	percent growth	18	37	—	38	—
Land						
Cultivated area	million hectares	212.2[e]	207.2[e]	- 2	211.0[f]	2
New irrigation	million hectares	0.5	1.4	280	3.2	129
New drainage	million hectares	1.2	3.8	321	5.0	32
Deliveries to agriculture						
Tractors	thousands	1,093	1,467	34	1,700	16
Trucks	thousands	418	717	72	1,100	53
Grain combines	thousands	385	469	22	543	16
Agricultural machinery	billion rubles[g]	6.6	9.1	38	15.5	70
Mineral fertilizers	million tons	90.8	184.9	104	303.0	64

[a]Constant prices of 1969.

[b]Derived from percent increases in Ninth Five-Year Plan: Gosplan and TsSU classifications cannot be wholly reconciled.

[c]In the public sector.

[d]At midpoint of five-year period.

[e]Five-year average.

[f]1971–73 average.

[g]Constant prices of 1955.

Sources: Drawn or derived from Narkhoz 65 through Narkhoz 72, Sel'skoe khozyaistvo SSSR (1971), and Gosudarstvenny pyatiletni plan razvitiya narodnogo khozyaistva SSSR na 1971-1975 gody (hereafter cited as Ninth Five-Year Plan), all passim.

total investment is set to rise by 59 percent. The explanation lies partly in the heavy weighting of the land improvement program, scheduled to account for over one-quarter of agricultural investment.[5] Moreover, outlays on equipment for use in animal husbandry and feed processing were scheduled to more than double from less than 3 billion rubles in 1966-70 to 6 billion rubles in 1971-75.[6] Finally, the prices of farm machinery and equipment have risen sharply— faster than their productivity[7]—while construction costs have also grown rapidly.[8] The second noteworthy feature is that none of the material inputs listed have been or will be supplied directly to the private sector.

In Tables 7.1 and 7.2 and throughout the rest of this chapter, official Soviet data are cited without further qualification. It is appreciated that these are not always comparable with Western statistics and this is especially true of output data. For example, the gross grain harvest totals in bunker weight terms contain a great deal of excess moisture and admixtures and they exclude postharvest losses: Discounts of 15-20 percent are often applied to bring them into line with Western dry, usable grain equivalents. Occasionally the required discount may be even higher. We have it on the authority of no less than Secretary-General Brezhnev that the postharvest losses in 1973 were so great that "nobody—neither the planning nor the other organs— could estimate the sum total of the losses."[9] In view of the unusually high moisture content of the harvested grain that year,[10] we feel that the dry, usable grain equivalent of the declared 222.5 million-ton bumper crop was probably closer to 170 million tons. And when reporting Soviet meat output data, the Food and Agriculture Organization (FAO) sees fit to apply a 20 percent discount in order to equate these with Western measures.[11]

The relative sobriety of the present administration's output targets contrasts starkly with Khrushchev's brand of "hurrah planning." Unwisely basing his projections on the bumper year of 1958, the latter had called for a 70 percent increase in the gross agricultural product during the Seven-Year Plan period of 1959-65; in the event, a 15 percent raise was reportedly achieved. With the poor harvest of 1963 and the concomitant mass slaughter of livestock in mind, Brezhnev aimed at a 25 percent increase in 1966-70 and attained a 21 percent growth.

It has now been acknowledged that a sustained average annual growth rate of about 4 percent is about as much as may be anticipated from a major, mixed agricultural sector, and thus future five-year growth targets for the gross agricultural product are unlikely to be set at much over the 20-22 percent level reached in 1966-70 and scheduled for 1971-75. However, the gross indicator does not give us the whole picture. With the gradual relative decline of the rural

TABLE 7.2

Soviet Agricultural Output, 1961-65, 1966-70, and 1971-75 (Plan)
(average annual totals)

Indicator	Units	1961-65	1966-70	Percent Growth	1971-75 (Plan)	Percent Growth
Value aggregates						
Gross agricultural product	billion rubles[a]	66.3	80.5	21	98.0	22
Public sector	billion rubles[a]	—	57.1	—	74.1	30
Private sector	billion rubles[a]	—	23.4	—	23.9	2
Net agricultural product	billion rubles[b]	57.1	69.3	21	—	—
Crops						
Grain	million tons	103.3	167.6	29	195.0	16
Cotton	million tons	5.0	6.1	22	6.8	11
Sugar beet	million tons	59.2	81.1	37	87.5	8
Sunflower	million tons	5.1	6.4	25	6.7	5
Potatoes	million tons	81.6	94.8	16	106.0	12
Vegetables and melons	million tons	16.9	19.5	15	24.7	27
Animal products						
Meat	million tons	9.3	11.6	25	14.3	24
Milk	million tons	64.7	80.6	25	92.3	15
Eggs	billions	28.7	35.8	25	46.7	30
Wool	thousand tons	362	398	10	464	17

[a]Constant prices of 1965.
[b]Constant prices of 1968.

Sources: Drawn or derived from Narkhoz 65 through Narkhoz 72, passim; Ninth Five-Year Plan, passim; net agricultural product estimates from Soviet Economic Prospects for the Seventies, U.S. Congress, Joint Economic Committee, 93d Cong., 1st Sess. (Washington, D.C.: U.S. Government Printing Office, 1973), p. 371.

population, the expansion of the state sector and with the introduction of specialized livestock, dairy, and vegetable farms, the marketed output has grown appreciably faster than the gross. During the 1960s for instance, gross agricultural output rose by 38 percent, while marketed output grew by 64 percent.[12] Against these gains must be set the increase in the number of mouths to be fed: Since the 1959 census, the total population has grown by 20 percent and the urban population by 50 percent.[13]

Despite the vicious setback inflicted by the combination of winterkill and drought in 1972, it is thought that the output levels attained in the period 1971-75 will come credibly close to meeting the targets. Nevertheless, a comparison of Tables 7.1 and 7.2 illustrates the great discrepancy between the growth of inputs into, and the increase of output from, the agricultural sector. The ten years that have elapsed since the March 1965 plenum have witnessed a doubling of inputs but a growth of some 50 percent in gross output. And, as has been noted, none of the material inputs listed have been supplied directly to the private sector, yet it continues to provide about one-quarter of the gross agricultural output and an even higher share of the fresh, high-quality items in the Soviet diet.

CAPITAL INVESTMENT

The allocation of resources, as exemplified by past and projected capital investment, reveals the Soviet leadership's true economic priorities far more cogently than volumes of agitprop. It is to be regretted, therefore, that official pronouncements on projected agricultural investment under the present administration have tended to be studiedly vague and sometimes contradictory.

Although published Soviet investment statistics are probably more comprehensive and more timely than in any other major economy, their use presents problems. For instance, the classifications and the absolute figures cited by the Soviet Gosplan cannot be wholly reconciled with TsSU (Tsentral'noe statisticheskoe Upravlenie—the Central Statistical Administration) data. The conversion ratios to be applied when relating past investment expressed in constant prices of 1955 to current and projected investment in constant prices of 1969 vary widely not only between sectors but also between sources.[14] Authoritative and roughly comparable figures generally appear too late and shed light upon current investment decisions, while these latter are often formulated to make the maximum political impact, and so on. These examples are listed not in sorrow but are cited merely to caution the user of Soviet investment statistics. With the above

reservations, certain tentative conclusions about agricultural investment since Khrushchev will probably be accepted by most observers.

Table 7.1 shows productive investment in agriculture rather
than the concept of total agricultural investment commonly cited. The
latter includes housing, hospitals, schools, and the like, and its use
can lead to double-counting in respect to resource allocation. Furthermore, its use could be misleading when assessing the priorities accorded to the various sectors: For example, expenditures upon the
housing of industrial workers and employees do not appear under the
heading of industrial investment. (This is not to deny the crucial
importance of nonproductive agricultural investment: In the absence
of markedly better living standards, the younger trained cadres will
not stay on the land.) In any case, it is clear that both total agricultural investment and productive agricultural investment have grown
faster than all investment throughout the economy under the present
administration. The 58 percent increase recorded for 1966-70 and
the 59 percent raise planned for 1971-75 in productive agricultural
investment are to be compared with increases of 43 and 42 percent,
respectively, for total investment throughout the economy. That the
priority accorded to agricultural inputs has not flagged was evidenced
by the plan for 1973: This provided for less investment for many
sectors than had been stipulated in the Ninth Five-Year Plan, but
left the agricultural allocation untouched.[15] During the Seventh,
Eighth and Ninth Five-Year Plan periods, the share of productive
agricultural investment in total investment has risen steadily from
16.1 to 18.3 to a planned 21.6 percent.[16]

The increase in agricultural investment since Khrushchev has
been attributable almost entirely to the state sector. This reflects
the expansion of the sovkhoz system (state farms), the marked increase in expenditures upon land improvement borne by the state and
the growing investment in specialized livestock facilities.

The need has at last been recognized for the wholesale industrialization of Soviet agriculture and for its fuller integration into the
economy, as in other developed nations. The claim that "the July
1970 plenum will go down in history as the plenum of agricultural
industrialization"[17] may well be merited. To be sure, the shift was
long overdue. Whereas in the United States in the early 1960s, 29.1
percent of the work force in all links of the agricultural complex were
engaged directly in agriculture, 27.6 percent worked in branches that
supplied vehicles, machinery, fertilizers, and services to agriculture
and 43.3 percent were in branches involved with processing, transportation, storage, and trade in agricultural products, the corresponding shares in the Soviet Union were 72.7, 4.5, and 22.8 percent,
respectively. Thus the United States had 6 million working directly
in agriculture and 7 million in branches that served agricultural

production, while the Soviet Union had 30 million in agriculture and little more than 2 million in the corresponding branches of industry.[18]

This structure is gradually changing and it is increasingly affecting the investment picture. Whereas the share of "agriculture and related sectors" reportedly accounted for 26.1 percent of all investment in 1961-65 and 29.7 percent in 1966-70, the share allocated for 1971-75 has been set variously at between 31 and 35 percent.[19] (The most recent, authoritative pronouncement was that "during the Ninth Five-Year Plan, 157.9 billion rubles are to be invested in the development of agriculture and branches related to it."[20] This would represent some 31.5 percent of total planned investment.) Whatever the outturn, such magnitudes will surely justify the assertion that "the proportions of the national income have altered in favor of agriculture."[21] Yet here again some qualification is in order. The declared shares of total investment going to the agricultural complex are unsupported by other data and may be manipulated for political effect. In the same way that the output growth rates of consumer goods vis-a-vis producer goods can be "adjusted" upward by a few percentage points to achieve the desired agitprop effect, the contribution of the machine-building, chemical, and defense industries to agriculture can be inflated. To cite just one example: The famous Shchekino chemical combine makes fertilizers and is therefore, presumably, counted under "branches supplying agriculture," but it also produces methanol, formaldehyde, caprolactum, and capron.

Despite the new priority accorded to agriculture since the March 1965 plenum, there is little doubt that it remains undercapitalized in relation both to Soviet industry and to the agricultural sectors of most developed Western nations. Furthermore, the internal discrepancy has continued to grow in recent years: During the period 1962-72, fixed productive capital throughout the economy grew by 120 percent, in industry by 130 percent, but in agriculture by 90 percent. Even after the March 1965 plenum, this imbalance persisted, with the respective figures in 1966-70 being 48, 52, and 40 percent.[22] Thus the availability of fixed assets per agricultural worker in 1972 was less than half of that available per industrial worker.[23]

One Soviet authority called for a trebling of the 1970 level of fixed capital in agriculture.[24] This would imply fixed productive capital valued at approximately 200 billion rubles (in constant prices of 1955). At the rate of growth recorded during the 1960s, it could be attained only in the mid-1980s and at some much more distant date if realistic rates of appreciation were to be applied. Another Soviet economist drew attention to the fact that, in the United States, industrial fixed capital per industrial worker amounted to some $6,000 while agricultural fixed capital—excluding the value of land—was $10,000 per farmer. In the Soviet Union, on the other hand, the

relationship was reversed: Agricultural fixed capital amounted to
about 3,000 rubles per farmer.[25] Yet agriculture should dispose of
higher capital/labor and power/labor ratios than industry, since so
many agricultural machines like seeders, combines, etc., can be
used for only a few days each year.

Nevertheless, opponents of the agricultural lobby can point to
the steeply falling capital productivity of the agricultural sector.
During the period 1950-70, fixed productive capital in agriculture
rose by 320 percent while output grew by only 120 percent.[26] In other
terms, for each ruble invested, the growth of the public sector's net
output was reportedly 1.32 rubles in 1956-60, 0.45 rubles in 1961-65,
and 0.42 rubles in 1966-68.[27] The capital productivity has continued
to decline in recent years. But here short-term measures can be
misleading since much of the current investment is directed not to
agriculture itself but to developing "those branches of industry which
create the material base for industrializing agriculture."[28] An illus-
tration of this trend is the recent renewed growth of investment in the
chemical industry after several years of capital constipation; much of
its increased capacity is destined for the production of agricultural
chemicals.

As in industry, part of the underfulfillment of agricultural
investment targets in 1966-70 could be ascribed not so much to the
shifting of resources to other recipients but to the lack of capacity
of construction organizations and to the shortage of producer goods
to meet unplanned, decentralized demand.[29] During the current plan
period, decentralized investment requirements are avowedly to be
treated with the same priority as centralized investment orders, at
least for construction materials.[30]

MECHANIZATION

F.D. Kulakov, the secretary of the Central Committee of the
Communist Party of the Soviet Union (CPSU) responsible for agriculture, told a VASKhNIL session: " . . . ours are mighty farms where
machinery can better be utilized . . . we do not need such a quantity
of tractors and combines per thousand hectares as possess, for instance, the Federal Republic of Germany or the U.S."[31] He was right,
of course, but there may have been a slight trace of sour grapes in
his pronouncement, for most Soviet agricultural economists would
argue that the timely completion of farm operations is especially vital
under the conditions of extreme climatic changes and the short sowing,
growing, and harvesting periods that prevail over much of the Russian
land mass. However, Kulakov did concede that plowing takes on

average more than 40 days, whereas it should be completed in 20. Lemeshev went further in putting the average duration of fall plowing at 50-60 days and calculated that an "optimal park" would include 4.25 million tractors and 2.7 million trucks.[32] Another economist, G. Ponomarev, called for a park of 3.2 million tractors, 2 million trucks, and 880 combines.[33] Both estimates represent a substantial escalation of Khrushchev's goals. Table 7.3 shows how far all three optima are removed from present reality. It also contrasts Soviet optima and reality with the U.S. inventories at the end of 1970: These have been declining in absolute terms in recent years and they serve an area of cultivated land that is some two-thirds of the Soviet level.

The growing discrepancy in recent years between the numbers of machines delivered and the rise in inventories bears eloquent witness to the wastage caused by amortization: For instance, 2,415,200 tractors were supplied to agriculture during the period 1966-73, but the tractor park rose by only 567,000 units.[34] In his striving toward any optimum park, Yezhevsky, the durable chief of Soyuzsel'khoztehnika, would go along with the Red Queen's admonition: "Now here, you see, it takes all the running you can do to keep in the same place. If you want to go somewhere else, you must run at least twice as fast as that." Yet so much more could be accomplished with the existing park if only enough trained personnel were available: In a two-year period, the shift coefficient of sovkhoz tractors declined from 1.17 to 1.12, while the daily output of kolkhoz tractors dropped from 2.4 to 2.27 hectares.[35]

In quantitative terms, the undermechanization of Soviet agriculture, when compared with the United States, is clear enough; in terms of quality, the situation is spotty to say the least. On the one hand, Belarus tractors are being exported to Western Europe and to the United States, where their ruggedness, simplicity, and competitive price are appreciated. Meanwhile, back at home, the exhortations and recriminations that appear daily in the Soviet press evidence the chronic unreliability of agricultural machinery and the perennial lack of spares. As one tractor driver put it, "Acquiring spare parts is the problem of problems."[36] To be sure, the Ninth Five-Year Plan did stipulate that "requirements for spare parts for tractors, automobiles, and agricultural machines will be fully met," but this was surely more of a pious hope than a planning directive. Designs have doubtlessly been perfected, while the average power of tractors supplied to agriculture will have grown by one-half in 1966-75.[37] What has not changed is the arbitrary allocation of machinery and equipment by Soyuzsel'khoztekhnika. Accustomed to a historic seller's market, its officials persist in allocating machinery that has not been requested,[38] while at the same time ignoring orders which have been placed.[39] Even if they enjoyed consumer sovereignty, farms would be largely

TABLE 7.3

Tractors, Trucks, and Combines—Deliveries and Inventories, Soviet Union
(thousands of units)

	Years	Tractors	Trucks	Combines
1. Delivered to farms	1961-65	1,093	418	385
2. Planned deliveries	1966-70	1,790	1,100	550
3. Actual deliveries	1966-70	1,467	717	469
4. Planned deliveries	1971-75	1,700	1,100	543
5. Inventories at end of 1965		1,613	945	520
6. Inventories at end of 1973		2,180	1,284	670
7. Khrushchev's "optimal park"		2,700	1,650	845
8. Ponomarev's "optimal park"		3,200	2,000	880
9. Lemeshev's "optimal park"		4,250	2,700	n.a.
10. United States inventories at end of 1970		4,562	2,968	760

Sources: 1. Ekonomika sel'skogo khozyaistva, no. 2 (1971), p. 45; 2. Pravda, April 10, 1966; 3. Ninth Five-Year Plan, pp. 182, 183; 4. Ibid; 5. SSSR v tsifrakh v 1973 godu, p. 123; 6. Ibid.; 7. Pravda, March 6, 1962; 8. Ekonomika sel'skogo khozyaistva, no. 2 (1971), p. 46; 9. Izvestia Sibirskogo Otdeleniya AN SSSR, no. 11 (1970), p. 78; 10. Statistical Abstract of the United States, 1972, p. 600.

ignorant of what was available because only three illustrated catalogs have been published during the past 13 years.[40] Supplies are channeled through a cumbersome network of stores and bases: These do provide employment for the toilers of Soyuzsel'khoztekhnika, but they also delay deliveries and add many millions of rubles to farms' outlays.[41]

Much has been made of the fact that the armaments industries have been coopted to help agriculture out of its difficulties: At the July 1970 plenum, pledges were made by the heads of the Aircraft, the Heavy, Power and Transport Engineering and of the Defense Industry. Indeed, the notion of beating T-62 tanks into plowshares renders some observers positively lyrical. However, these commitments were more of symbolic than quantitative significance. For example, the Defense Industry claimed to have supplied some 25,000 K-700 (Kirovets) tractors to agriculture in 1966-70;[42] yet this represented less than 2 percent of tractors supplied during that period.

Another aspect of farm mechanization that is of concern to the Soviet authorities is the shortage of auxiliary implements: For every ruble's worth of tractor, it has been estimated that some 2.50 rubles' worth of agricultural machinery is required, but inventories in 1970 were at about two-thirds of that level.[43] The gap has widened in recent years: During the period 1959-71, for example, the sovkhoz tractor park had risen in value terms by 96.5 percent while the inventories of auxiliary equipment had grown by 21.1 percent.[44] In view of the large capital expenditures that would accrue to farms, it has been proposed that Soyuzsel'khoztekhnika set up hiring points for agricultural machinery.[45]

Aggravating the shortage of farm machinery and trained operators is the historical Russian condition of bezdorozh'e: it has been claimed that up to 40 percent of farm power and labor is occupied with transport operations alone.[46] But "roadlessness" is a state that will take generations and vast resources to overcome.

A hidden cost of Soviet agriculture is the large number of trucks, tractors, and personnel that are "volunteered," "commandeered," or "borrowed" to help bring in each harvest. Total figures are not published, but they must run into the millions of extra hands and hundreds of thousands of vehicles. In 1970, for instance, some 120,000 trucks were requisitioned from industrial enterprises in the RSFSR for this purpose,[47] while another source reported that 600,000 trucks were transferred to the Virgin Lands each summer,[48] presumably from other farms and from industry. Of course, in other extensive agricultures, tractors, combines, and trucks "follow the harvest" each year, but surely not on the massive scale practiced in the Soviet Union to the detriment of many other sectors of the economy. Yet much of this transfer could be avoided if only the Stalinist practice of centralizing all state grain purchases within weeks of the harvest

were discontinued. The sixth consecutive "harvest decree" issued in
May 1974 suggests that the Soviet leadership may at last be prepared
to do just this.[49]

In most other respects, farm mechanization and electrification
is improving at a steady pace, even if it still has a long way to go to
attain current Western standards. In 1971, for instance, less than
10 percent of feeding operations and only 13 percent of manure-
clearing operations on kolkhozes were mechanized.[50] However,
despite the fact that there was a 50 percent shortfall in the scheduled
amount of electricity supplied to the countryside by 1970, virtually
all rural homes were reportedly supplied with electric power that
year.[51] And to judge from the profusion of television antennae, their
occupants have finally achieved cultural parity with their urban
cousins—at least by this widely accepted criterion.

MINERAL FERTILIZER

More than half of the projected increase in grain yields and
much of the gains in the output of fodder and technical crops during
the Ninth Five-Year Plan period are predicated on the planned rise
in the output, delivery, and application of mineral fertilizer. Output
was scheduled to rise from 55 million tons in 1970 to 72 million tons
in 1975 and to 120 million tons in 1980.[52] Up to mid-1974, the output
and delivery schedules had been maintained with only marginal
slippage.

Despite impressive growth rates during the past few years,
current Soviet levels of fertilizer application are still low, both
quantitatively and qualitatively, when compared with most Western
agricultures. In 1968, an average of 37.7 kg of mineral fertilizer—
in terms of nutrient content—was applied per hectare of plowed land
in the Soviet Union, against averages of 82 kg in the United States,
206 kg in West Germany, and 224 kg in the United Kingdom (1 kg
equals 2.2 pounds).[53] By 1973, the Soviet rates of application had
reached about half of the U.S. levels. Largely as a consequence of
the prevailing influence of the val or gross output indicator, the
quality of Soviet fertilizers is poor, although here again progress has
been recorded. Whereas the average nutrient content of U.S.-produced
fertilizers was 38.7 percent in 1968 and 40 percent in 1970, the Soviet
figures were 27.7 and 34.7 percent respectively, while only 6 percent
of the total was made up of compound, high-concentrate fertilizers.
However, by 1975 the average nutrient content is to be raised to 35-
37 percent, while by 1980 compound fertilizers will predominate in
the overall mix.[54] Furthermore, it is hoped to enhance the

effectiveness of fertilizers by a further 15-20 percent with the introduction of the relevant trace elements according to individual regions
and cultures.[55]

Up until now, the bulk of fertilizer supplied to agriculture has
been allocated to technical crops: Out of a total of 46 million tons
used by farms in 1970, only 16 million tons were applied to grain.
By 1975, it is expected that 32 million tons will be used on grain. With
an estimated minimum response of 1.2 tons of grain for each ton of
fertilizer, this should yield nearly 20 million tons more grain, that
is, over one-half of the total planned growth in output. Even so, this
quantity of fertilizer will still be less than one-half of the "optimal
agrotechnical norm."[56]

The economic rationality of applying fertilizer is easily demonstrated. One estimate put the average prime costs of one ton, including transportation and spreading expenditures, at 70-80 rubles,
while the average added value of produce thereby derived was some
160-180 rubles.[57] Why then do reports persist of miniature mountains
of fertilizer being left at railroad sidings or piling up at farms? There
are several possible explanations. Packaging is still poor or nonexistent, and so great blocks of concrete-like nongranulated fertilizer
may have to be blown or drilled out of freight cars (sometimes open
cars). The farms may lack the trucks to bring the fertilizer from the
station to the fields—or may be prevented from doing so by bezdorozh'e
(lack of roads). Specialized equipment is in short supply: Thus the
supply of fertilizer in 1965-68 rose by 30 percent, but the delivery of
spreaders grew by only 14 percent.[58] Fertilizer spoils from inadequate storage facilities: In 1973, it was reported that in many oblasts
less than one-third of mineral fertilizer supplies could be stored
under cover.[59]

However, one principal reason is probably a general apathy to
the stuff among farmers, stemming from a lack of direct interest and
incentive. In theory, on the basis of soil charts and crop rotation
schedules, farms should order given quantities of specific types of
fertilizer for delivery at a given time. In practice, all too often they
must just take what they are given and whenever it suits the supply
organs. Moreover, within such large operational units as brigades,
the link between the correct and timely application of fertilizer, high
yields, and higher earnings is just too tenuous.

With the increased emphasis upon livestock products, the availability of organic fertilizer is expected to rise by a further 100 million
tons by 1975 over the 1970 level: This is reckoned to be equivalent
to 6 million tons of mineral fertilizer and roughly one-third is to be
applied to grain.[60]

LAND IMPROVEMENT

Faced with the pressing requirement to raise food grain output as rapidly and as inexpensively as possible, without recourse to the world market, Khrushchev launched his grandiose Virgin Lands campaign, which brought some 30 million hectares of new land under the plow. Most observers would agree that, given the domestic and external context and constraints, this was the correct course. Indeed, on the twentieth anniversary of the inception of the program, the Soviet media hailed the success of this historic venture (without, of course, referring to the unperson who was its initiator). But by the end of the 1950s, the possibilities of further expansion were largely exhausted, and the setback of 1963 concentrated Khrushchev's mind wonderfully on the next stage: a shift of emphasis from extensive to intensive farming, with the prime determinants for raising yields being chemicalization and land improvement. He was not permitted to preside over the implementation of his impressive vision of land improvement, and the vast program of irrigation, drainage, clearance, and liming now under way and projected until the end of the century might be viewed as Brezhnev's salient contribution to the development of Soviet agriculture. The main thrust of land improvement in the near future is to be the nonchernozem (nonblack soil) region of the RSFSR (although it can be argued that this scheme represents merely redress for 60 years of neglect).[61] Looking further ahead, the chairman of the Soviet Academy of Sciences' Commission for Research into Production Potential and Natural Resources foresees the expansion of irrigated and drained lands covering 30 million and 50 million hectares respectively,[62] while another source refers grandly to 142 million hectares "suitable" for irrigation (1 hectare equals 2.47 acres).[63]

With the per capita average of arable land declining gradually—from 1.06 hectares in 1954 to 0.90 hectares in 1972[64]—and with over two-thirds of the existing stock of arable land prone to drought,[65] the rationale for land improvement in general and for irrigation in particular can hardly be disputed.[66] Here we would like to touch briefly on the most questionable aspect, namely the growing of food grains on irrigated land. Until now, the bulk of irrigated land has been allocated to cotton, rice, and to certain vegetables in the Central Asian and Transcaucasian regions. With due regard to the limitations of Soviet price formation, it may be conceded that these crops bring in a reasonable profit: Recent average profitability rates have been recorded of 40 percent for cotton and 69 percent for rice.[67] The economics of growing food grains, and especially wheat, on irrigated land is another matter.

Although there has been an understandable tendency to understate the true costs of irrigation, it would appear that these have risen substantially in recent years. No single all-union estimate has been published, but the average initial costs of irrigation have leaped from a declared 1,600 rubles per hectare in 1959,[68] to 2,600 rubles in 1963,[69] while an authoritative source in 1974 has put the average at between 5,000 and 6,000 rubles per hectare, with costs exceeding 10,000 rubles for the recovery of land gone barren.[70] In addition to the high and rising initial costs, the running costs are not negligible: These have been estimated at over 76 rubles per hectare per annum for water, application, cleaning, and other expenses.[71] Furthermore, numerous reports testify to the inadequate use of existing and new irrigation.

Since the average yield increment for wheat on irrigated land has seldom risen above 50 percent,[72] and since the average basic state purchase price for wheat is roughly 100 rubles a ton,[73] then it would seem impossible to justify the large-scale growing of wheat on irrigated land except as a break crop. Even if irrigation systems were correctly maintained, if adequately trained cadres were available, and if the correct amounts of fertilizers were applied in a timely fashion, the growing of food grains on irrigated land could not be vindicated by any normal cost-benefit analysis. Yet the irrigated area under grain is scheduled to expand to some 6 million hectares by 1975,[74] and much if not most of the vast irrigated territories envisaged for the next decade—the projected 1985 total ranges from 21 million to 40 million hectares depending upon the source[75]—will apparently be used for grain.

The explanation must surely lie in the determination of the Soviet leadership to attain and to retain autarky in staple foodstuffs almost regardless of cost. Moreover, in the light of behavior on the world commodity markets in recent times, of the high elasticity of demand for meat and animal products in all affluent societies, and of the international repercussions of the "great grain robbery" of 1972, this commitment is perhaps defensible.

AGRICULTURAL SUBSIDIES

A great deal of attention has, understandably, been paid to the topic of agricultural subsidies in non-Communist developed nations. For instance, the EEC's Common Agricultural Policy has been blamed (unjustly) for the recent alarming increases in food retail prices in Britain; Japan's rice "countermeasures" absorb more than 5 percent of budgetary outlays; while until recently the U.S. Sugar Bill was the vehicle for much political partisanship. But very little is known about the Soviet price support bill, which happens to be the largest in the world, both in absolute terms and in relation to the national income. This low profile is due primarily to the discretion of the Soviet media.

A relatively small subsidy for agricultural procurements was paid during Khrushchev's administration; this was financed under the omnibus "On the National Economy" heading of budgetary outlays. The annual subsidy started to climb dramatically with the substantial producer price increases of 1965 when food retail prices were left unchanged. At the March 1965 plenum, Garbuzov announced that "additional state assistance to the kolkhozes and sovkhozes" would be made available in 1965-70 to the amount of "over 22 billion rubles."[76] Some of this was to cover the writing off of bad debts and the loss of state budgetary revenue resulting from the reduction of kolkhoz income tax, but the bulk of this sum was destined for agricultural price support. Since then, no stenographic reports of CPSU Central Committee plenums have been published and to the author's knowledge most of the references to this delicate matter have appeared in the low-circulation house journal of the Soviet Ministry of Finances,[77] and in two little-known books.[78] From these specific and oblique references, it appears that the price support bill substantially exceeded Garbuzov's projection for 1966-70 and has since risen at a pace most disturbing to the orthodox souls at the Soviet Ministry of Finances. Figures cited have ranged from "over 4 billion rubles" in 1966, to a planned 6.5 billion rubles for 1969, to 9.3 billion rubles in 1971. At the Minsk conference of the International Association of Agricultural Economists in August-September 1970, the Soviet spokesman declined to give a direct reply to a direct (Western) question on the current scale of Soviet agricultural price support.

In the absence of authoritative and comprehensive Soviet data, Western observers have perforce made their own estimates, based on the known levels in previous years and adjusted in the light of purchase price increases and changes in the volume of procurements. The exercise is difficult, since so much depends upon the composition of state purchases in any given year. For example, in a bad year, a major grain-growing region may not fulfill its basic plan-quota while some marginal, high-cost producers may sell much of their grain at a 50 percent premium.[79] There is a 40-65 percent premium on the basic price for hard wheats and a 30-50 percent bonus for strong wheats.[80] Private producers now receive the same basic price for meat sold to the state as do kolkhozes and sovkhozes, but they do not qualify for the relatively new 50 percent premium for above-plan sales of meat, and so on. The "best Western estimate" is a calculation performed by Constance Krueger.[81] This concludes that the total subsidy on the procurement levels planned for 1974 would amount to 16 billion rubles. Since the procurement plans were reportedly overfulfilled at mid-1974,[82] the final outturn could be well in excess of 16 billion rubles.

This is no mean sum. At the official rate of exchange prevailing in August 1974[83] it represented over U.S. \$21 billion; it came close to the overt defense appropriation of 17.6 billion rubles budgeted for 1974;[84] it is equivalent to over 25 percent of the national income originating in agriculture,[85] and it is equal to about 5 percent of the national income (Soviet concept).[86]

It would appear that either the principle or the extent (or both) of agricultural price support have been questioned in Soviet ruling circles for, after the July 1970 plenum, Garbuzov delivered himself of the following, rather defensive statement:

> It should be noted that agricultural subsidies paid by the state are used in the U.S., Canada and in several other capitalist states. They are also widely used in the EEC, which has established a price level for agricultural products which has been coordinated between the individual nations. The subsidizing of the output of these products is one of the forms of intervention by capitalist states into the economy for maintaining a price level which will provide high profits for the major monopolies. For this purpose, they are working to reduce the output of agricultural products, and this has led to the collapse of an enormous number of farms. . . . Aid to the development of agriculture in the socialist nations has a fundamentally different nature. Expenditures for the purchase of agricultural products in these nations are directed not at reducing, but rather increasing, the output of agricultural products and are aimed at raising the workers' living standards.[87]

His pronouncement is not without merit, although he might have given credit to the United Kingdom's traditional—until 1971 at least—policy of using its price support system to keep food retail prices down. The mechanism of the market has only a limited influence upon agricultural producer prices and on food retail prices in many Western industrialized nations. More might have been made of the fact that the "capitalist states" are concerned with food surpluses and in few cases does the price support bill exceed one percent of the respective GNP. The Soviet Union, on the other hand, enjoys the dubious distinction of paying the largest subsidy in the world for a still irregular and uncertain supply of inferior foodstuffs. Meanwhile the Soviet housewife has to pay nearly twice as much—at the official rates of exchange—for a "family foodbasket" of staple foodstuffs as any of her American, British, French, or German counterparts.[88] The comparison in terms of take-home pay for the average industrial worker is even less favorable. It can be, and has been, argued by Soviet apologists that subsidies paid mainly on livestock products are offset by the profits derived by the state from crop products, for example, the turnover tax on sugar. However, this is a rather specious argument and is akin to the TsSU's practice of setting sovkhoz losses off against the profits generated by procurement organizations.[89]

What is to be done? The output and procurement of meat are expected to grow rapidly after the pause inflicted by the 1972 setback: Under the present system, this could lead to an annual price support bill of over 20 billion rubles by 1976. The straightforward economic and unpolitical solution would be to raise the retail prices of meat and milk: These would have to be more or less doubled to eliminate the subsidy completely.[90] But those in the Soviet leadership who might have forgotten the repercussions of the last overt increase in state retail prices in 1962 will have had their memories refreshed by the events of December 1970 in Gdansk and Szczecin. Besides, ever since the March 1965 plenum, the Soviet population has been repeatedly reassured that retail prices will not be raised. The alternative solution, long promoted by the authorities, is to raise labor and/or capital productivity, thereby lowering unit costs and thus enabling a reduction of state purchase prices.[91] But this remains a pious hope rather than a realistic plan of action; as one leading observer noted: "It is rather difficult to reduce purchase prices which have been in use for some time."[92]

Finally, one other category of subsidy might be mentioned here. This is the state subsidy paid to cover the discrepancy between the wholesale price paid to the manufacturer for agricultural producer goods and the price paid by the farms ever since the July 1967 price reform.[93] In 1971 this was expected to total about 1 billion rubles.[94]

PROCUREMENT AND DELIVERY PRICES

As in many Western nations, the formation and administration of agricultural producer prices in the Soviet Union is a rather complex matter, and here merely some of the more salient characteristics will be treated.

Broadly speaking, despite the very substantial increases in state purchase prices that were introduced during Khrushchev's administration, the output of most crops and animal products in the public sector was carried out either at a loss or at very low rates of profitability. Thus the more a farm sold to the state, the more losses it incurred: Sovkhozes required greater state operating subsidies, while kolkhozes either cut back on wage payments or went into debt or both. This, it was conceded at the March 1965 plenum, represented a very real disincentive to higher agricultural output.

The new purchase prices announced at that plenum went a long way to correct this state of affairs. For example, basic procurement prices for wheat and rye were raised by an average of 12 percent for most regions and by 53 percent for certain marginal high-cost areas. For all "voluntary" above-plan sales of grain, a 50 percent premium was instituted. "Temporary" supplements of from 32 to 36 percent were added to the price of meat purchased from kolkhozes and sovkhozes (but not from private producers). The state purchase price for milk was also raised by about 20 percent, although this concession was subsequently tempered by more rigorous regulations on milk grading.[95] Since state retail prices for all staple foodstuffs were left unchanged, this necessitated a large and growing annual subsidy, as we have seen, and especially on meat.

The initial effect of the producer price increases was to make the production of most grains and most other crops very profitable:[96] For instance, the average profitability of growing grain on kolkhozes in 1968 was 142 percent[97]—while most livestock products now returned a small profit in place of the former losses. However, labor costs rose quickly with the introduction of guaranteed pay and higher earnings for kolkhozniks and with increased wages for sovkhoz workers and employees. The growth in average earnings outstripped that of labor productivity and this had the greatest impact, understandably, on the labor-intensive livestock sector. By 1969, the average profitability of beef production on kolkhozes and sovkhozes was down to 14 and 3 percent, respectively, while for milk the figures were -8 and 12 percent.[98]

Another factor that adversely affected kolkhoz profitability was the change in the terms of trade effected by the July 1967 price reform. Whereas the prices of specifically agricultural producer goods such as farm tractors, grain combines, and fertilizers were deliberately left unchanged, necessitating a subsidy, farms had to pay more for producer goods that were in general use, such as fuel, construction materials, etc. And although at the time Sitnin promised that these latter price increases would be offset by "changes in procurement prices or by some other means,"[99] no such compensation appears to have been forthcoming.[100]

The large and growing discrepancy between the profitability of crop and livestock products inevitably manifested itself in the structure of output and sales. When it was 50 percent more profitable to sell grain to the state than to feed it to the pigs—and about 130 percent more profitable when the 50 percent premium was payable[101]—then it was hardly surprising that the output of pork in the public sector first stabilized then fell, despite a growing demand.

A few changes in purchase prices—invariably upward—were announced during the period 1967-69. For example, bonuses for hard and strong wheats were raised in 1967, [102] and the purchase prices paid to the public sector for poultry were substantially increased in 1969.[103] Nevertheless, the next major round of price increases came into effect during the first half of 1970, although the specific details were not promulgated until the July 1970 plenum.

The principal changes were as follows. The basic purchase prices for grain remained unchanged, but since a larger share of the total state purchases in 1971-75 (at least 35 percent) is to be sold at above-plan premium rates, the effective average producer price is expected to rise by about 10 percent. The "temporary" supplements to the basic meat purchase prices, which were announced at the March 1965 plenum, have now been permanently incorporated in the basic prices and were even increased with effect from May 1970: For instance, the previous supplement of 35 percent for the RSFSR, the Ukrainian, Moldavian, Tadzhik and Turkmen SSRs was increased to 40 percent; the Kazakh supplement rose from 20 to 35 percent, and so on.[104] As with grain, a premium of 50 percent is now offered to kolkhozes and sovkhozes for above-plan sales of meat, provided that their animal inventories do not fall below the January 1 count of that year; this premium was not offered to private producers. From May 1970, the purchase prices for mutton and lamb were raised in most instances to nearly the same level as for beef, [105] while milk and cream prices were increased by a further 20 percent.[106] New purchase prices, differentiated by zone, quality, and seasonality, for potatoes, vegetables, and fruit were introduced for kolkhozes and sovkhozes that were supposed to ensure them a profitability of at least 15 percent.[107] No systematic and comprehensive data are published on agricultural producer prices and it may be that not only external observers find the subject complex: One Soviet economist noted that four differing delivery prices (that is, those paid to sovkhozes) existed for one category of beef in one region—and none of them corresponded with the costs of production.[108] Since the 1970 round of purchase price increases, there appear to have been only two further changes of substance: In 1972, the purchase price in all regions for sugar beet was raised, [109] while new, higher prices were established for certain types of grain in parts of the non-chernozem zone.[110]

The effects of the price increases to mid-1974 may be summed up as follows. The purchase prices now paid for crops ensure high to very high profitability rates—at current production costs—for virtually all farms except in a few marginal regions. Some state purchases are still made in high-cost areas, since the higher prices are wholly or largely offset by economies in transportation. Animal products, on the other hand, should now bring a profit to practically all farms and regions, although in most cases the profit will not be as high as the 45-50 percent deemed necessary by many specialists to ensure extended reproduction and the high rates of planned growth.[111] Of course, provided that farms can increase their meat deliveries while maintaining livestock inventories, as Brezhnev stipulated at the July 1970 plenum, and thereby earn the 50 percent premium for above-plan sales, then the 45-50 percent level of profitability is surely attainable. But this has been difficult on the tight feed base. Moreover, the renewed emphasis upon the quantity of animals to the detriment of their productivity runs counter to the advice of many leading agricultural economists, expressed both before and after the July 1970 plenum.[112]

The continuing large discrepancy between the profits to be obtained from selling grain to the state and those to be derived from feeding it to livestock suggests that farms will persist in choosing the former course unless ordered to do otherwise: Even specialized livestock farms reportedly grow grain in order to sell some at above-plan rates.[113] No seasonal price differentiation has apparently been provided, although, as has been pointed out, this leads to an over-loading of the slaughter and processing facilities in the fall and their underutilization in the spring.

The economic rationale of many aspects of Soviet price forma-tion in the area of agricultural purchases is open to question—as are many Western producer prices for agricultural products. If the basic price for grain or meat ensures the correct rate of profitability for the farm, then surely the above-plan premium rate is wrong? The unscientific answer could be that it may be wrong in theory but that it works in practice. Soviet writers stress that the payment of a 50 percent premium for above-plan purchases is only a temporary ex-pedient and will be dropped when the effectiveness of production is raised and when prime costs fall.[114] But life has shown that many such "temporary" expedients have a habit of lingering on.

Many external observers might agree with the first part of Emelyanov's argument: "Under contemporary conditions, it is not the increase in purchase prices that is the prime factor in raising profitability and forcing agricultural growth. The prime factor is the transformation [that is, industrialization] of agricultural production and, on this basis, achieving an increase in the productivity of labor and a reduction in the prime costs of production, . . . " although most would view with scepticism his conclusion that "a stable base for a subsequent reduction in retail prices will be secured."[115]

The parallels with Soviet industry are evident. Industrial wholesale prices are set to provide an average rate of profitability for whole industries and sectors, but the profitability rates differ widely between enterprises and regions. Since the prices themselves are not allowed to guide the enterprise director in deciding what items and how many of them to produce, he must be given a plan-order covering most, if not all, of his plant's productive capacity. In agriculture, most producer prices now ensure a profit for each farm. But the rates of profitability vary from zero or below to over 300 percent (for sunflower seed, for example). If the kolkhoz chairman or sovkhoz director were allowed to choose the farm's output pattern, he would naturally tend to concentrate on the highly profitable items to the neglect of the loss-makers. Thus, even after the further refinements that were introduced at the July 1970 plenum, Emelyanov was justified in concluding:

> In the plans, the relationship between the structure of produce purchase and the requirements of the country is, to a great extent, determined by legal norms on the basis of which the interests of agricultural units are subordinated to the interests of the entire society. Kolkhozes and sovkhozes are obliged to fulfill the plan, even if the output of these products is inadequately profitable.[116]

STATE PURCHASES

Under Khrushchev, state purchase targets were frequently altered from year to year and even during the course of each year: This hampered meaningful perspective planning and crop rotation schedules. Acknowledging these defects, at the March 1965 plenum Brezhnev announced stable state purchase targets for the period until 1970. The basic grain purchase goals were stabilized at roughly the levels actually attained during the preceeding five-year period, with a 50 percent premium offered for above-plan sales, while the 1965-70 targets for animal products were evidently based upon a more realistic assessment of production potentialities rather than Khrushchev's earlier dream-like plans that attempted to impose output goals reflecting consumption requirements. In the event, the state purchases for all major products in 1966-70 were met, at least in terms of the overall five-year totals, even if a large proportion of the above-plan purchases of grain went to cover the underfulfillment of basic targets.[117]

The new system has shown itself to be a distinct step forward from the former methods, and it has been retained for the period 1971-75. Compared with average actual purchases in 1966-70, the new targets are 22 percent higher for grain (including anticipated above-plan purchases), 16 percent for sunflower seed, 6 percent for sugar beet, 26 percent for potatoes, 9 percent for raw cotton, 29 percent for cattle and poultry, 23 percent for milk, 66 percent for eggs, and 14 percent for wool. In absolute terms, the basic total for grain is 60 million tons each year, while the animal products targets rise to 17.7 million tons (liveweight) for cattle and poultry, 60 million tons for milk, 28.7 billion eggs, and 520,600 tons of wool by 1975.[118] The meat product targets for 1975 look unrealistically high.

Despite an overall improvement in the system of purchases, there are many admitted shortcomings. Complaints persist to the effect that procurement agencies issue purchase plans to farms for items that they do not produce at all or that are higher than the respective output plans. Purchase plans tend to cover the whole of the farms' production potential, thus leaving little or no discretion to the farm management as to the output mix. Furthermore, they often specify so many differing items that these make nonsense of the avowed official striving for greater specialization.[119] For their part, farms have not been slow to exploit the vagaries of the price system. Finding that the price of feed concentrates was much lower than the premium prices paid for above-plan sales of grain, the farms of the Central Economic Region of the RSFSR in 1966-69 sold 1.8 million tons of grain at premium prices, while at the same time purchasing 1.2 to 1.4 million tons of concentrates each year.[120]

More fundamental, however, are three developments that have diluted or negated the essence of the March 1965 program in respect to state purchases. The first is the enhanced powers of what was formerly the Soviet State Committee of Procurements and what has since been elevated to the Union-Republican Ministry of Procurements. The competence of its officials has now been extended beyond the sphere of procurements to permit them to participate in the farms' production planning. They must, for instance, "ensure that sowing plans are adequate to meet contractual obligations and that the capacity of every subunit is fully utilized."[121] Clearly, this represents a further diminution of the already limited operational autonomy of the farm managements.

The second is the growing tendency to plan the purportedly "voluntary, above-plan" deliveries: Indeed, these have been "built into" the Ninth Five-Year Plan.[122] These "voluntary" commitments are declared to be "a high duty for each farm,"[123] or even an "obligation."[124] The real nature of these assignments and, incidentally, the relationship between procurement agencies and farms

are summed up succinctly in the following citation from the procurement ministry's house journal: "However, as they themselves have
the best knowledge of the possibilities for overfulfilling the state
procurement plans assigned to them, kolkhozes and sovkhozes should
actively participate in determining above-plan procurements of agricultural products."[125] (Emphasis supplied.)

The third development has an immediate parallel in the implementation of the September 1965 reform program in Soviet industry;
a problem that has occupied the attention of, inter alia, the unfortunate
Yevsei Liberman. If a farm is offered a very high price for its above-
plan sales of grain or meat, then it will obviously strive to obtain an
"easy" basic plan and—in the eyes of the authorities—thereby "un-
deservedly" obtain excessive profits.[126]

On the positive side, every procurement point is now reportedly
obligated to purchase all marketable produce offered it by every farm
in its zone.[127] This should end the repeated complaints by farms that
have brought their livestock or produce, often over great distances,
only to have them turned down by the procurement officials for one
reason or another. The trucks are then obliged to return fully laden,
with resulting loss of weight in animals or spoilage of produce.

Finally, some bold spirits have even gone so far as to ask, in
an oblique manner, why obligatory purchases are still necessary if
procurement and delivery prices ensure a reasonable rate of profitability.[128] To date, however, no convincing reply appears to have
been offered.

THE PRIVATE SECTOR

The present leadership's attitude toward the private plots and
livestock holdings of the kolkhozniks, workers, and employees appears
to have been consistent throughout. Most of the relatively few de-
partures from the official policy of pragmatic tolerance of the private
sector in recent years have stemmed from objective causes or from
misplaced zeal on the part of local authorities. As Polyansky spelled
out in his Kommunist article of 1967 and again at the Third All-Union
Congress of Kolkholzniks, the private sector is still regarded as a
relic of private property instincts that will wither away with the
abundance ultimately to flow from the public sector and with the
growing socialist consciousness of the peasant. But, in the meantime,
people have to be fed, and the private sector supplies over one-quarter
of the gross agricultural product, including many of the attractive,
high-quality fresh items in the Soviet citizen's diet.[129] The widely
bruited formulation that the private sector occupies a mere 3 percent

of the sown area, yet yields nearly 33 percent of the agricultural
product, is, of course, misleading. The bulk of the private sector's
output in value terms consists of animal products, yet for their feed
inputs privately owned livestock are almost wholly dependent upon
the public sector. Thus the overall shortage of feed in recent years
has adversely affected the private sector's performance. Furthermore, with the transition to guaranteed monthly cash earnings, the
distribution of payments in kind has declined both relatively and
absolutely. By 1968, the natura payments (payments in kind) of
grain to kolkhozniks had fallen by 44 percent when compared with
1965, while the issue of potatoes and hay had dropped by 36 and 20
percent, respectively.[130] The share of the gross output of grain
distributed as in-kind payments fell from 16.8 percent in 1965 to 7.7
percent in 1969.[131] This rapid decline was doubtlessly accelerated
by the employment of state retail prices in valuing the natura distributions, a practice that was terminated in August 1969.[132]

The private sector's contribution to the gross agricultural
product is expected to decline gradually, as is its share of kolkhozniks' earnings. For instance, the Ninth Five-Year Plan envisages
a growth of 30 percent in the gross product emanating from the public
sector and only 2 percent from the private sector.[133] According to
the Gosplan's calculations, the average earnings from kolkhozniks
from the private sector are estimated to have decreased from 41.3
percent of their total incomes in 1965 to about 32 percent in 1970, and
are expected to drop further to 25 percent by 1975.[134]

Two of the principal reasons for the falling share in total output
of the private sector are the steady annual decline in the number of
kolkhoz households and the rural reconstruction program. This latter
aims to consolidate the present 705,000 rural inhabited localities into
roughly 120,000 perspektivnye communities (those with a future).[135]
In many of these, a concomitant of urban-type amenities and comfort
will be the physical separation of the plot and livestock shed from the
dwelling.

A further objective factor is that, as the kolkhoznik's earnings
from work in the public sector increase to a meaningful sum and no
longer represent a form of barshchina (work performed in payment)
for the privilege of keeping a private plot, then the very young as well
as the aged and infirm will tend voluntarily to relinquish their rights
to a cow and some chickens, preferring instead to buy their milk and
eggs at the local store.[136] Such a process will not take place over-
night, and in general the authorities are wisely refraining from ex-
pediting it. Furthermore, it is a moot point just when—and if—the
rural retail trade network will be in a position to meet such increased
demand: For instance, of the estimated 30 million tons of milk produced in the private sector in 1969, only 1.1 million tons was marketed.[137]

Whereas the elderly might be prepared to give up their cow and their pigs, "private property instincts" are clearly still tenaciously rooted in many modern Soviet citizens. In one sovkhoz, where private plots had not been assigned to newcomers, one resourceful resident of an apartment building planted onions on the roof, while his tractor-driver neighbor built some large sledges, fixed sties on them, and towed his pigs around with him behind the tractor.[138]

Despite the disappointing and rather negative results of the Third Congress of Kolkhozniks with regard to recommended provisions on the private sector, there appears to have been little subsequent official pressure directed against the plots and livestock holdings. Complaints are occasionally aired when the plots "wander" beyond the prescribed norms,[139] but other pronouncements have stressed that these norms may be raised for exceptionally diligent kolkhozniks or for those with large families. Moreover, the kolkhozes are exhorted to help out with the provision of draft animals, transport and construction materials.[140]

As has been mentioned, the 1965 "temporary" supplements to meat purchase prices were payable until 1970 only to the public sector. Thus whereas in 1968 the average price paid to farms for one hundredweight of beef on the hoof was 117.40 rubles, private producers received 90.70 rubles; the respective sums for pork were 140.50 and 123.80 rubles.[141] The temporary supplements have been increased, incorporated into the basic prices and are now payable also to the private sector. Whether this will attract a substantial response will depend to a large extent upon the way in which kolkhoz markets are regulated.

Prices in these markets are traditionally free to move with supply and demand: This was restated in a decree published shortly after the March 1965 plenum.[142] Yet, in 1969, top limits of twice the state retail price level were set in the markets of Moscow and other cities.[143] And although this was subsequently denounced,[144] later sources confirm that similar or even more severe restrictions were again applied in 1970[145] and again in 1972.[146] The reaction of the kolkhoznik was prompt and understandable. It is hardly worth his while to slaughter a pig and to hump it to market if he knows that he will get only, say, 3.40 rubles a kilo for the meat. Consequently, meat just disappeared from the kolkhoz markets in many cities for weeks at a time.

Despite their widespread use in Yugoslavia and recent modest beginnings in Poland and Czechoslovakia, the provision of minitractors for private plots in the Soviet Union is not even an issue: Indeed, no mention of small, powered agricultural implements appears to have been made for over seven years.[147]

However, to end on a positive note, the Ninth Five-Year Plan did stipulate that "kolkhozes and sovkhozes are to extend to the rural population the necessary assistance in running their private subsidiary farms and in increasing their inventories of livestock and poultry." And in view of the enormous backlog to be overcome before an efficient transportation and distribution system can be created, it would seem that the private sector is assured of a reasonably secure existence for many years to come.

MANPOWER AND MATERIAL INCENTIVES

In a seeming paradox, the Soviet agricultural sector employs about 24 million hands, if labor in the private sector is excluded,[148] and yet there is an acute labor shortage on many farms and throughout many regions. Only part of this is attributable to the uneven distribution of the work force; the chief cause is its composition. In 1965, an estimated 71 percent of labor inputs into the public sector of the kolkhozes consisted of unskilled manual labor.[149] Even today, a large proportion and probably the bulk of the kolkhoz labor force is made up of unskilled, elderly women, many of whom are staying on past the minimum retirement age in order to qualify for at least a modest pension.[150] Thus there is no shortage of elderly, sometimes infirm, and generally unskilled farm hands. What are in short supply are the younger trained mechanizers and specialists, and especially those who are flexible and versatile enough to acquire the new skills and to adapt themselves to the new models of machinery and to the bewildering array of farm chemicals. Yet it is among these more skilled and resourceful cadres that the labor turnover and the flight from the land is the most critical.

By 1966, the number of trained mechanizers had reportedly fallen below the level needed to maintain one-shift working of the available tractors.[151] Since then the situation has deteriorated further. By 1969, the tractor park had grown by 18 percent when compared with 1965 and yet the number of trained mechanizers had increased by only 8 percent.[152] During the five years from 1967 to 1971, 3,721,000 new tractor drivers and combine operators were trained, yet by the end of that period their number employed on the farms had grown by only 190,000.[153] A predictable response of the Soviet authorities has been to issue decrees: One of these provided for the expansion of mechanizers' schools and offered shorter courses for those joining immediately after their demobilization from the armed forces.[154] The response to date has been disappointing. A further 600,000 mechanizers completed their training in 1971-73, but

the number employed on farms rose by a mere 3,000.[155] Of course,
the flight from the land is not peculiar to the Soviet Union; it is a
problem shared by many developed Western nations. But it is of
especially serious concern for a Soviet leadership that has already
invested much treasure and prestige—and is planning to invest even
more—in the belated industrialization of its agricultural sector. When
367 senior pupils in village schools in the Crimea were asked what
they wanted to do in life, only 15 opted for agriculture.[156] The sample
may well have been representative for the whole country.

Improvements have been made in rural working hours and conditions: One source proudly cited a poultry sovkhoz where the conditions and hours of work were similar to those in industrial plants.[157]
As Emelyanov pointed out, modern livestock farms with all-round
mechanization of labor are really just factories for the industrial
production of meat and milk.[158] To work on such a farm requires
as much knowledge and skill as the average industrial worker pos-
sesses. He might have gone further to add that it often takes more
on-the-spot initiative and a greater degree of motivation, in view of
the unsupervised nature of many farm operations and the necessary
exposure to the elements. What is obviously required is the provision of enhanced material incentives.

In every major industrialized nation, the average earnings of
farm workers are below those of industrial workers, even when
allowance is made for payments in kind, free or cheap housing, lower
transportation expenditures, etc. However, during the past two
decades, that is, commencing during Khrushchev's administration,
there has taken place a significant, albeit overdue, closing of the
gap between urban and rural incomes in the Soviet Union. During the
period 1960-68, the average earnings of kolkhozniks from the public
sector in cash and kind rose by 150 percent and those of sovkhoz
workers and employees by 71 percent; over the same period, industrial earnings grew by 33 percent.[159] Pay is no longer a residual
charge on kolkhoz income after all other operating expenditures are
met; nearly all kolkhozes are now paying guaranteed wages, and the
trudoden (workday) system has virtually disappeared. In the Eighth
Five-Year Plan period, the gross incomes of kolkhozes and sovkhozes
rose by 35 percent, while the average earnings of kolkhozniks grew
by 46 percent and those of sovkhoz workers and employees by 36
percent.[160] For the current five-year plan period, a further 30-35
percent rise in the average earnings of kolkhozniks is foreseen, while
the pay of sovkhoz workers and employees is planned to grow by
nearly 30 percent, against raises averaging 22 percent for all other
workers and employees, and at mid-1974 this closing of the differentials was being implemented on schedule.[161]

Now it is hardly equitable to emulate the practice of many Soviet writers[162] and add the kolkhoznik's earnings from his private plot and livestock holding to his pay from the public sector in any direct comparison of average urban and rural earnings. Nevertheless, under current conditions of scarcity, and when the private sector is virtually the sole source of many of the high-priced items of consumption, these subsidiary earnings do represent a source of considerable legitimate additional income. Thus, all things being considered, the present pay differentials between rural and urban workers, for comparable skills and effort, in the Soviet Union are probably now as low and possibly lower than in many industrialized nations.

Clearly then, what is needed to attract and to retain skilled cadres down on the farm is not merely parity or near-parity with factory workers. It is a level of remuneration greater than that offered to industrial workers and employees in order to compensate for irregular and longer working hours, the primitive living conditions, the exposure to the elements and for the political and social discrimination still practiced against the majority of rural residents, that is, the kolkhozniks. Equally clearly, such a course is wholly unacceptable to orthodox Marxist-Leninists. The deputy head of the CPSU Central Committee's Agricultural Department was evidently shocked to learn of instances where "the wages of kolkhozniks had been allowed to exceed the earnings of sovkhoz workers."[163] And yet sovkhoz wages are some 14 percent below those of industry. Moreover, if the money earnings of agricultural workers are still below those of their urban cousins, their total incomes—including transfer payments—are relatively much lower. This ideological barrier to the granting of parity or more may prove to be immovable.

ORGANIZATION AND POLICY

The "campaigning" and unpredictable switches in policy and organization, which marked Khrushchev's term of office, have given way to a more sober and consistent style of agricultural management. It makes for duller reading for external observers, but it also must give rise to far fewer ulcers for Soviet farm managers and local officials. Indeed, perhaps the only major "subjective" policy switch in recent years has been Brezhnev's decision of 1970 to emphasize the numbers of livestock kept, to the possible detriment of the animal's productivity and to the short-term detriment of the livestock sector's labor productivity. Other policies may be questioned by agricultural specialists—the irrigation program is a case in point—but at least these goals have been unwaveringly pursued.

The trend toward concentration and specialization begun under Khrushchev and enshrined in the Party Program of 1961 has been expedited by Brezhnev, especially since the reassuring harvest of 1973. In developments roughly parallel with those in industry, individual farms are being merged into gigantic agroindustrial associations: These are held to represent the "highest synthesis and union of industry and agriculture . . . a qualitatively new stage in combining industry and agriculture."[164] To the decision-makers in Moscow, the economies of scale to be derived from further merging kolkhozes and sovkhozes, together with processing plants, may be self-evident. As Brezhnev sees it: "The time is now ripe for step-by-step transition from small farms and brigades to large-scale specialized production using industrial methods and extensive application of the achievements of science and technology."[165] Many Western (and Soviet) observers might not agree, feeling that the existing production units are already far too large and cumbersome.

For the foreseeable future, the two basic forms of agricultural production unit—the kolkhoz and the sovkhoz—are expected to coexist and to retain their separate identities within the framework of the vast agroindustrial complexes. To be sure, in recent years the sovkhoz sector has been gradually expanding, largely at the expense of the kolkhozes, although not with the momentum or underlying motivation of Khrushchev's sovkhozizatsiya. Between January 1966 and January 1974, the number of kolkhozes dropped from 36,900 to 31,500 and kolkhoz households from 15.4 million to 13.9 million, while the number of sovkhozes grew from 11,681 to 17,300.[166] Most of the new sovkhozes are specialized dairy, poultry, fruit, or vegetable farms established near large towns and industrial centers; an increasing number are gigantic livestock complexes with up to 16,000 head of cattle.[167]

A marked sblizhenie, or convergence between the two forms of agricultural enterprise, has taken place under the present administration. Sovkhozes operating under full khozraschet (financial autonomy) receive the same purchase prices as do kolkhozes for their output sold to the state, and they also finance their own investments. Both forms draw on Gosbank credits for replenishing their working capital. With the introduction of a guaranteed wage at scales roughly comparable with those obtaining on sovkhozes, and with improved pension and social security schemes, the remuneration of kolkhozniks for work performed in the public sector has drawn close to that of sovkhoz workers and employees. The formal differences between kolkhozes and sovkhozes are more apparent than real. Alec Nove lists two: "cooperative as opposed to state ownership, and elected as opposed to appointed management."[168] But one wonders if these subtleties are perceptible from the worm's eye view of the rank-and-file

kolkhoznik? In the judgment of the present author, the more meaningful distinction lies in the continuing discrimination practiced against
the kolkhoznik. He still has no assured right to an internal passport,
he is not guaranteed the freedom to change his employment whenever
he thinks fit, and many aspects of his every-day life are subject to
the arbitrary whim of the kolkhoz chairman, against whom he has no
effective redress.

As a vehicle for "perfecting kolkhoz democracy," the institution
of kolkhoz councils at all levels by the Third All-Union Congress of
Kolkhozniks has proved to be the bomb predicted at the time. When
the chairman of the all-union council is none other than the Soviet
Minister of Agriculture, then it is hardly surprising if its resolutions
mirror and augment party and state decrees. In the field of safe-
guarding their members' rights, the councils so far have been even
less effective than the industrial trade unions—if that is possible.
For example, a pronouncement of the All-Union Kolkhoz Council
condemned those kolkhozes that had allegedly distributed too much
of their gross incomes on pay and too little on accumulation.[169] The
hope that these bodies might provide at least a platform for pressure
groups to air the common interests of kolkhozes and kolkhozniks has
to date remained unfounded.

The present leadership can take much of the credit for the
expansion and development of the ancillary or subsidiary enterprises
of kolkhozes and sovkhozes. These are of great mutual benefit to the
whole economy and to the agricultural work force. Their gross output
in 1970 was estimated to be worth about 8.4 billion rubles, that is,
nearly one-tenth of the gross agricultural product, and it is expected
to grow to about 15 billion rubles by 1975.[170] These often tiny enterprises—employing only three on an annual average basis[171]—are
more responsive to consumer demand than are the cumbersome state
retail trading network and the Soviet Gossnab, and they tend to concentrate upon the simpler consumer and producer goods that are in
short supply. Their capital intensity is low—in 1968 the industrial
ancillary enterprises of kolkhozes accounted for only 2 percent of
the farms' fixed assets—and yet their profitability rate in that year
was 94.9 percent.[172] Moreover, they help to provide year-round
employment for the farmers. Of course, abuses occur—at least in
the eyes of the authorities—such as the kolkhoz ancillary enterprise
employing 230, of which only 21 belonged to the kolkhoz. This farm's
income from its ancillary enterprise in 1969 was twice as much as
from agricultural production.[173] But on the whole there is little
doubt that many of the more affluent farms are those with well-
developed ancillary enterprises—and it is these that have the most
chance of retaining their skilled cadres.

The discussion concerning the optimal size of an operational subunit is being carried on in a desultory fashion, although it is clear that many of the participants find it difficult to comprehend that diseconomies of scale can exist and equate optimal with maximal. Undeterred by their distinct setback at the kolkhozniks' congress in 1969, the proponents of the beznaryadnoe zveno, or "nonscheduled link, "[174] have kept up their lobbying, usually reserving their biggest guns for the slack season before plowing commences—and perhaps when the diet of their urban readers is least attractive.[175] Favorable references appear from time to time in the more authoritative specialist journals.[176]

Of course, the zveno has a great deal to be said for it: Clearly much could result from granting "meaningful operational autonomy to subunits where hard work and care for the land cultivated and for the implements utilized bring commensurate and tangible rewards." But critics—or sceptics—can point with some justification to the obverse side of the coin. Where is the additional equipment to come from? How are land and the available equipment to be apportioned between the subunits? What will happen to the millions of elderly, unskilled women who will, presumably, be left outside the zvenos? What raison d'etre would remain for the staffs of the parent farms?

The doughtiest champion of the zveno, Voronov, was unceremoniously retired. Neither the secretary-general, the secretary of the CPSU Central Committee responsible for agriculture, nor the current Soviet minister of agriculture appear to have said anything encouraging about the zveno and thus the prospects for its large-scale adoption are not bright.

The debate on land rent, initiated by Strumilin in 1967, [177] seems to have remained on a purely academic level and no party or government spokesman took a position. The discussion in Voprosy ekonomiki was purportedly closed, but subsequently a further article appeared that attacked the introduction of land rent on the grounds that it would imply adaptation to the present situation and would reinforce the existing weaknesses of specialization.[178]

In another realm of agricultural policy, namely rural reconstruction, battle has been joined by the opposing factions and the smoke is still too dense for us to see which side is winning. In theory, all nonproductive agricultural investment is to be allocated only to the 120,000 or so communities designated as perspektivnye (those with a future).[179] But the inhabitants of the remaining 600,000 neperspektivnye localities have either not been canvassed for their opinions on the matter or else they have been confronted with distinctly loaded questionnaires. For instance, one of these asked in effect: "Would you rather live in a two- or three-storied building complete with all amenities such as water, gas, electricity, heating, and sewage, or would you prefer to live in a one-family house without any amenities?"[180]

The shining urban-type settlements envisaged in the plans are evidently predicated on the construction of some 300 million square meters of living space, costing 40-45 billion rubles. Who is to finance this and how has not been made clear. About one-half of the new residential construction is expected to take the form of multistoried apartment buildings, but this type of accommodation has not always found favor with the prospective inmates. Indeed, in one sovkhoz, some of the new apartments remained empty, since the workers and employees preferred to pay rental for private accommodation where they could keep their own cattle.[181]

An increasing share of rural housing construction is to be financed through cooperatives: These enjoy more favorable deposit and credit terms than their urban counterparts.[182] Nevertheless, individual construction in the countryside has recently fallen sharply: During the period 1960-70 the completion of individual homes had dropped by nearly half for sovkhoz workers and employees and by 40 percent for kolkhozniks.[183] An obvious precondition to the full industrialization of agriculture is the construction of a network of all-weather roads. Yet no final decision appears to have been taken as to who shall pay for these roads: The costs will run into tens of billions of rubles and the time span into decades. The implied thrust of an article by the RSFSR deputy minister of Road Construction and Utilization was that the major burden of financing new rural roads must fall upon the rural population.[184] This could represent an intolerable load on the resources of the kolkhozes and khozraschet sovkhozes, akin to the strains imposed by the compulsory purchase of the machine-tractor station machinery after 1958.

The leadership's drive for autarky in all foodstuffs embraces some rather marginal products, and Soviet boasts of self-sufficiency in such items as rice and tea must be galling for the major third-world producers of these commodities, although their spokesmen have so far been remarkably reticent on this point at UNCTAD sessions.

Finally, despite the lip-service paid at the March 1965 plenum to the need for real operational autonomy for the farmer on the spot and the condemnation of "petty tutelage," sovkhoz directors and kolkhoz chairmen continue to be subjected to constant detailed supervision, "control," and meddling by local party, state, and procurement officials. During their lunch breaks, tractor-drivers are reportedly subjected to pep talks on their transistor radios.[185]

FOREIGN TRADE

As in the United States, Soviet external trade in agricultural products plays a marginal role in purely economic terms: The value of agricultural imports or exports in any given year probably never exceeds, say, 5 percent of the gross agricultural product. However, its political and strategic impact can be enormous. Thus, the 10.4 million tons of grain ordered from Western supplies in the wake of the 1963 setback was a major factor in Khrushchev's downfall. Similarly, the political repercussions of the over 40 million tons of grain imports ordered by the present Soviet leadership after the shortfalls of 1972 are too well known to require further elaboration here. The whole topic of Soviet foreign trade in agricultural products merits detailed analysis: Here we will merely touch upon the most sensitive aspect of grain exports and imports.

The abrupt switch in the Soviet grain trade in 1964-66 and the dramatic reversal in 1972-73 should be viewed in the perspective of Czarist and Soviet Russias that have traditionally been major net exporters of grain. It should be stressed that Soviet grain exports and imports cannot be equated in value terms: Exports go primarily to soft-currency areas, while imports come overwhelmingly from hard-currency nations.

Table 7.4 shows that during the three lean years (in terms of the grain trade balance) that followed the poor harvests of 1963 and 1965, the reduction of Soviet grain exports to its traditional customers—other than Cuba—was marked; at the same time, offerings on the hard-currency markets virtually ceased. Much the same happened in 1972 and 1973.

Nevertheless, with the bumper crop of 1973, the prospects for the grain trade balance are bright, and we may expect the Soviet Union to move comfortably into the black by 1975. The 2-million ton "loan" to India is just a harbinger of future Soviet largesse. Once the current import orders have been delivered, the prime requirement will be for high-quality feedstuffs. If it is to meet the animal products goals for 1975 and its "scientific norms" of meat consumption in the 1980s, the Soviet Union will need all the feed imports that it can afford.[186] Their volume will be limited by competition on the world market, by the Soviet hard-currency balance, and by the availability of credits. On the other hand, despite assurances to the contrary given to U.S. Secretary of Agriculture Butz by Eksportkhleb,[187] this observer would not be surprised if growing quantities of Soviet food grain were once more to be offered on the world market. Much will depend upon substitution possibilities and on the domestic and world relationships between the prices for food and feed grains.

TABLE 7.4

The Soviet Grain Trade Balance, 1961-73
(excluding groats and flour; thousands of metric tons)

	1961-63 Average	1964-66 Average	1967-69 Average	1970-71 Average	1972-73 Average
Total exports	7,185	3,800	6,286	7,169	4,707
of which to					
Cuba	375	491	507	562	546
Czechoslovakia	1,386	1,104	1,385	1,434	1,092
Egypt	—	—	533	—	—
East Germany	1,850	1,131	1,310	1,755	1,022
Hungary	284	131	222	270	—
North Korea	130	73	162	200	169
Poland	762	368	1,048	1,603	1,125
United Kingdom	511	—	226	293	—
Total imports	1,276	7,136	1,477	2,850	19,700
of which from					
Argentina	2	771	72	98	—
Australia	91	926	—	134	662
Canada	936	3,896	977	1,720	4,443
France	—	667	57	219	1,362
United States	—	595	—	—	11,305
Grain trade balance	+5,909	-3,336	+4,809	+4,319	-9,995

Note: For the record, this table assembles the official Soviet
data for the period 1961-73 on grain trade from the foreign trade handbooks for the respective years.
   Sources: Vneshtorg 62, 64, 65, 67, 69, 71, 73, passim.

Finally, in this connection a postscript might be added concerning Soviet cooperation on the world grain market. Although one
of the U.S.-Soviet agreements of 1972 provided for a much fuller
exchange of information about grain stocks, trade, and prospects,
as late as March 1974 it was reported that Moscow was not observing
its side of that particular bargain.[188] A further breach occurred
when a U.S. Department of Agriculture team was prevented from
touring certain virgin land regions in August 1974.[189] Masses of
data are promulgated on the condition of the soil, crops, and the
weather in all kinds of regions, but never a complete picture or an
overall authoritative estimate.[190] Of course forecasts are made, but
they are not published in advance! Thus, with great aplomb, one
authority patted himself on the back in 1973 for having predicted with
accuracy the outturn of 1972's poor harvest.[191] Another source

claimed, in 1974, "Life already proves the correctness of the predictions by Soviet scientists; for instance, the 1972 drought for these
areas [the Volga and Caspian] was predicted back in 1969."[192] We
have yet to see a Soviet prediction published in advance of the event.

FOOD CONSUMPTION

   The approach march to what are known to the "scientifically
determined norms of consumption"—not to mention what the Soviet
consumer feels he would like to eat—is proving to be a very
long haul. It is, perhaps, not accidental that the goals have been
trimmed somewhat in recent years. But, as Table 7.5 indicates,
even the reduced targets for meat, eggs, vegetables, and fruit are
hardly to be reached much before 1990 at the earliest at the anticipated
rates of progress.
   Soviet and U.S. categories and classifications differ so widely
that the juxtaposition in Table 7.5 should be taken merely as indicative. For instance, the TsSU's concept of edible meat and meat products is believed to embrace fats, offal, subproducts, and slaughter
fats that are generally excluded from Western measures.[193]
   The principal deficiency in the Soviet diet is the lack of high-
grade protein from meat. Although a leading member of VASKhNIL
believes that this shortfall can be made good by 1985 or so,[194] many
Western observers would be less optimistic. On the other hand, the
Soviet consumer's intake of protein is already being augmented from
other sources. His consumption of fish is already at or near the
optimum level. Meanwhile, much is being done in the area of synthetic
foods. One leading practitioner, Academician A.N. Nesmeyanov,
perfected the art to the stage where he could distribute artificial
meat, rice, and caviar to his audience.[195] However, most of the
output of synthetic protein from petroleum and gas is destined to take
the longer route through the animals' stomachs and it is apparently
not being sold direct to the public in the form of meat "extenders."[196]

CONCLUSION

   During the Seven-Year Plan period (1959-65), the growth of the
Soviet gross agricultural product (15 percent) and net agricultural
product (14 percent) barely kept pace with that of the population (12
percent). With the program outlined at the March 1965 plenum and
rather consistently implemented since then, Khrushchev's successors

TABLE 7.5

Soviet Per Capita Consumption of Selected Staple Foodstuffs
(kilograms per annum)

Foodstuff	Norm 1965	Norm 1969	1965	1973	1975P	U.S. 1971
Bread and grain products	120	120	156	145	—	65
Potatoes	120	97	142	124	—	66
Vegetables and melons	164	146	72	85	109	81*
Meat and meat products	87	82	41	52	59	110
Milk and milk products	467	433	251	307	340	254
Eggs (units)	365	292	124	194	192	321
Sugar	44	36	34	41	43	46
Fish and fish products	—	18	13	16	22	5
Fruit and berries	—	112	28	40	—	48

*Excludes melons and certain categories of vegetable.
Sources: "Scientifically determined norm" 1965: Planirovanie
narodnogo khozyaistva SSSR (Moscow: Ekonomika, 1965), p. 421;
"Scientifically determined norm" 1969: Planovoe khozyaistvo, no. 12
(1969), p. 49; Ekonomika sel'skogokhozyaistva, no. 12 (1969),
pp. 18-24; Literaturnaya gazeta, no. 8 (1971), p. 10. The "milk
norm" has apparently been further reduced to 405 kilograms per
annum, Vestnik selskokhozyaistvennoi nauki, no. 4 (1974), p. 107;
1965 & 1973 actual: SSSR v tsifrakh v 1973 godu, p. 190; 1975P:
Ninth Five-Year Plan, p. 300; U.S. 1971: Statistical Abstract of
the United States, 1972, p. 84 and U.S. Department of Agriculture
data.

have provided the preconditions for a more stable, sustained rate of
agricultural growth. In the ten years from 1966 through 1975, the
gross agricultural product is expected to rise by nearly one-half and
the marketed output by much more. This has been achieved at a
tremendous and incommensurate cost.

With practically no more new land to be brought under the plow,
the prime determinants for this restored growth have been massive
material inputs of machinery, chemicals, and land improvement
together with higher earnings for farmers that have substantially
narrowed the income differentials between country and town. To
ensure profitability for high-cost agricultural operations, the authorities have raised producer prices while keeping retail prices for
agricultural products stable. The consequence has been an agricultural price support bill that is the highest in the world, both in

absolute terms and in relation to the national income. In addition to
the above overt costs, there are the large but incalculable hidden
costs of the agricultural sector arising from the mobilization and
transportation of millions of men and women and hundreds of thousands
of trucks and tractors from other sectors of the economy and often
from distant locations to aid with the harvest each year.

The setback of 1972 was attributable to a combination of unpre-
cedentedly vicious weather, low stocks, and to the usual inefficiencies
that were aggravated and highlighted by the climate. Apart from this
aberration, the present leadership may be said to have largely resolved the food grain problem where its predecessors had failed. Its
main task for the foreseeable future is to raise the output and consumption levels of meat from their quantitatively and qualitatively
low levels. The course chosen for the rest of this administration at
least is the further concentration and industrialization of the agricultural sector and its fuller integration into the economy.

Most of the over 40 million tons of grain imported in 1972-74
was food grain. From 1975 on, the Soviet Union is expected to resume
its traditional role as a net exporter of food grains, although it will
have a continuing requirement for as much imported feedstuffs as it
can afford if the long-term consumption goals for meat and animal
products are to be met.

For decades the Soviet rural population has served as a reser-
voir of manpower for industry. This is virtually over and, for the
most part, the current labor surplus in the Soviet countryside consists
of elderly and predominantly female unskilled hands. With the belated
switch to the industrialization of agricultural production and the fateful
decision to substitute capital for labor, the remaining skilled and
flexible younger cadres, as well as the rural youth coming onto the
labor market, must somehow be induced to remain on the farms.
Without these skilled cadres, the capital inputs already made and
those projected for the future cannot effectively be exploited. But
how can they be persuaded to stay on the farm? This is now the most
crucial problem of Soviet agriculture to be resolved by the leadership.
Ideological barriers prevent the award of parity, let alone a higher
scale of remuneration for the farmer than is awarded to his industrial
counterpart, yet some form of additional compensation will be needed
to offset the irregular working hours, the seasonality of employment,
the exposure to the elements, and the primitive living conditions
throughout much of the countryside.

A respectable rate of growth of agricultural output by international standards has been achieved at an immoderate cost. This
might be viewed as a partial redress for the decades during which
the peasant bore most of the burden of financing Soviet industrialization: Now other sectors are being denuded to finance the

industrialization of agriculture. The plans that have been promulgated
for the future envisage further modest rates of growth, again at an
exorbitant cost in terms of scarce resources and alternatives foregone.
But short of changing its system of socialized agriculture, the Soviet
leadership has no visible alternative. On political, strategic, and
economic grounds, it has opted for a course of virtual autarky in all
staple foodstuffs and agricultural raw materials for industry.

In the absence of basic changes in agricultural planning and
management, the forthcoming decade may witness again a more than
doubling of material inputs into the agricultural sector in order to
obtain less than a 50 percent increase in output. Capital productivity
in the public sector of agriculture will continue to diminish at a rapid
rate with inevitable effects upon overall economic growth.

The task of creating a modern infrastructure throughout the
countryside to complement the industrialization of agriculture has
been largely deferred by the authorities, although the nonchernozem
program represents a belated start in this direction. The produce of
sophisticated agrotechnology is often prevented from reaching the
consumer by an archaic transportation and distribution system, and
the need for the private sector is thereby ensured for many years to
come.

Finally, it is understandable that Soviet agricultural performance
should be compared with that of the United States or of Western Europe.
Yet it must not be overlooked that the Soviet Union is comparatively
poorly endowed in terms of agricultural land and climate. Thus under
any system of farming, agricultural labor and/or capital productivity
would probably be appreciably lower than in the United States or
Western Europe. Nevertheless, so much more could be done with the
existing labor and capital resources if a distinction could be made
between the optimal and the maximal size of production unit, if
meaningful operational autonomy were ceded to the farmers on the
spot, if the potential of the private sector were to be freed from the
ideologically imposed limitations, and if a more tangible link were
to be established between effort and reward. But these may have to
wait upon a change in the style and content of Soviet leadership.

NOTES

1. For further details, see Keith Bush, "The Eighth and Ninth
Five-Year Plans for Soviet Agriculture," L'Est, no. 3 (1970) and
"Soviet Agriculture in the 1970s," Studies on the Soviet Union, no. 3
(1971).

2. This was spelled out in Finansy SSSR, no. 3 (1969), p. 16.

SOVIET AGRICULTURE: NEW MANAGEMENT   197

3. Pravda, July 20, 1974.
4. Ibid.
5. Ekonomika selskogo khozyaistva, no. 2 (1971), p. 37.
6. Sotsialistichesky trud, no. 10 (1970), p. 24.
7. See, for instance, Ekonomika sel'skogo khozyaistva, no. 12 (1973), p. 8.
8. For example, the construction costs of livestock buildings rose on average by 65-70 percent between 1964 and 1969, (Sel'skaya zhinan', July 24, 1970).
9. L.I. Brezhnev, Voprosy agrarnoi politiki KPSS i osvoenie tselinnykh zemel'Kazakhstana (Moscow: Politizdat, 1974), p. 351.
10. See Zakupki sel'skokhozyaistvennykh produktov, no. 9 (1973), p. 44.
11. See, FAO, Monthly Bulletin of Agricultural Economics and Statistics, no. 2 (1970), p. 21.
12. Ekonomika sel'skogo khozyaistva, no. 1 (1974), pp. 47, 48.
13. SSSR v tsifrakh v 1973 godu, p. 7.
14. Thus conversion ratios for agricultural investment ranged from 9 percent (Vestnik statistiki, no. 5 [1970], p. 89) to 19 percent (Pravda, December 9, 1970).
15. Pravda, December 19, 1972.
16. For detailed examination of Soviet investment in recent years, see Keith Bush "Soviet Capital Investment Since Khrushchev," Soviet Studies, July 1972, pp. 91-96 and "Resource Allocation Policy: Capital Investment," in Soviet Economic Prospects for the Seventies, U.S. Congress, Joint Economic Committee, 93d Cong., 1st Sess. (Washington, D.C.: U.S. Government Printing Office, 1973), pp. 39-44.
17. Izvestia Akademii Nauk SSSR—Seriya ekonomicheskaya, no. 6 (1970), p. 28.
18. Ibid., p. 24.
19. See Finansy SSSR, no. 10 (1970), p. 4; Ekonomika sel'skogo khozyaistva, no. 11 (1970), p. 5 and no. 2 (1971), p. 37.
20. Finansy SSSR, no. 12 (1973), p. 33.
21. Finansy SSSR, no. 10 (1970), p. 4.
22. Voprosy ekonomiki, no. 4 (1973), p. 58.
23. Ekonomika sel'skogo khozyaistva, no. 5 (1972), p. 96.
24. Voprosy ekonomiki, no. 2 (1971), p. 26.
25. Izvestia Akademii Nauk SSSR—Seriya ekonomicheskaya, no. 6 (1970), p. 27.
26. Ekonomika sel'skogo khozyaistva, no. 12 (1973), p. 8.
27. Voprosy ekonomiki, no. 3 (1970), p. 117.
28. Izvestia Akademii Nauk SSSR—Seriya ekonomicheskaya, no. 6 (1970), p. 26.
29. Voprosy ekonomiki, no. 2 (1971), p. 29.

30. Ekonomika sel'skogo khozyaistva, no. 1 (1971), p. 37.
31. Vestnik sel'skokhozyaistvennoi nauki, no. 11 (1970), p. 2.
32. Izvestia Sibirskogo Otdeleniye AN SSSR, no. 11 (1970), p. 78.
33. Ekonomika sel'skogo khozyaistva, no. 2 (1971), p. 46.
34. Gosudarstvenny pyatiletni plan razvitiya narodnogo khozyaistva SSSR na 1971-1975 gody (hereafter cited as Ninth Five-Year Plan), pp. 182, 183; SSSR v tsifrakh v 1973 godu, p. 123.
35. Finansy SSSR, no. 10 (1970), p. 10.
36. Sel'skaya zhizn', April 26, 1973.
37. Ekonomicheskaya gazeta, no. 14 (1973), p. 2.
38. See Finansy SSSR, no. 10 (1970), p. 11.
39. Ekonomika sel'skogo khozyaistva, no. 11 (1970), p. 44.
40. Selskaya zhizn', April 26, 1973.
41. See Finansy SSSR, no. 10 (1970), p. 11.
42. Sotsialisticheskaya industriya, October 1, 1970.
43. Vestnik sel'skokhozyaistvennoi nauki, no. 11 (1970), p. 2.
44. Voprosy ekonomiki, no. 7 (1973), p. 42.
45. Finansy SSSR, no. 12 (1970), pp. 18, 19.
46. Izvestia, August 6, 1970.
47. Sel'skaya zhizn', July 12, 1970.
48. Ekonomika selskogo khozyaistva, no. 9 (1970), p. 64.
49. Pravda, May 11, 1974.
50. Ekonomika sel'skogo khozyaistva, no. 8 (1973), p. 26.
51. Agitator, no. 3 (1971), p. 10.
52. Drawn from Ekonomika sel'skogo khozyaistva, no. 2 (1971), p. 39; Ninth Five-Year Plan, pp. 346, 350, and Pravda, March 16, 1974.
53. Izvestia Sibirskogo Otdeleniya AN SSSR, no. 11 (1970), p. 82.
54. Khimicheskaya promyshlennost, no. 9 (1970), pp. 3, 4 and Kommunist, no. 18 (1970), p. 54.
55. Vestnik Akademii Nauk SSSR, no. 11 (1970), p. 18.
56. Ekonomika sel'skogo khozyaistva, no. 12 (1970), p. 6.
57. Voprosy ekonomiki, no. 2 (1971), p. 25.
58. Izvestia Sibirskogo Otdeleniya AN SSSR, no. 11 (1970), p. 84.
59. Ekonomika sel'skogo khozyaistva, no. 7 (1973), p. 32.
60. Ekonomika sel'skogo khozyaistva, no. 12 (1970), p. 8.
61. For a detailed study, see Radio Liberty Dispatch (RL 153/74), "The Belated Decision to Develop Agriculture in the RSFSR's Nonchernozem Zone," May 27, 1974.
62. Radio Moscow-1, 1130 GMT, January 16, 1974.
63. Vestnik sel'skokhozyaistvennoi nauki, no. 3 (1974), p. 10. (Of course, it all depends on what you mean by "irrigation.")

64. Voprosy ekonomiki, no. 11 (1973), p. 30.
65. Vestnik sel'skokhozyaistvennoi nauki, no. 5 (1973), p. 120;
See Znanie, no. 12 (1971), p. 13.
66. A comprehensive survey of the mid-1974 status of the
land improvement program in the Soviet Union is given in Radio
Liberty Dispatch (RL 187/74), "The Program for Land Development
in the U.S.S.R.," June 25, 1974.
67. Ekonomika sel'skogo khozyaistva, no. 11 (1973), pp. 9,
10.
68. Gidrotekhnika i melioratsiya, no. 1 (1959), p. 9.
69. Pravda, October 2, 1963.
70. Anatolii Ivashchenko, Radio Moscow-1, 1200 GMT,
February 24, 1974.
71. Using a shadow price of 34-40 kopeks per cubic meter of
water (Ekonomika sel'skogo khozyaistva, no. 12 [1969], p. 59). A
more recent source has priced water at 1.60 rubles per cubic meter
(Izvestia, December 15, 1973).
72. Derived from Zemledelie, no. 6 (1969), p. 53; Narkhoz
68, p. 349; Pravda, February 5, 1971; and Ekonomika selskogo
khozyaistva, no. 3 (1974), p. 14.
73. Zakupki sel'skokhozyaistvennykh produktov, no. 3 (1968),
p. 10.
74. Pravda, May 25, 1966.
75. The lower end of the bracket was given by TASS, December 10, 1970 and Ekonomika selskogo khozyaistva, no. 2 (1971),
p. 39, while the higher is taken from Znanie, no. 11 (1973), p. 40.
76. Plenum TsK KPSS, 24-26 marta 1965 g. Stenografichesky
otchet (Moscow: Politizdat, 1965), p. 130.
77. Finansy SSSR, no. 2 (1967), p. 34; no. 3 (1969), p. 16;
no. 10 (1970), p. 7; no. 5 (1971), p. 65; no. 9 (1972), p. 45; no. 12
(1973), pp. 31, 35; and no. 5 (1974), pp. 37-47.
78. A.M. Birman, Ocherki teorii Sovetskikh finansov, Vypusk
vtoroi (Moscow: Finansy, 1972), p. 72; V.N. Semenov, Rol'finansov
i kredita v razvitii sel'skogo khozyaistva (Moscow: Finansy, 1973),
passim.
79. Thus three billion rubles were paid out in 1965-69 for above-
plan grain surpayments (Finansy SSSR, no. 10 [1970], p. 6).
80. Voprosy ekonomiki, no. 10 (1970), p. 49.
81. Constance B. Krueger, "A Note on the Size of Subsidies on
Soviet Government Purchases of Agricultural Products," The ACES
Bulletin Fall 1974, pp. 63-69.
82. Pravda, July 20, 1974.
83. Izvestia, August 2, 1974
84. Pravda, December 13, 1973.
85. Krueger, op. cit., p. 63.

86. The national income in 1973 was 337.8 billion rubles (produced) and 333.8 billion rubles (utilized): SSSR v tsifrakh v 1973 godu, p. 175.

87. Financy SSSR, no. 10 (1970), p. 7.

88. See Keith Bush, "Les prix de detail a Moscou et dans quatre villes occidentales en novembre 1971," Revue de l'Est, January 1974, pp. 55-57.

89. See, for instance, Narkhoz 72, p. 697.

90. Based on procurement and retail prices for meat given in Voprosy ekonomiki, no. 8 (1970), p. 42.

91. For example, A.M. Emelyanov, Ekonomicheskie sotsial'nye problemy industrializatsii sel'skogo khozyaistva, no. 12 (1973), pp. 63, 64.

92. Izvestia Akademii Nauk SSSR—Seriya ekonomicheskaya, No. 6 (1970), p. 31.

93. Details were given in Ekonomicheskaya gazeta, no. 25 (1967), p. 11; Selskaya zhizn, July 14, 1967; Sel'sky mekhanizator, no. 11 (1967), p. 37.

94. Finansy SSSR, no. 10 (1970), p. 6. A later article in Ekonomika selskogo khozyistva, no. 8 (1974), pp. 17-24, suggested that this subsidy had grown substantially in subsequent years.

95. See Keith Bush, "Agricultural Reforms Since Khrushchev," in New Directions in the Soviet Economy (Washington: U.S. Government Printing Office, 1966), pp. 456-61.

96. A loss-making exception remains potatoes: see Voprosy ekonomiki, no. 7 (1973), pp. 46, 47.

97. Izvestia Akademii Nauk SSSR—Seriya ekonomicheskaya, no. 6 (1970), p. 22.

98. Finansy SSSR, no. 10 (1970), p. 6.

99. Ekonomicheskaya gazeta, no. 25 (1967), p. 11.

100. For a recent complaint, see Voprosy ekonomiki, no. 7 (1973), pp. 46-48.

101. Izvestia Akademii Nauk SSSR—Seriya ekonomicheskaya, no. 6 (1970), pp. 29-30.

102. Voprosy ekonomiki, no. 10 (1970), p. 48.

103. Voprosy ekonomiki, no. 12 (1970), p. 56. It might be noted that the private sector still accounts for most of the poultry.

104. Ibid., p. 53.

105. Ibid., p. 57.

106. Ibid., p. 56.

107. Zakupki sel'skokhozyaistvennykh produktov, no. 11 (1970), p. 29.

108. Vestnik sel'skokhozyaistvennoi nauki, no. 1 (1971), p. 61.

109. Zakupki sel'skokhozyaistvennykh produktov, no. 4 (1972), p. 3.

110. Zakupki Sel'skokhozyaistvennykh produktov, no. 3 (1973), p. 6.

111. See, for instance, Izvestia Akademii Nauk SSSR—Seriya ekonomicheskaya, no. 6 (1970), p. 22.

112. For example, Voprosy ekonomiki, no. 8 (1970), p. 5.

113. Izvestia Akademii Nauk SSSR—Seriya ekonomicheskaya, no. 6 (1970), p. 24.

114. Ibid., p. 31.

115. Ibid., p. 24.

116. Ibid., p. 25.

117. See Agitator, no. 16 (1970), p. 7.

118. Ninth Five-Year Plan, p. 349; see Zakupki sel'skokhozyaistvennykh produktov, no. 10 (1970), p. 17; Agitator, no. 16 (1970), p. 6.

119. See, for instance, Zakupki sel'skokhozyaistvennykh produktov, no. 11 (1970), p. 20 and no. 12 (1970), p. 22; Voprosy ekonomiki, no. 7 (1974), p. 49.

120. Voprosy ekonomiki, no. 10 (1970), p. 63.

121. Ekonomika sel'skogo khozyaistva, no. 7 (1970), p. 14.

122. Ninth Five-Year Plan, p. 349; See Zakupki sel'skokhozyaistvennykh produktov, no. 12 (1970), p. 22.

123. Zakupki, op. cit., p. 3.

124. Ekonomicheskaya gazeta, no. 40 (1970), p. 18.

125. Zakpuki sel'skokhozyaistvennykh produktov, no. 10 (1970), p. 18.

126. Ibid., p. 17. For a recent criticism, see Ekonomika sel'skogo khozyaistva, no. 12 (1973), p. 84.

127. Sovetskaya Rossiya, January 5, 1971.

128. For example, Novyi Mir, no. 9 (1965), pp. 212-29.

129. The definitive work on this subject is Karl-Eugen Waedekin, The Private Sector in Soviet Agriculture (Berkeley: University of California Press, 1973).

130. Izvestia Akademii Nauk SSSR—Seriya ekonomicheskaya, no. 6 (1970), p. 32.

131. Ekonomika sel'skogo khozyaistva, no. 1 (1971), p. 41.

132. Ibid.

133. Derived from Ninth Five-Year Plan, p. 193.

134. I.A. Gorlanov, Torzhestvo Leninskogo kooperativnogo plana (Moscow: Znanie, 1970), p. 27.

135. Voprosy ekonomiki, no. 11 (1970), p. 94.

136. See the ambivalent treatment of this topic in Literaturnaya gazeta, no. 28 (1970), p. 10.

137. Zakupki sel'skokhozyaistvennykh produktov, no. 11 (1970), p. 33.

138. Sel'skaya zhizn', February 3, 1970.

139. For instance, Sovetskaya Kirghiziya, December 9, 1970.

140. Ekonomika sel'skogo khozyaistva, no. 11 (1970), pp. 38, 39.

141. Izvestia Akademii Nauk SSSR—Seriya ekonomicheskaya, no. 6 (1970), p. 33.

142. Izvestia, May 14, 1965.

143. Handelsblatt, June 19, 1969.

144. Sovetskaya torgovlya, May 23, 1970.

145. For instance, Izvestia, July 31, 1970.

146. Sel'skaya zhizn', May 15, 1973.

147. The last mention seems to have been in Kommunist (Lithuania), no. 1 (1967), pp. 5-11.

148. SSSR v tsifrakh v 1973 godu, pp. 127, 131.

149. Voprosy ekonomiki, no. 9 (1970), p. 101.

150. The pension is based on the average annual earnings during the five highest-paid years of service.

151. Kommunist, no. 4 (1968), pp. 53-59.

152. Derived from Narkhoz 69, pp. 389, 427.

153. Voprosy ekonomiki, no. 7 (1973), p. 43.

154. Ekonomika sel'skogo khozyaistva, no. 2 (1971), p. 40. A more recent decree stipulates the establishment of centers on kolkhozes and sovkhozes for the purpose of retraining those cadres who have remained on the land (Pravda, August 10, 1974).

155. Trud, May 11, 1974.

156. Pravda, June 5, 1970.

157. Ekonomika sel'skogo khozyaistva, no. 12 (1970), p. 101.

158. Izvestia Akademii Nauk SSSR—Seriya ekonomicheskaya, no. 6 (1970), p. 30.

159. Sotsialisticheski trud, no. 10 (1970), p. 21.

160. Planovoye khozyaistvo, no. 2 (1971), p. 53 & no. 3, (1971), p. 14.

161. Izvestia, August 3, 1974.

162. Such as N. Ya. Bromley in Voprosy istorii, no. 7 (1966), pp. 3-17 and even the invaluable Emelyanov in Izvestia Akademii Nauk SSSR—Seriya ekonomicheskaya, no. 6 (1970), pp. 20-33.

163. Zhurnalist, no. 5 (1970), p. 28; See Sovetskaya Kirghiziya, March 25, 1970.

164. Ekonomika sel'skogo khozyaistva, no. 1 (1974), pp. 50, 51.

165. Pravda, December 16, 1973.

166. SSSR v tsifrakh v 1973 godu, p. 131.

167. Ekonomika sel'skogo khozyaistva, no. 10 (1973), pp. 45, 46.

168. Alec Nove, "Soviet Agriculture Under Brezhnev," Slavic Review, September 1970, p. 390.

169. Sel'skaya zhizn', January 20, 1971.

170. Literaturnaya gazeta, no. 8 (1971), p. 3.
171. Voprosy ekonomiki, no. 8 (1970), p. 136.
172. Ibid., pp. 135, 136.
173. Finansy SSSR, no. 12 (1970), p. 17.
174. The system rejoices under the full title of beznaryadnaya akkordnopremialnaya sistema, which could be translated as "the nonscheduled-payment-by-job-plus-bonus system"!
175. For instance, Sovetskaya Rossiya, March 17, 1970 and January 7, 1971; Kosomolskaya pravda, March 17, 1970; Leninskoye znamya, March 25, 1970; Izvestia, July 17, 1974.
176. See Planovoye khozyaistvo, no. 8 (1970), p. 5; Voprosy ekonomiki, no. 10 (1970), p. 45. The latest seems to have been in Ekonomika sel'skogo khozyaistva, no. 12 (1973), pp. 24, 25. For an excellent historical review of the zveno debate, the reader is referred to Dimitry Pospielovsky, "The 'Link System' in Soviet Agriculture," Soviet Studies, April 1970, pp. 411-35.
177. Voprosy ekonomiki, no. 8 (1967), pp. 60-72.
178. Voprosy ekonomiki, no. 10 (1970), p. 45.
179. Voprosy ekonomiki, no. 11 (1970), p. 94.
180. Ibid., pp. 94-104.
181. Ibid., p. 100.
182. Zhilishchnoye stroitelstvo, no. 11 (1970), p. 12.
183. Voprosy ekonomiki, no. 5 (1973), p. 41.
184. Pravda, March 15, 1971.
185. Sel'skaya zhizn', July 11, 1973.
186. A study by David Schoonover of the USDA's Economic Research Service suggested a "feed gap" of some 100 million tons by 1985, Prospects for Agricultural Trade with the U.S.S.R. (Washington, D.C.: USDA, 1973), p. 39. However, this projection was made before the announcement of the program for land improvement in the nonchernozem area of the RSFSR, which should correct part of the feed deficit.
187. USIA, November 20, 1973.
188. Washington Post, March 22, 1974.
189. International Herald Tribune, September 7/8, 1974.
190. Modesty almost prevents us from recording that Radio Liberty has forecast the Soviet grain crop to within 5 percent of the declared outturn in nine out of the ten past years. The exception was in 1973, when our estimate was 10 percent down.
191. Vestnik sel'skokhozyaistvennoi nauki, no. 5 (1973), p. 112.
192. TASS, May 14, 1974.
193. On this, see Luba Richter, "Some Remarks on Soviet Agricultural Statistics," The American Statistician, June 1961.
194. Sel'skaya zhizn', December 25, 1973.
195. Vestnik Akademii Nauk SSSR, no. 4 (1970), p. 98.

196. Recent reports on Soviet progress in the field of synthetic foods have appeared in Izvestia, March 27, 1973; Pravda, August 5, 1973; Izvestia, October 23, 1973; TASS December 27, 1973, and Radio Leningrad, 0650 GMT, March 7, 1974; Vestnik sel'skokhozyaistvennoi nauki, no. 4 (1974), p. 113; Sel'skoya zhizn', September 5, 1974.

8

THE PROBLEMS OF THE "AGRARIAN-INDUSTRIAL COMPLEXES" IN THE SOVIET UNION
Arcadius Kahan

In their quest for increased efficiency in agricultural production, the Soviet decision-makers have subjected the farms during the last two decades to a variety of pressures and transformations. One is reminded of the measures to increase the level of agricultural prices, of the policy of farm mergers, that resulted in a reduction of the number and spectacular growth of the average size of farms, followed by a mass conversion of collective farms into state farms. These measures coincided with the expansion of the grain area into the so-called new lands and the attempts to increase the production of feed grains to raise the level of livestock production. It is also necessary to mention the introduction of economic accounting (Khozraschet) into the state farms, on the one hand, and the major increases in the supply of mineral fertilizers as well as the huge investments in land amelioration and land improvement on the other. It is necessary to keep all this in mind in order to appreciate the combination of efforts designed to increase the quantity and quality of conventional inputs into agriculture and the organizational or institutional changes that were directed to act as stimuli to increase the level of efficiency either via higher prices and farm incomes or via less arbitrary planning practices.

The purpose of this chapter is to consider the issue of the so-called agrarian-industrial complexes within the context of the search by Soviet decision-makers for new solutions to the problems of relative inefficiency of the performance of the agricultural sector. The fact that the problems of "agrarian-industrial complexes" might be at this point only peripheral to the task of solving problems of greater urgency is not significant. It indicates on the decision-makers' part an increased awareness that there is no single panacea to difficult problems.

VERTICAL INTEGRATION OF AGRICULTURAL AND
INDUSTRIAL SECTORS

The decision to instigate and to encourage a debate on the role of agrarian-industrial complexes, which is a debate on the problems of vertical integration of agricultural and primary processing industry, seems to indicate that the Soviet planners and decision-makers have concluded that there are no more economies of scale to be achieved either in the horizontal integration of farm units, or in the transformation of collective into state farms, and especially with respect to the latter that there is not much magic left in the distinction between the cooperative property principle upon which the collective farms are based and the "higher" stage of national or social property principle of the state farms. The a priori past assumption that a national property arrangement results automatically in higher output at lower costs could simply not be supported by available evidence. Thus, the discussion that began in the last few years has turned toward a number of options, none very revolutionary in their nature, many directed toward the solution of "minor" ills plaguing Soviet agriculture for decades.

The problems of vertical integration deal with the links of the agricultural and industrial sectors. They include the area of both inputs in the agricultural process (fuel, energy, machinery, construction materials), as well as the food processing and raw material supply to industry and thus are related to the consumer goods market, as well as to the problems of labor force utilization. Therefore, they constitute a convenient vehicle for the exchange of views and ideas, leading by implication to some fundamental problems of the role of agriculture in the Soviet economy. Since the discussions are still under way, while the actions to be implemented are still not decisive to make much difference either in the actual pattern of resource allocation, or in the basic institutional arrangements, one ought to reserve judgment as to the final outcome and its likely impact. In addition, keeping in line with the recent policies in agriculture, the solutions will most probably be applied gradually, leaving room for a process of learning by doing, rather than in the form of a major institutional and policy break. In fact, Soviet economists and officials participating in the debate thus far do not use any specific, uniform definition of the "agrarian-industrial complex." The various authors feel free, after providing the dictionary translation of the Latin term "complex," to provide their own interpretation of what an agrarian-industrial complex is or ought to be. Some of the writers include in the definition a contractual arrangement of trade and exchange between farms, as an embryonic form of activity leading toward the subsequent

establishment of a "complex."[1] But for the majority of Soviet economists the term denotes a variety of interactions between institutions
of two branches of the economy, agriculture and industry.

It is, however, characteristic of the debate so far that one of
the most important aspects of the agrarian-industrial complex, which
is hardly touched upon in the discussions by the Soviet economists, is
that of supply of capital goods and some of the important current inputs
to the agricultural sector.

According to the data on capital investment, the shares of investments in agriculture are impressive, and in terms of the flow of
machinery to the farms, reclaimed or irrigated land or mineral
fertilizer, no one would claim that agriculture is being starved of
funds or of goods. Nevertheless, economists have no reason to re-
joice or the policy-makers no reason to rest on laurels given the rate
of return of this flow of capital investments or current inputs. To put
this in other words, the decline of the rate of return on capital in
Soviet agriculture, as far as one could make sense out of the published data, started earlier than it would have been warranted given
the relative size of the capital or the rate of its increment. It is
possible, and perhaps probable as some Soviet economists claim, that
the distribution of capital among the various sectors of production,
or the composition of its supply, is suboptimal.[2]

A closer reading of the literature suggests that much of the
"new" technology does not meet the expectations or specifications of
the farms. Thus, Soviet agricultural organization has not yet resolved
the fundamental problem of responsiveness of the industrial sector
to the demands by the farms. There is no doubt that in this very
important area of interindustry relationships, the mere establishment
of agrarian-industrial complexes as a form of vertical integration of
agriculture and the food industry will not resolve the problems that
are much more fundamental and can be changed only by the supreme
decision-makers on a national level rather than on the local level. It
is therefore other problems, namely those on interaction between
agriculture and industry, at the stage of utilization of the agricultural
output, that the Soviet economists emphasize. It harks back to the
old problem of "links" between the two sectors, a problem that, at
least the Soviet historians would continuously assure everyone, was
solved a long time ago.

THE RURAL INDUSTRIES

As with so many of the issues raised in recent Soviet discussions
the problems of agrarian-industrial complexes have historical

precedents in debates or abortive attempts of the 1920s and 1930s.
But it is not the history that is of interest in our considerations, but
rather the circumstances that left a lasting impact upon the subsequent
development. In this particular case, the indisputable fact was that
the rapid pace of collectivization and the social conditions under which
it took place caused the virtual destruction of most of the rural industries, which either provided during the earlier period necessary inputs
into the small-scale peasant economy or specialized in the primary
processing of a substantial portion of the marketable agricultural
output. The labor force of the rural industries was either dispersed,
shifted to agricultural production, or entered large-scale industry;
the capital equipment of such industries was either merged into larger-
scale enterprises or went into disrepair. Under such circumstances,
until large-scale industry was achieving the capacity to supply inputs
for agriculture or until larger-scale centralized food processing
plants could absorb and process at relatively low costs the agricultural
products, the idea of vertical integration between agriculture and
industry remained wishful thinking, or a utopia to be accomplished
by future generations.

A cursory view of the number and type of industrial enterprises
existing within the farms in the Soviet Union during 1970 might provide
some background for the following discussion.

However, after 1953 when the Soviet decision-makers had
rediscovered the rural areas and faced up to the most urgent needs
of the farms, a gradual and slow revival of the rural small-scale
industry started. Industrial shops for the repair of equipment (later
amplified by the transfer of the machine-tractor station repair shops
to the farms), electrical energy generating plants, flour mills, wood-
working shops, flax-scutching establishments, small-scale dairy
plants, etc., began to be developed by the collective and state farms
that were themselves growing in size. The difficulties in obtaining
spare parts for their machinery, the low-density of an electrical
network previously designed to supply large-scale industry and larger
population centers, coupled with the insufficient capacity of the food-
processing industry, not prepared to handle an increased output of
agricultural commodities, dictated the development of small-scale
industrial shops and establishments in order to meet urgent needs,
even in the short run, because of the imperfection of the links between
agriculture and industry affecting both production and distribution.

A cursory view of the number and type of industrial enterprises
existing within the farms in the Soviet Union during 1970 might provide
some background for the following discussion.

Table 8.1, although far from complete, suggests that the productive capacity of this small-scale industry network was being
utilized for the following tasks: (1) to produce raw materials for
construction that takes place within the farms; (2) to repair agricultural
machinery and equipment; (3) to generate electrical power for farm
operations and household use;[3] (4) to provide primary processing for

TABLE 8.1

1970 Selected Industrial Enterprises of Soviet Collective and
State Farms by Major Regions

	Soviet Union	RSFSR	Ukraine	Kazakhstan	Moldavia
Electric stations	19,249	12,913	1,232	3,729	100
Machine repair shops	56,073	29,878	12,760	1,305	828
Saw mills	39,635	21,609	9,028	1,664	533
Woodworking	17,679	7,383	6,302	1,517	303
Bricks and ceramics	2,952	1,387	935	318	14
Other construction materials	3,162	1,085	1,139	526	93
Flour and grist mills	39,422	20,149	9,560	719	527
Vegetable oil and fats	2,391	572	1,240	11	212
Vegetables and fruits	2,405	798	1,018	70	97
Wine making	1,740	234	856	25	333
Total above	184,708	96,008	44,070	9,884	3,040

Source: TsSU SSSR, Sel'skoe Khoziaistvo SSSR (Moscow, 1971), pp. 572-73, 656-57.

209

products that are being used as inputs within agriculture itself (for example, preparation of grain feed); (5) to provide primary processing of agricultural products for the consumption of the agricultural population; (6) to provide primary processing of agricultural products for the urban market.

Thus, we are confronted with a decentralized network of enterprises engaged in industrial production, integrated within the particular farms, that is primarily providing vital services for the farms and for the agricultural population, and only secondarily for the rest of the economy. That the role of those industrial enterprises was not at all negligible either on a national scale or in terms of the total utilization by the agricultural sector can be gauged from available data provided for the year 1970.[4]

The economic and organizational rationale for the existence of small-scale industrial enterprises, as it appears from the available data, can perhaps be found as based upon the following considerations: (1) the availability of raw materials in quantities that would make small-scale output feasible; (2) availability of skills or relative ease of skill acquisition for a labor force utilizing the limited productive capacity of such enterprises; (3) savings on transportation costs on bulk products; (4) priorities of the planners and decision-makers to invest in capital goods that would provide employment in the short-run for some members of the agricultural labor in labor-intensive branches of material supply for agriculture; (5) more efficient utilization of labor with special emphasis on the decrease of the seasonal peak; (6) better utilization of by-products and decrease of waste.

Given the traditional bias in favor of large-scale production, the intrafarm industrial shops and establishments were never presented as models of efficiency, although the degree of their relative inefficiency was hardly studied in a rigorous manner.[5]

This dearth of information on the activities of the industrial shops and establishments within the farms is underscored by the scanty economic data that are available for such institutions in the collective farms only for the year 1971. The data presented by I.F. Suslov are presented in Table 8.2.

Although it is not easy to reconcile the data from Table 8.2 with another authoritative source,[6] they have to be used as a basis for some of our considerations of the problem, on the assumption that the economic conditions of this set of data are not atypical for the larger universe. The chief characteristic of the enumerated collective farm industrial enterprises is their small size with less than three workers per shop (their average size would increase if the construction workers would be included). The capital endowment of the industrial enterprises is also limited, so that an estimated value added per worker exceeds the yearly wage by about 20 percent.

TABLE 8.2

Productive Capacity of the Industrial Enterprises of the Soviet
Collective Farms as of 1971

	Number of Enterprises (in 1,000)	Average yearly Number of workers (in 1,000)	Value of Capital (in million rubles)	Capital per Worker (in rubles)	Output (in million rubles)	Output per Worker (in rubles)	Output/ Capital Ratio
Total	162.5	571.5	1,223	2,140	2,990	5,230	2.44
Including flour milling, oil crushing	37.6	56.5	189	3,340	895	15,850	4.74
Including fruit, vegetable processing	3.3	15.3	60	3,920	98	6,400	1.63
Including processing of livestock products	8.4	13.4	26	1,940	227	16,900	8.73
Including sawmills and woodworking	33.8	130.4	129	990	503	3,870	3.88
Including construction materials	3.5	44.0	75	1,700	73	1,662	.97
Including electrical generating stations	8.5	9.6	57	5,950	31	3,170	.54
Including machinery repair shops	40.3	192.9	618	3,210	739	3,842	1.19

Source: I.F. Suslov: Ekonomicheskie Interesy i Sotsialnoe Razvitie Kolkhoznogo Krestianstva (Moscow: Mysl', 1973), p. 120.

While the demand of the collective farms for the services of the industrial shops appears to increase, if one is to judge by the rapidly rising wages of these categories of labor (62 percent per man-day and about 60 percent per yearly worker during 1965-71), it is not at all clear that the expansion of capital and labor ought to occur indiscriminately in all directions. That the further development of services for the collective farms can be decided jointly by the farms and the government authorities would be desirable and possible is beyond doubt. However, the proposed framework of the agrarian-industrial complexes leaves this issue largely unresolved.

Apart from the general characteristic of size, it should come as no surprise to students of Soviet agriculture that the largest single category of industrial employment in the collective farms is the preparation of construction materials. Somehow, between the giant construction trusts and the private individual mason or carpenter, the teams of builders capable of erecting farm buildings disappeared in the whirlwind of rapid industrialization and collectivization, and they had to be recreated or reassembled when buildings for livestock were demanded, storage facilities expanded, or machinery sheds constructed. As one could see from glancing at Table 8.3, which presents the numerical growth of intercollective farm processing and industrial associations, over a half of them are devoted to construction tasks.

INDUSTRIAL ESTABLISHMENTS OF THE FARMS AND VERTICAL INTEGRATION

So much for the raw data. What do they indicate for the future of the industrial establishments of the farms and for the possibility of developing a vertical integration of input supply for the agricultural sector, agricultural production proper, and the processing of agricultural commodities? With respect to one type of industrial activity of the farms a probable decline could be expected, namely the machinery repair. There is good reason to assume that at least capital repairs (as distinct from current repairs) will be assumed increasingly by the large shops of the Soyuzsel'khoztekhnika organization. Although this writer does not consider the solution as an optimal one, but only as a second-best substitute for capital repairs and spare-part production by the industrial producers themselves, [7] there is every reason to believe that the substitution of major machinery repairs by Soyuzsel'khoztekhnika for the local farm repair shops will take place.

It is much more difficult to predict the likely prospects for the production of construction materials and the rate of construction

TABLE 8.3

Growth of Numbers of Soviet Intercollective Farm
Cooperative Associations and Enterprises,
1960-72, Selected Years

	1960	1963	1965	1967	1970	1972
Total number	3,095	3,055	3,355	3,884	4,554	5,068
Participating collective farms	35,265	44,311	47,296	54,722	64,329	67,813
Single purpose associations	2,382	2,397	2,660	2,881	4,255	4,861
including construction	1,215	1,234	1,470	1,622	2,432	2,625
including production of construction materials	116	62	53	54	146	182
including processing of agricultural products	1	6	7	9	14	29
including processing of feed			11		77	153
including feed lots	181	181	187	202	272	320
including poultry production		522	616	589	574	584
including artificial insemination of livestock		46	34	29	57	63
including electrical stations	211	170	121	68		
including machinery repair shops	92	33	25	24		
Multipurpose associations	713	658	695	1,003	299	172

Sources: I. Sigov, Formy Obobshestvlenia Proizvodstva na Sele (Moscow: Ekonomika, 1970), pp. 116, 117; V.I. Arefiev, "Nekotorye Voprosy Vzaimootnoshenii Mezhkolkhoznykh i Gosudarstvenno-Kolkhoznykh Predpriatii," in Vsesoiuznyi NauchnoIssledovatelskii Institut Ekonomiki Sel'skogo Khoziaistva: Doklady i Soobshchenia, no. 64 (Moscow, 1972), p. 97; TsSU SSSR, Narodnoe Khoziaistvo SSSR v 1972 godu (Moscow: Statistika, 1973), pp. 396, 397.

activities within the farms. In this case the element of transportation costs might favor the use of local resources and local labor for a long time to come. Thus, at least in part, the farms will maintain in the areas of construction only a partial dependence upon resources or services from the other sectors of the economy. With regard to the supply of mixed feeds, as an input in the production of livestock, a general policy of regional development that would determine the levels of livestock output by type in the various regions could provide guidance for the location and scope of appropriate milling establishments, based upon the savings of transportation costs, availability of the raw materials and perhaps final demand, although the transportation of the final output is conceivably less expensive than the transportation of the inputs. As one would imagine, the emphasis here is upon an economic calculation in which the various parameters have to be taken into account. This leads us to a set of more fundamental considerations with respect to the problems of vertical integration. Much of what the Soviet economists are writing about can be subsumed under a number of headings, some explicit and some implied.

UTILIZATION OF LABOR

Among the most explicit elements is the one of a more optimal utilization of labor on the farms and perhaps in the rural areas in general. The Soviet authors seem to oscillate between an assumption of labor surplus on the farms, topped by a still-considerable seasonal peak, and a view of a labor scarcity in some regions, and faced by outmigration of the younger age groups into the towns and cities motivated by the lack of certain cultural amenities in the countryside and by the lower level of agricultural and rural wages compared with wages in industry and urban areas.

The Soviet economists assume that the agricultural-industrial complexes can help to resolve the employment and income problems of the agricultural labor force by offering additional employment opportunities for the labor force and profits for the farms. There are a number of problems with this assumption, some of them related to the methodology and some of a factual nature.

The majority of examples are selected from such areas as wine-making and fruit and vegetable canning, obviously areas in which either the value added or processing can be captured by the agricultural labor force or in which the price structure favors the processing industries and the capital/labor ratio is relatively low. In terms of factual evidence, for example, the increase in the employment of the agrarian-industrial complexes or industrial shops and construction does not help to decrease the seasonal peak in agricultural labor; in fact an increase in employment of the industrial and construction sectors could only aggravate the seasonal peak.

As far as the long-term problems of agricultural employment and income are concerned, a cursory review of the agricultural population and composition of the agricultural labor force seems to imply that a further improvement in the conditions of employment and income would depend to a considerable extent upon the continuity and effectiveness of labor force training in skills and on the ability of the farms to retain the skilled labor force.

While in the past the sex imbalance of the agricultural labor force was a major obstacle to the increase of modern skills and incomes, and thus to higher productivity and incomes, the present ratio of low-skilled to middle- and high-skilled labor, especially on the collective farms, calls for massive training in modern skills. Within the context of such urgent demands the role of the agrarian-industrial complexes is minute indeed. It is needless to point out that while one stresses the importance of skill acquisition for the labor force, the unspoken accompanying assumption is a high rate of investment in the physical capital stock and increased economic effectiveness of its utilization built into the set of the optimistic assumptions.[8]

A test for the continuation of high rates of investment in both physical and human capital in agriculture and its channelling through the institution of agrarian-industrial complexes may be provided by the new crash program to develop the agricultural economy of the Central Nonblack-Soil Region. The agrarian-industrial complexes are designated to play a significant role in the augmentation of feed and livestock resources,[9] and the experience gained from their performance might affect to a considerable extent their future development.

RELATIONSHIP BETWEEN THE CENTRAL AND LOCAL DECISION-MAKERS

Among the host of implied, rather than explicit, benefits of the agrarian-industrial complexes carefully suggested or hinted at by Soviet economists, two deserve special scrutiny. One of the implied benefits suggests a changed relationship between the central and local decision-makers, as though it is assumed that the present system of strict control and supervision over the activities of the collective and state farms is detrimental to their present and future performance. This writer sympathizes with such views, while admitting that some of the more recent measures of the central planners and decision-makers, such as the extended insurance of farm output against natural calamities, or the extension of pension-benefits covering the collective farmers, were without any doubt beneficial to the farms and the farm population. Thus the problem is not one of extremes, tight controls versus no controls at all, but one of the proper mix of supervision and self-government or degrees of autonomous decision-making authority. In fact, many of the ills that the agrarian-industrial complexes are expected to remedy can be overcome by what this writer called "freedom of interfarm trade and interfarm mobility of resources."[10] One does not have to invoke the formula of an agrarian-industrial complex to allow farms either to barter or to sell to each other an economic surplus of feed or young animals for fattening. Freedom to migrate from farm to farm or to transfer land from one farm to another might be a more economical solution to local problems of the land/labor ratios than the setting up of new enterprises designed to deal indirectly with those problems at an acute stage on the local level. There is no need to elaborate that one of the basic preconditions of granting the farms such freedoms is the abolition of the system of centralized, detailed planning of delivery quotas of agricultural output for each farm and the insistence that most or all of the transactions in agricultural commodities pass through the state's procurement agencies. The legal right of entering into contractual relationships between farms, or between farms and state-owned industrial or trading institutions, when granted or enforced, might help to increase farm incomes by stimulating production of commodities in demand more than the agrarian-industrial complex organizations per se. The second, implied but not revealed, concern on the part of the economists writing on the subject of the agrarian-industrial complexes is the problem of pricing of both the agricultural commodities and the processed products.

PRICING OF AGRICULTURAL COMMODITIES

The problem of pricing agricultural commodities, a prerogative of the central planners and decision-makers, was a source of uncertainty and irritation for the collective farms and became one for the state farms when economic accounting (khozraschet) was introduced. If during the Stalinist period the price policy was largely an instrument of taxation, the situation has changed radically in this respect during the last two decades. The problem of uncertainty, however, remains because the farms are not only facing a given (or sometimes changing) schedule of prices, but it is combined with a demand schedule for quantities of products to be delivered at those prices to the state. Thus, the mix of obligatory sales of goods that contain differing weights of profitable and nonprofitable components of output creates the uncertainty about the overall profitability of the farm operations that is independent of the decisions at the farm level. Therefore, as long as the central authorities reserve for themselves the right of simultaneously determining both the prices and the quantities of the farms' commercial output, the actual autonomy of the farms in reaching optimal output decisions exists more on paper than in reality. To the extent that the pricing of processed agricultural products is also within the authority of the state, but perhaps modified by some margins allowed the local state organs, the two policies would have to be brought into some harmony. Decisions about subsidizing the consumption of dairy and meat products would have to be adjusted if a meaningful integration between the farm sector and the industrial sector would take place.

Apparently the implicit hopes of some Soviet economists writing about the prospects of the agrarian-industrial complexes are that the establishment of such institutions might allow the farms and industrial establishments to negotiate among themselves the intermediate prices for the agricultural output, or that it may free the farms participating in such arrangements from the obligatory sales of farm products now demanded by the state, but produced at costs exceeding the government set price. To the extent that the state plan would stipulate the output of processed agricultural products in total value terms, even at the existing levels of relative prices, the farms would gain much more flexibility in adjusting their output mix to maximize their incomes, the degree of specialization of the farms would be enhanced, and the heavy hand of minute government interference might be eased. With respect to liberalization of the pricing policies the hope of setting a precedent through the agrarian-industrial complexes seems to be the moving spirit behind the support for the vertical integration institutions.

There is one additional aspect of the agrarian-industrial complexes that appears still very unclear in the minds of its proponents, namely the aspect of administration. In contradistinction to other countries of Eastern Europe, specifically Hungary and East Germany, where a number of steps were already undertaken to create an administrative framework for such an integration, [11] nothing definitely was proposed for the Soviet Union. Given the strong attachment to existing bureaucratic structures, the creation of another, additional administrative framework for agrarian-industrial complexes might bureaucratize and stifle the initiative of the local farms or food-processing plants in trying to achieve a measure of vertical integration combined with autonomy for management at the local level and end in increased bureaucratic red tape and supervision.

LONG-TERM SOCIAL EFFECT

There is, however, one area of Soviet policy that is in harmony with the attempts to set up the various agrarian-industrial complexes, an area that deals with the long-term social effect, rather than with the shorter-term economic effects, namely the policy of narrowing down the "differences between town and countryside." Observers of Soviet agriculture remember the debate of the early 1950s about the setting up of the so-called agro-goroda (agrarian cities), and also the various utterances by Khrushchev about the construction of multi-apartment dwellings, particularly in the state farms. Critics pointed out not only the heavy costs of this type of construction, but also its likely effects upon the private auxiliary plots and privately maintained livestock, as necessary sources of income for the farm families, incomes to the farmers that could not be compensated for by the farms.

It is this writer's strong impression that the attempts to reconstruct the existing villages in the Soviet Union were only postponed by the decision-makers until the time when for economic and noneconomic reasons such a reconstruction will become feasible. When debates about agrarian-industrial complexes coincide with plans to integrate relatively small villages (with less than 100 or 200 inhabitants) into larger population centers, it augurs well for further steps to provide relatively large rural population centers with some of the amenities of modern life. To be sure, such measures will differ from the Stalinist sweeping haste of liquidating the old homestead-type farming habitat of the 1938-39 years in Belorussia and North-West of the RSFSR when hundreds of thousands were moved into existing villages, increasing the misery of the collective farmers of those regions. The measures may be more gradual, perhaps supported by the resources of the farms themselves and the state construction agencies, but the tendency and the direction seem to be unmistakable, namely, to bring about a change in the style of life and the standard of living that would become more or less uniform within the rural areas and in which the differences between agricultural and nonagricultural settlements would tend to disappear.[12] If such a policy appears in the view of the decision-makers to justify the organization of agrarian-industrial complexes, then the arrangements for using the labor force of such settlements for either agricultural or industrial work, or even interchangeably, would make greater sense. In addition, administrative problems could be much more easily resolved, existing institutional barriers might be disregarded or changed, and new more liberal and more economically sound principles of pricing of supply and investment could be developed.

    Thus, if the agrarian-industrial complexes are not to be considered as a goal per se, but as merely a component of a major social reconstruction of the rural areas, they can be justified by the total benefits of the social reconstruction. Taken out of this broader context, a justification on purely economic grounds looks rather pale to this observer.

NOTES

    1. See S.I. Semin, Ekonomicheskie Osnovy Agrarno— Promyshlennykh Kompleksov (Moscow: Kolos, 1973).

    2. For example, P.E. Streletz argues that the ratio of farm machinery to tractors, or the ratio of trucks to tractors, is an insufficient one, and production cannot achieve the desired level of efficiency unless such disproportions would be corrected. See P.E. Streletz, Problema Sezonnosti Truda v Sotsialisticheskom Sel'skom Khoziaistve (Omsk: Omskii Politekhnicheski Institut, 1973).

    3. The share of locally produced electrical energy has tended to decline since about 1963 as a result of the inclusion of the rural areas in the all-Soviet electric grid as indicated by the following figures of electrical energy supply (in million kwh):

	Produced on the Farms	Received from Outside	Total Supplied
1960	4,191	4,078	8,269
1965	5,259	10,354	15,613
1970	2,193	24,777	26,970

    Source: TsSU SSSR, Sel'skoe Khoziaistvo SSSR (Moscow, various years).

    4. The volume of physical output for selected commodities by the industrial enterprises of the farms, when compared with total reported output is as follows:

	Total Output	Farm Output
Flour	42 million tons	9.2 million tons
Dried Fruits	34.7 thousand tons	14.5 thousand tons
Bricks	32,373 million	1,775 million
Construction stone	27.9 million cubic meters	4.1 million cubic meters
Construction wood	298.5 million cubic meters	15.3 million cubic meters
Firewood	86.5 million cubic meters	13.9 million cubic meters
Peat	54.3 million cubic meters	3.4 million cubic meters

Source: TsSU SSSR, Sel'skoe Khoziaistvo SSSR (Moscow, 1971), pp. 574-75, 658-59.

5. Such a study might reveal that the intensive utilization of a simple technology under the existing circumstances is more efficient than one would suspect; it might also reveal relatively low opportunity costs of labor of a particular age or sex or skill composition. In any event, judgment has to be suspended until a proper analysis is carried out.

6. The other source, S.I. Semin, states,

In 1970 there existed in the rural areas 261 thousand auxiliary enterprises and industrial establishments, of which in the collective farms 173 thousand; in the state farms 75 thousand, and in intercollective organizations 11 thousand. They had a total steady employment of 1,230 thousand persons, including 457 thousand in collective farms, 545 thousand in state farms and 228 thousand in the intercollective organizations. Their combined output, which includes canned vegetables and fruits, wine, construction materials increased (in 1967 comparable prices) from 4.3 billion rubles in 1965 to 6.6 billions in 1968 and constituted in 1970 8.4 billion rubles, or about 10 percent of the total output of agriculture.

S.I. Semin, Ekonomicheskie Osnovy Agrarno-Promyshlennykh Kompleksov (Moscow: Kolos, 1973), p. 47.

In the absence of references to primary sources or applied methodology it is difficult to speculate about the degree of comparability of the two estimates. One could speculate that the output of the state farm repair shops is included since Suslov included their output in his classification of the collective farms. Given an employment figure of about 285,000 in the repair shops of the state farms, another 1.2 billion rubles could be added to the Suslov figure of 3 billion rubles. If the output of construction of the intercollective farm organizations estimated at 2.5 billion rubles together with the construction work of the state farms of 1.5 billion rubles are added to the 4.2 estimated output of the previous categories, the total rises to about 8.2 billion rubles and the figures of both Suslov and Semin would belong to the same universe.

7. A contractual guarantee of quality performance, of spare parts availability, and repair services by the machinery producers appear to this writer to be the most elementary conditions of a more satisfactory relation between the capital goods suppliers and their agricultural clients. This obviously does not address itself to the more fundamental problem of the impact of the clients' choices and demand upon the quality and type of capital goods supply.

8. While a continuously high rate of investment of physical capital in Soviet agriculture can perhaps be assumed for the foreseeable future, there are some reasons to doubt a continuous rise of the rate of return on capital in Soviet agriculture. A number of studies in the increased costs of capital equipment revealed that the increase in prices for such equipment exceeds the actual efficiency gain of the new models of machinery and equipment.

9. The planned program envisages over a half of projected capital construction for livestock production and ought to take place through the agrarian-industrial complexes. Within the collective farms alone, 819 new enterprises for milk production, 211 for raising calves, 177 for beef fattening, 125 for sheep raising, and 63 for hog fattening are projected. L. Florentiev, "Nechernozemnaia Zona RSFSR, Itogi Razvitia Sel'skogo Khoziaistva," Voprosy Ekonomiki no. 10 (1974), pp. 44-47.

10. See A. Kahan, "The Present State of Soviet Agriculture," in Soviet Economic Outlook, Hearings before the Joint Economic Committee, U.S. Congress, July 17, 18, 19, 1973 (Washington, D.C., 1973).

11. In Hungary, for example, the ministries of food production and of agriculture have been merged.

12. The following table reproduces the results of the population census data about the distribution by size and population of the rural settlements in the Soviet Union:

	1959		1970	
	Number of Settlements	Population (in 1,000)	Number of Settlements	Population (in 1,000)
Up to 5 inhabitants	212,076	644.0	94,296	277.7
6-10 inhabitants	71,617	541.2	39,206	299.2
11-25 inhabitants	69,675	1,191.4	51,607	887.3
26-50 inhabitants	67,410	2,517.5	50,709	1,887.7
51-100 inhabitants	80,924	5,897.7	56,781	4,121.4
101-200 inhabitants	76,402	10,983.8	55,373	7,989.0
201-500 inhabitants	74,762	23,688.4	64,753	20,815.8
501-1,000 inhabitants	31,763	22,105.9	33,032	23,116.8
1,001-2,000 inhabitants	14,218	19,337.0	16,677	22,785.4
2,001-3,000 inhabitants	3,482	8,398.1	3,911	9,424.2
3,001-5,000 inhabitants	1,807	6,732.1	2,040	7,656.4
Over 5,000 inhabitants	675	4,973.2	868	6,446.7
Total	704,811	107,010.4	469,253	105,697.6

Sources: TsSU SSSR, Itogi Vsesoiuznoi Perepisi Naselenia 1959 godu
(SvodnyiTom) (Moscow: Gosstatizdat, 1962), pp. 44, 45; TsSU SSSR, Itogi
Vsesoiuznoi Perepisi Naselenia 1970 godu, Vol. I, Statistika (Moscow, 1972),
pp. 146-47.

The table indicates that the process of concentration of the rural
population in larger settlements was going on during the period 1959-
70. It is true that the most spectacular reduction of private homesteads took place in the area where they still exist, namely the Baltic
republics of the Soviet Union. But the shift from small villages, with
less than 200 inhabitants, or roughly less than 60 households, took
place in many other parts of the Soviet Union and is likely to continue.

Apparently, the long-range plans for the Nonblacksoil Region
envisage a reduction of the number of existing rural cattlements by
five times, to about 29,000. In the Lithuanian republic, according to
reports, the number of individual homesteads was recently reduced
by 24,300 and the population resettled in the larger villages.

See V. Stern, "Puti Razuitia Sel'skikh Poselkov Nechernozem-
noi Zony RSFSR," Voprosy Ekonomiki, no. 10 (1974), pp. 50-61.

9

THE SOVIET FEED-LIVESTOCK
ECONOMY: PROJECTIONS
AND POLICIES
David M. Schoonover

The Soviet leadership basically must choose between limiting growth in demand for livestock products (perhaps by higher prices) and importing deficit amounts of feeds. Basing projections largely on linear extrapolations of relationships in the production of feeds and livestock products, a large and growing feed gap is evident during the remainder of the 1970s.

However, the leadership has undertaken a wide array of internal policies, to counter the tendency toward increasing feed deficits. Policies affecting feed supplies range from those with an immediate impact to others that may not greatly affect production until well into the 1980s. Policies also are being implemented to reduce feed demand, primarily through an attempt to increase efficiency in feeding, but the effect on average efficiency may not be felt for several years. The projected feed deficits, of course, already assume usual rates of change in feed supply and demand. The closing of the gap requires policies that will accelerate growth in feed crop areas and yields and changes in feed efficiency.

In view of the large budgetary subsidization of livestock product consumption, as well as the foreign exchange costs of feed imports, demand limitation through price increases must be considered a possible policy alternative. Evidence is not available to measure the probability of this policy, but it can be considered a relatively unpopular course of action.

In the past few years, the Soviet Union has imported deficit quantities of grains, but generally has not imported to cover feed protein shortages. Crop shortfalls in 1972, which required imports in 1972-73 of more than 20 million tons of grain, have tended to mask the magnitude of the basic Soviet supply/demand situation. Additional imports of about 10 million tons during 1973-74 also may be partly attributed to the desire to purchase insurance against a possible further shortfall. Wheat dominated imports during this period. Beginning in 1971-72, however, feed grain imports have held rather steady at about 5 million tons annually. Despite apparent steady levels of feed grain imports, overall grain trade is subject to the vicissitudes of weather, which can bring annual swings of 50 million tons or more in Soviet grain output.

The pattern of Soviet grain imports is insufficiently well established to base projections on historical experience. Assuming that Soviet policy is represented by an attempt to attain reasonable satisfaction of consumer demands for livestock products, then an analysis of relationships in the Soviet feed-livestock economy can be useful in reaching conclusions about probable future trade patterns. In any specific year, of course, the general conclusions are modified by the impact of weather on domestic feed supplies.

This chapter briefly reports the findings of a quantitative study of the Soviet feed-livestock economy and the projected feed supply and demand situation. The principal purpose in this study, though, is to look at the policies, which have been undertaken by the Soviet government, that will modify the trends in relationships and cause actual results to differ from those projected.

FEED-LIVESTOCK ECONOMY PROJECTIONS

At a seminar held at the U.S. Department of Agriculture in 1974, I reported the preliminary findings of a study on the Soviet feed-livestock economy.[1] The study consisted of a historical analysis of Soviet livestock product and feed supply/demand relationships and a projection of these relationships over the next decade or so, focusing especially on 1980. It would be helpful to summarize briefly the findings to better illustrate the decisions concerning the feed-livestock economy that are now being faced, and still must be faced, by Soviet policy-makers.

Although planning in the Soviet Union has focused more heavily on supply, in the cited study the demand analysis and projections were the principal bases for the projections of livestock product supply and, hence, feed requirements. Future per capita levels of consumption of livestock products were projected using income elasticities of demand calculated largely from time-series regression analysis. Although it can be argued that such calculations understate true elasticities in an economy of queues and shortages, such as the Soviet Union, it was found that most calculated elasticities appeared quite reasonable in international comparisons with countries of various regions of Europe. For example, the selected income elasticity on meat of about .7 is very similar to the elasticities used for Italy and Spain in a recent study by FAO.

Calculation of aggregate consumption required the use of projections both of population and per capita consumption. The former assumed constant fertility. The latter was based on an assumed 5 percent annual growth in per capita disposable money incomes. The 1975 per capita projections approximated the 1975 plans and the 1985 projections generally approached the long-term norms specified by the Soviet Academy of Medical Sciences.

Livestock production projections in the study generally were set at the level required to cover projected consumption. The projected 1980 requirements were: meat, 19 million tons; milk, 114 million tons; eggs, 63 billion. The 1975 plan now calls for the following levels of output: meat, 16 million tons; milk, 100 million tons; eggs, 52 billion.

Feed supplies were determined by constructing balances of grains, other concentrates, milk, and forage crops. Feed was aggregated in terms of oat-equivalent feed units and digestible protein, using Soviet standards. Livestock products were aggregated in terms of total feed- and concentrate-consuming livestock production units, similar to those in use in U.S. feed balance statistics, using Soviet feeding rates for 1970 or other recent years. Aggregate total feed supplies were divided by aggregate livestock production units to determine patterns or trends in aggregate feeding rates. The calculations indicated that there has been very little change over time in aggregate feed consumption per total feed-consuming livestock production unit, but there has been a marked increase since the mid-1960s in concentrate use per concentrate-consuming livestock production unit. According to these calculations, the ratio of digestible protein per oat-equivalent feed unit has improved only slightly during the past 15 to 20 years.

In the projections of feed requirements, total feed per livestock unit was assumed to remain constant at the 1960-71 average level. The uptrend in concentrate feed units per concentrate-consuming livestock unit, however, was extrapolated to 1980 and 1985. The required ratio of digestible protein was calculated using Soviet norms. The calculated absolute protein deficit in 1970-71 was 3.5 million tons—roughly equivalent to the digestible protein content of 10 million tons of soybeans.

Determination of expected future feed supplies required projection of feed crop production, which largely was based on separate linear extrapolations of area and yield data. The extrapolated downtrends in grain and uptrends in forage crop areas were shifted as a result of the structural changes in 1973, but the trend rate was left

unchanged. The grain area trend, for example, was shifted upward
by 8 million hectares and extrapolated from this revised position.

In the grain yield projections, the steeper uptrends of 1960-71
were preferred over the longer-term trends of 1955-71. Alternative
regressions of yields on fertilizer and their projection based on
fertilizer plans suggested that linear extrapolations over the next
decade are relatively conservative. The projections indicated that
Soviet gross grain production may well be around 240 to 250 million
tons by 1980 and 270 to 280 million tons by 1985—given the usual
assumption of normal weather in those years—compared with the
1971-73 average of just over 190 million tons.

Although uptrends in forage crop yields were evident, in contrast
to grain little acceleration was apparent. The forage production
projections diverged greatly from Soviet plans on feed availabilities
from forages, suggesting a probable major feed deficit in this area.

The separate projections of feed production and requirements
indicated a substantial and growing deficit of feed units and a continuing chronic deficit of digestible protein over the next decade. This
growing deficit can be expected to evoke a response. One response is
to import feeds. Other responses are to increase supplies or reduce
requirements. The initial response of Soviet policy-makers, in my
judgment, would be feed imports. Other policies must be adopted,
however, to eventually close the gap or prevent it from widening
beyond bearable limits. On the supply side, policies to sharply improve forage crop production and use in the Soviet Union seemed a
good possibility. On the requirement side, increased efficiency
through modernization of the livestock industry and increased emphasis on the protein balance in feed seemed likely. As a last resort,
of course, requirements can be reduced by a reduction in consumption through price changes or shortages, but these are not popular
policies.

Most observers of the Soviet economic scene will agree, I
believe, that the Soviet leadership recognizes the general problem it
faces in the feed-livestock sector, and it has been actively seeking
policies to deal with the problem. In the remainder of this chapter
I will discuss the internal policies that have been adopted, especially
those announced or pursued more aggressively during 1974. Finally,
I will attempt to assess the implications of these policies on the
projected feed gap.

NONCHERNOZEM PROGRAM

A major program that will impact on the feed-livestock economy
is the plan for development during 1976-90 of the nonchernozem soil

zone (Nonblacksoil Region) of the Russian Federation (RSFSR), which
was first made public by Secretary-General Brezhnev on March 15,
1974.[2] Although this zone contains only 14 percent of the cultivated
area of the Soviet Union, it assumes greater weight in the overall
feed-livestock development because of its heavier concentration of
livestock. In 1971, for instance, farms in this zone accounted for the
following percentage shares of Soviet livestock production: milk, 21;
beef, 16; pork, 17; poultry meat, 20; and eggs, 22. Besides contributing roughly one-fifth of livestock product output in the Soviet Union,
the zone contains about one-fourth of the country's permanent hay
meadows, drained land, and potato-vegetable area.

Rural areas in this long-settled zone have remained relatively
neglected as population has migrated to industrial centers. The
proposed program involves a combination of rural and agricultural
development, requiring inputs into infrastructure as well as agricultural production, consolidation of villages, and other measures
to attempt to raise the attractiveness of the region to rural workers,
as well as to increase agricultural productivity. Farming productivity
in the region has remained relatively low. During 1970-72, for example, grain yields in the zone ranged from 83 to 89 percent of the
national average.

A host of measures have been planned to increase agricultural
production in the nonchernozem zone of the RSFSR. During 1976-80
investments of 35 billion rubles—1.8 times the 1971-75 level—will
be directed into the zone's agriculture.[3] (For comparison, national
investments in agriculture are planned to increase less than 1.6
times during 1971-75.) The planned level of agricultural investments
in the zone during 1976-80 is more than one-fourth of planned national
investments in agriculture during 1971-75, but evidently would be
less than one-fifth of national investments during 1976-80. In addition
to the 35 billion rubles in agricultural production, investments will
include 8 billion rubles in food and light industries and 5 billion rubles
in infrastructure, housing, and amenities.[4] During the five-year
period, planned equipment supplied to the zone's agriculture will
include 380,000 tractors, 94,000 grain combines, and 230,000 trucks.
Infrastructure investments during 1976-90 will provide for the construction of 25,000 kilometers of hard-surface roads.[5]

Planned fertilizer deliveries to agriculture in the zone during
1976-80 are set at 120 million tons—roughly one-fourth of the planned
national total. Applications per hectare of cultivated land are scheduled to increase from 3 quintals (standard gross weight; 1 quintal
equals 220.46 pounds) in 1970 to 10 quintals in 1980.[6] The scheduled
rate of increase exceeds the national rate by about one-fourth. During
1976-90, about 23 million hectares will be treated with lime, compared
with about 10 million hectares in recent years.[7] (Total agricultural

area is 50 million hectares; 32 million are cultivated. One hectare equals 2.47 acres.)

Reports on the nonchernozem program do not clearly indicate the planned expansion of agricultural or cultivated land, and it may be that the area of agricultural land will change only slightly, but it is clear that the cropping condition of the land will improve markedly if the program is implemented. The 50 million hectares of agricultural land currently include 9.4 million that are swampy or waterlogged, 6.5 million covered with brush, and 28 million with highly acid soils.[8] During the 15-year period, the program calls for drainage of 9 to 10 million hectares (7 to 8 million with tile or pipe), irrigation of pastures and vegetable fields on 2 to 2.5 million hectares, and renovation of an additional 8 to 10 million hectares.[9] The zone in 1972 contained only 2.8 million hectares of drainage systems. One report stated that about 14 million hectares of sandy soil would be plowed up during 1975-80, with a 50 percent expansion of cultivated area in some districts, but it does not seem likely that the 14 million hectares represents a net addition to cultivated land.[10] For example, targeted grain yields and outputs suggest little intended grain area expansion from the current level of about 15 million hectares.

A fundamental part of the program to develop agriculture in the zone is the move toward large-scale, specialized complexes for production of milk, pork, and poultry. Improvement of hay meadows, pastures, and seeded forage crops is an essential part of this program. Special emphasis has been placed on the development and management of clovers in crop rotations.[11]

Gross agricultural output in the zone is scheduled to expand 38 percent from 1975 to 1980.[12] (This compares with a planned growth at the national level of about 23 percent from 1970 to 1975.) Planned grain output is 31 million tons in 1980 and 43 million tons in 1990.[13] This compares with average output of 18.6 million tons during 1970-72. (A similar percentage increase in national production would bring output to 298 million tons by 1980 and 412 million tons by 1990, although, of course, such rapid expansion is not expected at the national level.) The grain yield target (apparently for 1980) is 20 quintals per hectare, compared with 12.8 quintals during 1970-72.[14]

OTHER POLICIES TO BOOST FEED SUPPLIES

The Soviet leadership has adopted or retained a number of additional policies to boost feed supplies during the next several years. These include the expansion of grain areas, the increase of fertilizer deliveries to agriculture, an irrigation program, and the search for domestic sources of higher-protein feeds.

One of the major supply-boosting developments in 1973 was the sharp increase in areas seeded to grain. The increase represented a reversal of the downtrend of the previous decade. In the feed-livestock economy projections, the increase was treated as an upward shift in the trend line, but a declining area was extrapolated to 1980 and 1985. Developments in 1974, however, suggest there is a determined policy to maintain grain area at the higher level, by means both of an overall expansion in cultivated land and a permanent reduction in some other crops, especially annual grasses. Seeding plans, for example, called for a further area expansion to more than 130 million hectares.[15] Although slightly less than the full increase was attained, grain area seeded expanded almost 2 million hectares in 1974. Even prior to 1973, several governmental organs reportedly had suggested that grain area should increase to 125 to 127 million hectares by 1975 and, subsequently, to 129 to 130 million hectares or more. Gosplan and the Soviet Ministry of Agriculture reportedly expected cultivated land to increase 3 million hectares from 1970 to 1975 and an additional 7 million hectares by 1980.[16]

Success in maintaining the area at the higher level could substantially raise projected grain output. Assuming the projected average yields still would be attained on the larger area, projected production in 1980 would be increased about 10 million tons on an area of 125 million hectares and 20 million tons on an area of 130 million hectares. Although this probably would not be attained without some sacrifice of forage crop production, the net gain still should be considerable if an area is removed from the least productive forage uses.

Total fertilizer deliveries to agriculture jumped 69 percent from 1965 to 1970 and are planned to increase 64 percent from 1970 to 1975. Fertilizer delivery targets generally have been met during the 1971-75 plan. The 1976-80 plan calls for a further increase in deliveries of 60 percent. Although deliveries in 1965 were only 27 million tons (standard gross weight), the planned level by 1980 is at least 120 million tons.[17]

The rate of application (nutrients) per harvested hectare in 1973 was 63 kilograms—half the U.S. application rate—but if 1980 targets are reached the application rate will exceed the current U.S. level by about 10 percent.

Although projected increases in grain and forage crop yields in the feed-livestock economy study already are based largely on growth in fertilizer use, it is possible that they are understated, owing to the more rapid increases on these crops in the past few years. From 1970 to 1975, for example, plans call for fertilizer use on grain to more than double—from 15 to 32 million tons. With realization of the expected response of 1.2 million tons of grain per ton of fertilizer, this alone would account for more than 20 million tons of added grain output.[18] At a constant response rate, if the entire increment of fertilizer from 1975 to 1980 were applied on grain it would boost output more than 50 million tons—considerably more than the projected increase. It seems likely, however, both that response will decline and that an increasingly larger share will be allocated to forage crops, thus accelerating forage yield increases.

In May 1966 the Soviet Union adopted a major long-term program of irrigation, drainage, and other land improvement. The effort in this area is illustrated by the following data on land improvement investments (constant 1969 prices) by five-year periods:[19]

	Billion rubles
1956-60	1.4
1961-65	4.1
1966-70	10.1
1971-75 plan	26.6

During 1966-70 about 1.8 million hectares of land were newly irrigated and about 3.9 million hectares newly drained. The net increments were less—1.2 million hectares additional irrigated land and an estimated 3.0 million hectares additional drained land in the Soviet Union. The ratio of net to gross additions to improved land generally appears to have increased, though. The 1971-75 plan calls for new irrigation of 3.2 million hectares (including almost 2.0 million of cultivated pastures) and new drainage of 5.0 million.[20] Aggregate progress was about as scheduled during the first three years of the plan. With a better net/gross ratio, net additions during 1971-75 could reach 2.5 million hectares of irrigated land and 4 million hectares of drained land. These net additions could bring Soviet irrigated land to almost 14 million hectares by 1975 and drained land also to about 14 million hectares. Developments in the non-chernozem zone probably will account for the largest share of additional drainage during the next decade or so.

Major irrigation projects are under construction or discussion, however, that could greatly increase the quantity of irrigated land during subsequent plan periods. The most grandiose scheme is the proposed diversion of water from Siberian rivers—Irtysh, Ob, and Yenisey—south through Kazakhstan to the Caspian Sea and to the basins of the Central Asian rivers—Syr-Darya and Amu-Darya. Although plans for the project still are being drawn up, work already has begun on the Ob-Pavlodar Canal, which will be included in the system.[21] If and when the project is implemented, it is expected to increase irrigated land in the Kazakhstan steppes and in Central Asia by 10 million hectares.[22] Even without the river diversion, the area of irrigation in the Syr-Darya and Amu-Darya basins of Central Asia is expected to increase by 3 million hectares during the next ten years.[23]

Construction of the Volga-Ural Canal was scheduled to begin in 1974. When completed—the target date is 1985—the canal will irrigate 2.5 million hectares.[24] In the Volga Valley, as a whole, a long-term plan has been drawn up to expand the irrigated area by 8 million hectares, including 3 million in Saratov Oblast, 1.6 million in Uralsk Oblast, and 1.5 million in Volgograd Oblast.[25] Of this 8 million hectares, 2 million are to be brought into cultivation during 1976-80.[26] Several major irrigation projects now are under construction in South European Soviet Union. The Kakhovka system, which now irrigates 260,000 hectares, eventually will supply water to about 1 million hectares.[27]

This incomplete enumeration of Soviet irrigation projects should be sufficient to demonstrate that impressive developments in irrigation probably can be expected during the remainder of this century. Academician Melnikov of the Soviet Academy of Sciences' Commission for Research into Production Potential and National Resources has stated that by 1985 it has been proposed to bring irrigated area up to 21 million hectares and drained area up to 27 million hectares. In the long-term, these proposals call for 30 million irrigated hectares and 50 million drained hectares.[28] Raskin claims the long-term potential irrigated area in the Soviet Union is 90 million hectares.[29]

Another ongoing program designed to improve the feed supply is the search for additional sources of protein for livestock feeds. The program takes a wide variety of forms including: (1) breeding higher-protein grains; (2) breeding higher-yielding, high-protein pulses; (3) expanding area of pulses and higher-protein crops; (4) improving technology and management in handling harvested feed crops; (5) increasing production of animal and synthetic forms of protein. A major restraint on protein growth, however, is the apparent lack of any program for major expansion of protein meal from oilseed crops.

Soviet plant breeders are working on barley varieties with 1.5 to 2 percent more protein and up to 3.5 percent more lysine. They reportedly have found forms of wheat with 18 to 22 percent protein. High-lysine corn hybrids with 14-15 percent protein also are scheduled for production in the next few years.[30] Experimental plot data on a nonalkaloid lupine—Kievskiy Mutant—reportedly yielded 20 to 40 quintals of grain or 40 to 80 tons of green mass.[31] It has been suggested that total pulse area be increased from the current level of about 6 million hectares to 10 million in 1980 and 13 to 14 million in 1990.[32]

Scientists at the All-Union Scientific Research Institute on Corn reportedly have suggested that 50 to 75 percent of silage area in the next few years should consist of mixed corn and soybean plantings to boost silage protein levels.[33] Alfalfa and clovers are replacing grasses in hay crop sowings. Production of dehydrated grass meal is expanding rapidly and is scheduled to reach 4 million tons in 1975, compared with less than 1 million in 1970.[34] Targets on fish meal output are 675,000 tons in 1975 and a million tons in 1980, compared with less than 400,000 tons in 1970.[35] Production of synthetic feed yeasts is planned to reach nearly a million tons in 1975, compared with 260,000 tons in 1970.[36]

SPECIALIZED LIVESTOCK ENTERPRISES AND INTERFARM ASSOCIATIONS

Turning from policies that will affect the supply of feeds to those that influence feed demand, the most prominent program is the shift toward large-scale specialized livestock operations. The movement toward specialized operations theoretically would be expected to improve allocation of resources and, hence, increase efficiency in feeding. On the other hand, concentrate use may increase in confined feeding operations as the concentrate/roughage ratio increases markedly.

Poultry operations have led the way toward livestock specialization in the Soviet Union. In the early 1960s, poultry farming largely was a "backyard" operation on the household plots of collective and state farms. During 1966-70, poultry "factories" were completed with a capacity of 23 million layers and 73 million broilers annually.[37] By January 1, 1971, the Ptitseprom system (created in 1964) encompassed 502 poultry factories, 302 specialized state farms, 172 breeding farms, and nearly 900 incubator stations.[38]

In April 1971 the Soviet party and government adopted a decree on the further development of industrialized production of eggs and poultry meat and also a decree on the industrialized production of other livestock products.[39] The decree called for government construction during 1971-75 of 1,170 specialized meat and dairy complexes and the construction or expansion of 585 poultry factories (of the 585, apparently 394 represent expansion or reconstruction).[40] Planned 1975 production from these specialized enterprises—compared as follows with specialized enterprise output in 1975—represents about 37 percent of the total production plan on eggs, 34 percent on poultry meat, 5 percent on other meat, and 2 percent on milk.[41]

	1970	1975
	1,000 metric tons	
Milk	—	2,100
Meat (excluding poultry)		
Live weight	—	1,300
Carcass weight (estimate)	—	825
Poultry meat		
Live weight	294	600
Carcass weight (estimate)	235	480
	Billions	
Eggs	10.7	19.2

The 1971-75 output from specialized government enterprises will account for the following percentage shares of the total planned increases from government farms: milk, 18; beef, 47; pork, 57; poultry meat, 100; eggs, 71. These complexes do not include specialized collective farm operations. About 1,500 large collective farm and intercollective farm complexes also are to be built during 1971-75.[42] During 1971-75, the plan calls for completion of construction of the following capacities in specialized government livestock enterprises: layers, 48 million; broilers, 193 million annually; beef cattle, 351,000 head; and hogs, 5.9 million head.[43]

The 1,170 specialized government livestock complexes to be constructed during 1971-75 include 307 for beef, 228 for pork, and 635 for milk. The beef complexes include 47 with an annual capacity of 10,000 head each, 20 mechanized feed lots with capacities of 20,000 to 30,000 head each, and 240 beef state farms fattening their own calves from 600 cows each. Hog complexes with four different sizes of annual fattening capacities are being constructed: 12,000; 24,000; 54,000; and 108,000 head. The largest complexes reportedly can provide the needs of a city of almost a half million people. The 635 dairy farms are to include 558 state farms with 800-cow capacities and 77 state farms with 1,200-cow capacities.[44] Larger dairy farms also have been mentioned. Egg poultry factories range from 50,000 to 1 million layers and broiler factories from 1 to 8 million birds.[45] Common sizes apparently are 200,000 to 400,000 layers or 3 million broilers.[46]

As of early 1973 eight complexes reportedly had been put into operation and 205 were under construction; including 66 for hog production, 32 for beef production, and 107 for milk production. The eight completed complexes were: 10,000-head beef complexes in Moscow and Leningrad oblasts and the Bashkir ASSR; 108,000-head hog complexes in Moscow, Gorkiy, Belgorod, and Kiev oblasts; and a

2,000-head dairy state farm in Moscow Oblast. Mixed feed plants attached to the large hog complexes were under construction.[47] At the beginning of 1973 there were 547 poultry factories—445 for eggs and 102 for meat—with an average of 248,000 birds per factory. The 3 percent largest egg factories (about 13 enterprises) averaged more than 1 million birds each with an average rate of lay of 227 eggs.[48]

Planning now is underway for the construction of meat and dairy complexes during the 1976-80 plan. Beef complexes will continue to be based chiefly on dairy calves in zones around major cities and industrial areas. A beef fattening sector, unrelated to the dairy sector, also will be developed. By the beginning of the 1981-85 plan most pork production will be located on specialized hog complexes. Dairy herds, however, will continue to be held widely by collective and state farms. During 1976-80, both dairy and fattening operations will be developed in regions with more moderate climates, especially those where large-scale irrigation systems are being constructed.[49]

The development of specialized livestock enterprises seems closely intertwined, but not synonymous, with the movement toward interfarm and agroindustrial associations, integrating a number of collective farms, state farms, or collective and state farms in a raion (local government), together with other enterprises, such as feed mills, feed lots, and, perhaps, processing plants. Interfarm and agroindustrial associations also integrate other types of enterprises—for example, fruit and vegetable production and processing— but they now are receiving special emphasis in the livestock sector. Such associations facilitate both horizontal integration of smaller livestock farms and vertical integration enabling separate production units for calves or pigs, feeders, fattening, feed production, mixed feed mills, and processing. They also have facilitated the use of by-product feeds, such as beet pulp, by means of ties between farms and sugar plants or other mills. Many livestock complexes, of course, are not now members of such associations.

Clear approval for the expansion of cooperative arrangements among farms was given by Secretary-General Brezhnev at the December Plenum of the Central Committee of the CPSU, when he stated: "I think that the time has come to give interfarm enterprises, as we say, the green light, to render help from the state by means of technology and equipment to those collective and state farms that are ready to assign resources to this matter."[50]

Interfarm associations now appear to be more active in livestock production throughout the South European zone of the Soviet Union, especially in the Central Nonchernozem Region and Moldavia. The major pioneer efforts in interfarm livestock production appear to have occurred in Moldavia and in Tambov Oblast. In the latter, for example, the first intercollective farm feeding center—for cattle—was organized in 1960. Intercollective operations in both cattle and hog feeding developed during the 1960s, and in 1970 the feeding base was reorganized into a collective-state farm complex. From 1971 the Tambov Oblast agroindustrial associations has united the raion specialized farm associations, which, in turn, incorporate specialized livestock complexes and affiliated enterprises.[51] Intercollective farm associations for production of meat also apparently were first organized in 1960 in Moldavia. Raion interfarm fattening associations are united in a republic association. Beginning in 1973 the republic collective farm union was experimentally entrusted with the overall management of collective and intercollective farm activities in Moldavia.[52]

The intent of the move toward specialized livestock operations—both individual enterprises and interfarm associations—is increased efficiency. At the 84 interfarm enterprises for beef and pork in the RSFSR in 1972 the average daily weight gain of cattle was 705 grams compared with 470 grams in republic collective farms, and on hogs was 425 grams, compared with 303 grams on collective farms.[53] The more rapid gains are associated with lower costs, which originate both in feed and labor savings. In three raions in Moldavia in 1970, for example, average feed use per kilogram of gain of cattle was 7.2 kilograms at the intercollective enterprises and 10.5 kilograms for all collective farms. Similarly, for hogs, the feed use range was 5.8 to 10.6, in favor of intercollective units.[54] Compared with these results, greater efficiency is intended on the new large complexes coming into operation in the Soviet Union.

OTHER POLICIES TO REDUCE FEED DEMAND

Other policies to reduce feed requirements have included a drive to utilize more balanced rations, which is based primarily on a rapid expansion of the mixed-feed industry, and an intensified effort to improve the breeding herd both through domestic achievements and imported breeding stock.

The Soviet mixed-feed industry is relatively new. Production during the first half of the 1960s barely exceeded 10 million tons annually and consisted heavily of milling by-products. Production has increased rapidly to 24 million tons in 1970 and 32 million tons in 1973. Mixed-feed availability as a share of total concentrate consumption has increased from 17 percent in 1960 to about 28 percent in 1973. The share of concentrate consumption accounted for by mixed feeds has grown slowly since 1965, however. As pointed out recently by V. Chemm, Soviet Deputy Minister of Procurements,

"The thing holding up the increasing production of feeds at the present time is the shortage of protein raw materials. . . . "[55]

According to the plan, by 1975 state mixed feed plants will produce about 41 million tons of mixed feed and 1.2 million tons of protein-vitamin supplements, which will be used by farms to produce another 6 or 7 million tons of mixed feed.[56] Current plans reportedly call for mixed-feed output to reach 100 million tons by 1990.[57] Some economists, however, have emphasized the economies of developing a substantial share of feed mixing on farms by supplying them with protein-vitamin supplements. The need for supplements in 1975 reportedly is 7 to 7.5 million tons instead of the planned 1.2 million tons.[58]

As of early 1973 the number of mixed feed plants and shops in the system of the Soviet Ministry of Procurements reportedly was 546, with an additional 172 plants to be built during the current five-year plan.[59] This system excludes a substantial number of inter-collective farm mixed-feed plants. The percentage distribution of state mixed-feed production in 1972 by category of livestock was as follows: hogs, 50; poultry, 28; cattle, 18; other, 4.[60]

Soviet studies have indicated that use of well-balanced rations would result in considerable feed savings. Burlakov, for example, concluded that the potential savings in grain feed is 20 million tons in 1975 and almost 40 million tons in 1980.[61]

The major effort to improve livestock performance through breeding apparently has been focused on beef production. Specialized beef breeds have represented an almost insignificant share of the Soviet cattle herd. In 1968 there were only 2.3 million head of beef cattle, including 707,000 cows—about 2 percent of all Soviet cattle.[62] Plans call for 7.5 to 8.0 million head of beef breeds by 1975.[63] Specialized beef herds are scheduled to account for 15 to 20 percent of total beef output.

Artificial insemination has been used extensively to increase the breeding power of the improved herd. In 1970 in the RSFSR, the semen of 2,000 beef bulls was used to inseminate 1.35 million cows and heifers. Soviet specialists expect 4 to 5 million head of beef cows in the RSFSR to be inseminated by about 1975.[64]

The USSR has made substantial use of imports to upgrade the breeding quality of the cattle herds. During the 1964-73 decade, the Soviet Union imported 28,900 heads of breeding cattle, apparently primarily beef breeds.

The dairy herd will continue to furnish the major supply of beef during the next several years. Soviet specialists recommend the breeding of dairy and dual-purpose cows with beef bulls to attain hybrid vigor in calves. Leading farms reportedly can produce 450- to 500-kilogram crossbred yearlings in 15 to 18 months.[65] According to Ministry of Agriculture specialists, within a few years 12 to 15 million head of crossbred calves will be produced annually.[66] Repetitive crossbreeding with beef bulls also will be used to develop a beef herd in the Soviet Union.[67]

NARROWING THE FEED GAP

The feed-livestock economy study, to which I referred at the beginning of this chapter, projected for 1980 a feed deficit of 53 million tons (in oat-equivalent feed units), including 22 million tons of concentrates. It also projected a slightly increasing deficit of digestible protein, which was calculated at 3.5 million tons in 1970-71. The projections in the study assume a great deal of linearity in domestic feed production and requirement relationships, for example, in grain yields and in feed-livestock product input-output ratios.

Policy actions by the Soviet government seem likely to increase supplies and reduce requirements at a more rapid rate, however, than implied by the assumptions of linearity. On the supply side, major policies discussed in this chapter include the nonchernozem program, the expansion of grain areas, the increase of fertilizer deliveries to agriculture, an irrigation program, and work on higher-protein feeds. On the demand side, policies include specialized livestock enterprises (including interfarm associations), development of a mixed-feed industry, and an effort to improve the breeding herd.

The impact from many of these policies will be slight at first and probably will only gradually build up sufficiently to alter the results suggested by linear projections. By 1980 considerable progress probably will be attained, although it seems doubtful that the feed gap will be closed.

The expansion in grain areas has had the most immediate impact. As indicated earlier, if this area is maintained at the higher level, output in 1980 could be boosted 10 to 20 million tons above previous projections. Response to accelerated fertilizer use on grains and forage crops already is occurring, and by 1980 yield increases could move measurably above the longer-term rates of growth. The nonchernozem and irrigation programs require massive and slower-maturing investments. It seems likely that heavier-than-normal impacts from these programs will not be felt before the 1980s. Work in finding better protein sources may keep the protein gap from widening, but is not likely to close the gap unless exceptional technological discoveries are made.

Similarly, on the demand side, the development of specialized livestock enterprises and efforts to improve the breeding herd may bring little improvement to national average efficiency in feed use before 1980, although a considerable improvement may occur during that decade. The mixed-feed industry now is undergoing rapid growth and may help bring improvement in typical rations, although, as noted previously, it is held back by limited availability of protein feed sources. It seems unlikely, also, that state output of mixed feed will reach one-third of total concentrate use by 1980. Farm and interfarm production, however, may increase dramatically and upgrade the overall quality of rations.

A qualitative analysis of Soviet internal policies in the feed-livestock sector can enable little more than a qualitative assessment of success in closing the projected feed gap. On balance, though, it seems likely that the Soviet Union will succeed in covering from domestic sources well over half of the projected feed energy deficit by 1980. Greater progress may be made in the 1980s, and eventual self-sufficiency seems likely to be attained. The adequacy of domestic protein sources in the Soviet Union seems much more questionable, however. No clear-cut trend to cover this deficit is now evident, and external sources probably will be necessary to provide this critical element of the feeding program.

NOTES

1. David M. Schoonover, "The Soviet Feed-Livestock Economy: Preliminary Findings on Performance and Trade Implications," in Prospects for Agricultural Trade with the USSR (Washington, D.C.: U.S. Department of Agriculture ERS-Foreign 356, April 1974).

2. Pravda, March 16, 1974.

3. Trud, April 3, 1974.

4. Leonid Florentyev, Moscow, Domestic Radio, April 6, 1974.

5. Angel O. Byrne, "Soviet Plan Large-Scale Farm Development in European USSR," Foreign Agriculture, May 20, 1974.

6. N. Baybakov, ed., Gosudarstvenniy Pyatiletniy Plan Razvitiya Narodnovo Khozyaystva SSSR na 1971-75 gody (Moscow, 1972).

7. Sovetskaya Rossiya, April 5, 1974.

8. Ibid.

9. Byrne, op. cit.

10. Foreign Broadcast Information Service, Daily Report, Soviet Union, May 15, 1974.

11. Sovetskaya Rossiya, April 5, 1974.

12. Ibid.

13. Sovetskaya Rossiya, April 11, 1974.

14. Florentyev, op. cit.

15. K. Khoroshilov, "Polneye Ispolzovat Reservy Zernovovo Polya," Ekonomika Sel'skovo Khozyaystva, no. 3 (1974).

16. K. Kuznetsov, "Puti Resheniya Zernovoy Problemy v Strane," Zemledeliye, no. 2 (1971).

17. Pravda, March 16, 1974.

18. V. Manyakin, "Tempy Rosta Proizvodstva Produktsii Rasteniyevodstva," Ekonomika Sel'skovo Khozyaystva, no. 4 (1972).

19. V.N. Semyenov, Finansy SSSR, no. 12 (1973).

20. Bayakov, op. cit.

21. Theodore Shabad, New York Times, October 29, 1973.

22. Foreign Broadcast Information Service, Daily Report, Soviet Union, May 15, 1974.

23. Moscow Domestic Radio, June 2, 1973.

24. Sel'skaya Zhizn, February 6, 1973.

25. Moscow Domestic Radio, July 1, 1973.

26. Leningrad Domestic Radio, December 1, 1972.

27. Moscow Domestic Radio, January 14, 1974.

28. Moscow Domestic Radio, January 16, 1974.

29. G.F. Raskin, Sel'skoye Khozyaystvo Sovetskovo Soyuza (Moscow, 1970).

30. V.D. Kabanov, "Proizvodstvo i Ispolzovaniye Belka v Zhivotnovodstve," Zhivotnovodstvo, no. 2 (1974).

31. V. Martynovskiy, "Uvelichit Proizvodstvo Vysokokachest-vennykh i Deshevykh Kormov," Zemledeliye, no. 2 (1974).

32. I. Shatilov, "Sovershenstvovat Kormoproizvodstvo", Zemledeliye, no. 1 (1973).

33. Martynovskiy, op. cit.

34. Baybakov, op. cit.

35. Kabanov, op. cit.

36. Baybakov, op. cit.

37. Ibid.

38. V. Onisovets, Politicheskoye Samoobrazovaniye, July, 1972.

39. Pravda, April 26, 1971.

40. A. Dubrovin, Zhurnalist, no. 3 (1972).

41. Pravda, April 26, 1971.

42. Dubrovin, op. cit.

43. Baybakov, op. cit.

44. P.A. Yesaulov, "Nauchno-Tekhnicheskiy Progress v Zhivotnovodstve," Zhivotnovodstvo, no. 12 (1971).

45. V.I. Akulinin, Mekhanizatsiya i Elektrifikatsiya Sotsial-isticheskovo Sel'skovo Khosyaystva, no. 8 (1971).

46. Dubrovin, op. cit.

47. K. Makurin, Mezhdunarodniy Sel'skokhozyaystvennyy Zhurnal, no. 2 (1973).

48. V. Galashova, Vestnik Statistiki, no. 11 (1973).

49. Ibid.

50. L.I. Brezhnev, Speech at the Plenum CC-CPSU, December 10, 1973, Voprosy Agrarnoy Politiki KPSS i Osvoyeniy Tselinnykh Zemel Kazakhstana: Rechi i Doklady (Moscow, 1974).

51. N. Yumashev, Ekonomicheskaya Gazeta, no. 49 (1973).

52. V. Golikov and G. Dolgoshey, Kommunist, no. 18 (December 1973).

53. Sel'skaya Zhizn, February 6, 1973.

54. N. Burlakov, "Effektivnost Proizvodstva Produktsii Zhivotnovodstva," Ekonomika Sel'skovo Khozyaystva, no. 5 (1972).

55. V. Chemm, Mukomolno-Elevatornaya i Kombikormovaya Promyshlennost, no. 2 (1973).

56. V. Annenkov, Ekonomika Sel'skovo Khozyaystva, no. 3 (1973).

57. Roger E. Neetz, Foreign Agricultural Service Report (Moscow: American Embassy, June 12, 1974).

58. Burlakov, op. cit.

59. V. Annenkov, Ekonomika Sel'skovo Khozyaystva, no. 3 (1973).

60. Kabanov, op. cit.

61. Burlakov, op. cit.

62. V. Desyatov, Voprosy Ekonomiki, no. 5 (1971).

63. Baybakov, op. cit.

64. S. Dudin, "Uvelichit Proizvodstvo Vysokokachestvennoy Govyadiny," Ekonomika Sel'skovo Khozyaystva, no. 4 (1972).

65. V. Matskevich, "Uskorennoye Razvitiye Sel'skovo Khozyaystva," Ekonomika Sel'skovo Khozyaystva, no. 3 (1971).

66. Ministry of Agriculture USSR, "Obespechit Dalneysheye Razvitiya Zhivotnovodstva," Ekonomika Sel'skovo Khozyaystva, no. 4 (1972).

67. Dudin, op. cit.

10

SOVIET FARMER PRODUCTIVITY, 1950-70, AS MEASURED BY A U.S. BAROMETER

Roy D. Laird

The central interest of this chapter is to analyze Soviet agricultural changes between 1950 and 1970 in terms of productivity per farmer. U.S. performance is used as a barometer of the Soviet achievement.[1]

If all conditions under human control were made equal, the U.S. farmer ought to out-produce his Soviet counterpart because the U.S. climate is more favorable to agriculture. However, in spite of climate differences, equal input advances ought to result in similar growth changes.

In 1970, U.S. farmer aids (for example, tractors and mineral fertilizers) still remained significantly higher than such Soviet aids. However, Soviet investments in agricultural production increased much more rapidly than did U.S. investments during the preceding 20-year period. This being the case, if the two systems were equally efficient on all accounts, production per farmer in the Soviet Union should have increased more rapidly than U.S. production per farmer. As we shall see, the opposite was the case.

As argued elsewhere, we believe the primary human advantage enjoyed by the U.S. farmer over his Soviet counterpart lies in the decision-making realm.[2]

A farm is a managerial unit. In 1950 there were 5.5 million U.S. farms and 9.9 million farm workers for a ratio of 1.8 workers per farm.[3] Thus there were something less than 5.4 million farm managers (some managers operate more than one farm) in charge of

The author wishes to thank Betty Laird, Alec Pirogow, and Darlene Heacock for enormous assistance in the preparation of this study.

managing the farms, themselves, and something less than one other worker (in the vast majority of cases a member of the same family). By 1970 there were 2.9 million farms and 4.5 million farm workers for a lower ratio of 1.6 workers per farm.

In 1950 in the Soviet Union there were 111,400 kolkhozy and sovkhozy and (excluding peasants engaged in private plot operations) 31 million farm workers, a ratio of 278 workers per farm. As a result of the 1950s amalgamations, by 1970 there were only 48,000 farms and some 26.8 million state and collective farm workers, resulting in a ratio of 558:1. In our view one farm manager responsible for himself and 278 workers has an impossible task, and enormous losses in worker efficiency will result. If this is true, problems of efficiency would be doubly impossible for a manager responsible for 558 workers.

A GRAIN PER FARMER INDICATOR

If, as we shall attempt to demonstrate, increases in total grain output as related to the changed total number of agricultural workers is used as a barometer of agricultural success, when measured by U.S. achievements, the Soviet Union made significant progress between 1950 and 1960.[4] Indeed, growth so measured equaled U.S. growth in the 1950s when both the area sown to grain and grain yields advanced significantly in the Soviet Union. However, if the United States provides a barometer as to what growth can be achieved in spite of even greater Soviet increases in agricultural inputs between 1960 and 1970 (Brezhnev's intensification campaign), when little new grain area was added, production per farmer growth in the Soviet Union lagged by some 68 percent behind U.S. growth. Moreover, with all the new emphasis given to Soviet agriculture during the 20-year period, the growth in productivity per farmer lagged 118 percent behind the U.S. barometer.

Why do we believe grain per farmer is a key measure? In 1970 grain occupied 58 percent of the total sown area in both nations. Beyond the importance of grain in direct consumption, it is the major key to modern livestock production. Fertilizers, combines, and other inputs to grain farming can be crucial, but the ultimate determinant of the amount of grain available is farmer efficiency.[5] The amount of food ultimately available for a population (where grain is the key crop) is very closely correlated with the total amount of grain produced per total number of farm workers. The base for a test of this assertion is provided by a USDA time series recording calculations (based in part on food dollar values) as to changes in the number of people fed per U.S. agricultural worker:

	1950	1960	1970
Number of people fed by one U.S. agricultural worker	14.6	25.2	47.1

When the percentage increases during the period are compared with the percentage increases in grain per farmer, a striking correlation is revealed:

Percent Increases	1950-60	1960-70	1950-70
Number of people fed by one U.S. farmer	173	187	323
Grain produced by one U.S. farmer	174	209	364
Grain produced by one Soviet farmer	175	140	246

If the 1960-70 and 1950-70 production data were corrected for the greater consumption of meat than in 1950 (which advanced 22 percent by 1970), the parallel in the latter years would be even closer.[6]

Utilizing the barometer to compare Soviet advances with those of the United States, we see that the Soviet Union kept pace between 1950 and 1960, and that the gap significantly widened after 1960.

FOOD PRODUCTION, 1950-70

Although our prime interest is in changes in terms of production per farmer, in order to examine these changes we need first to look at total production.

Production in both countries, excepting eggs and milk in the United States and potatoes in the Soviet Union, was up substantially. Moreover, in most instances the Soviet advances were very substantially higher than those achieved in the United States (Table 10.1).

In spite of the sown area changes, such a comparison would imply that the Soviet Union had gone a long way toward correcting its major agricultural shortcomings and (minus natural differences primarily due to climate) is well on the way toward matching U.S. achievements. However, when output growth in the two countries between 1960-70 is compared, a shift in the pattern is discovered (Table 10.2). The growth in grain production is equal, while U.S. potato and sugar beet growth is slightly higher; yet the sown area in

TABLE 10.1

U.S. and Soviet Production Changes, 1950-70

| | Million tons | | | | Changes, 1950-70 (1950 = 100) | |
| | United States | | Soviet Union[a] | | United States | Soviet Union |
	1950	1970	1950	1970		
Crops						
Grains	148.9	246.5	77.9	173.6	165	223
Potatoes	10.0	14.0	80.2	92.4	140	115
Sugar beets	9.8	24.5	19.0	78.6	250	413
Livestock						
Meat[b]	12.6	20.6	4.9	12.3	164	253
Milk	52.8	53.0	25.3	83.0	100	243
Eggs (billions)	64.8	68.3	11.7	40.7	105	347

[a]No adjustment has been made in grain to allow for a conviction among Western observers that because of a failure to account adequately for moisture and foreign matter, Soviet usable grain is some 10-15 percent below the official accounting presented here.

[b]U.S. meat adjusted upward by 26 percent to make accounting comparable to Soviet accounting (for example, which includes offal).

Source: Calculated from Agricultural Statistics (Washington, D.C.: Department of Agriculture, Government Printing Office, 1960-73); Narodnoe khozyaistvo SSSR (Moscow: Statistika, 1956-72); Sel'skoe Khozyaistvo SSSR (Moscow: Statistika, 1960, 1971).

TABLE 10.2

U.S. and Soviet Production Changes, 1960–70

| | Million tons | | | | Changes, 1960–70 (1960 = 100) | |
| | United States | | Soviet Union | | United States | Soviet Union |
	1960	1970	1960	1970		
Crops						
Grains (metric tons)	186.2	246.5	131.2	173.6	132	132
Potatoes (metric tons)	12.1	14.0	82.3	92.4	116	112
Sugar beets (metric tons)	15.3	24.5	50.8	78.6	160	155
Livestock						
Meat	16.1	20.6	8.7	12.3	128	142
Milk	55.8	53.0	61.7	83.0	95	134
Eggs	61.6	68.3	27.4	40.7	110	149

Source: Calculated from Agricultural Statistics (Washington, D.C.: Department of Agriculture, Government Printing Office, 1960–73); Narodnoe khozyaistvo SSSR (Moscow: Statistika, 1956–72); Sel'skoe Khozyaistvo SSSR (Moscow: Statistika, 1960, 1971).

245

the Soviet Union advanced another 2 percent (grain 3 percent) while in the United States it declined 7 percent (grain 2 percent).

Two explanatory points should be stressed at this juncture. First, most farm changes from year to year are normally small. Therefore, comparisons used here in all instances but for crops are just for the years indicated. However, weather changes can significantly alter crop yields (especially grain in the Soviet Union). Therefore, in every instance where crop data is used it is for the average of five years in both countries (for example, the two years prior to the year indicated, the year itself, and the two years subsequent to the year indicated). Thus, 1970 crop, yield, and area figures for both countries are actually an average for the years 1968, 1969, 1970, 1971, and 1972.[7] Second, in the United States, lagging prices and various government programs were not exactly conducive to all-out production expansion during the two decades, while in the Soviet Union unprecedented new investments were poured into agriculture, especially after 1964 when Khrushchev was ousted.

A point that must be stressed here is that although sugar beets and potatoes are important and they are included here as examples of other crops (often full Soviet data is not available, especially on many important feed crops), the focus of the comparison should be on grain. As shown by Table 10.3, in terms of the total sown area, even in 1970 sugar beets and potatoes together only occupied 6.7 percent of the Soviet sown area (.8 percent in the United States), while grain occupied 57.8 percent of the area (also 57.7 percent in the United States).

YIELD CHANGES, 1950-70

Output per unit of sown land is crucial in any country. In the United States during the period under study, vast tracts of crop land were held idle in various programs. In the Soviet Union no similar idle lands existed, although once-virgin lands were ploughed up during the 1950s. Since 1964 the Brezhnev leadership has been right in stressing intensification. Little usable virgin land remained after 1960, and for the period 1960-70 nearly all of the Soviet advances in productivity came from yield per hectare increases.

Since the late 1950s Soviet agricultural investments have been directed toward achieving higher yields, especially in grain. Yet a most interesting picture emerges when the 1950-60 yield advances for grain and meat (per unit of sown land) are contrasted with similar yield changes in the United States (Table 10.4).

TABLE 10.3

U.S. and Soviet Sown Area and Key Crops, 1950, 1960, and 1970
(million hectares and percent)

	1950		1960		1970	
	United States	Soviet Union	United States	Soviet Union	United States	Soviet Union
Sown area, hectares	156.6	145.3	145.3	203.0	134.8	206.5
Sown in Grain, hectares	88.3	102.9	78.6	115.6	77.8	119.3
percent	56.4	70.8	54.1	56.9	57.7	57.8
Sown in Potatoes, hectares	.66	8.5	.56	9.1	.56	8.1
percent	.4	5.8	.4	4.5	.4	3.9
Sown in Sugar beets, hectares	.29	1.3	.39	2.9	.57	3.4
percent	.2	.9	.3	1.4	.4	1.6

Source: Calculated from Agricultural Statistics (Washington, D.C.: Department of Agriculture, Government Printing Office, 1960–73); Narodnoe khozyaistvo SSSR (Moscow: Statistika, 1956–72); Sel'skoe Khozyaistvo SSSR (Moscow: Statistika, 1960, 1971).

TABLE 10.4

U.S. and Soviet Yield Changes, 1950–70

| | Yield per Hectare | | | | Changes, 1950–70 (1950 = 100) | |
| | United States | | Soviet Union | | | |
	1959	1970	1950	1970	United States	Soviet Union
Crops (centners per hectare)						
Grain	16.8	31.7	7.5	14.4	189	192
Potatoes	151	251	93	114	166	123
Sugar beets	336	429	146	231	128	158
Livestock						
Meat (kgs per hectare)	80	153	34	60	191	140
Milk (liters per hectare)	337	393	241	402	117	167
Eggs (no. per hectare)	414	507	76	197	122	259

Source: Calculated from Agricultural Statistics (Washington, D.C.: Department of Agriculture, Government Printing Office, 1960–73); Narodnoe khozyaistvo SSSR (Moscow: Statistika, 1956–72); Sel'skoe Khozyaistvo SSSR (Moscow: Statistika, 1960, 1971).

A substantial increase in the number of chickens and milk cows (cows by 165 percent) in the Soviet Union and a substantial U.S. decline in these numbers (cows by 31 percent) did allow the Soviet Union to surpass the United States in output of milk and eggs per hectare sown. However grain yields grew only 3 percent more than U.S. yields (although Soviet farms received an 8.5 increase in fertilizer while the U.S. increase was 1.9 times). When measured in terms of kilograms of meat produced per sown hectare, U.S. output advance of 91 percent surpassed the Soviet advance of 40 percent.

When yield advances between 1960-70 are compared, the pattern again changes for the key crop grain (Table 10.5). The peak of Soviet yield growth occurred during the earlier period. True, U.S. grain yields advanced only 1 percent more than Soviet yields per hectare, but this is a reverse of the 1950-60 picture when Soviet yields increased 3 percent more than U.S. yields.

PRODUCTION PER CAPITA

Perhaps too much has been made here of shifts in Soviet grain yield advances, particularly over a seemingly small percentage differential change in the growth of grain yields. However, these changes need to be put into the perspective of the population's food needs.

Perhaps 1 percent is small, but had the grain-short Soviet Union grown 1 percent more grain per year during 1960-70, the total output during the period would have been more than 8 million metric tons greater, enough to supply more than 8 million people for a year at the level of the stated Soviet goal of producing 1 ton per capita annually or some 10 million people for a year at the level of the 1970 production of .72 tons per capita. Further reminder of the importance of every ton of grain is the fact that twice during the period accounted for here, in 1963 under Khrushchev and in 1972 (1968-72 averages used) under Brezhnev, massive grain purchases were made abroad.

Let us draw some contrasts between 1970 U.S. and Soviet production per capita. Of course imports and exports have been important, but throughout the period the vast bulk of food in both countries was domestically produced.

1970 PRODUCTION AND COMMENTS

As noted above, in 1970 the Soviet Union produced .72 tons of grain per capita. The Soviet leaders' long-run goal of producing 1 ton

TABLE 10.5

U.S. and Soviet Yield Changes, 1960–70

| | Yield per Hectare | | | | Changes, 1960–70 (1960 = 100) | |
| | United States | | Soviet Union | | | |
	1960	1970	1960	1970	United States	Soviet Union
Crops (centners per hectare)						
Grain	23.7	31.7	10.8	14.4	134	133
Potatoes	215	251	90	114	116	127
Sugar beets	392	429	175	231	109	132
Livestock						
Meat (kgs per hectare)	111	153	43	60	138	140
Milk (liters per hectare)	384	393	303	402	102	133
Eggs (no. per hectare)	424	507	135	197	120	146

Source: Calculated from Agricultural Statistics (Washington, D.C.: Department of Agriculture, Government Printing Office, 1960–73); Narodnoe khozyaistvo SSSR (Moscow: Statistika, 1956–72); Sel'skoe Khozyaistvo SSSR (Moscow: Statistika, 1960, 1971).

of grain per capita annually was achieved in the United States in 1950, and by 1970 the United States was producing 1.2 tons of grain per capita.

U.S. potato output per capita has been virtually stable since 1950 (in 1950 there were 66 and in 1960 there were 69 kg produced per capita). Most Americans (and most nutritionists) think there is probably too much starch in the U.S. diet. Large amounts of Soviet potatoes go into animal feed. Nevertheless, the Soviet tendency to run to dumpling shapes is partially a result of their consumption of a large amount of potatoes, much more than that consumed by U.S. citizens. In 1970, U.S. potato production per capita was 69 kg as contrasted to 382 kg in the Soviet Union. (One kilogram equals 2.2 pounds.)

Both the Soviet Union and the United States import large quantities of sugar. In spite of the Cuban source of sugar, however, the Soviets continue to produce more sugar beets per capita than does the United States. Much of the Soviet production undoubtedly goes into animal feed. In 1970, U.S. production of sugar beets per capita was 120 kg versus Soviet 325 kg.

Perhaps, as some have suggested recently, in eating too much, the U.S. citizen also eats too much meat. However, Soviet medical authorities assert that the average annual consumption per person should be some 82 kg of meat per capita.[8] In 1970 the U.S. produced 101 kg of meat per capita as contrasted with 51 kg per capita for the Soviet Union.

Whereas in 1950, U.S. output of milk was substantially higher per capita (337 kg) than Soviet output per capita (198 kg), the relationship was reversed during the two decades. Thus milk production in terms of liters per capita in 1970 was U.S. = 260 and Soviet = 343. On the U.S. side, many citizens became disenchanted with milk, particularly in the form of butter, and in the struggle against animal fat (and asserted cholesterol dangers) turned increasingly to vegetable oil. In contrast, the bulk of the Soviet table spread is butter, while relatively little by way of vegetable oil is available.

For multiple reasons, Americans (again including cholesterol fears) eat fewer eggs now than in 1950, when some 427 eggs were produced per capita. In contrast, although Soviet output per capita has increased 2.5 times (from 66 per capita in 1950), at least two times the present Soviet production level seems desirable, for as we see in the United States in 1970, 335 eggs were produced per capita as compared to only 168 per capita in the Soviet Union.

PRODUCTION PER FARMER

As indicated in the opening paragraph of this chapter, during the decades involved, the gap between farmer productivity in the two countries increased significantly.

Official Soviet accounts of the total labor force engaged in agriculture are lower than Western estimates, which include a substantially larger number of peasants engaged in private food production. In our view the higher Western estimates are closer to the truth. Comparisons made on this higher basis do show a greater absolute difference in terms of production per farmer in favor of the U.S. farmer. However, the prime measure we are interested in here is in relative changes over time, and as shown in Table 10.6, whether one uses the higher or lower labor count, the U.S. versus Soviet changes are substantially the same.

Relative changes in production per agricultural worker are as shown in Table 10.7.

Table 10.8 reflects the 1950-70 changes in terms of the number of times the U.S. farmers' output exceeded that of the Soviet farmers.

Clearly the Soviet agricultural workers have gained somewhat in the milk and egg realms, although the ratios are still more than

TABLE 10.6

U.S. and Soviet Agricultural Workers, 1950-70
(Millions; 1950 = 100)

	1950	1960	1970
Soviet, Eason estimate	42.1	40.5	38.1*
1950 = 100	100	96	90
Soviet, Official estimate	32.4	32.0	29.2
1950 = 100	100	99	90
U.S., USDA estimate	9.9	7.1	4.5
1950 = 100	100	72	45

*Eason's data ends with 1968, therefore, using his same percent of additional workers in private over the official Soviet total 1968, 38.1 is our own Eason derived estimate for 1970.

Sources: Warren W. Eason, "Demography," in Handbook of Soviet Social Science Data, ed. Ellen Mickiewicz (New York: The Free Press, 1973).

TABLE 10.7

U.S. and Soviet Output per Farmer, 1950–70

| | United States | | Soviet Union* | | Changes 1950–70 (1950 = 100) | |
	1950	1970	1950	1970	United States	Soviet Union
Crops (tons)						
Grain	15.04	54.78	1.85(2.40)	4.56(5.94)	364	246(247)
Potatoes	1.01	3.12	1.90(2.48)	2.43(3.16)	309	128(128)
Sugar beets	.98	5.44	.45(.59)	2.06(2.69)	555	457(456)
Livestock						
Meat (tons)	1.27	4.57	.12(.150)	.32(.420)	360	267(280)
Milk (tons)	5.33	11.78	.84(1.09)	2.18(2.84)	221	260(261)
Eggs (number)	6,545	15,178	278(361)	1,068(1,393)	232	384(386)

*The figures not in parentheses are derived from the Eason estimate (see Table 10.7); those in parentheses are derived from the official Soviet estimate.

Source: Calculated from Agricultural Statistics (Washington, D.C.: Department of Agriculture, Government Printing Office, 1960–73); Narodnoe khozyaistvo SSSR (Moscow: Statistika, 1956–72); Sel'skoe Khozyaistvo SSSR (Moscow: Statistika, 1960, 1971).

TABLE 10.8

U.S. and Soviet Sown Area per Farmer and Output per Farmer, 1950, 1960, and 1970

	1950			1960			1970		
	Soviet	U.S.	Difference U.S. x Soviet	Soviet	U.S.	Difference U.S. x Soviet	Soviet	U.S.	Difference U.S. x Soviet
Sown area (hectares)	3.5	15.9	4.5	5.0	20.5	4.1	5.4	29.9	5.5
Output Grain (tons)	1.85	15.04	8.1	3.24	26.22	8.1	4.56	54.78	12.0
Potatoes (tons)	1.90	1.01	- 1.9	2.03	1.69	- 1.2	2.43	3.12	1.3
Sugar beets (tons)	0.45	0.98	2.2	1.25	2.15	1.7	2.06	5.44	2.6
Meat (tons)	0.12	1.27	11.5	0.21	2.26	10.8	0.32	4.57	14.3
Milk (tons)	0.84	5.33	6.3	1.52	7.85	5.2	2.18	11.78	5.4
Eggs (number)	278	6,545	23.5	676	8,676	12.8	1,068	15.17	14.2

Source: Calculated from Agricultural Statistics (Washington, D.C.: Department of Agriculture, Government Printing Office, 1960-73); Narodnoe khozyaistvo SSSR (Moscow: Statistika, 1956-72); Sel'skoe Khozyaistvo SSSR (Moscow: Statistika, 1960, 1971).

254

TABLE 10.9

U.S.-Soviet Agricultural Data, 1950, 1960, and 1970[a]

	1950		1960		1970		1950-70		1950-60 (1950 = 100)		1960-70 (1960 = 100)	
	United States	Soviet Union	United States	Soviet Union	United States	Soviet Union	United States	Soviet Union	United States	Soviet Union	United States	Soviet Union
1. Population, millions	151.7	178.5	179.9	212.4	203.8	241.7	134	135	119	119	113	114
2. Farmers U.S. & Eason Soviet, millions	9.9	42.1	7.1	40.5	4.5	38.1	45	90	72	96	63	94
3. Population per farmer, Eason	15.3	4.2	25.3	5.2	45.2	6.3	300	150	165	124	179	121
4. Farmers as percent of population, Eason	6.5	24.0	3.9	19.0	2.2	16.0	34	67	60	79	56	84
5. Total labor force, Eason	58.9	80.1	65.8	95.7	78.6	119.1	133	149	112	119	119	124
6. Farmers as percent of labor force, Eason	17	53	11	42	6	32	35	60	65	79	55	76
7. No. Workers per farmer, Eason	5.9	1.9	9.3	2.4	17.5	3.1	297	163	158	126	189	124
8. Farmers, U.S. & official Soviet	9.9	32.4	7.1	32.0	4.5	29.2	45	90	72	99	63	91
9. No. Kolkhoz, 1,000s		111.4		44.0		33.0						
10. No. Sovkhoz, 1,000s		5.0		7.4		15.0						
11. Total farms, 1,000s	5,388.4	116.4	3,962.5	51.1	2,954.2	48.0						
12. Sown area, million hectares	156.6	146.3	145.3[b]	203.0	134.8[b]	206.5	86	141	93	139	93	102
13. Hectares sown per farm	29.1	1,256.0	36.7	3,973.0	45.6	4,302.0	157	343	126	316	124	108
14. Hectares sown per agricultural worker	15.9	3.5	20.5	5.0	29.9	5.4	188	154	129	143	146	108
15. Hectares sown per capita	1.03	0.82	0.81	0.96	0.66	0.85	64	104	78	117	86	89
16. Grain, million hectares	88.3	102.9	78.6	115.6	77.8	119.3	88	116	89	112	98	103
17. Grain, million tons	148.9	77.9	186.2	131.2	246.5	173.6	165	223	125	168	132	132
18. Grain, centners per hectare	16.8	7.5	23.7	10.8	31.7	14.4	189	192	141	144	134	133
19. Grain, hectares per farmer	8.92	2.44	11.1	3.12	17.3	3.13	194	128	124	128	158	100

(continued)

(Table 10.9 continued)

	1950 United States	1950 Soviet Union	1960 United States	1960 Soviet Union	1970 United States	1970 Soviet Union	1950-70 United States	1950-70 Soviet Union	1950-60 (1950 = 100) United States	1950-60 (1950 = 100) Soviet Union	1960-70 (1960 = 100) United States	1960-70 (1960 = 100) Soviet Union
20. Grain, hectares per capita	0.58	0.58	0.44	0.54	0.38	0.49	66	84	76	93	86	91
21. Grain, tons per capita	0.98	0.44	1.03	0.62	1.21	0.72	123	164	105	140	117	116
22. Grain, tons per farmer	15.04	1.85	26.22	3.24	54.78	4.56	364	246	174	175	209	141
23. Potatoes, million hectares	0.66	8.5[c]	0.56	9.1	0.56	8.1	85	95	85	107	100	89
24. Potatoes, million tons	10.00	80.2	12.06	82.3	14.03	92.4	140	115	121	103	116	112
25. Potatoes, centners per hectare	151	93	215	90	251	114	166	123	142	97	116	127
26. Potatoes, kgs per population	66	449	67	387	69	382	104	85	102	86	103	99
27. Potatoes, tons per agric. worker	1.01	1.90	1.69	2.03	3.12	2.43	309	128	167	107	185	120
28. Sugar beets, million hectares	0.29	1.3[c]	0.39	2.9	0.57	3.4	196	262	134	223	146	117
29. Sugar beets, million tons	9.8	19.0	15.3	50.8	24.5	78.6	250	413	156	267	160	155
30. Sugar beets, centners per hectare	336	146	392	175	429	231	128	158	117	119	109	132
31. Sugar beets, kgs per capita	65	106	85	239	120	325	185	306	130	225	141	136
32. Sugar beets, tons per farmer	0.98	0.45	2.15	1.25	5.44	2.06	555	457	219	278	253	165
33. Cattle, millions	77.9	58.1	96.2	74.2	112.4	95.2	144	164	123	128	117	128
34. Hogs, millions	58.9	22.2	59.0	53.4	57.0	56.1	97	253	100	241	97	105
35. Sheep and goats,[e] millions	29.8	93.6	33.2	144.0	20.4	135.8	68	145	111	154	61	94
36. Milk cows,[d] millions	21.9	24.6	17.5	33.9	12.0	40.5	55	165	80	138	69	119
37. Milk, million tons	52.8	35.3	55.8	61.7	53.0	83.0	100	253	106	178	95	134

38. M per capita, liters	348	198	310	290	260	343	75	173	89	146	84	118
39. M per farmer, tons	5.33	0.84	7.85	1.52	11.78	2.18	221	260	147	181	150	143
40. Milk per cow, litersd	2,410	1,370	3,188	1,779	4,421	2,110	183	154	132	130	139	119
41. Milk per liters sown area	337	241	384	303	393	402	117	167	114	128	102	133
42. Meat, million tons	12.6	4.9	16.1	8.7	20.6	12.3	164	253	128	178	128	142
43. Meat per capita, kgs	83	27	89	41	101	51	122	189	107	152	113	124
44. Meat per farmer, tons	1.27	0.12	2.26	0.21	4.57	0.32	360	267	178	175	202	152
45. Meat per sown hectare, kgs	80	34	111	43	153	60	191	181	139	130	138	140
46. Cattle-cows	56.0	33.5	78.7	40.3	100.4	54.7	179	163	140	120	128	136
47. Animal units, f cattle-cows	44.8	26.8	62.9	32.2	80.3	43.8						
48. Animal units, hogs	10.6	3.9	10.6	9.6	10.3	10.1						
49. Animal units, sheep and goats	2.7	8.4	2.9	12.9	1.8	12.2						
50. Total animal units-cows	58.1	39.1	76.4	54.7	92.4	66.1	159	169	131	140	121	121
51. Animal units per capita	383	219	425	258	534	273	139	125	111	118	126	107
52. Animal units per farmer	5.87	0.93	10.76	1.35	24.22	1.73	413	186	183	145	225	128
53. Meat per animal units, kgs	216	130	211	159	189	186	88	143	98	122	90	117
54. Units per sown hectares	0.371	0.267	0.526	0.269	0.809	0.320	218	119	142	101	154	119
55. Eggs, billions	64.8	11.7	61.6	27.4	68.3	40.7	105	347	95	234	110	149
56. Eggs per capita	427	66	342	129	335	168	78	255	80	195	98	130
57. Eggs per farmer	6,545	278	8,676	676	15,178	1,068	232	384	133	243	175	158
58. Eggs per hen	174	n.a.	209	n.a.	218	199	122		120		109	
59. Eggs per sown area	414	76	424	135	507	197	122	259	102	178	120	146
60. Tractors, 1,000s (U.S. + garden Soviet, all)	3,610	595	5,138	1,127	5,424	1,927	150	332	142	189	106	170
61. Grain combines, 1,000s	1,170	211	1,834	497	1,425	623	122	295	158	236	78	125
62. Fertilizer,g 1,000 tons	18,453	5,350	22,107	11,404	36,191	15,649	196	853	119	213	163	400

(continued)

257

(Table 10.9 continued)

aCrop and area data averages for five years (for example, 1970 is really 1968, 1969, 1970, 1971, and 1972). All other data is just for the year indicated.

bPrevious census year.

c1950 only.

dIn determining cows and milk per cow only dairy herds used in official determinant of milk per cow are included.

eExcluding goats in United States.

fOfficial Soviet weights, all cattle 0.8 (cows 1), hogs 0.18 and sheep and goats 0.09 as cited by Douglas Whitehouse and James Havalka, in Soviet Economic Prospects for the Seventies, U.S. Congress, Joint Economic Committee, 93rd Cong., 1st Sess. (Washington, D.C.: U.S. Government Printing Office, 1973). Excludes goats in United States. See note d for cow count.

gTon for ton Soviet and U.S. mineral fertilizer are not directly comparable since the amount of usable nutrients in a ton of fertilizer is not the same. Thus a ton of Soviet mineral fertilizer has something like only one-half the usable nutrients that are in a ton of U.S. fertilizer. See Whitehouse and Havalka, op. cit. Further, the quantities recorded here for the Soviets is the amount of fertilizer delivered to the farms and in the U.S. accounting it is the total fertilizer consumed.

5:1 for milk and 14:1 for eggs in favor of the U.S. farmer. On balance, however, an examination of the 1950–70 Soviet record when measured by the U.S. barometer leaves little doubt that in spite of enormous new investments in agricultural productivity, the gap between the U.S. and Soviet agriculture widened significantly in favor of the U.S. farmer (Table 10.9).

Again, we believe that as long as the Soviet farmer is held captive by the enormously inefficient kolkhoz and sovkhoz, the enormous potential of the Soviet land for producing food cannot be achieved.

NOTES

1. For an excellent look at comparative output in general between the two countries, 1950–71, see F. Douglas Whitehouse and Joseph Havalka, "Comparison of Farm Output in the US and USSR, 1950–71," in Soviet Economic Prospects for the Seventies, U.S. Congress, Joint Economic Committee, 93rd Cong., 1st Sess. (Washington, D.C.: U.S. Government Printing Office, 1973), pp. 340–74.

2. See especially, Roy D. Laird and Betty A. Laird, Soviet Communism and Agrarian Revolution (Harmondsworth, Middlesex: Penguin Books, 1970), p. 158.

3. A note on sources: Unless otherwise indicated, all of the data presented here is either cited from or calculated from data presented in the annual statistical volumes: Agricultural Statistics (Washington, D.C.: U.S. Department of Agriculture, U.S. Government Printing Office, 1960 through 1973), Narodnoe khozyaistvo SSSR (Moscow: Statistika Moskva, 1956 through 1972), Sel'skoe khozyaistvo SSSR (Moscow: Statistika, 1960 and 1971).

4. Total grain output in the Soviet Union includes not only what is normally thought of as grain, but also other crops as well. Therefore to make a grain bag comparable to the Soviet bag, we have included in the U.S. grain data, wheat, corn, sorghum, oats, barley, rye, rice, soybeans, and field peas and beans.

5. As Khrushchev bitterly noted during his tenure in office, even when scarce mineral fertilizer was shipped to some farms, often it was left lying in piles on the open ground.

6. Calories consumed in terms of meat produced from grain are several times less than calories derived from the direct consumption of grain.

7. Where, for example, grain output per farmer in 1970 is shown, it will reflect the average grain output in 1968–72 per farmer in 1970.

8. S. Dudin, "Razivat' myasnoe skotovodstvo," Ekonomika sel'skovo khozyaistva, no. 2 (1971), pp. 9-14.

11

AGRICULTURAL PERFORMANCE
COMPARED: BELORUSSIA
AND EASTERN POLAND
Alec Nove

This chapter represents the preliminary results of some work undertaken in connection with a large comparative study of Communist agriculture. The underlying idea, so far as performance is concerned, is to compare like with like. We feel that the Soviet Union itself is too huge, too diverse in climate and culture, as well as agriculture, to be a suitable basis of comparison. We all know that the farms in the United States are more efficient than Soviet farms on any known basis of measurement, but it is not clear what morals should or could be drawn from this: The natural conditions and human factors are so different. We must all surely suspect that, under any conceivable regime, and whether collective or private, Soviet farms would be inferior to those of the United States. It therefore follows that the inferiority as such is not "evidence of system," and cannot be used without careful qualification to measure the effects of private enterprise versus the collective and state farms.

More meaningful results would be obtained, we thought, by comparing the comparable. Let us take territories that are broadly similar in climate, in soil, in the cultural background of the inhabitants, but are different in their agricultural organization. Let us then compare their outputs, inputs, yields, and see what conclusions

---

The author wishes to express thanks to G.A.E. Smith and J.G. Zielinski for help in sorting out data. He is conscious that much more work needs to be done and hopes that the preliminary results presented will be regarded as a slice of unfinished work in progress.

will emerge, which may serve as an indication of the difference made by the given type of organization. This approach is not based on any preconceived notions: We simply do not know, in advance of doing the work, what the outcome of the research will be. It may point to quite other variables, such as the application of fertilizer per hectare, but it seemed that the comparisons were worth trying.

Among the areas chosen were the territories of the Belorussian republic and the two adjoining Polish provinces (Wojwodztwa) of Bialystok and Lublin. The detailed study will contain an analysis of soil differences, which do exist, but these are not of great importance as far as the principal cultivatable areas are concerned (the Pripet marshes are not greatly used for agriculture). The crop and animal husbandry patterns on both sides of the border seem reasonably comparable.

Table 11.1 shows a substantial transfer of land to the state sector in Belorussia, due to conversion of kolkhozy into sovkhozy, a process that was particularly rapid in the 1960s and has continued at a reduced pace since. The total area under private plots has fallen from 482,000 to 445,000 hectares, and the smaller share of kolkhozy in the land area (and work force) is reflected in the much smaller share of kolkhoz members in the area of private plots.

Since Table 11.1 is intended merely to indicate the relative importance of state, collective, and private agriculture, this degree of detail seems sufficient. We shall, of course, return to the livestock sector, to analyze numbers and output more systematically, later in the chapter. Since no significant changes have occurred in the pattern of land ownership in Poland, it seems sufficient to cite figures conveniently available for a recent year (see Table 11.2, part A). This is sufficient to demonstrate the quite overwhelming predominance of private agriculture in the Wojwodztwa of Eastern Poland. Consequently it would be statistically justifiable to use statistics of output and yields, insofar as these relate to Bialystok and Lublin, as representing private-peasant agriculture. The corrections that might have to be made for the exiguous state sector and even smaller cooperatives can make no difference worth measuring. It is otherwise in Belorussia: The private sector is of evident importance (particularly if one notes the large numbers of private poultry and goats, and the high-value vegetable crops and fruit that occur on the private plots), and we also have to note the possibility of significant contrasts between kolkhozy and sovkhozy.

The average size of holding in Poland is quite small, contrasting with state and collective farms. This is shown in Table 11.2 (parts B and C). Clearly these are smallholdings. A not untypical peasant would cultivate six hectares, and own maybe two cows and a horse.

TABLE 11.1

Organization of Agriculture in Belorussia, 1959 and 1971

	Year	Total	Total State	of which: Sovkhozy	Kolkhozy	Total Private	Kolkhoznik Private Plots	Other Private Plots
Arable land (thousand hectares)	1959	6,022	1,164	1,026	4,374	482	362	120
	1971	6,143	2,175	2,012	3,553	445	250	195
Cattle (thousand head)	1959	3,361	248	195	1,406	1,706	—	—
	1971	5,383	1,414	1,286	2,603	1,366	—	—
Cows (thousand head)	1959	1,957	87	71	574	1,496	—	—
	1971	2,544	n.a.	450	926	1,139	—	—
Pigs (thousand head)	1959	2,741	231	162	855	1,655	—	—
	1971	4,004	n.a.	736	1,407	1,754	—	—

Source: Narodnoe khozyaistvo BSSR, for 1959 and 1971.

TABLE 11.2

Organization of Agriculture in Bialystok and Lublin, 1969

A. Arable Land (thousand hectares)

Province	Total	Individual Peasants	Cooperatives	State Farms
Bialystok	1,483.3	1,380.7	3.6	96.0
Lublin	1,775.7	1,703.7	13.2	56.1

B. The Number of Holdings According to the Size of Agricultural Land (thousands of holdings)

Province	Total Number of Households	Households with Agricultural Land in Hectares									
		Below 0.5	0.5 -1.5	1-2	2-3	3-5	5-7	7-10	10-18	15-20	20 and over
Bialystok	168.2	10.6	5.0	9.6	9.9	24.5	29.2	38.5	30.5	7.8	2.6
Lublin	348.6	15.7	17.4	44.2	51.9	101.7	63.6	39.2	13.0	1.5	0.3

C. The Number of Households According to the Number of Cows and Horses Owned

Province	Cows					Horses			
	None	One	Two	Three	Four and More	None	One	Two	Three and More
Bialystok	23.5	40.6	54.5	30.3	19.3	42.9	69.5	43.7	12.1
Lublin	53.8	131.3	122.7	31.9	8.8	122.8	164.3	54.9	6.6

Source: Part A: Przestrzenne zroznicowanie kraju (Warsaw: Glowny Urzad Statystyczny, 1971), p. 90; Parts B and C: Rocznik statystyczny, 1973 (Warsaw: Glowny Urzad Statystyczny, 1973), p. 289.

The average Belorussian farms were rather larger:

Size of Farms, 1972

	Sown Area (hectares)	Peasants/Workers	Cows	Pigs
Sovkhozy	2,360	520[a]	570	880
Kolkhozy	1,600[c]	381[b]	410	580

[a]Employed [b]Households [c]2,700 hectares of agricultural land.
Source: Narodnoe Khozyaistvo, 1972 (calculated).

Private plots are very small: 0.20-0.25 hectares per household is normal (1 hectare equals 2.47 acres).

We will now proceed successively to compare output (Table 11.3) and yield (Table 11.4), and also principal inputs (labor, fertilizer, power, etc.), before dismissing causes and arriving at any conclusion.

It will be observed that the Polish figures relate only to six years. This is entirely due to the availability at the moment of writing of Polish statistical annuals, and this will be put right in the full study. The years are quite random. The difficulty was that the series for a set of years appear only for the country as a whole. As a guide to weather variations, in a medium-sized country, the statistics on grain yields for Poland as a whole are of interest (Table 11.5). This also enables one to see how our two eastern Wojwodztwa compare with the national data (and also compare with the whole Soviet Union.

A calculation of yields on private plots is only worth making for potatoes, since their contribution to grain crops in Belorussia (as elsewhere in the Soviet Union) is not significant.

Some very striking conclusions may be reached even from the incomplete comparisons.

1. Belorussia has shown some remarkable progress, from a very low starting point. Thus, the average yield of grain in 1959-64 was below even the poor all-Union levels and roughly half the yields in Bialystok and Lublin, which were and are somewhat below average for Poland. In the past five years, however, Belorussia has surpassed the all-Union average grain yields and has come close to the Lublin-Bialystok levels for grain, while still far behind in potatoes, sugar beets and (probably) flax. The large rise in barley production is particularly notable.

2. The Soviet figures consistently show sovkhozy behind kolkhozy in yields per hectare, whenever they are distinguished. This could be because the weaker kolkhozy were transformed into sovkhozy in the early 1960s. More research is needed here.

TABLE 11.3

Crops, Area Sown: Belorussia and Poland
(thousand hectares)

Crops	Belorussia			Poland (Lublin and Bialystok)	
	1959	1955	1972	1966	1972
All grain	2,743	2,832	2,659	1,415.9	1,474.1
Wheat (winter)	59	146	341	232.9[a]	333.9[a]
Wheat (spring)	129	13	8		
Rye	1,389	1,519	693	724.5	561.4
Barley	237	435	859[b]	99.4	162.0
Oats	499	282	291[b]	264.6	276.0
Maize (for grain)	69	—	—	n.a.	n.a.
Pulses	200	266	200	n.a.	n.a.
Sugar beet	25	50	54	74.7	66.9
Flax fiber	282	275	258	n.a.	n.a.
Potatoes	1,023	1,000	945	451.8	445.7

[a]Polish breakdowns for Wojwodztwa do not distinguish between winter wheat and spring wheat. National figures show that winter wheat predominates in the proportion of roughly 7:1.

[b]1971.

Source: Narodnoe khozaistvo SSSR and Rocznyk statistyczny for requisite years.

TABLE 11.4

Yields of Principal Crops, Belorussia and Poland, 1959–73

A. Belorussia

	All Grains			Winter wheat	Spring Wheat (all farms)	Rye	Barley	Oats	Sugar beets			Flax			Potatoes			
	All Farms	Kolkhozy	Sovkhozy						All Farms	Kolkhozy	Sovkhozy	All Farms	Kolkhozy	Sovkhozy	All Farms	Kolkhozy	Sovkhozy	Private
1959	7.1	—	—	10.3	5.6	8.2	8.0	5.2	119	—	—	2.0	—	—	92	—	—	—
1960	8.7			9.4	8.5	8.6	10.8	8.5	132			3.1			104			140
1961	8.3			10.8	6.7	9.5	8.7	6.6	117			2.8			109			144
1962	6.9			7.6	6.5	7.0	9.4	6.5	112			3.0			76			
1963	8.0			9.9	7.0	8.9	9.8	6.9	129			3.0			105			
1964	7.2			9.8	3.4	8.1	6.9	4.6	170			2.4			134			
1965	11.3	11.7	10.6	13.8	11.6	11.3	14.1	12.6	152	157	123	4.1	4.3	3.0	121	95	83	160
1966	10.5	10.5	9.8	10.7	11.8	9.6	14.3	12.3	197	201	175	3.8	3.9	3.0	134	108	98	
1967	11.3	11.5	10.4	15.9	14.2	9.8	15.4	12.8	254	258	222	4.1	4.2	3.4	137	119	106	
1968	11.0	11.2	10.2	14.7	13.1	8.7	15.6	10.3	211	214	182	3.8	4.0	3.2	150	135	121	
1969	15.9	16.3	14.7	16.4	21.9	11.9	23.5	18.9	187	190	161	4.4	4.6	3.6	139	123	111	
1970	16.9	17.7	15.2	17.9	20.3	13.9	21.2	18.7	221	226	192	3.9	4.1	3.2	138	121	111	162
1971	21.4			21.8	26.4	18.5	—	—	168	—	—	4.7			130	—	—	—
1972	17.3			19.7	15.0	18.1	—	—	272	—	—	4.2			138	—	—	—
1973	21.9			—	—	—	—	—	(230)			(4.3)			(148)			

B. Bialystok

	Main Grains	Wheat	Rye	Barley	Oats	Potatoes	Sugar Beets
1959	13.2	13.0	13.9	11.9	12.0	135	203
1962	12.0	13.6	10.8	14.2	13.9	123	198
1965	16.6	17.7	16.8	17.7	15.6	157	252
1969	19.3	20.8	18.1	23.7	19.9	162	269
1972	22.2	21.4	22.2	24.3	21.4	207	355
1973	23.6	25.2	22.9	25.2	23.1	226	262

C. Lublin

	Main Grains	Wheat	Rye	Barley	Oats	Potatoes	Sugar Beets	Flax
1959	16.3	18.3	15.4	17.8	16.2	137	238	—
1962	13.2	17.9	9.9	18.1	16.2	131	269	4.9
1965	18.7	19.2	18.0	20.8	19.1	169	280	6.8
1969	21.2	22.7	18.6	26.5	22.2	185	298	5.7
1972	23.9	26.9	20.9	27.6	22.2	205	392	6.6
1973	25.1	26.9	22.6	27.3	24.6	181	323	6.6

Sources: Narkhoz (Belorussian SSSR), Rocznik statistyczny (Warsaw), and Sovetskaya Belorussia, January 29, 1974.

TABLE 11.5

Yields of Principal Grains, Poland and
Soviet Union, 1960-73

Year	Poland	Soviet Union
1960	16.1	10.9
1961	18.0	10.7
1962	16.1	10.9
1963	17.3	8.3
1964	16.2	11.4
1965	19.2	9.5
1966	19.0	13.7
1967	19.5	12.1
1968	21.4	14.0
1969	21.6	13.2
1970	19.6	15.6
1971	23.7	15.4
1972	24.2	14.0
1973	26.5	(17.2)

Source: Narodnoe khozaistvo SSSR and Rocznyk statistyczny
for requisite years.

3. It is obviously necessary to compare inputs, in order to see
at what cost the higher output was achieved. If this comparison were
being undertaken ten years ago, we might well have concluded that
the striking superiority of the Polish areas was proof of superiority
of private smallholder agriculture. Now things are not so clear.

LIVESTOCK PRODUCTS

In the absence of large year-by-year variations, figures will be
given for a few selected years (see Table 11.6, part A).
The following preliminary comments seem called for:
1. The superiority of state and collective as against private
milk yields in Belorussia must be due partly to priority in feed
supplies, and partly also to breeds.
2. There is no significant difference between kolkhozy and
sovkhozy.
3. Bialystok and Lublin are ahead, but not greatly so, in milk
production per cow, with a general tendency toward higher yields in

TABLE 11.6

A. Production of Milk, Belorussia and Poland

Belorussia

	All Farms			Kollkhozy and Sovkhozy					Private		
Year	Output (thousand tons)	Cows (thousand)	Yield (kg)	Output (thousand tons)	Cows (thousand)	Yield (kg)	Kollkhozy	Sovkhozy	Output (thousand tons)	Cows (thousand)	Yield (kg)
1960	3,219.2	1,958.8	1,607	1,400.5	732.4	1,818	—	—	1,818	1,226.4	1,500
1966	4,402.7	2,364.5	1,766	2,412.1	1,179.8	2,040	1,934	2,015	1,991	1,184	1,688
1970	5,264	2,522	2,087	3,085	1,358	2,304	2,306	2,300	2,179	1,164	1,870
1972	5,467	2,593a	2,120	—	—	2,279	2,301	2,233	—	—	—

Bialystok

Year	Output (thousand tons)	Cows (thousand)	Yield (kg)
1965	648.8	363.8	1,783
1969	792.5	413.7	1,915
1972	868.7	393.7	2,210

Lublin

Year	Output (thousand tons)	Cows (thousand)	Yield (kg)
1965	1,027	550.3	1,934
1969	1,242.3	592.2	2,098
1972	1,281.9	556.8	2,304

(continued)

269

(Table 11.6 continued)

B. Production of Meat, Belorussia and Poland
(dead weight)

Belorussia (selected years; thousand tons)[b]

Year	All	State	Kollkhozy	Private	Per 100 Hectares[c] All
1960	402	62.7	113.9	225	42
1965	508	105.8	133.9	268	54
1970	685	172.0	256.9	256	70
1972	765	—	—	—	—

	Bialystok		Lublin	
	Thousand tons	Per 100 Hectares[c]	Thousand tons	Per 100 Hectares[c]
1969	124.0	90.2[d]	178.6	108.4[d]
1972	162.1	109.7	230.1	131.3

C. Numbers of Cattle and Pigs, Belorussia and Poland
(thousands)

Belorussia (1 January)		1961	1966	1973
	Cattle	3,666	4,704	5,769
	Pigs	3,164	3,688	4,115

Lublin + Bialystok (1 June)		1965	1969	1973
	Cattle	1,431.5	1,658.2	1,785.8
	Pigs	2,189.0	2,573.0	3,520.0

aJanuary 1974

bThere are minor contradictions between figures for Belorussia, according to Narodnoe Khozyaistvo of different years. They are not significant.

cOf agricultural land, in centners (quintals).

d1968.

Sources: Narodnoe Khozyaistvo (Moscow), and Rocznik statystyczne (Warsaw) for relevant years.

all the areas under consideration. The fact that the Soviet figures are for January and the Polish ones are for June affects comparability, especially for pigs.

4. Output of meat per 100 hectares of agricultural land is still very much higher in the Polish wojwodztwa.

5. Careful research is evidently required into supplies of feed, and one must also seek figures on slaughter weights of various types of animals, where there is the probability of considerable Polish superiority.

Meat production has risen substantially in both Belorussia and Poland. It is noteworthy that considerable subsidies are paid in both countries to keep retail prices below costs of production.

INPUTS[1]

Labor, Belorussia

Total number of kolkhoz members "participating in collective production" (thousands) declined between 1960 and 1970.[2]

1960	1965	1970	1972
1, 269	1, 144	1, 020	997

The total number of workers and employees in sovkhozy (average for year), in thousands (some not engaged in agricultural work) were as follows:[3]

1950	1965	1970	1972
227?	385/403?	415?	437

To these must be added labor inputs in the private sector.

Agricultural Labor, Polish Figures

The data are deficient, as is often the case in peasant economies. Part of the problem can be seen in the data on size of holdings given above. Thus of Lublin's 348,000 peasant households, no less than 129,000 have 3 hectares or less, which means that some of the members of these (and of other) households work the whole or part of the year outside agriculture (see Table 11.7).

TABLE 11.7

Active Rural Population in Bialystok and Lublin, 1966

	Engaged in Agriculture	Not Engaged in Agriculture	Partly Agricultural and Partly Non-agricultural
Bialystok	394,814	28,715	34,046
Lublin	721,888	52,350	85,139

Source: Przestrzenne zroznicowanie Kraju (Warsaw, 1971), Table 20.

If the partly employed were regarded as half-time, then the total labor force in the two wojwodztwa would be of the order of 1,176,000. But the first column in Table 11.7 does not necessarily relate to full-time equivalents. Consequently these figures must be regarded as very rough. Judging from general statistics for Poland, the numbers are declining, but only slowly.

These figures suggest high labor inputs in the Polish areas. Let us relate this to agricultural land, while uncomfortably aware of statistical deficiencies in measurement (see Table 11.8).

There is little year-by-year variation, as might be expected. Taking 1970 as a sample year for labor inputs, the Soviet figures look like this:

	(thousands)
Kolkhoz "participants"	1,028
Sovkhoz workers and employees	415
Private and other	?

However, these figures are misleading. The labor inputs include nonagricultural work (such as construction, etc.), and, as already explained, there are not full-time equivalents. In 1970, 212 million man-days were expended in kolkhozy in Belorussia, 196 million of them in agricultural work.[4] Defining a full-timer as one who works 280 days a year, this would represent 700,000 persons engaged in kolkhoz agriculture, and not 1,028 thousand. The same source gives labor inputs in sovkhozy as 104 million man-days, of which 95 million are devoted to agriculture.[5] On the same 280 day basis, this would represent 340,000 man-years. A few thousand must be added to this to take into account the existence of state agriculture other than sovkhozy. Two other upward corrections require to be made. First, and most important, there are labor inputs in private plots. Scattered

TABLE 11.8

Agricultural Land and Arable Land in Belorussia
and in Bialystok and Lublin, 1969
(hectares)

	Agricultural Land*	Arable Land
Belorussia	9, 859, 000	6, 204, 000
Bialystok + Lublin	3, 258, 000	2, 411, 000

*Uzytki rolne, or Sel'skokhozyaistvennye ugodiya.
Sources: Selskoe khozyaistvo SSSR (Moscow, 1972) and
Prezestrzenne zroznicowanie Kraju (Warsaw, 1971).

evidence suggests that private plots are responsible for something
between 25 and 30 percent of the output of agriculture. Arbitrarily
assuming approximately similar labor productivity, this would require
us to add roughly 30 percent or a little more to the labor inputs we
have calculated for sovkhozy and kolkhozy. Second, it is likely that
extra labor drafted in at harvest time (village school children, urban
"volunteers," students, etc.) is not counted or is incompletely counted.
Allowing for all this, a total labor input in full-time equivalents of
something like 1.7 or perhaps 1.8 million would seem to be implied
by these figures. This is not a reliable estimate and can only be taken
as a rough order of magnitude.

How can we compare productivities? We can attempt to add up
the principal products, using some common price base. No doubt
results will differ according to the prices used.

Let us take, from the FAO annual production survey, the U.S.
farm prices of 1970 as weights (except that for flax, which has no
American price, we have used Belgian export prices instead; a rough
adjustment had to be made from live weight to dead weight for meat,
with some averaging for different types of meat and grain). Output
figures are for 1969. The calculation works out as shown in Table
11.9, and, rough and ready though it is, it does seem to have
significance.

It is doubtful if omitted items would greatly change the picture.
To take one example, eggs per hen were 222 in 1972 in Belorussia, [6]
while the reported average for all Poland was only 103;[7] one wonders
at the completeness of Polish reporting. The Poles should do better,
however, in vegetables and fruit.

If the above figures are anywhere near correct, Belorussia
produces double the total output of Lublin-Bialystok, with a labor

force probably around 70 percent greater. Labor productivity is therefore higher as might be expected from the comparative levels of mechanization (see below). And, of course, the Polish areas use a great deal more labor per unit of land.

But what of other inputs?

Fertilizer

The Belorussian figures show a very large increase in mineral fertilizer application, which correlates quite well with the impressive gains in yields per hectare:

Belorussia[8] (mineral fertilizer)	Total (thousand tons)*	Per Hectare of Arable Land
1960	248	45.6
1965	456	76.7
1970	929	160.2
1972	1,025	176.2

*100 percent nutrient.

TABLE 11.9

Production of Selected Agricultural Commodities in Belorussia and in Bialystok and Lublin

	Belorussia			Lublin-Bialystok	
	Thousand Tons	Price per Ton ($)	Value ($ millions)	Thousand Tons	Value
Grain	4,328	45	194.7	2,713	122.1
Potatoes	13,531	49	663.0	8,072	395.5
Sugar beets	905	19	17.2	1,975	37.5
Flax	116	595	69.0	(20)	(11.9)
Meat	678	860	583.1	302.6	260.2
Milk and products	5,204	131	659.7	2,035.7	266.7
Total value			2,186.7		1,093.9

Source: Narodnoe khozaistvo SSSR and Rocznyk statystyczny for requisite years.

Organic fertilizer application has remained virtually static, at around 7 to 8 tons per hectare (much more than this on private plots).[9]

Bialystok	(Mineral fertilizer, in kg per hectare of sown area)
1959-60	23.5
1968-69	106.8
1971-72	169.5
Lublin	
1959-60	38.0
1968-69	116.2
1971-72	165.6

The pattern is thus more or less parallel: In Poland, too, the quantity of mineral fertilizer has risen fast, but Belorussia has tended to be just ahead of its use. On the other hand there have been many complaints about supplies of the wrong type of fertilizer in Belorussia, and also of lack of packaging, means of transport and storage, and of equipment, leading to much waste. These complaints may well relate especially to the mid-1960s, when the big rise in fertilizer output was not matched by investments in related items. There is also some evidence that the application of fertilizer to acidic soils, inadequately limed, has harmed them in some instances.

The smaller Polish farms doubtless benefit from more organic fertilizer, though no statistics have been found as yet. This helps to explain why Polish yields were higher in 1959-60, at a time when they had much less mineral fertilizer than Belorussia (but the latter may have concentrated the small supplies on flax). There are many more horses, and the manure of private livestock is not diverted into the private plots of the collective and state peasantry, as it is in the Soviet Union.

Tractor and Other Sources of Power

The contrast between Belorussia and the two Polish wojwodztwa is notable:

Tractors (thousands)

	Belorussia			Lublin and Bialystok		
1960	1965	1970	1972	1960	1970	1972
34.0	55.4	81.6	90.8	4.3	22.3	30.3

Grain Combines (thousands)

10.6	13.5	27.5	29.0	n. a.	n. a.	n. a.

Combines appear to be few in number in Poland, as national data show. There were in 1972 about 300 combine-harvesters in the "agricultural circles" of our wojwodztwa[10] and probably only a handful more on the farms.

Tractors in Bialystok and Lublin in 1972 were divided as follows by ownership (thousands):[11]

Ministry of Agriculture	Agricultural Circles	Individual Peasants
3.85	16.44	8.75

These figures do not quite add up to the total, since I have omitted some minor organizations. It is highly probable that the average horsepower per tractor in Poland is well below the Soviet level.

The Polish figures give agricultural land per tractor as follows:[12]

	Hectare, 1972
Poland	53
Bialystok	93
Lublin	77

Clearly, the eastern areas are less well supplied with tractors than the center and west.

For Belorussia a (probably more powerful) tractor cultivated an average of 57 arable hectares in 1972, which is much better than Lublin-Bialystok, but comparable with the average for Poland as a whole.

However, it must always be noted that the private plots in Belorussia, as in the rest of the Soviet Union, are mostly unmechanized, and indeed their cultivators do not even have the help of a horse, since private horse-ownership is to all intents and purposes forbidden.

Horses present an interesting contrast:

Belorussia	329,000 horses, all ages	(1971)
Bialystok	201,500 horses, all ages	(1972)
Lublin	301,600 horses, all ages	(1972)

Obviously, in terms of arable land areas, the number of horses in Poland is very much greater.

This emerges in the contrasting sources of haulage power. In Belorussia, energy and haulage in thousand mechanical horsepower in 1970 was as follows:[13]

Mechanical, Total	13,300
of which:	
Tractors	4,472
Combines	1,806
Motor vehicles	5,123
Live animals	179
Total	13,479

Polish statistics on haulage power per 100 agricultural hectares (horsepower) for 1972 show a higher proportion of live power in 1972:[14]

	Total	Live	Mechanical
Bialystok	15.9	10.5	5.4
Lublin	21.4	14.9	6.5
(Poland)	(19.9)	(10.5)	(9.4)

On the few state and cooperative farms, the level of mechanization of haulage power is, of course, much higher. (The ratio of mechanical to animal, which is 1:2.5 on individual peasant holdings in Bialystok, is 14:1 on state farms in this same wojwodztwa; but such farms are very few.)

The figures for Belorussia and Poland are on a different basis (sown as against agricultural area) and probably convert horsepower into horsepower by a different formula. But the contrast is nonetheless very great. It is clear that the total haulage power per 100 hectares is much higher in Belorussia.

The figures so far found on the use of electricity are neither complete nor comparable.

SOME PRELIMINARY CONCLUSIONS

The following are essentially preliminary, in the nature of notes for further research. Yet we hope that they are of some interest even in their present unfinished state.

1. The place of the respective regions in their respective countries: Lublin and Bialystok are backward by Polish standards, usually below average in virtually every respect as far as inputs and productivity are concerned. Belorussia in 1960 was a backward republic also by Soviet standards, but has advanced strikingly. A note on this dynamic aspect is clearly in order.

2. Belorussia's past backwardness was a function of several mutually reinforcing factors. This can be deduced from the literature, and it also emerged from discussions the author had in Minsk in 1970. These factors certainly included the following:

a. War damage and loss of males, belatedly "repaired." Some parts of Western (ex-Polish) Belorussia collectivized around 1949-50, with some negative results initially.

b. Low prices for typical Belorussian products until relatively recently.

c. Exceedingly low pay for collective work; in the late 1950s Belorussia was among the lowest in the Soviet Union. Thus payment per man-day was only 0.91 rubles in 1960.[15] This changed radically. Some of the least successful kolkhozy became sovkhozy, with appropriate rates of pay. The average per man-day in the rest increased to 2.16 rubles by 1965, and I was informed in Minsk in 1970 that the figure then exceeded 3.50 rubles.

d. Under Khrushchev, mineral fertilizer tended to be sent to southern areas. But even when available, it was often of the wrong type, there was lack of storage space, transport, and machinery for spreading it on the fields. Liming was essential on acidic soil, but was also neglected. All this took time to correct, indeed is still only partially corrected, but much more fertilizer is now used as the figures already cited plainly show.

e. Fodder shortage was, and to some extent still is, a serious bottleneck. Natural pastures were neglected, there were serious shortages of gross seeds. Mechanization was particularly backward in the livestock sector, and this is being put right, though machines are too often of poor quality. A particular cause of trouble is breakdown in electricity supply; thus in Grodno province in six months in 1970 there were 1,645 unplanned breakdowns in supply registered in rural areas, the average length of cut-off being 4.25 hours.[16] How, then, can one rely on mechanization, when cows might at any time have to be milked by hand?

f. Land improvements, drainage, and clearance are vital in Belorussia, and were neglected for too long.

g. There were, and to some extent still are, acute supply problems: building materials, spare parts, etc. Tractors were much too few. Improvements in supply seem real enough.

A striking improvement in output and yields was thus achieved for a combination of reasons, underlining the dangers of using

Cobb-Douglas functions or simple correlations in explaining complex phenomena. More and better use of fertilizer, better incentives, land drainage, more and better tractors and other machinery, probably more efficiency in management, less interference from the center (for example, in demanding more maize and less sown grasses)—after Khrushchev's fall, all these made their contribution. We simply cannot quantify the relative importance of each of these factors, on the evidence. We should, however, certainly examine cost, and ask the question: Were the achievements worthwhile, in terms of alternative uses for the resources used?

3. Polish smallholder agriculture evidently presents some features that can hold back its efficiency. It showed up very well compared with the depressed Belorussian kolkhozy in the first 15 postwar years, but this suggests that individual peasants can do better than neglected, undercapitalized, and underpaid kolkhozniki, a conclusion easy to reach. The problem is: Can they do better than a reorganized and more intensive form of kolkhoz-sovkhoz agriculture? If some Soviet farms are so large that diseconomies of scale set in, the opposite must be true in Poland. The following, then, are disadvantages that affected and still affect the Poles.

a. The political situation influences peasant attitudes to improvements in their holdings. The specter of a future collectivization is not altogether exorcized.

b. Many tractors and some other equipment belong to cooperative "circles," regarded by many peasants with suspicion. This affects their desire to use tractors, and their faith in their availability. This, in turn, encourages the preservation of nonmechanized methods, and with them the horses. True, horses provide useful organic fertilizer, but they eat a lot of grain.

c. As already mentioned, Polish farm size, certainly in Lublin and Bialystok, is very small. The state is against excessive fragmentation, which is because of forces working within peasant society. Anyhow, the figures clearly demonstrate that a numerically important proportion of the peasants in Lublin and Bialystok are cultivating holdings that are of a dwarf type, and this also adversely affects mechanization. The argument on the advantages and disadvantages of large scale is unlikely to be clearly resolved if one compares farm sizes of 6,000 hectares with 6 hectares. Some Polish holdings are similar to Soviet private plots and are presumably to be seen as an auxiliary source of family income, worked largely by women and largely by hand.

d. This is connected with problems of relative rural overpopulation, and with the alternative use actually available to the possibly surplus manpower (and especially womanpower), a factor that also must affect one's judgment of Soviet manpower utilization in rural areas. The Poles' labor inputs do seem a good deal higher, though the word "seem" must be reemphasized, in view of the ambiguities of agricultural labor statistics of both countries.

e. Polish peasant agriculture has also greatly increased its utilization of mineral fertilizer. The incomes of the producers have risen; comparison is very difficult when figures are in zloty and rubles (and incomplete), but it does appear that in both countries the improved results have coincided with a large increase in incomes, the increases being larger (from much lower levels) in Belorussia. Research is needed as to relative costs. Statistics, when published, can be ambiguous: Thus large investments in agricultural inputs may or may not be recouped through the prices charged, and agricultural subsidies of various kinds (especially in the livestock sector in the Soviet Union) can be very important and do not lend themselves to regional analysis.

4. Comparison between types of farms in the same country can only be meaningfully attempted in Belorussia, because of the relative insignificance of the state and cooperative sector in Eastern Poland. As already indicated, sovkhozy do not show up too well vis-a-vis kolkhozy, either in yields or in the utilization of inputs (thus sovkhozy have considerably higher amounts of energy per employee), but this may be due to the declared policy of converting the more depressed kolkhozy into sovkhozy. As usual, the private sector's yields of crops tend to be higher than the collective or state sector, a consequence of the concentration of human effort and manure on a limited area.

5. Potential for improvement: It is interesting to speculate about the further improvements that could occur, in efficiency and productivity, within the existing systems of the respective countries. There remain numerous remediable weaknesses. The Belorussian press refers to the continuation of difficulties over equipment and spare parts, shortages in some areas of trained "mechanizers" and maintenance staff, the need for more roads and means of transport, lack of good seeds, weed infestation, the need for more drainage, lack of storage and processing facilities. Reports speak of bureaucratic troubles: Thus vegetables and fruit, which could be sent profitably to Leningrad by rail, cannot be transported until the republic's purchase plan for these items has been fulfilled, and this is delayed by the official purchasing agencies owing to shortage of storage space, handling equipment, and packaging. As a result, some produce goes bad and production is discouraged. Publicity for these defects suggests a desire to remedy them. In Poland it would seem that any major improvements would depend on some reduction in the number of dwarf holdings; one cannot expect either mechanization or adequate capitalization on 2- to 5-hectare farms.

TABLE 11.10

Cost of Production of Selected Agricultural
Commodities in Belorussia
(rubles per ton)

	1960	1965	1972
Sovkhozy			
Grain (excluding maize)	93	87	102
Potatoes	34	49	69
Cattle*	957	1,088	1,493
Pigs*	1,630	1,304	1,545
Milk	144	159	194
Kolkhozy			
Grain (excluding maize)	83	70	83
Potatoes	32	39	59
Cattle*	1,109	1,009	1,375
Pigs*	1,534	1,273	1,511
Milk	148	152	180

*Increase in live weight (per ton).
Sources: Belorusskaya SSSR v. tsifrakh (1963); Sel'skoe khozyaistvo SSSR (Moscow, 1970); Narodnoe khozyaistvo SSSR (Moscow, 1972).

Finally, we must consider cost. Evidently, improved yields per hectare are not of themselves evidence of improved efficiency. Polish (and German and French) wheat yields per hectare are above those of Canada, but Canada is a lower-cost producer, and by no stretch of the imagination could be described as less efficient than European wheat producers.

A major element in cost is labor cost, and this has risen, since the improvements in peasant income (especially in Belorussia) have exceeded the rise in productivity per head. Some research effort is needed to compare the incomes of Belorussian and Polish peasants, and the efforts will be complicated by the income from private plots in Belorussia and the contribution of nonagricultural incomes to the peasant family budgets in both countries.

Perhaps the following could form the basis of comparison. For Poland, we have figures for the pay for casual male labor on farms: about 120 zloty per day for digging potatoes. Average wages in Poland in the same year 1972 were 2,634 zloty per month, in state agriculture, 2,231 zloty ($30.03 = 100 zloty official parity as of March 1974).[17] The pay rates have risen rather slowly; in terms of rye, the average for all Poland in 1972 was 39 percent above the level of 1960, but no doubt the 1960 level was well above that of Belorussia at this period. However, pay rates for casual labor may not be a useful indication of incomes of individual peasants working in their own holdings. (There is likely to be some relationship, in that some peasants with very small holdings work as laborers for part of the year.)

Soviet cost-of-production figures are published, in rubles per ton, separately for kolkhozy and sovkhozy. Some examples are given in Table 11.10.

Again, sovkhozy do not show up well. Unfortunately, no comparable data on Poland has yet been found or analyzed. There is also more research needed on the costs of various inputs other than labor.

NOTES

1. Data on feed exist, but seem not readily comparable. This will be the subject of more research.

2. This is not the same as full-time equivalents, in that an individual who worked in any month is entered as having worked for that month, nor are they all engaged only in agricultural production. However, it excludes extra labor (nonmembers), hired at peak periods.

3. Series for state farms are ambiguous; some figures relate only to sovkhozy, others include auxiliary farms or other state enterprises. Some may exclude nonagricultural labor.

4. Selske Khozyaistvo SSSR (Moscow, 1971), p. 430.

5. Ibid., p. 431.

6. Narodnoye Khozyaistvo (Moscow, 1972), p. 385.

7. Rocznik statystyczny 1973 (Warsaw, 1973), p. 273.

8. Narodnoye Khozyaistvo, 1972, op. cit., p. 356.

9. Przestrzenne zroznicowanie kraju (Warsaw, 1971), p. 116 and Rocznik Statystyczny 1973, op. cit.

10. Rocznik statystyczny 1973, op. cit., p. 309.

11. Ibid.

12. Ibid., p. 302.

13. Narodnoye Khoziaistvo (Moscow, 1970), pp. 372, 374.

14. Rocznik statystyczny 1973, op. cit., p. 302.

15. Martinkevich et al., Ekonomika sovetskoi Belorussii (Moscow, 1967), p. 466.

16. Sovetskaya Belorussia, June 26, 1971.

17. Rocznik statystyczny 1973, op. cit., p. 570.

CHAPTER

12

ORGANIZATION AND
MANAGEMENT OF AGRICULTURE
IN EASTERN EUROPE, 1967-74
Everett M. Jacobs

The face of East European agriculture has changed significantly
in recent years, though perhaps not as dramatically as during the
earlier periods of collectivization or mass farm amalgamations.
The economic reforms that were introduced throughout the area in
the 1960s have been constantly revised and modified in an effort to
improve the efficiency of Communist agriculture. At the same time,
there have been moves in new directions, most noticeably the attempts
to introduce some form of economic integration between agriculture
and industry. It is the purpose of this study to examine some of the
recent developments in the organization and management of the
socialist sector of agriculture in Bulgaria, Czechoslovakia, East
Germany, Hungary, and Romania.[1]

It is clear from Table 12.1 that changes in the number of state
or cooperative (collective) farms in Eastern Europe in recent years
have had little or no effect on the proportion of each country's arable
area occupied by one or the other kind of farm. The only noticeable
change had been within the cooperative farm sector of East Germany,
where there has been a rapid diminution of the number of Type I and
Type II cooperatives in favor of Type III cooperatives. In Type I
and Type II cooperatives, less work is done collectively by the members than in Type III cooperatives, which resemble Soviet kolkhozes.[2]
Since the completion of mass collectivization in East Germany at the

––––––––––––

The author gratefully acknowledges the financial support he
has received in his research for this study from the Knoop Economics
Research Fund of the University of Sheffield.

284

TABLE 12.1

Selected Statistics for East European Agriculture, 1967 and 1972

	1967						1972					
	Sector's Share of Country's Arable Area (%)[a]	Total Number of Farms	Average Size of Farm (hectares of arable land)[a]	Average Number of Permanently Active Farmers per Farm	Average Arable Area (hectare) per 15-h.p. Tractor Unit[a]	(sector)	Sector's Share of Country's Arable Area (%)[a]	Total Number of Farms	Average Size of Farm (hectares of arable land)[a]	Average Number of Permanently Active Farmers per Farm	Average Arable Area (hectare) per 15-h.p. Tractor Unit[a]	(sector)
Bulgaria												
State farms	12.5	151	3,446	949[b]	58	56	12.6[c]	149[c]	3,499[c]	846[b,c]	47[c]	43[c]
Coop farms	79.5	866	3,808	1,236[d]	56[e]		77.7[c]	725[c]	4,426[c]	1,180[c,d]	42[c,e]	
Czechoslovakia												
State farms	20.7	344	3,038	570	25	24	20.3	305	3,321	549[d]	20	20
Coop farms[f]	64.6	6,395	509	112[d]	24[e]		65.5	5,318	614	125[d]	20[e]	
East Germany[g]												
State farms	6.8	650	668	114[h]	40[i]		7.1	500	893	170[h]	40[i,j]	
Coop farms												
Types I and II	24.2	7,129	216	36[k]	46[i]	46[i]	7.8	1,939	253	32[h]	43[i,j]	43[i]
Type III	61.6	5,944	658	104[k]	46[i]		78.1	5,636	872	113[h]	43[i]	
Hungary												
State farms	13.1	210	3,160	835[h]	n.a.	52[i]	13.0	179	3,653	n.a.	n.a.	42[l]
Coop farms[f]	76.7	3,033	1,282	261[h]	n.a.		76.9[m]	2,321	1,653[m]	n.a.	n.a.	
Romania												
State farms	16.8	343	4,800	751[b]	35	59	17.1	364	4,572	754[b]	29	45
Coop farms	75.1	4,678	1,570	736[d,n]	69[e]		74.3	4,549	1,587	759[d,n]	51[e]	

a Including personal plots of farm members; figures for East Germany relate to agricultural land.
b Workers only.
c 1971.
d Not including independent machine–tractor station (MTS) work force.
e Including tractors owned and operated by MTS (or equivalent).
f Excluding lower-level cooperatives.
g All data from statistical yearbooks of corresponding years.
h Including apprentices.
i Hectares of agricultural land per physical unit.
j Estimate.
k Excluding apprentices.
l Based on country's entire arable area and total tractor park.
m Estimate based on arable area of common fields for 1972 and personal plots for 1970.
n Families.

Sources: Statistical yearbooks.

end of 1960, the number of simpler type cooperatives has fallen continuously through amalgamation and through upgrading these farms to
Type III status.[3] Both tendencies were apparent between 1967 and
1972 as the average size of the remaining Type I and Type II cooperatives increased, while the Type III sector gained around 1 million
hectares of agricultural land as a result of upgrading.

The policy of amalgamating farms in the socialist sector has
had its setbacks as well as success in Eastern Europe in recent
years. The most interesting case is Romania, where the average
size of cooperative farms hardly changed between 1967 and 1972,
and the average size of state farms actually dropped. However, when
the figures are examined on an annual basis, it turns out that the
number of state farms in Romania reached an all-time high of 731 in
1966, fell to 343 after an intense amalgamation campaign in 1967,
and then rose to 370 by the end of 1970.[4] The state farms, which
were already the largest in Eastern Europe, grew even bigger as a
result of an aggressive amalgamation campaign begun in February
1971. The original intention was to reduce the number of farms to
218 (145 nonspecialized and 73 specialized farms, the latter group
concentrating on pig fattening, poultry raising, combined fodder
production, and hothouse crop production), but the actual number of
farms remaining at the end of 1971 was only 200.[5] In connection with
this reform, the county inspectorates for state agricultural enterprises
were abolished, and the farms were placed under the direct control
of the Department of State Agriculture of the Ministry of Agriculture,
Food, Forestry, and Water Administration. The specialized state
farms were also answerable to specialized state farm trusts.[6] Another
reform of the state farm system took effect on January 1, 1972, less
than a year later. The farms were redivided into 364 units on the
grounds that many of the enterprises created in the February 1971
reorganization were too large, causing management problems. Also,
there was said to be excessive centralization in the operation of the
state farm system.[7] Another factor contributing to the collapse of
the 1971 reform was the failure to provide sufficient material and
technical resources to improve the efficiency of the state farms.

The state farm sectors of Bulgaria and Czechoslovakia have
been comparatively stable in recent years, whereas amalgamations
have greatly increased the average size of Hungarian and East German
state farms. It should be mentioned here that for some reason, the
East German statistical yearbook in 1968 gave the number of state
farms at the end of 1967 as 650, whereas subsequent editions put the
figure for that year at 548 and also greatly reduced the figures for
earlier years.[8] There are, it appears, many ways to carry out farm
amalgamations. In the collective farm sector, all the countries under
review except Romania have pursued a vigorous policy of

amalgamations. In Czechoslovakia, the scope of the amalgamation campaign is slightly obscured because of the creation of new cooperatives in Slovakia, especially in the central region, as a result of the new collectivization drive that began in 1971.[9] As late as 1970, more than 17 percent of Slovakia's agricultural area was still uncollectivized, and some 662 Slovak communities had neither cooperative nor state farms located in them.[10] The policy of eliminating these anomalies has given the post-Dubcek regime a good opportunity to prove its devotion to orthodox communism.

It is clear that in recent years, the size of cooperative farms in Eastern Europe has usually increased at a faster rate than the size of state farms in each county.[11] This trend can be expected to continue for some time, since the cooperative farms still are usually much smaller than the state farms, and are also more numerous. The only exceptions to the size rule are Bulgaria, where the cooperatives are now very much bigger than the state farms, and East Germany, where Type III cooperatives are only slightly smaller than state farms. The slowdown or reversal of amalgamations in the state farm sector may indicate, as in the Romanian case, that the practical limits of amalgamations are now being reached. On the other hand, it may be the result of a greater interest by the regimes in interfarm cooperation, or even horizontal integration, both of which can be viewed as a way of creating larger economic units without the necessity of formal merger. The Hungarians seemed to favor interfarm cooperation and the merging of capital rather than territory at the end of 1969,[12] but this has not stopped the constant reduction in the number of cooperative farms through amalgamation.

The stability observed in the proportional use of the arable area of each country between 1967 and 1972 may be somewhat misleading, since all the countries suffered noticeable losses in total arable area during the period (see Table 12.2). The most dramatic case is Romania, which lost 208,600 hectares of arable land between 1962 and 1972, of which 87,000 hectares were lost between 1967 and 1972 (1 hectare equals 2.47 acres). In the latter period, the area of the state farm sector increased by 19,000 hectares, while that of the cooperative sector fell by 127,900 hectares, not including a loss of 9,200 hectares accounted for by personal plots. After much criticism of this trend, which undermined the country's efforts to boost production through the expansion of area under irrigation, a law was passed in March 1974 to give the local people's councils greater responsibility in protecting areas designated for agricultural use.[13] Complete data for arable area are unavailable for East Germany, though it is clear that 51,000 hectares of such land fell out of use between 1967 and 1972. In terms of agricultural land, which includes arable land, 59,000 hectares were lost. The net drop of 45,000 hectares of

TABLE 12.2

Decline in Arable Area in Eastern Europe, 1967–72
(hectares)

	Total Change	State Farm Sector	of which		Personal Plots of Cooperative Farm Members
			Cooperative Farm Sector, Excluding Personal Plots		
Bulgaria[a]	-13,800	+ 1,000	- 97,100		+8,300
Czechoslovakia	-59,000	-32,000	+ 10,000		no change
East Germany[b]	-59,000	+12,000	Type I + II	-1,047,000	n.a.
			Type III	+1,002,000	n.a.
Hungary	-40,000	-10,000	- 26,000		+7,000[c]
Romania	-87,000	+19,100	-127,900		-9,200

[a]Changes between 1967 and 1971.
[b]Agricultural land.
[c]Estimate.
Sources: Statistical yearbooks of corresponding years.

288

agricultural land in the cooperative sector reflects the fact that many
farmers who were in Type I and II cooperatives gave up farming
altogether when their farms were upgraded. In Czechoslovakia, the
total arable area fell mainly as a result of 63,000 hectares of privately farmed land going out of use. The drive against private farming
in 1972 accounted for 56,000 hectares of this decline. In Bulgaria,
much of the large drop in arable area in the cooperative farm sector
seems to be the result of the transfer of land totaling 117,800 hectares
to workers, employees, and nonagricultural cooperative members
for use as personal plots. The arable area farmed by these groups
in 1971 reached 138,600 hectares, or 3.4 percent of the country's
arable land. The overall figures show only a slight decline in arable
area in Bulgaria, although the land-loss problem is in fact quite
acute there. Each year, between 400,000 and 500,000 hectares of
arable land are left uncultivated because of migration from mountain
regions to industrial centers or because of insufficient machinery
suitable for cultivating such terrains.[14] Construction projects and
erosion also contribute significantly to the loss of arable area.[15]
District People's Councils have been given special responsibility for
protecting arable land,[16] but tackling the erosion problem, which is
said to threaten more than 70 percent of the country's arable area,
is clearly a national, not a local, task.[17] Hungary's arable area has
fallen by 40,000 hectares in recent years, mainly through losses in
the socialist sector.

   Table 12.1 shows quite clearly that the level of mechanization
is steadily increasing in East European agriculture. It is interesting
to note that in 1972, the rank order of countries in terms of the level
of mechanization was much the same as in 1967, with Czechoslovakia
and East Germany far in the lead.[18] However, because of the great
progress in mechanization in Bulgaria and Romania, the gap between
the countries has lessened. As far as it is possible to ascertain,
Romania is the only country under consideration that still maintains
a large difference in the level of mechanization between state farms
and collective farms. The very close correlation observed in the
past between an East European country's rate of fertilizer application
per hectare of arable land and its level of mechanization is still valid.
The rate of fertilizer application is still highest in East Germany
(332 kg of active ingredients per hectare), followed by Czechoslovakia
(254 kg), with Romania in bottom position (69 kg). Despite significant
improvements in fertilizer consumption since the 1960s, especially
by Bulgaria and Hungary, there is hardly a difference in rank order.[19]

   The mechanical and technical improvements in East European
agriculture in recent years have facilitated the transfer of labor from
the rural areas to the industrial centers. In Bulgaria, the size of the
agricultural work force has shrunk very quickly, to the point that

there is now a shortage of agricultural labor. Between 1967 and 1971, around 238,300 people left the agricultural sector in Bulgaria, which is a drop of about 19 percent in only four years. The size of the work force on state farms in East Germany dropped by about 2,900 between 1967 and 1972, while the number of persons in the Type III cooperatives grew by about 7,500. However, the number of farmers in Type I and II cooperatives fell by about 196,000, making the net transfer from agriculture during the period (around 186,800 persons, or 19 percent of the 1967 figure) quite sizable and further exacerbating the agricultural labor shortage. In Czechoslovakia, another industrialized country with a shortage of agricultural workers, more than 159,000 people, or 13.3 percent of the agricultural labor force in 1967, left agriculture by the end of 1972, including 29,000 people from state farms, 46,000 from cooperative farms, and 68,000 from private farms. In Romania, the picture is somewhat different, since between 1967 and 1972 the number of persons employed on state farms increased by 9,700 (the number of workers rose by 17,000, while the administrative staff fell by 7,300), the staff working for Stations for Mechanizing Agriculture grew by almost 17,700, and the number of families belonging to cooperative farms increased by 11,300. However, the figures do not necessarily imply an increase in the total active work force in Romanian agriculture since it is reasonable to assume that some attrition occurred during the period in the number of independent farmers and the number of cooperative farmers permanently engaged in agriculture, though no precise data are available. Moreover, even if the agricultural work force did in fact increase by around 45,000 persons, or by a mere 0.8 percent, during the five-year period, there would be very good reason to conclude that there had been a significant transfer of labor from the expanding rural population to nonagricultural spheres of the economy.

MANAGEMENT

The management of East European agriculture has on the whole become more centralized in recent years. Hungary still has the most decentralized and liberal agricultural policy among the collectivized countries of Eastern Europe, and little has been done in the past five years or so to intensify central supervision.[20] A possible exception to this are the attempts that have been made since 1969 to upgrade the agricultural associations (lower-level cooperatives) so that they more closely resemble the kolkhoz-type farmers' cooperatives.[21] In 1972 the agricultural associations were renamed "specialized agricultural groups" and were brought more firmly into the cooperative system

administratively.[22] Specialized agricultural groups can now be formed
and operated under several parent cooperatives (including the General
Consumer and Marketing Cooperatives, within a farmers' cooperative,
or a branch agricultural cooperative). They are supposed to be self-
governing, but their semiautonomous status may well limit their
independence.[23] The policy of upgrading lower-level cooperatives
is being vigorously pursued in East Germany as stated above, and is
also part of the overall agricultural policy of Romania.[24]

Agricultural administration in East Germany is probably the
most centralized in Eastern Europe. Decision-making on the cooperative farms is limited through the direct imposition of compulsory
production tasks for grain, potatoes, sugar beets, milk, meat, and
eggs, and through compulsory contracts with purchasing bodies for
other agricultural products.[25] Moreover, the centrally determined
production plans for each local area are quite specific, even indicating
the levels of fertilizer application.[26] The operation of the price bonus
system makes it financially more advantageous for a farm to under-
fulfill an unrealistically ambitious plan than to overfulfill an unrealistically pessimistic plan.[27] This tends to discourage a careful
evaluation of a farm's potential, although political and administrative
pressures on farm leaders, it must be said, often counterbalance
this fault in the system of incentives. As will be seen below, in the
important matter of agroindustrial integration, the organizational
setup in East Germany gives the individual farms very little room to
maneuver independently. The interesting thing is that even with this
degree of central control, East German agriculture is still the most
efficient and productive in the Communist world, probably because
of the relatively small size of the farms and the high level of
mechanical-technical inputs.[28]

The Romanians also have a very centralized system of agricultural administration. In recent years, the search for an effective
administrative formula has led the Romanians into one agricultural
reform after another. For example, in October 1969, the Ministry
of Agriculture and Forestry replaced the Higher Council for Agriculture and at the same time took over several responsibilities
(including investments, supply, production organization, and norm-
setting) previously belonging to the National Union of Agricultural
Production Cooperatives.[29] At the end of November 1970, Ceausescu
announced that some of the ministry's planning prerogatives were to
be transferred to the county agricultural directorates, leaving only
plans for the delivery of basic products to the state, arable areas,
and the number of livestock subject to central planning.[30] Furthermore, Inter-Cooperative Councils would be established to determine,
among other things, the crops to be sown, production specialization,
and the best use of the machinery of Enterprises for the Mechanization

of Agriculture. The latter body, which had been reformed in 1968, was to be reorganized into smaller units to serve the farms more efficiently.[31] The state farm reforms of February 1971 and January 1972 have already been discussed. Meanwhile, the Ministry of Agriculture and Forestry was reorganized in January 1971 into the Ministry of Agriculture, the Food Industry, Forestry, and Waters. This body then lost its responsibilities for forestry in a January 1972 change that followed a further major reorganization of the ministry at the end of 1971.[32] The net result of these shifts was that the limited decentralization that began in November 1970 was reversed, with the ministry now once again closely supervising the farms.

There appears to have been some attempt in Romania to counterbalance the greater administrative centralization with greater incentives for the farmers on the farms. At the December 1969 plenum of the Central Union of Agricultural Production Cooperatives, the decision was taken to abolish the workday unit as a measurement of farm labor and substitute a contract payment system of remuneration in which payment depended on output in terms of volume or value.[33] Under the contract payment system, large work brigades with 120-150 members were all but abandoned in favor of smaller work units such as teams (25-30 members), families (1-3 members), or groups of families (5-7 members), and individual cooperative farm members who sign one-year contracts (renewable) with the cooperative farm.[34] A sample of 316 cooperatives in 1972 revealed that 52.2 percent of the cooperative members chose to enter into contracts with the farms as individuals, although in practice, such individuals often represented a family group or worked in association with other individual contractors. Only 19.2 percent of the cooperative members chose to join teams, and the remaining 28.6 percent belonged to some kind of family-based unit.[35] Family-based work units continue to be rejected by all the other East European countries except Hungary, presumably because of the desire to mechanize work and the potential problems of labor discipline with family work groups. However, in Romania in particular, the family-based groups are seen as a way of mobilizing the part-time labor force, thereby making better use of farm resources. Toward the end of 1970, it was decided that the small work units should become permanent, complete with mechanization where possible, and should be responsible for the entire production process.[36] Another concrete incentive for the farmers was the provision at the start of 1971 of a guaranteed minimum monthly wage of 300 lei ($20.12 = 100 lei at the official rate as of March 1974) for all cooperative members working a minimum number of days, and increases of between 39 and 67 percent in the pensions of cooperative farm members.[37] In 1973, for those working under the piece-rate

system and meeting centrally set norms of production in fruit growing,
vegetable growing, or animal breeding, the guaranteed minimum
monthly income was raised to 800 lei, 900 lei, or 1, 200 lei respectively.[38] The introduction of the piece-rate system in cooperative
agriculture was to be made general in 1973: Only 33 percent of the
farms had applied the system in all sectors in 1971, rising to 75
percent of the farms in 1972, although such branches as the production
of maize, sunflowers, and sugar beets were 90 percent covered.[39]
In addition, the party decided to introduce the piece-rate system
experimentally into the state farm system in the course of 1973.[40]

    Greater centralization of agricultural management has also
been evident in Czechoslovakia and Bulgaria. The new collectivization
drive in Czechoslovakia is one example of the process there. Another
is the June 1972 reform that swept away the district agricultural
associations and the regional departments of the Ministry of Agriculture and Food, replacing them with district and regional agricultural boards under the ministry. This reform was undertaken,
it was said, mainly so that the state could influence every phase of
production and at every level.[41] In Bulgaria, a limited decentralization of the state farm system was carried out in February 1969 to try
to eliminate the overconcentration of responsibility typical of the old
system.[42] The major change was to create district amalgamated
enterprises of state farms in 18 of the country's 27 districts. These
then became the intermediate link between the state farms and the
State Farms Economic Concern, which still was responsible for
central supervision. The district enterprises were subordinate to
both the central Concern and the district People's Councils. The latter
could then exercise influence over the local state farms as it did over
local cooperative farms (through the district cooperative union). In
the change, the state farms were also put on the same planning,
financing, and crediting basis as the cooperative farms. A subsequent
reorganization in June 1970 reversed the limited decentralization by
abolishing the district amalgamated enterprises of state farms and
putting the state farms directly under the central Concern and the
local district People's Councils.[43] In addition, responsibility for
central control over the cooperative farms was switched from the
Central Cooperative Union to the Ministry of Agriculture and the
Food Industry, while local responsibility went from the district
cooperative union to the district People's Council.[44] These moves
were in keeping with the party's 1968 decision to make People's
Councils responsible for all enterprises within their territory.[45]

    There has been less change in the sphere of farm prices in
Eastern Europe in recent years than when the economic reforms
were just beginning.[46] The Romanians have continued their practice
of increasing only a few prices at a time (meat and milk in June 1970;

rice and wool, in February 1972; wheat and maize, April 1973; meat
and milk, July 1973), [47] whereas East German procurement prices
have remained relatively stable, changing last in 1972 for beef,
potatoes, and sugar beets. [48] New bonuses for sales of beef were
introduced at the beginning of 1974. [49] In October 1972, the scale of
prices for grain deliveries in Czechoslovakia was simplified, although
the average price was not increased, despite reported rises in production costs. [50] In contrast, the Hungarians have tried to maintain
the level of profitability of all branches of agricultural production in
the hope of encouraging greater output, and so raised procurement
prices for meat, milk, and wool in December 1969, and introduced
a temporary premium for the sale of fattened pigs in September
1970. [51] However, the Hungarians have made no important changes
in their agricultural price system since that time. In Bulgaria, more
than two years of discussion and planning culminated in a major
reform of the price system in 1972. [52] No longer were agricultural
prices to be based directly on average national costs. Instead, the
Ministry of Agriculture was to set norms for the cost of production
of agricultural products, differentiated by regions. A standardized
profitability rate was then added to obtain the basic procurement
price. The idea behind the change was to encourage farms to keep
costs below the norms, thereby encouraging efficiency and greater
profitability. In conjunction with the reform, the price per ton for
hard wheat was raised to 250 leva from 150 leva ($103.09 = 100 leva
at the official rate of exchange as of March 1974), but the premia on
hard wheat were discontinued. The procurement price on deliveries
on highly profitable sunflower seeds was cut in an attempt to reduce
the differences in the profitability of various crops and thus force the
farms to think more carefully about concentration and specialization. [53]
Procurement prices were still to be correlated with quality, [54] but
the premium system was totally revised. Premia are now paid after
60 percent of the contracted quantities have been delivered, with the
highest premia when deliveries reach between 70 and 100 percent of
the contract. Premia for above-contract deliveries are at a lower
level in order to encourage farms to conclude realistic contracts, a
feature still missing from the East German scheme. [55] In May 1974,
purchase prices for cow's milk, beef, and veal were increased, along
with bonuses paid for cow's milk, for sheep raised in mountainous
regions, and for fattened pigs bought from private plots for farmers. [56]

AGRICULTURAL INTEGRATION

Despite persistent calls over the years for production specialization in agriculture, most East European farms have had little real

opportunity to specialize because of their more or less compulsory contractual obligation to deliver to procurement agencies a wide range of agricultural products. For example, most cooperative farms in Bulgaria have been producing between 50 and 60 different crops and several different kinds of farm animals.[57] Moreover, even with the price increases in recent years, many farms have been unable to accumulate sufficient capital for investment in new technology and in new areas of production. In an effort to overcome these persistent problems, the East European regimes have adopted new measures to encourage horizontal and also vertical integration in agricultural production.

In general terms, horizontal integration implies greater economic and financial cooperation and coordination between farms in production work and product specialization. Farms operating under similar conditions are brought together in some form of association or complex, which then becomes integrated within itself but is not integrated with related industrial processing enterprises or sales organizations. With vertical integration, the already integrated agricultural sector becomes fully integrated with the industrial sector relating to it so that the whole economic process, from producing the primary product to selling the final product, is the responsibility of a single corporate unit. The eventual goal of vertical integration is to make agriculture into a branch of the food industry and light industry.[58]

Horizontal integration has proceeded farthest in Bulgaria, where it has been expressed in the creation of agroindustrial complexes. The aim of these complexes is to stimulate the concentration and specialization of Bulgarian agriculture through the formation of very large production associations using industrial methods of production. Almost all farms in Bulgaria are now members of agroindustrial complexes, which can be made up of cooperative farms, state farms, or both cooperative and state farms.[59] At the start of 1971, there were 160 agroindustrial complexes in Bulgaria, of which 86 were composed only of agricultural cooperatives, 12 only of state farms, and 62 of both cooperative and state farms.[60] Each complex had an average of 5 or 6 farms, between 25,000 and 30,000 hectares of cultivated land, around 7,000 workers, and basic funds worth between 25 and 30 million leva. Before 1971, in each farm there had been up to 1,200 workers, and basic funds totaling between 3 and 3.5 million leva.[61] Some complexes were much larger than average (up to 50,000 hectares and more), and some were even smaller than the average size of a single cooperative.[62] Each district usually has between 5 and 7 agroindustrial complexes within its borders.[63] In keeping with the emphasis on specialization, the complexes usually grow only between 3 and 5 crops, and limit themselves to only one branch of livestock production.[64]

There are two types of agroindustrial complexes in Bulgaria, reflecting different stages of economic and organizational development. In the lower form of agroindustrial complex, member farms retain their economic and legal independence. At the same time, the complex itself is an economic and juridical entity separate from its members and having its own property and assets, which are also separate from those of its members. The complex operates on the basis of economic accountability, and it is supposed to be self-supporting. The eventual goal is to transform the lower form of agroindustrial complex into the higher form, in which there is a complete merging of the participants so as to form a unified economic and legal entity. The formerly independent member farms become self-supporting sections of the new unified farm, and the mode of management changes from territorial to branch (that is, section managers are concerned with spheres of specialization rather than separate territorial units).[65] There have been warnings that the transformation of a lower-form agroindustrial complex to a higher form should not be done until the necessary production-technical, economic, and political conditions exist.[66] One obvious problem would undoubtedly be to define the new status of cooperative property when a lower form complex containing both cooperative and state property became a higher-form agroindustrial complex. Another problem is to ensure that such a large farm unit is administratively governable and economically viable. Because of these problems, only two complexes had been reorganized into the higher form by the beginning of 1974.[67]

Romania is moving forward with horizontal integration through the creation of intercooperative councils, which then assist in setting up intercooperative associations.[68] The associations are supposed to be established at the initiative of a number of cooperative farms with the assistance and approval of the local intercooperative council, the county branch of the Ministry of Agriculture, the Food Industry, and Water, and the county Union of Agricultural Production Cooperatives. The intercooperative council participates in the preparation of the plan indicators of the cooperatives and the intercooperative associations. The council is responsible for checking on the fulfillment of each cooperative's plans and also, together with the local agricultural machinery station, allocates machinery to the cooperative farms.[69] Ceaucescu recently criticized these councils, which control areas of between 10,000 to 15,000 hectares, for excessive interference in the autonomy of the cooperative farms. It appears that in some cases, the councils even engaged in asset-stripping, taking away land or animals from the farms but leaving them with their debts.[70] This sort of abuse, while unfortunate, cannot be unexpected when so much authority is vested in one body.

There are two kinds of intercooperative associations in
Romania. The so-called ordinary intercooperative association provides guidance and supervises the coordination of production.[71] The
more important economic intercooperative association engages in
production activities such as servicing work, the sale of produce,
and the construction and operation of production, storage, and processing facilities.[72] At the start of 1971, there were 254 intercooperative associations in Romania, including 9 large hothouse units, 50
pig fattening units, 6 cattle fattening units, and 23 poultry farms.[73]
Associations also engage in milk and meat production and wine-
making. It has been reported that the best results are obtained when
no more than 6 or 7 farms are linked together;[74] the optimum number
of livestock on intercooperative associations specializing in animal
husbandry was said to be between 15,000 and 30,000 for pig fattening
farms, 2,700 (maximum) for cattle fattening farms, and around
15,000 for sheep fattening farms.[75]

Members of intercooperative associations retain their autonomy,
but each farm must contribute cash and equipment to the association's
social fund to ensure fixed assets and necessary operating funds.[76]
It is possible for associations to be formed from cooperative farms
alone or from cooperative farms and, seemingly, one state enterprise.[77] Where only cooperative farms are members of the association, an association council is established, whose chairman is the
director of the local agricultural mechanization station. Where the
association is between a number of cooperatives and a state enterprise, the director of the state enterprise is to serve as head of the
association's council. This provides an additional measure of state
control since state employees directly subordinate to the Ministry of
Agriculture, the Food Industry, and Water head the associations,
whatever their composition.[78] Thus, Romania's intercooperative
associations to some extent resemble Bulgaria's lower form of agroindustrial complex, except that more central control appears to be
exercised over the units in Romania.

The East Germans are also enthusiastic about horizontal integration in agriculture, but favor a looser form of arrangement than
the Bulgarians or Romanians. A preference has been shown for
integration rather than large-scale amalgamation of East Germany's
relatively small cooperative and state farms, presumably because
their plan is to develop specialized production units instead of merely
increasing the size of nonspecialized farms. Production cooperation
associations, which can link either cooperative or state farms, or a
mixture of both, have been set up for the joint performance of different
kinds of tasks, such as melioration, chemicalization, plant protection
work, livestock raising and fattening, construction and operation of
warehouses and mixed feed plants, etc. The production cooperation

associations can also be very simple, formed merely to enable the joint purchase and use of machinery or equipment.[79] In 1970, there were about 5,000 production cooperation associations, joining 85 percent of all the agricultural enterprises in the country.[80] It appears that the organizational structure is loose enough to allow one farm to participate in more than one association.[81] In contrast to the Bulgarian agroindustrial complexes, the East German production cooperation associations are not permanent bodies (in that the partners are only temporary members), nor are they economic units in the eyes of the law. The plans of the member farms are coordinated with government agencies which then confirm them, and the relations between members are regulated by contracts they conclude with each other.[82] Thus, members of the association have very little room to maneuver. The production cooperation association acts as a vehicle and coordinator of all this activity.

Much emphasis has been given to cooperation in East Germany in the production of beef, pork, milk, poultry, sugar, fruit, and vegetables. Since the beginning of 1974, the state has provided capital investments, grants, and reduced annual interest rates on long-term loans for agricultural and livestock complexes operating on an industrial basis.[83] What is more, because of the costs of building and equipping the interfarm complexes and running them in (and the effect that this would have on the income of the members of the farms), the state also pays bonuses for produce from the complex for the first three years of its operation if the complex meets certain standards.[84] For example, in order to receive the special financial benefits and incentives, all newly constructed livestock farms must be large, modern enterprises run on an industrial basis with a minimum of 1,930 cows in a dairy complex, 16,000 animals in a beef fattening unit, 24,000 pigs in a pig fattening unit, and so on.[85] Although these cooperative ventures are obviously of some scale, there is no idea yet that the individual members will lose their identity or independence in the production cooperation association. At the same time, the scale of investment and length of time required to repay the investment indicate that membership of farms in some of the associations will be for a fairly long period.

Loose forms of horizontal integration are also favored in Hungary and Czechoslovakia. In Hungary, interfarm cooperative associations carry out a wide range of functions, although most of the associations are not involved directly in agricultural production. For example, in 1970 there were 462 interfarm cooperative associations in Hungary, of which 117 were engaged in construction, 141 in agricultural work, 42 in the processing of agricultural produce, 55 in trade, and 107 in repair work and other services.[86] Each cooperative association usually has 10-15 members, a number of which belong to several associations. In the sphere of agricultural production, joint ventures have been started for corn production, sugar beet production, pig fattening, broiler production, and processing such items as milk, fruit, and vegetables. Members retain their independence but agree to concentrate on specified areas of production along the lines agreed by the association, quite often employing the "closed production system," that is, industrial-type farming. Departments and bureaus to coordinate the activities of the interfarm associations have been created (for instance, there is a Central Bureau of cooperative enterprises for the processing and sale of milk, the members of which are 9 intercooperative enterprises for milk processing).[87] There seems to have been little interest in Hungary in joint projects between cooperative and state farms. In Czechoslovakia, the emphasis is on the pooling of financial, material, and manpower resources between farms. Contracts link together the partners (solely cooperative or state farms, or a combination), who retain their individual identity. At the beginning of 1973, there were said to be 243 joint agricultural enterprises in the entire country, combining 5,936 members, of which 5,391 were agricultural cooperatives. There was a great concentration on animal husbandry, with 115 of the enterprises specializing in livestock production, 39 in pork production, and 31 in egg production. An additional 53 dealt with construction work, and 33 produced animal fodder. A further 109 joint enterprises had been formed and were in the process of readying themselves to start production.[88] However, at the end of 1972, there were said to be 154 joint agricultural enterprises in full operation in the Czech republic,[89] and "more than 100" in the Slovak republic,[90] which somewhat surprisingly produces a sum higher than the reported national total of 243. At the beginning of November 1973, the number of joint agricultural enterprises in operation in the country was placed at a mere 146, with 196 more reported to be about to go into operation in the Czech lands.[91] As with other forms of loose cooperation in Eastern Europe, it is possible for a farm in Czechoslovakia to belong to more than one joint enterprise.[92]

In terms of vertical integration of agricultural production, the East Germans have progressed farther than the other East European Communist countries. In the East German model, the processing enterprises have a more prominent role than those cooperating in production, and the partnership is therefore based on the final product (for example, the Poultry Industry Combine). The cooperating partners in these combines remain legally independent, but the combine itself is a legal entity and operates under the system of economic accountability. The combine members, which often include both cooperative and state farms as well as processing and trade enterprises, enter into contracts with each other, basing these on their centrally approved overall production plans. The contracts usually run for two to three years, and nonfulfillment carries with it financial penalties and legal responsibilities. A joint material and financial fund is maintained by the combine to finance joint projects.[93] In 1969, about 20 percent of the Type III cooperatives participated in some form of vertical integration.[94] There were some 265 vertically organized combines in operation in 1971, in which almost one-quarter of all the country's agricultural enterprises participated.[95] Although this form of collaboration in East Germany is more structured than the production cooperation associations, a serious fault is that the competence of the combines is restricted to a given area, whereas effective vertical integration most often cuts across narrow territorial boundaries.

Having devoted most of their efforts to implementing horizontal integration, the Bulgarians have only recently created their first industrial-agricultural complexes (not to be confused with the agro-industrial complexes). The industrial-agricultural complexes are distinguished by the predominance of an industrial enterprise in their organizational structure. At the end of 1972, it was announced that an industrial-agricultural association controlling the country's sugar production would be set up. This association would be based on seven industrial-agricultural complexes, each of which would be built around one of the country's existing sugar refineries.[96] Two agroindustrial complexes and the Ruse sugar refinery were organized into Bulgaria's first industrial-agricultural complex. A very interesting innovation was that the property of the two agroindustrial complexes, although they were of the pure cooperative type and did not include any state farms, was reclassified as state property, and the cooperative members became state workers.[97] However, the farms themselves do not yet seem to have been classified as state farms. Two other industrial-agricultural complexes have recently been created in Bulgaria, but the status of the farm property is not yet known.[98]

In principle, there are three different kinds of vertically integrated combines in Hungarian agriculture: the state enterprise, in which all components are owned by the state; the joint enterprise, combining state enterprises and cooperative farms under the rules relating to economic associations; and a combine-type enterprise set up by a specialist producer to process the raw materials it turns out and then market the end product.[99] In practice though, the state-owned food-processing industry has tried to preserve its monopolistic position by opposing the development of vertical integration of state enterprises with cooperative farms.[100] For example, in a number of towns, the Milk Industry Trust, with the help of local councils, has prohibited the marketing of dairy products produced by cooperative state associations.[101] Another disincentive to cooperatives is that such joint associations come under the tax laws relating to state enterprises, which are disadvantageous for cooperatives. Last, most Hungarian cooperatives are reported to lack sufficient capital to participate in joint enterprises.[102] In the export branches of agricultural production, state-owned enterprises have formed vertically organized combines. For instance, the Tokaj Wine Combine operates as an independent enterprise, subject only to the direct supervision of the Ministry of Agriculture and Food.[103] All the same, vertical integration has not progressed very far in Hungary, and has hardly been developed at all in either Czechoslovakia or Romania.[104]

It is clear that the implementation of horizontal or vertical integration can provide the farms with greater opportunities to develop production. However, one of the problems is that farms that need the most help, the weak farms, cannot benefit greatly from most of the schemes because these farms have so little capital to invest. The development of production specialization through integration could be a potential boon to each farm, and yet some of the looser forms of horizontal integration provide only weak incentives for farms to make large investments in new areas since the partnerships are temporary and the integration is so incomplete. It would seem likely that more formal and permanent arrangements will be introduced in this area as the process of integration develops.

One of the reasons for the looser forms of integration is of course the difference in the status of the property of some of the partners. The emphasis of horizontal integration has been on getting nearby cooperative and state farms to collaborate, which is not overly difficult as long as each partner remains independent. However, once partners of a mixed association surrender their independence to the association, as is foreseen in the higher form of Bulgarian agroindustrial complex, the natural tendency would be to upgrade the cooperative property to some form of state property. The same tendency operates in relation to vertical integration, as seen in the creation of the sugar industrial-agricultural complexes in Bulgaria. However, any large-scale change in the status of cooperative property through horizontal or vertical integration would have deep economic, political, and social repercussions, which the regimes apparently want to avoid at this time. Instead, they are content to promise the continued existence of both forms of property for the foreseeable future, while at the same time praising integration for bringing the two forms of property closer together. It would not be at all surprising to see action taken, perhaps gradually at first, to unify the status of the property in the various joint enterprises.

Were it not for the huge amount of new capital investment required, vertical integration would undoubtedly be more common in Eastern Europe than it is now. The demand of other areas of the economy, as well as the need to look after more mundane investment needs in the agricultural sector (for example, roads, irrigation, chemicalization, mechanization, etc.), will most likely mean that progress toward full vertical integration in East European agricultural production will be slow, but nevertheless apparent.

NOTES

1. Poland and Yugoslavia have been omitted from the study because of the relatively minor role of the socialist sector of agriculture in those countries; Albania, because of scarcity of information.

2. See Everett M. Jacobs, "Ownership and Planning in Soviet and East European Agriculture," in The Prediction of Communist Economic Performance, ed. Peter J. Wiles (London: Cambridge University Press, 1971), pp. 51-52.

3. Ibid.

4. Ibid., p. 57.

5. Romania Libera, February 17, 1971. The report on the reform broadcast by Radio Bucharest on February 15, 1972 said that 144 reorganized farms would be created.

6. Ibid.

7. Ibid., January 11, 1972.

8. Statistisches Jahrbuch, 1968 (Berlin, 1968), p. 255; Statistisches Jahrbuch, 1973 (Berlin, 1973), p. 188.

9. Rolnicke Noviny, February 8, 1972; Zivot Strany, no. 1 (1973).

10. Rolnicke Noviny, January 8, 1972; Lud, March 10, 1970.

11. In East Germany there was little difference between 1967 and 1972 in the rate of increase in size of state farms and Type III cooperatives.

12. Dunantuli Naplo, September 23, 1969; Nograd, February 10, 1970.

13. Romania Libera, April 2, 1974.

14. Rabotnichesko Delo, January 6, 1973.

15. Pogled, April 24, 1972.

16. Rabotnichesko Delo, January 6, 1973.

17. Kooperativno Selo, October 29, 1970.

18. See Jacobs, op. cit., pp. 42-43. The author estimates that East Germany had around 27 hectares of arable land per 15-horsepower tractor unit in 1967, and around 22 hectares per unit in 1972.

19. Ibid., pp. 42, 44.

20. Ibid., pp. 44, 69-72

21. Ibid., p. 53.

22. Magyar Kozlony, September 27, 1972.

23. Nepszabadsag, September 22, 1972. This source stated that the change would broaden the independence of the specialized agricultural groups.

24. Jacobs, op. cit., pp. 40, 57.

25. Ekonomika Selskogo Khozyaistva, no. 4 (1973), pp. 114-15.

26. Ibid., p. 114.

27. Ekonomika Selskogo Khozyaistva, no. 10 (1971), pp. 110-11. The bonus is paid on increases over the previous year's production. If a farm overfulfills its deliveries plan, the farm's original calculations are used to determine the level of the bonus, which would be lower than would have been paid had the plan been more accurate in its predictions. If a plan is underfulfilled, the bonus on any increase in deliveries over the previous year would be paid as if such an increase had been accurately predicted.

28. Jacobs, op. cit., pp. 42-45.

29. Buletinul Oficial, November 13, 1969.

30. Speech of November 23, 1970, published in Scinteia on November 28, 1970.

31. At the beginning of 1971, an average of six cooperative farms were served by each of the Stations for the Mechanization of Agriculture, which operated as local branches of the county Enterprises for the Mechanization of Agriculture. See Buletinul Oficial, January 5, 1971.

32. Buletinul Oficial, December 31, 1971.

33. Scinteia, December 25, 1969.

34. Mihail Cernea, "The Large Scale Formal Organization and the Family Primary Group," Revue Roumaine des Sciences Sociales: Serie de Sociologie, Vol. 18 (1974), pp. 87-91.

35. Ibid., pp. 91-92.

36. Scinteia, November 28, 1970. In particular, emphasis was placed on mechanizing the work of teams.

37. Ibid.

38. Scinteia, March 11, 1973.

39. Viata Economica, no. 49 (1972), p. 6.

40. Scinteia, March 11, 1973.

41. Zemedelske Noviny, September 2, 1972.

42. Rabotnichesko Delo, February 20, 1969.

43. Rabotnichesko Delo, June 26, 1970.

44. Ibid.

45. Rabotnichesko Delo, December 1, 1968.

46. Jacobs, op. cit., pp. 61-86.

47. Ibid., pp. 76-77; Radio Bucharest, February 2, 1972; Buletinul Oficial, April 10, 1973; Radio Bucharest, July 13, 1973.

48. Neue Deutsch Bauernzeitung, no. 39 (1972); reference by courtesy of Karl-Eugen Wadekin.
49. Ekonomika Selskogo Khozyaistva, no. 6 (1974), p. 107.
50. Radio Prague, October 17, 1972.
51. Magyar Hirlap, December 5, 1969; Dunatuli Naplo, September 11, 1970.
52. Rabotnichesko Delo, June 27, 1972; and Ikonomicheski Zhivot, June 28, 1972.
53. Ikonomicheski Zhivot, June 28, 1972.
54. See Ekonomika Selskogo Khozyaistva, no. 1 (1969), pp. 112-13.
55. Ikonomicheski Zhivot, June 28, 1972.
56. Darzhaven Vestnik, May 28, 1974.
57. Voprosy Ekonomiki, no. 5 (1972), p. 148.
58. Ekonomika Selskogo Khozyaistva, no. 3 (1973), p. 116.
59. Kooperativno Selo, October 27, 1970.
60. Voprosy Ekonomika, no. 5 (1972), p. 148.
61. Ibid.
62. Rabotnichesko Delo, September 22, 1970.
63. Ibid.
64. Voprosy Ekonomiki, no. 5 (1972), p. 148.
65. Kooperativno Selo, October 27, 1970.
66. Kooperativno Selo, January 14, 1971.
67. Otechestvan Glas, March 1, 1972.
68. See Buletinul Oficial, April 15, 1972.
69. Ibid.
70. Scinteia, February 28, 1974.
71. Buletinul Oficial, April 15, 1974.
72. Voprosy Ekonomiki, no. 4 (1972), p. 110.
73. Ibid.
74. Era Socialista, no. 3 (1972), p. 8.
75. Romania Libera, May 7, 1974.
76. Buletinul Oficial, April 15, 1974.
77. Ibid.
78. Ibid.
79. Ekonomika Selskogo Khozyaistva, no. 5 (1970), p. 114. Type I and II cooperatives, as well as horticultural garden cooperatives, can join production cooperation associations.
80. Ekonomika Selskogo Khozyaistva, no. 3 (1973), p. 116.
81. Ekonomika Selskogo Khozyaistva, no. 5 (1970), p. 114.
82. Kooperation, April 1973, pp. 171-74.
83. Ekonomika Selskogo Khozyaistva, no. 6 (1974), p. 106.
84. Ibid., pp. 106-07. The Ministry of Agriculture and Forestry has even given additional subsidies to a dairy complex which ran at a loss in its first year because of the cost of running in the new facilities.

85. Ibid., p. 105.

86. Voprosy Ekonomiki, no. 4 (1972), p. 111.

87. Ibid.

88. Tribuna, January 31, 1973.

89. Zemedelske Noviny, Feburary 1, 1973. In all, there were said to be 282 joint agricultural enterprises, of which 181 were engaged in livestock production. Of the latter, 43 were fully operational and 138 were not.

90. Rolnicke Noviny, April 11, 1973.

91. Rude Pravo, November 2, 1973.

92. See Rolnicke Noviny, April 11, 1973.

93. Ekonomika Selskogo Khozyaistva, no. 5 (1970), pp. 115-17.

94. Voprosy Ekonomiki, no. 4 (1972), p. 112.

95. Ekonomika Selskogo Khozyaistva, no. 3 (1973), p. 117.

96. Rabotnichesko Delo, December 19, 1972.

97. BTA in English, January 19, 1973, cited by Harry Trend, "Agriculture in Eastern Europe: A Comparative Study," Radio Free Europe Research, May 15, 1974, Part VI, p. 10.

98. Darzhaven Vestnik, April 9, 1974.

99. Figyelo, February 10, 1971.

100. Szabad Fold, November 30, 1969; Magyar Hirlap, April 27, 1973.

101. Magyar Hirlap, April 27, 1973.

102. Ibid.

103. Figyelo, February 10, 1971.

104. For a Czechoslovak example, see Ekonomika Selskogo Khozyaistva, no. 3 (1973), p. 118.

13

EFFICIENCY IN HUNGARIAN AGRICULTURE AFTER SIX YEARS OF ECONOMIC REFORM
Lewis A. Fischer

In the wake of World War II, agriculture was the most dev-
astated segment of the Hungarian economy. Direct losses through
military actions amounted to 65 percent of fixed assets. The German
occupation followed by the looting by the Soviet forces decimated
livestock and other movable inventory. The new regime adapted the
Soviet pattern of ruthless collectivization without being prepared to
make the necessary capital investments to give the enterprises a
reasonable chance of success. Investment policy attached highest
priority to the development of heavy industry while agriculture was
neglected. Subsequent plan modifications reduced the originally
stipulated 20 percent of agricultural investment to 9.8 percent of
the total by the end of 1951. Consequently, the production volume of
the farm industry in 1949 and 1950 represented a mere 85 and 89
percent, respectively, of that in prewar years.[1] The years after
Stalin's death marked the advent of a slow recovery; however, the
revolution of 1956 brought about substantial setbacks. Several collective enterprises were disbanded, and in the atmosphere of re-
pression in 1956-57 a great many agricultural experts and specialists
left the country forever. Collectivization was resumed in 1959 and
continued in yearly steps until its completion in 1961-62.

Restructuring of the farm industry started prior to the official
inception of the New Economic Mechanism (NEM). The "production
for production's sake" concept has been gradually abandoned, and
modernization of the product mix appeared in encouraging better
supplies adjusted to market demand. Yet, during the first half of
the 1960s there was marginal progress only in socialized agriculture.

INSTITUTIONAL AND STRUCTURAL EFFECTS
OF THE REFORM

The major institutional change was the merger of the Ministries of Agriculture and of Food into one Ministry of Agriculture and Foods. Simultaneously, however, the authority of the ministry to define indicators mandatory on enterprises was narrowed. As one leading Hungarian agricultural economist stated, "Under the earlier system of management the enterprise should not deviate from the line of instructions contained in the plan. . . . The economic reform opened instead of unilinearity a highway implemented with delimitations, permissive and prohibitive signals."[2] These "signals" are considered as economic regulators determining the decision-making power of the manager. In the institutional framework the isolation of enterprises from the international market was terminated. Organizations under authority of the Ministry of External Trade cooperate with the Ministry of Agriculture and Foods in efforts to create an advantageous supply position by adjusting production to international market conditions.

Basic changes occurred in the application of administrative measures. In the words of Csikos-Nagy, "the economic guidelines stipulate that it is unnecessary and useless to limit or to regulate the movement of products in cases of monetary disequilibrium. Limitation both to production and marketing should only be induced by the Government where approving the annual plans for people's economy."[3] Indeed, the 1971 Plan provided regulations only in marketing of meat and meat products of all agricultural commodities.

The striking feature of structural changes is the decline in the number of enterprises. The material incorporated in Table 13.1 indicates that total land area in state farms and cooperatives remained practically unchanged, while the number of enterprises declined by 18 percent in state farms and by 29 percent in cooperatives. This development reflects the trend toward economies of scale by integration.

Another important structural change affecting productivity is the shrinkage of the labor force and accelerated mechanization. Active earners in agriculture, forestry, and water conservancy contributed 52 percent of the total labor force in 1950. Their rate diminished to 28 percent in 1968 and was 25 percent in 1972.[4] Since the inception of the NEM some 150,000 young people (under 26) joined the cooperatives, partly permanently, partly temporarily. Because of that, the average age of working people in cooperatives was lowered from 47.5 to 42.5 years. In an effort to keep workers on the farms by giving them opportunity to earn higher incomes and

TABLE 13.1

Hungary: Major Data on Agriculture

	1965	1970	1971	1972
I. Number of agricultural units of management				
State farms	214	180	181	175
Agricultural producers' cooperatives	3,278	2,441	2,373	2,315
Private and auxiliary farms (over 0.6 hectares per thousands)	120	110	120	120
II. Land area (1,000 hectares)				
State farms	1,019	n.a.	999	997
Cooperative sector:	5,840	n.a.	5,908	5,912
of which common farms	4,753	n.a.	4,872	4,888
household plots	767	n.a.	723	712
Private and auxiliary farms	518	n.a.	553	554

	1966-70	1970	1971	1972
	(million forints)			Percentage
III. Production of agricultural products (at 1968 prices)				
Social sector	14,838	15,244	16,319	15
Cooperative sector	70,781	69,764	76,602	72
of which: producers' cooperatives	66,750	65,837	72,420	68
of which in common land	43,867	42,761	48,473	47
on household plots	22,883	23,076	23,947	21
Private and auxiliary farms	11,606	12,521	13,603	13
Agricultural production total	97,225	97,529	106,524	100

Sources: Statistical Pocket Book of Hungary, 1972 (Budapest: Statistical Publishing House, 1972), p. 151; Statistical Pocket Book of Hungary, 1973 (Budapest: Statistical Publishing House, 1973), p. 167.

to get some of the necessary industrial and construction work done, many types of auxiliary work have been developed under the auspices of the farm collectives. Industrial and service-type activities performed by the cooperatives increased between 1966 and 1970 by 335 percent. About 92 percent of these auxiliary industrial activities are performed by male workers.[5] Measurement of labor productivity has been aggravated by the complicated labor structure in the cooperatives. There we have to distinguish between permanently settled manpower and so-called mobile workers' groups. The settled labor force has been recruited from the membership and accounts for approximately one-third of all work done on the common farm. It receives about half of its income from the household plots and devotes a great deal of its labor to the labor-intensive works there. The "mobile" labor force is the successor of the "migrating agricultural laborers" of the pre-Communist farm industry. According to a country journal's report, in 1973 more than 400,000 of the 1,000,000 farmers' cooperative members are retired and some 120,000 people are employed to work with the remaining 600,000 members.[6] According to the reporter, the increase in the number of employees is attributable in part to the fact that modern production technologies demand considerable expertise, and young experts demand regular wages. There are considerable discrepancies in wages and social benefits between members who have their household plots and employed workers.

MECHANIZATION

The attempt to establish a model to calculate a coefficient for labor productivity has been aggravated by scarcity of reliable data on the distribution of machinery. The economic reform included a favorable trend toward investment for agricultural improvement. In the past, the selection of machinery was determined by the capacity of the supplier—who must have been a socialist country—and not by actual needs. Some of the models soon went out of production. Thus, the replacement of parts or repairs represented grave difficulties. The Fourth Five-Year Plan (1971-75) indicates that "agricultural development shall be supported by an investment expenditure of about 61-62 billion forints. In the large-scale agricultural units the tractor park and other machinery shall be updated and extended; mechanized harvesting of maize and rough fodders, as well as sugar beet and potato shall be introduced—in addition to grain harvesting."[7] Of the total agricultural investment, 18 billion are to be spent on mechanization. In 1973 about one-third of the agricultural machinery requirement was supplied by domestic manufacturers and 40 percent was Soviet-manufactured. The introduction of the "closed production system" (CPS) postulated acquisition of sophisticated modern machinery. Consequently, machinery purchases from nonsocialist countries—primarily the United States, West Germany, and France—increased from 9 percent of the total in 1971 to 29 percent in 1973.[8]

Table 13.2 reveals the trend toward mechanization that has been considered as the major avenue to efficiency, that is, higher productivity. The material indicates a gradual increase in tractor park, and measured on average land per tractor, Hungary has surpassed its socialist neighbors; however, it is still behind West European countries such as the neighboring Austria, also Italy and France, not to mention West Germany and the Benelux countries. The statistics show that a substantial part of the machinery has been used to replace traditional—horses and oxen—hauling power. The reform with its new investment policy enabled the enterprises to mechanize crop production. Experts maintain, however, that much more must be done to reach the desired grade of efficiency. Ianos Felfoldi, head of the scientific section of the Research Institute for Agricultural Economics, stated, "In recent years it was proven that there is only a limited possibility for the extension of new complex machine systems like CPS. The most frequently applied method of mechanization is the partial periodical, or if you like, continuous reconstruction activity."[9]

CHANGING INPUT MIX—CHANGING OUTPUT

On the road toward efficiency the changing input mix is the major characteristic of modern agriculture. The provision of NEM brought about substantial changes both in production and application of fertilizers. The 1971-75 Plan foresees 80 percent increase in domestic production and continuing imports to meet the growing demand on the farms. Indeed, application by hectare in kilograms of active substance shows substantial growth since the inception of the NEM as reflected in the following figures:[10]

Year	Kilograms
1970	150
1971	171
1972	190
1973	215 (estimated)[11]

The reform has combined the proposition for technological progress and material supply with a clever wage and price policy to stimulate

TABLE 13.2

Hungary: Major Data on Mechanization in Agriculture

	1960	1965	1970	1971
Arable land per tractor, hectare	129	79	73	74
Mechanical hauling power as percentage of total hauling power	50.2	74.7	85.4	87.2
Machinery—substituted peasants' work days, thousands	61,603	120,437	160,508	173,602
Degree of mechanization (percentage) in grain harvesting				
State farms	97.4	99.2	100.0	100.0
Common farms of agricultural producers' cooperatives	53.3	83.1	98.7	100.0
in corn cob harvesting				
State farms	—	24.0	89.0	97.2
Common farms of agricultural producers' cooperatives	0.1	0.9	40.4	56.7

Source: Statistical Pocket Book of Hungary, 1973 (Budapest: Statistical Publishing House, 1973), p. 177.

intensive farming in the social sector (see Table 13.3). The measures resulted in conspicuous improvement of yields, particularly in commodities that quickly respond to mechanization and fertilization. Specified data in Table 13.4 reveal this trend. Average wheat yields jumped during the first reform years and reached an estimated 3,500 kg in 1973. The projected target for 1980 is about 4,000 kg.[12] Taking the 1972 averages, Hungary still ranks after East Germany (3,980 kg), Bulgaria (3,730), and Czechoslovakia (3,360) among the Comecon countries. However, it fulfilled the foremost target, that is, self-sufficiency in its prime bread grain. Of course, it is still a far cry from the prewar situation when Hungary was one of the quality wheat-exporting nations in Europe. Corn productivity has also

TABLE 13.3

Hungary: Value of Per Unit Production by Sectors of Agriculture, 1965 and 1971

	1965	1971	Percent Change
	Production of One Hectare, in 1968 Forints		
State farm	14,561	16,335	12.0
Producers' cooperatives	9,229	9,949	7.8
Household plots	29,834	33,121	11.0

Source: Calculated from data presented in Statistical Pocket Book of Hungary, 1973 (Budapest: Statistical Publishing House, 1973), p. 169.

TABLE 13.4

Hungary: Average Yields of Major Crops (quintal* by hectare)

	Average of		1970	1971	1972
	1961–65	1966–70			
Wheat	18.6	24.3	21.3	30.7	31.0
Barley	18.7	21.2	19.5	26.2	27.6
Grain corn	26.1	32.3	33.8	35.4	39.7
Sugar beet	246.4	325.2	287.3	277.7	370.1
Alfalfa hay	29.7	43.0	49.9	41.7	44.8
Onions	100.5	135.9	102.7	122.8	147.6
Red pepper (paprika)	49.3	65.1	55.2	56.1	68.6

*1 quintal = 100 kilograms, or 220.46 pounds.
Source: Statistical Pocket Book of Hungary, 1973 (Budapest: Statistical Publishing House, 1973), p. 175.

shown substantial improvement as a result of the introduction of the closed production system. In view of growing protein requirements in animal production, particular importance must be attached to the improvement of alfalfa yields.

Yield increasing technological change in agriculture is usually accompanied by increased use of purchased inputs and greatly increases the returns to them. Under these circumstances, it is essential that input supplies be increased rapidly as the demand curve shifts.[13] When these requirements are met, productivity and efficiency of the industry grow accordingly. The foregoing discussion has demonstrated that technological changes created favorable conditions to substantial growth of the crop production in Hungarian agriculture. The reform's provisions embodied in actual plans enabled crop producers to meet the increased demand for purchased inputs. However, the situation is entirely different in the sector of animal and animal products, although livestock expansion is one of the principal goals of every five-year plan. The NEM also attaches priority to the sector that has to fulfill a dual task: (1) to improve the nutritional level of the population, that is, to meet the demand for meat; (2) to expand animal and meat export since a considerable proportion of the country's foreign exchange originates from it.[14] Both plan and reform call for quantitative and qualitative improvement of the cattle stock. Cattle breeding has been in the state of stagnation since neither cattle stock nor milk production shows a positive trend during the past five years or so. Table 13.5 reveals the complexity of the cattle economy. While total number has been reduced, there is a tremendous increase from 1960 on, on the common farms of the cooperatives; 120 percent in total number of cattle and 89 percent in dairy cattle. During the same time, the numbers decreased on the household plots by 33 and 35 percent, respectively. It is not intended here to dwell on the present and future role of household plots, which still provided 22.5 percent of the value of gross farm products in 1973.[15] They experienced several ups and downs during the last decade. There is, however, unmistakable trend of their diminishing economic importance mirrored in the reduction of their number from 923,975 in 1966 to 782,000 by March 1972.[16] Young cooperative members opt for cash instead of opportunity for working long hours on the private plots. This trend influences primarily dairying, which postulates permanent attendance, while hog production allows more relaxation. The lack of efficiency in the dairy and beef industry is reflected in the figures on both total and per cow milk production (see Table 13.5). Sales of cattle for slaughter, which amounted to 310,000 tons in 1970, have decreased to 287,000 by 1972. Experts attribute the current situation to economic constraint. In the words of a specialist: "This coercive force

TABLE 13.5

Hungary: A. Livestock by Social Sectors
(thousands)

Date	State Farms	Common Farms of Agricultural Producers' Cooperatives	Household Plots
		Cattle	
1960	208	448	738
1965	247	816	699
1970	229	982	526
1971	221	971	520
1972	228	985	492
		Of which: Cows	
1960	72	167	358
1965	97	275	330
1970	90	310	247
1971	86	315	240
1972	91	315	233
		Pigs	
1960	564	606	2,144
1965	825	2,018	2,594
1970	856	1,554	2,156
1971	887	1,797	2,723
1972	877	1,870	2,702

B. Milk Production and Yields

	1960	1965	1970	1971	1972
Milk production, million liters	1,899	1,709	1,807	1,749	1,783
Milk production, per cow, liters	2,190	2,150	2,420	2,354	2,400

Source: Statistical Pocket Book of Hungary 1973 (Budapest: Statistical Publishing Company, 1973), p. 179.

is due to the high investment costs of an up-to-date dairy farm. According to estimations a minimum increase by 250 liters in milk production without any surplus cost is required for the reimbursement of the 10 thousand forints additional investment costs of the accommodation per one cow at normal pace."[17] Obviously, the relationship between investment and return has deteriorated as a result of the inefficient allocation of resources. The current Five-Year Plan calls for increase and qualitative improvement of the dairy cattle population. Also, beef cattle production is to increase by 25 percent and wholesale procurement by 37 percent. Long-term estimates of meat and beef cattle requirements pointed to a 40 to 50 percent increase for both domestic and export markets. Fundamental restructuring and reorganization both of the beef cattle and dairy industry are the preconditions to reach these targets.

Major success has been in the industrialization of hog production. In every sector of the farm industry, the number has increased (see Table 13.5), and at the end of 1973 the country's total stock of pigs amounted to 8 million head. Since the inception of the NEM, 265 specialized pig farms have been established, and some of them have been operating their own processing plants. While the cattle sector struggles with the problem of accommodation, the Hungarian Central Statistical Office reported allocation of investment to put into operation the following number of pigsties:

1970	299,030
1971	254,084
1972	446,758

Obviously specialized farms with vertically integrated operations necessitate a higher-than-average level of management, organization, and labor. According to Jeno Vancsa, "one of the greatest worries is the organization of feedstuff production and supply. . . . Cooperation with the processing industry is recommended by superior authorities but it does not work. It does not work because—apparently in lack of financial resources—the meat industry holds itself aloof."[18] Therefore, specialized farms make every effort to establish their own processing plants.

Losses caused by the 1972 hoof and mouth epidemic greatly add to the difficulties in assessing efficiency in cattle and hog economy. Nevertheless, it seems to be a fair statement that the hog industry has a bright prospect, efficiency, and profitability for the years to come. Concerning the dairy industry and meat production, basic structural changes are necessary to reach the level of efficiency that secures profitability and meets the requirement of domestic and international markets.

For many years poultry meat and egg production in Hungary were superior in profitability to all other agricultural branches. State farms have adopted modern methods of production and disseminated both breeding material and know-how to the cooperatives. The layer stock increased, for example, between 1965 and 1970 by 3.5 million birds, and egg production grew from 2,393 million in 1965 to 3.3 billion by 1972. There was a setback in 1973 to 2,094 million as some producers reconsidered expansion. Since 1970, signs of market saturation began to appear; the prices fell and the profitability decreased on farms where production costs surpassed returns. However, poultry production is the sector in which Hungarian farmers achieved the highest efficiency and became competitive on international markets.

PROSPECTS

In the fifth year of its operation, economists and other social scientists along with party ideologists began to assess the positive and negative results of the reform. B. Csikos-Nagy, who remained the authentic and authoritative representative of the reform, provided a comprehensive review of the first five years' effects on the national economy.[19] He emphasized the detrimental effect of the prevailing tax system that makes technological progress very expensive and labor cheap. (This has, of course, greatly affected agriculture's search for higher efficiency.) The national revenue is excessively centralized, hindering the highly desired self-financing of the enterprises. He submits that the reform has succeeded as agricultural productivity has increased. He attributed that to the adjustment of wages to those earned in other sectors and to the price policy that provided the incentive to the producer. Specific agricultural problems inherent in the reform were thoroughly examined in the 1972 report that the minister of agriculture and foods submitted to the Parliament. It concentrated on the problem of still-existing weak agricultural cooperatives that, despite extensive support, were unable to improve their financial status. He also referred to the weaknesses of the food industry discussed in the foregoing section of this study.

In summary, increases both in production and in the income level of the agricultural population are the positive results of the reform. In the words of J. Marton, "These results however are bearing several contradictions and imperfections in the particularities. . . . Extension achieved in production, on the one hand, is not incarnated in the same assortment as scheduled in national economic plans or required by inland and foreign markets, inputs, on the other hand, and investments more particularly exceeded the planned level."[20] The recognition of emerging problems of this nature fruited in the trend toward limitations, restrictions, and the claim for new controls. The latter were incorporated into so-called economic regulators, the criterion of which never has been clearly defined. Consequently, they attained some flexibility according to the need of their application. Discussions both on economic equilibrium and structural problems have dominated the meetings of politicians and civil servants involved during all of 1972 and part of 1973. Some leading architects and founding fathers of NEM were replaced in early 1974. Prior to that, in November 1973, however, the Central Committee of the party announced that new regulations were likely to be introduced by 1975 at the advent of the new Five-Year Plan.[21] It seems that the basic concept of the NEM will be maintained, yet restrictions in the scope and allocation of investment will be extended. Forthcoming regulative interventions of the state authorities are likely to combat undesirable side effects such as inflation-like price increases and wage discrepancies on the enterprise level, phenomena that caused microeconomic disequilibrium and social discontent in several segments of the population.

NOTES

1. T.I. Berend, Gazdasagpolitika az elso oteves terv meginditasakor, 1948-1950 (Economic Policy at the Launching of the First Five-Year Plan, 1948-1950) (Budapest: Kozgazdasagi es Jogi Konyvkiado, 1964), p. 106.
2. T. Marton, "Economic Regulations—The Interest of the Enterprises," Bulletin No. 33, (Budapest: Research Institute for Agricultural Economics, 1973), p. 23.
3. B. Csikos-Nagy, Magyar Gazdasagpolitika (Hungarian Economic Policy) (Budapest: Kossuth Konyvkiado, 1971), p. 389.
4. Computed on the basis of Statistical Pocket Book of Hungary 1973 (Budapest: Statistical Publishing House, 1973), p. 167.
5. H. Trend, Agriculture in Eastern Europe: A Comparative Study (New York: Radio Free Europe Research, 1974), mimeo, Part IV, p. 19.
6. Veszprem Megyei Naplo, May 27, 1973, quoted in Radio Free Europe, Hungarian Situation Report 29, August 21, 1973, p. 7.
7. "The Fourth Five-Year Plan of the Hungarian National Economy," Hungaropress, no. 19-20 (1970), mimeo, p. 13.
8. Budapress Bulletin 12, no. 47 (1973), p. 9.
9. Bulletin No. 33, p. 58.

10. Statistical Pocket Book of Hungary, 1973, op. cit.

11. Personal communication in Hungary.

12. Personal communication in Hungary.

13. J.W. Mellow, Accelerated Growth in Agricultural Production and the Intersectoral Transfer of Resources (Ithaca, N.Y.: Cornell University, Occasional Paper No. 34, 1972), p. 3.

14. Magyar Export's September 1973 issue stated that exports of live cattle and meat products yield every fourth foreign trade dollar that Hungary earns, p. 5.

15. Personal communication in Hungary.

16. Negyedeves Statisztikai Kozlemenyek: "Mezogazdasagi Adatok," several issues; Radio Free Europe, Hungarian Situation Report 44, November 28, 1972, p. 15.

17. K. Dobos, "Situation and Development of Cattle Breeding," Bulletin No. 33, op. cit., p. 95.

18. Ibid., p. 102.

19. B. Csikos-Nagy, in the September 1972 issue of Kozgazdasagi Szemle, reproduced in Radio Free Europe Research, No. 2244 (December 7, 1972), pp. 1-16.

20. Marton, op. cit., p. 22.

21. "Tragheitsmomente in der Ungarischen Wirtschaftspolitik," Neue Zurcher Zeitung, March 15, 1974, p. 18.

PART

III

CONFLICT IN THE
PUBLIC SECTOR

Alan Abouchar

It may be helpful to start with a few words to explain the title
of this section, which may appear somewhat mystifying or redundant.
Redundant to those of us accustomed to thinking as political scientists
who find inter-group conflict under every stone—party, scholarly
institutions, bureaucracy, business, and so on—and redundant, also,
within the framework of an almost all-pervasive state machine that
manages the economy. From these points of view it goes without
saying that the story of the Soviet Union is the story of conflict in the
public sector.

It was never the intention of this section to assume such an
ambitious mandate. Rather, it was intended to limit the scope to the
kinds of administrative and/or income distribution-resource allocation
conflicts that one encounters in the public sector in Western economies.
While in some economies this public sector might include crown cor-
porations or government producing firms to a greater or lesser degree,
many of whose problems would be analytically similar to those of the
Soviet firm, it was really the intention to stress those aspects of
public sector policy that have to do with income distribution and efficiency in those areas that, for one reason or another, Western societies have come to expect to be provided in the public sector. It is
hard to be more precise than this since there is still so much disagree-
ment in the West about both the descriptive and the normative analysis
of the public sector: (1) why are things in the public sector provided
in the public sector in the first place? (2) what things should be provided in the public sector? and (3) what are the implications of the
foregoing questions for pricing and financing policies? Thus, apart
from general agreement that the public sector does or should do what
it does for purposes of income distribution, economic efficiency,
and stabilization—as conceived by Musgrave 16 years ago—there is
very little further operational normative guidance in Western capital-
istic economies. These issues have been little studied in socialist
economies and it was the hope that, if problems could not be answered,
at least they could be specified.

This, then, is the amorphous framework within which the panel
was conceived. What questions in the Soviet Union present dilemmas
that are similar to those we find in the West? How should we price
and finance the highway or school systems? Who should pay and how?
What kind of federal/provincial income transfers should be made and
why? Indeed, as many studies in the West have shown, we must first

ask more elementary questions to determine what is the size of federal/provincial or federal/state transfers before we can begin to ask whether such transfers accord with normative rules. This is usually a very difficult job.

The chapters in Part III all focus on interesting sources of conflict in the public sector. They all do yeoman (or perhaps, given the composition of this panel, one should say "yeoperson") work in mining new statistical and institutional information concerning their chosen subjects and bring into focus some of the conflicts that public financial authorities face.

Elizabeth Clayton has done an admirable job surveying the rules and regulations affecting property holdings and transfers in the Soviet economy. She goes on to analyze the real income effect of public expenditure policy on urban and rural populations. Her essential conclusion is that present policies give a better break to the city than to the country. The institutional information she has brought together will be valuable for her own and others' future work in the analysis of public expenditure policies, including both the income distribution aspect as well as the efficiency of provision of certain public sector services; and the statistical tables she has compiled provide very useful regional expenditure data that, to my knowledge, have never been so conveniently summarized before.

Gertrude Schroeder's contribution provides a copious survey of the financial relations and changes therein over the past decade, comparable in scope and thoroughness to her previous studies on price and organizational reforms. It illustrates somewhat different kinds of conflicts from those above, conflicts in which the questions of resource utilization are paramount, for example, could the free remainder be better used for investment body enterprise or by centralized allocation? Again, administrative-bureaucratic motives and conflict are operative in the backgrounds.

We turn next to Vladimir Treml's chapter. He has focused on a problem that beautifully illustrates the kinds of conflict that the panel intended to examine. These include conflict between desires for increased productivity, on the one hand, and the recognition that alcohol is a low-cost way to satisfy consumer demand, all compounded by implications for inflation, criminal behavior, and tax revenue objectives. And, once again, scholars will for long be grateful for the tremendous storehouse of data concerning various aspects and dimensions of the alcohol problem that Treml has brought together.

CHAPTER

14

PROPERTY RIGHTS, TAXATION, AND THE SOVIET CITIZENS' USE OF PUBLIC LAND

Elizabeth Clayton

THE PRIVATE USES OF PUBLIC LAND

Soviet socialist property rights in land and other means of production belong to the state, but the state may yield the use of these properties to individuals. On the one hand, Article 6 of the constitution declares that land is social wealth:

> The land, its minerals, waters, forests, mills, factories, mines, quarries, rail, water and air transport, banks, communications, large state-organized agricultural enterprises and municipal enterprises, and the bulk of housing in the cities and at industrial sites, shall constitute state ownership, that is, the wealth of the entire people. [1]

On the other hand, Articles 9 and 10 of the Constitution declare that land use may be granted to individuals, for it permits the "small scale private economy of individual peasants and handicraftsmen" and guarantees the "right of personal ownership in . . . a dwelling house and subsidiary household economy. . . ." Thus, the land, which is owned by the state, is granted to individuals for uses that benefit the individual. The benefits of the land may be valued in kind or in money, but they are reduced by taxes on land use paid to the state. It is the

The support of the Center for International Studies at the University of Missouri-St. Louis is gratefully acknowledged. Ronald Pennington assisted with the collection of regional data.

323

net relationship between state and user, between benefits and costs, that is the focus of this chapter.

Whereas the nationalization of industry is common among socialist economic systems, the nationalization of land is rare. The data are sketchy, but Frederic Pryor has estimated the extent of public ownership in advanced industrialized economic systems.[2] Using the employment of labor in the public sector of an industry as an index of the public ownership of property in that sector, he demonstrates that the nationalization of property is most common in the industrial sectors of transportation, communications, and utilities. He accounts for the nationalization of these specific industries by arguments of, respectively, externalities, political sovereignty, and natural monopoly. He concludes that the nationalization of land is rare, since agriculture, the major land-using industry, is subject to none of these phenomena. Indeed, the Soviet economic system is one of only three systems to nationalize land and even it relinquishes the use of some land to individuals for use in housing and agriculture (the private subsidiary household plots).

The allocation of public land to a private individual increases his net worth and provides a benefit or grant. The Soviet allocation of land is a process of granting and contrasts with market exchange. A grant occurs when the net worth of the recipient is increased, when there is no counterflow of payment or goods, and when the terms of the grant are nonnegotiable.[3] A grant of land, for housing or agriculture, increases the net worth of the user; if not, the grantee may may relinquish the land. Soviet land grants are "free" in that there is neither a transfer price nor a rental charge. There is a land tax, but this is not a price, for there is no bargaining or trading between the grantor and grantee and there is no direct nexus between the tax and the acquisition of land. Finally, the rules for allotting the land are made by an administrative hierarchy; they differ between users and classes of users. Qualifying to receive land means meeting the requirements of administrative rules, rather than of markets.

When land is granted by the state to an individual, property rights are transferred. Property rights are the accumulation of duties, or costs, and rights, or benefits, which attach to the use of the land. In economic terms, the costs may be deducted from the benefits to get net rights. In general, the rights in land are those of use, of possession, and of wealth or the claim on income.[4] When property rights are assigned to the state, they are administered through political or bureaucratic control. When they are assigned to the individual, they are administered by personal choice and decision. In the Soviet Union, "land funds" are assigned to enterprises, institutions, organizations, or local government (urban or rural raiony). Land from these funds is assigned to individuals on the basis of residence. Thus, an employee of a state farm may receive a garden plot from the state farm, from the local government (raion) or from a collective farm, depending on his place of residence, rather than his place of work.[5] Assignments from land funds are regulated by the land codes of the Soviet Union and each republic.[6]

The quantity of land that is given to individuals is specified by the land code of each republic. In the RSFSR code, which serves as a prototype for other republics, agricultural land is allotted in small plots for pensioners (.15 hectare), increasing for rural intelligentsia (.25 hectare), and state employees (.30 hectare). Land for one- or two-family housing ranges from .03-.06 hectares in urban areas to .07-.12 hectares in suburban areas.[7] Land for pasturing, haying, and orchards may be allotted separately. If the land is irrigated, allotments are halved. These allotments from the land code are maximums that may be reduced by the grantor agency. The size of a house erected on state land also is prescribed. In the RSFSR, the maximum is 60 square meters. In Georgia, the maximum is 40 square meters. Exception may be made for large families. The RSFSR also has a minimum of 25 square meters.

If land under private use is returned to state use (roads, hydro-electric projects, or electric lines), the private user is compensated, but only through the granting agency. Compensation is paid for restoring the original land or developing new land. It includes buildings, equipment, land improvement projects such as irrigation, orchards, and crops. In most republics, compensation is paid into a land improvement fund of the granting agency. The agency compensates the individual either in money or, more frequently, in land. In a few republics (Azerbaijan, Latvia), the compensation goes to a centralized land improvement fund, and there is no restitution, even in kind, to the individual. Compensation may not be paid if the granting institution has exceeded the land grant norms set by the republic. The compensation price in the RSFSR was set by the Council of Ministers in 1962. The price for forest land under cultivation is 359 rubles per hectare. If we assume this price is a capitalized value at 6 percent, it implies an infinite income stream of 21.5 rubles per year from the land. In one lawsuit, the court dropped this price to 200 rubles per hectare on the basis of low fertility. This lower price was denied by the court; it said that a reduced price for low fertility had no basis in law.

The decision not to compensate for land location or fertility is consistent with the Marxian view of land rent. J. Wilczynski, studying the Marxist problems of valuing land, distinguishes three Marxist rents:[8] (1) Differential Rent I is based on natural differences in the quality of land, such as location or fertility. The individual cannot be compensated for the loss of this rent, for if he were, it would

become (2) Absolute Rent and the economic system would be capitalis-
tic. (3) Differential Rent II is based on man-made differences in the
quality of land and the person making the improvements may be compensated. The administrative determination of the source of fertility,
that is, man-made or natural, would be difficult. New provisions for
compensation replace land and preclude the need for such a decision.

Soviet land users must be employed in order to receive a land
grant. Only employment gives the required legal status (pravosposob-
nost') for land use. Pensioners and students are given legal exemptions from this requirement. An individual peasant (edinolichnye
krest'ian) has an employment status, but the tax rates for this group
are doubled. While the right to receive land is determined by employment, the granting agency is determined by the residence of the
recipient. In one court case, a collective farm was subject to criminal
action for granting land to an urban resident in exchange for 10 days
of weeding or 25 working days. The land grant is terminated when the
enabling employment ends, or when the collective farm workday requirement is unfulfilled. The land grant also ends if the land is not
used for two years, or if the land is used illegally (including hiring
labor for productive purposes).

While a private user may not sell public land, he may sell the
house or other structures on the land. The garden plot attached to a
house may be transferred to the purchaser of the house with the consent of the granting agency. This delineation follows the Soviet ideological distinction between personal (lichnaia sobstvennost') property
of an individual (the house) and socialist (sotsialisticheskaia sobstvennost') property of the state (the land). (Private [chastnaia] property
applies only to the means of production, such as land, and is forbidden.) The sale of personal property is governed by the civil codes,
whereas the transfer of land is governed by the land codes.[9] Houses
may be sold, given away, bartered, or inherited.[10] There are contracts for each kind of transaction. Houses and cooperative apartments often are sold in shares, equal or unequal, as a result of
divorce or inheritance. The coowner has some rights in choosing
the purchaser. Sales of a house are limited to one sale each three
years and are registered with the land-granting agency. Houses may
be rented, but a rental contract may not extend past five years.
Rentals of state-owned housing are contingent upon work status, but
private rentals are not.

Land use may be transferred between users, but there are
complex restrictions. The requirement of employment must be met
and the permission of the granting agency must be given. Transfers,
particularly of housing, often are made by barter, rather than
exchange. In one court case, Lumel'skii exchanged his two-room
apartment and his mother-in-law's one-room apartment for a three-

room apartment. The first apartment was held as a result of his
employment at the Birobidzhanskii trust. The new apartment came
from the land fund of the local soviet, which approved the exchange.
The exchange was held to be invalid because the consent of the trust
was not obtained. [11]

The regulation of private land is extensive. Permissible private
uses of land are few. While public control of land use occurs in all
economic systems, for example, land use zoning, the Soviet system
is distinguished by the extreme narrowness of permissible private
uses, that is, in housing and small-scale agriculture. Production of
commercial crops, such as cotton, is forbidden. Hiring of nonfamily
labor is forbidden. The regulation is bolstered by the tax system.
There are two symmetrical taxes on land use. They apply to agricultural and urban land uses. A detailed examination of these taxes
forms the subject of the next section.

LAND USE TAXES

Taxes on housing and agricultural land use are part of local
budget revenues. Local budget finance is important not for its exten-
siveness, for it is a small share of total budget financing, but for its
direct impact on Soviet citizens. In some rural areas, three-fourths
of the population live in private housing, which is taxed. The subsidiary agricultural sector provides much of the truck-farm food for
the population. Finally, the revenues of local budgets provide health,
education, and cultural services to the population.

Local budget revenues come from taxes imposed and retained
at the local level and from taxes imposed by a higher-level authority
but retained (in whole or in part) at the local level. Table 14.1 gives
the sources of local budget revenues in the Soviet Union for 1950,
1960, 1965, and 1968. More recent data, for RSFSR sources only,
are given in Table 14.2. R. W. Davies notes that the dependence of
local governments on state funding combines maximum control of
local expenditures, usually through expenditure norms, with some
flexibility and local autonomy. [12] Local governments receive less
than 10 percent of their total revenues from taxes that they themselves
impose. The share of local taxes in local budgets has fallen from
9.8 percent in 1950 to 3.0 percent in 1968. Local budget revenue
increasingly depends upon deductions from the turnover tax and
profits of local enterprises. [13]

Taxes on land use are the agricultural tax, imposed on rural
land use, and the land and building rent, imposed on urban land use.
The agricultural tax is imposed by the state, but in recent years has

TABLE 14.1

Local (Mestnye) Budget Revenues, Soviet Union, 1950, 1960, 1965, and 1968

	Percent				Million Rubles			
	1950	1960	1965	1968	1950	1960	1965	1968
Turnover tax	26.7	30.4	38.3	33.8	1,829.4	4,696.2	8,735.8	9,604.8
Tax on profits	10.7	18.7	17.3	19.0	731.9	2,878.4	3,938.6	5,415.9
Income tax (enterprises and organizations)	5.8	9.2	5.3	3.3	394.8	1,413.4	1,215.6	938.8
Taxes on the population	21.8	15.6	15.1	16.0	1,499.8	2,405.8	3,432.7	4,538.7
Income tax	12.5	10.6	11.0	12.5	858.7	1,630.8	2,514.8	3,546.8
Agricultural tax	4.4	2.6	1.6	1.2	301.5	396.2	356.3	341.9
Tax on small families and bachelors	4.9	2.4	2.5	2.3	339.4	375.6	561.6	650.0
Local taxes	9.8	4.3	3.3	3.0	673.5	660.7	754.8	850.0
Tax on land and building rent	3.8	0.9	0.8	0.7	259.5	140.9	181.2	197.6
Entertainment tax	2.7	2.4	1.8	1.6	187.9	374.1	418.7	457.9
State fees and miscellaneous charges	3.3	1.0	0.7	0.7	149.0	135.7	141.9	179.6
Other (lotteries, forest income, loans and subsidies)	25.2	21.8	20.7	24.9	1,734.8	3,368.8	4,704.6	7,067.5
Total	100.0	100.0	100.0	100.0	6,864.2	15,423.3	22,782.2	28,415.7

Note: Items given as details, for example, the agricultural tax, do not add to subtotals.

Source: Mestnye Biudzhety SSSR (Moscow: Izdat Finansy, 1970), pp. 10–13.

TABLE 14.2

Local (Raion) Budget Revenues, RSFSR, 1967 and 1972

| | 1967 | 1972 | 1967 | 1972 |
	(million rubles)		(percent of total)	
Deductions from turnover tax	1,228	1,871	29.9	34.6
Deductions from profit	280	388	6.8	7.2
Income tax (enterprises and organizations)	340	422	8.3	7.8
Taxes on the population[a]	1,266	2,030	30.9	37.6
Fees (customs) and local taxes[b]	120	143	2.9	2.6
Other income	117	384	2.9	7.1
Subsidies from higher-level budget	749	166	18.3	3.0
Total	4,100	5,404	100.0	100.0

[a]Includes income tax and agricultural tax.
[b]Includes building and land rent.
Source: Ia. N. Stepanov, E. A. Chernyskeva, and S. A. Vishniakov, Sostavlenie i ispolnenie Biudzeta Raiona (Moscow: Izdat Finansy, 1972), p. 9.

been retained wholly at the local level.[14] The building and land tax is imposed within norms established by a national enabling tax law.[15] Time series for both taxes, by republic, are given in Tables 14.3, 14.4, and 14.5. Agricultural tax revenues declined after 1953, when rates were cut. Building and land tax revenue has increased slightly over the period 1950-68. Land use taxes remain a minor and declining share of total local budget revenues, since indirect tax revenue has grown faster.

The agricultural tax is levied upon the household of a collective farm member.[16] Membership in the collective farm and the tax obligation continue even if the member moves from the farm. Exemptions are made for the elderly, invalids, military personnel, and collective farmers entering specified occupations, among which are mining, lumbering, and medical or technical professions. Workers and employees of state enterprises do not pay the agricultural tax, but pay land rent or income tax.

Agricultural tax rates are fixed. They are differentiated by the degree of use of land, by yields, by market sales, and by level of income. Surcharges or discounts may be made at the discretion

TABLE 14.3

Agricultural Tax Revenue by Republic, Soviet Union, 1940 and 1950-55

	1940	1950	1951	1952	1953	1954	1955
Soviet Union	162.7	398.9	434.9	238.3	253.8	159.1	176.4
RSFSR	71.6	234.6	244.9	131.4	134.8	80.2	87.4
Ukraine	46.9	89.3	112.1	63.9	71.0	46.8	53.8
Belorussia	19.6	22.7	22.4	10.9	12.0	8.0	7.5
Uzbekistan	5.4	7.6	9.3	4.9	5.9	4.6	5.4
Kazakhstan	5.0	10.7	10.5	5.8	5.5	3.1	3.5
Georgia	4.1	9.0	10.1	5.5	5.9	4.3	5.2
Azerbaijan	1.9	3.5	4.0	1.6	1.9	1.4	1.7
Lithuania	—	5.1	4.8	3.0	3.7	2.1	2.1
Moldavia	2.6	2.2	2.6	2.1	3.2	2.1	2.6
Latvia	—	3.0	2.9	2.3	2.6	4.4	1.4
Kirghizia	1.6	2.6	3.0	1.8	1.8	1.2	1.4
Tadjikistan	1.7	2.5	2.4	1.4	1.5	1.0	1.2
Armenia	1.0	2.1	2.2	1.2	1.4	.9	1.1
Turkmenistan	1.0	1.4	1.7	1.2	1.3	1.2	1.4
Estonia	—	2.6	2.0	1.4	1.4	.7	.7

Source: Gosuderstvennyi Biudzet SSSR i Biudzety Soiuznykh respublik (Moscow: Gosfinizdat, 1957), pp. 11, 23, ff.

TABLE 14.4

Agricultural Tax Revenue by Republic, Soviet Union, 1956–70
(million rubles)

	1956	1957	1958	1959	1960	1961	1962	1963	1964	1965	1966	1967	1968	1969	1970
Soviet Union	322.1	306.5	421.6	416.2	376.6	388.2	376.6	364.2	351.5	356.6	352.5	347.9	342.2	334.1	326.9
RSFSR	158.2	149.9	204.5	198.9	188.5	183.2	175.7	167.8	158.8	161.8	158.5	155.5	151.6	146.8	141.7
Ukraine	99.4	96.9	130.1	129.9	124.1	123.3	118.6	115.5	112.0	111.9	110.0	108.2	105.5	102.4	99.8
Belorussia	13.7	13.4	18.7	18.0	17.3	17.2	16.5	16.2	14.4	15.2	14.9	14.6	14.2	14.0	13.7
Uzbekistan	10.5	10.1	16.0	16.6	17.2	16.7	16.8	17.5	18.2	18.3	18.9	19.3	20.1	20.2	20.6
Kazakhstan	5.9	4.8	7.5	7.5	7.2	7.3	7.0	6.6	7.2	6.8	6.9	6.9	7.2	7.1	7.0
Georgia	9.8	8.3	12.0	12.2	10.5	10.4	10.3	10.5	10.7	10.9	11.0	11.1	11.0	10.9	11.2
Azerbaijan	3.2	2.8	4.2	4.4	4.6	4.6	4.5	4.2	4.6	4.9	5.0	5.1	5.2	5.4	5.6
Lithuania	3.8	3.7	5.1	5.1	5.0	7.5	7.3	7.6	4.5	5.0	5.0	4.8	4.7	4.5	4.4
Moldavia	4.6	4.6	6.3	6.2	5.8	3.2	3.0	3.0	5.4	5.3	5.4	5.5	5.5	5.3	5.3
Latvia	2.5	2.4	3.4	3.3	3.1	3.0	2.9	2.5	2.7	2.7	2.6	2.6	2.6	2.5	2.4
Kirghizia	2.5	2.3	3.3	3.4	2.4	1.8	1.7	1.7	2.2	2.9	3.1	3.1	3.1	3.2	3.1
Tadjikistan	2.1	2.1	3.2	3.0	3.2	3.2	3.5	3.7	4.0	4.0	4.3	4.4	4.5	4.7	5.0
Armenia	2.0	1.8	2.6	2.8	2.7	2.6	2.6	2.5	2.5	2.5	2.5	2.5	2.6	2.6	2.7
Turkmenistan	2.6	2.1	3.0	3.1	3.2	2.5	2.6	3.0	3.1	3.0	3.0	3.1	3.2	3.3	3.3
Estonia	1.3	1.3	1.7	1.7	1.6	1.6	1.5	1.5	1.4	1.4	1.3	1.2	1.2	1.2	1.1

Source: Gosndar stvennyi Biudzet SSSR i Biudzhety Soiuznykh respublik (Moscow: Gosfinizdat, 1962), pp. 98ff; Izdat Finansy, 1966, pp. 101, ff; and 1972, pp. 108 ff.

TABLE 14.5

Building Tax and Land Rent Revenue by Republic, Soviet Union, 1940, 1950, and 1955–70
(million rubles)

	1940	1950	1955	1956	1957	1958	1959	1960	1961	1962	1963	1964	1965	1966	1967	1968	1969	1970
Soviet Union	79.1	259.5	330.5	359.1	378.7	422.5	477.2	145.8	153.3	163.1	170.8	180.1	181.2	186.0	191.5	197.6	204.3	211.4
RSFSR	51.5	164.1	206.7	225.0	242.3	263.4	298.5	73.9	77.3	82.2	86.4	90.9	93.7	95.6	97.6	99.8	102.6	105.0
Ukraine	17.6	57.5	71.0	76.6	82.3	88.9	99.7	36.9	38.2	40.6	42.4	44.5	46.0	47.0	48.4	50.1	51.7	53.5
Belorussia	2.1	4.8	7.3	8.1	8.8	9.7	11.1	8.8	9.5	9.6	9.2	9.9	5.5	5.7	5.9	6.2	6.5	6.9
Uzbekistan	2.2	6.1	6.8	7.6	8.2	9.1	10.4	4.8	5.5	5.7	6.3	6.5	6.7	7.0	7.4	7.9	8.2	8.7
Kazakhstan	1.4	8.3	12.8	14.0	15.6	17.8	20.4	6.5	7.1	7.8	8.4	9.1	9.4	9.8	10.2	10.5	11.0	11.5
Georgia	1.6	3.6	5.1	5.5	6.0	6.6	7.1	2.5	2.7	3.0	3.2	3.4	3.4	3.5	3.7	3.9	4.3	4.5
Azerbaijan	1.2	2.6	3.7	3.8	4.2	4.7	4.9	1.4	1.5	1.7	1.8	2.0	2.1	2.3	2.6	2.8	2.9	3.1
Lithuania	—	1.7	2.5	2.7	3.0	3.3	3.8	1.8	2.1	2.2	2.3	2.4	2.4	2.5	2.6	2.8	2.9	3.0
Moldavia	.1	1.0	1.7	1.9	2.1	2.4	3.0	1.4	1.6	1.8	1.8	1.9	2.0	2.2	2.3	2.5	2.7	2.8
Latvia	—	3.6	4.0	4.2	4.4	4.7	5.1	2.0	2.1	2.1	2.2	2.3	2.4	2.4	2.5	2.5	2.6	2.8
Kirghizia	.3	1.3	2.0	2.1	2.3	2.5	2.8	1.2	1.3	1.6	1.7	1.7	1.8	1.9	1.9	2.0	2.0	2.2
Tadjikistan	.3	1.0	1.2	1.4	1.5	1.8	1.9	1.1	1.1	1.2	1.3	1.4	1.5	1.6	1.7	1.8	1.9	2.1
Armenia	.5	1.3	1.9	2.1	2.3	2.6	2.9	1.2	1.3	1.4	1.5	1.5	1.6	1.7	1.8	1.9	2.0	2.1
Turkmenistan	.3	.8	1.3	1.4	1.5	1.7	1.9	.6	.7	.8	.8	.9	1.0	1.0	1.1	1.1	1.1	1.2
Estonia	—	1.8	2.5	2.7	3.0	3.3	3.7	1.2	1.3	1.4	1.5	1.7	1.7	1.8	1.8	1.8	1.9	2.0

Source: Gosndar stvennyi Biudzet SSSR i Biudzhety Soiuznykh respublik (Moscow: Gosfinizdat, 1962), pp. 98ff; Izdat Finansy, 1966, pp. 101, ff, and 1972, pp. 108 ff.

TABLE 14.6

Soviet Agricultural Tax Rates, by Republic, 1965
(rubles and kopecks per .01 hectare)

| | Average Rate | Limits for Oblast Discretion | |
		Low	High
RSFSR	0.85	0.30	1.40
Ukraine - east	0.85	0.50	1.20
west	0.40	0.20	0.60
Belorussia - east	0.60	0.30	0.90
west	0.30	0.20	0.50
Uzbekistan - irrigated	2.20	—	—
- not irrigated	0.80	—	—
Kazakhstan	0.80	0.40	1.30
Georgia	1.30	0.40	2.50
Azerbaijan	1.20	0.60	1.80
Lithuania	0.30	—	—
Moldavia - left shore	0.80	—	—
- right shore	0.40	—	—
Latvia	0.40	—	—
Kirghizia	0.90	0.40	1.30
Tadjikistan - irrigated	2.20	—	—
- not irrigated	0.80	—	—
Armenia	1.30	—	—
Turkmenistan - irrigated	2.00	—	—
- not irrigated	0.80	—	—
Estonia	0.40	—	—

Source: D. B. Burmistrov, S. I. Vinokur, and S. V. Svoikin, Spravochnik nalogogo rabotnika (Moscow: Gosfinizdat, 1967), p. 102.

of the oblast, as long as total revenue for the oblast is unchanged.[17] Limits for surcharges and discounts are established by the law. Surcharges also are added to the tax rate of those who do not complete the collective farm work requirement (50 percent), those who exceed the land allotment (100 percent), and those not working on the collective farm but not working for hire (75 percent). Rates may be reduced for natural disaster such as drought or late frost. The tax is paid in four installments: 20 percent on March 1; 20 percent on June 1; 30 percent on September 1; 30 percent on November 1. Rates for irrigated land are much higher. The most recent rate schedule is given in Table 14.6. Rates in the Caucasus region (Georgia, Azerbaijan,

Armenia) are higher than average. Rates in the Baltic region are lower.

The building and land tax is the urban worker's equivalent of the agricultural tax on rural collective farmers. Taxes are levied on the homes and other buildings of workers and employees. Buildings may be owned privately or cooperatively, and taxes are levied on the owner (sobstvennik) rather than the user. Religious buildings are taxed under this category. There are exemptions for collective farm buildings, foreign diplomatic buildings, state-owned enterprises, unused land or land with incomplete buildings under construction, military personnel, and pensioners and elderly persons.

The building tax rate is 0.5 percent on cooperatives and 1.0 percent on all others, levied on the original cost of the building. Both rates may be applied to different parts of the same building if there are multiple uses. In an example from a tax manual, a residential building of 900 square meters is owned, in equal shares, by three persons. The value of the building, 1,200 rubles, was determined from the insurance payment of the previous years. One owner is excused from the tax because he works for the Ministry of Finance. Each of the others pays building tax based on 400 rubles of value and land rent based on 300 square meters of space, the pro rata shares.[18] Building tax and land rent data were merged after 1954. The present shares are not known, but in 1954 the revenues from building rents were twice those of land rents.[19]

Land rent rates are divided into six classes:[20]

> Class 1: 1.8 kopecks per square meter
> Class 2: 1.5   "
> Class 3: 1.2   "
> Class 4: 0.9   "
> Class 5: 0.6   "
> Class 6: 0.4   "

The Ministry of Finance assigns the classes on the basis of population density, growth in trade in the area, and "other economic conditions." The primary basis for judgment seems to be the administrative assignment of city, worker settlement, etc., to the area. There is a 100 percent surcharge on the tax rate for land use above the established norm.

PROPERTY RIGHTS AND TAXATION OF LAND

The private use of public land creates an asset for Soviet citizens. In economic terms, the value of an asset is the discounted stream of net income (explicit or implicit) accruing to the individual, minus charges for the opportunity cost of mobile inputs, plus the sale price at the end of the use period. To an individual, the asset's value is limited by his property rights to claim services income, and to transfer the property. The right to use public land has value because the individual has the right to use the land and to receive income from this use. It is valuable also because the individual may transfer the land in a sale, barter, or gift.

Property rights in Soviet land differ between users for housing and for agriculture. Both sets of users may claim the stream of services and income from land use. The house owner may rent his house. The collective farmer may sell his product. Their property rights are the same on this account, although the value of the rights may differ. Neither set of users may sell the land outright. However, the user of land for housing may sell his complementary property (the house) and transfer the land at the same time. The user of agricultural land has not the same opportunity. Other things equal, the property right to transfer land raises the value of one land parcel over another. The asset value of the citizen using public land for housing is enhanced over that of the agricultural user.

Taxation of land reduces its asset value. Since the stream of income or service is reduced by the tax, the capitalized value of the asset is reduced. Tax rates may be capitalized even on a tax base that cannot be sold. From the Soviet case, we can generalize the capitalization of taxes at the time of sale into capitalization at any transfer. A taxable asset is valuable if it is transferred by barter or inheritance, as well as sale. While an asset that can be transferred only by barter or inheritance is less valuable than an asset transferable by sale, the value is positive. Property rights are truncated, but not reduced to zero. Civil suits regarding inheritance, barter, gift, and sharing testify to the validity of this proposition. The value is the capitalized income stream, net of taxes.

The Soviet land-grant system requires complementary inputs as a condition of keeping the land. These inputs have alternative uses and are mobile. To use agricultural land, the user must give up leisure and other goods to have labor and agricultural raw materials, including livestock. To use land for housing requires labor and raw materials as well. Using the land must return at least the value of these inputs in their alternative uses. Returns may be in money or in kind. Labor must receive its opportunity cost either as wages or leisure. Raw materials must receive their cost plus interest over the time of the investment. The relevant interest rate is the alternative use of these funds, probably the rate on savings accounts at the state bank.[21] After these opportunity costs are met, the residual is a return to the land and is taxed.

The Soviet land tax differentiates between parcels of land by rates, rather than by assessed valuations of the capitalized asset. Agricultural land tax rates are differentiated by republic on the basis of location and marketings, with surcharges for irrigated land. Rates are over 50 percent higher in the trans-Caucasus region than in other republics. Only three republics (Ukraine, Moldavia, Belorussia) differentiate rates within the republic. Land tax rates in housing are differentiated by population density. There are no adjustments for intracity differences, nor for differences between cities in the same density class. The effective agricultural tax rate (revenues divided by base) is slightly less than the stated rate. No similar comparison could be made of the housing tax rate.

The taxation of land by rate differentials reflects a principle of taxation based on consumer surplus. Tax rates differentiated by location and fertility capture Marxian Differential Rent I, which is from natural (that is, not man-made) differences in land. This Marxian rent is economic rent, which is identical to consumer surplus.[22] In the classical theory of the Physiocrats, Ricardo, and Marx, consumer surplus could be taxed without changing land use. There is, however, a substitution effect relative to other, untaxed assets. The maximum tax on consumer surplus is that amount of other goods that the individual is willing to give up in order to keep the land. The lower the price on land, the greater is the consumer surplus that may be taxed. All things being equal, tax revenues are maximized under the Soviet system, which sets the price of land at zero and taxes consumer surplus. There are practical difficulties with such a system. It is difficult to identify pure consumer surplus apart from a land price and to develop tax instruments that can capture it.[23] However, the rate structure of Soviet land taxes, differentiating between classes of users, provides a rough instrument for capturing consumer surplus.

Housing taxes on land may be distinguished from housing taxes on operations. Taxes on operations are shown in Tables 14.7 and 14.8; they do not come from consumer surplus, but are user charges for electricity, water, and other services. Most of these charges (89 percent) are retained by republics for local use. Only the Baltic republics retain less. This may be due either to redistribution from the Baltics to general fiscal revenues or to peculiarities of the communal housing sector in that area.

The Soviet land tax system may be analyzed according to the principles of the benefit criterion.[24] The reduction in capitalized value due to taxes may be offset by expenditures in the public sector. Land taxes are retained for local use in educational, cultural, and health activities. Regrettably, space does not permit a detailed analysis in this framework. One source compares urban and rural education relevant in this context. A. Vucinich asserts that education facilities

TABLE 14.7

Taxes on Housing and the Communal Economy, by Republics, Soviet Union, 1940, 1950, and 1955–70[*]
(million rubles)

	1940	1950	1955	1956	1957	1958	1959	1960	1961	1962	1963	1964	1965	1966	1967	1968	1969	1970
Soviet Union	113.2	250.7	444.3	456.6	473.5	544.2	595.0	704.5	776.8	831.2	803.5	843.2	918.4	992.1	1051.5	1259.3	1387.7	1568.6
RSFSR	77.6	171.5	299.9	307.6	332.9	383.2	413.8	476.6	518.6	544.6	537.6	568.5	622.1	676.0	710.5	857.7	924.1	1026.7
Ukraine	18.7	34.0	68.5	74.3	65.2	76.3	92.8	109.3	125.9	151.5	149.1	157.1	167.2	173.1	177.3	217.1	260.0	297.4
Belorussia	1.8	4.4	9.6	9.8	8.8	11.2	8.1	8.8	10.6	13.0	12.9	15.6	17.4	18.3	13.6	19.1	20.9	23.7
Uzbekistan	2.8	7.2	11.4	10.7	12.7	12.5	13.4	17.3	15.2	18.8	14.1	14.6	18.4	23.2	23.9	29.9	32.4	39.3
Kazakhstan	1.6	3.4	4.7	4.5	5.3	5.8	7.9	11.1	12.2	14.5	17.3	15.8	15.4	19.3	24.1	23.7	30.8	35.9
Georgia	4.0	4.8	8.5	8.8	9.0	12.3	9.1	12.6	13.3	15.3	11.8	12.4	12.4	14.1	18.0	26.6	25.6	30.0
Azerbaijan	4.0	4.5	8.6	8.2	8.3	10.1	11.4	23.3	33.0	18.0	15.8	11.9	14.1	10.6	14.6	15.4	19.3	27.8
Lithuania	—	1.8	2.7	3.3	4.6	3.8	4.7	5.7	6.5	8.5	6.4	7.6	7.4	9.1	10.1	6.6	9.2	10.0
Moldavia	.1	1.5	3.9	3.0	3.9	4.9	6.4	8.0	7.8	8.0	7.0	7.1	8.2	7.8	9.2	11.4	12.5	14.7
Latvia	—	7.8	11.0	10.6	9.3	8.6	10.0	11.2	11.1	11.9	9.9	10.2	10.7	10.5	12.4	13.4	14.0	15.3
Kirghizia	.2	2.6	4.1	3.7	1.7	1.8	1.9	2.4	2.4	2.9	2.4	2.4	3.0	3.7	4.3	5.2	6.5	7.2
Tadjikistan	.6	2.1	1.9	1.8	2.5	3.3	3.8	4.7	5.1	5.7	4.4	4.0	4.6	5.4	4.8	6.7	4.6	5.8
Armenia	1.0	2.2	3.9	4.3	4.7	5.2	5.6	5.8	6.6	8.8	7.7	8.2	8.9	8.9	10.3	14.0	17.7	20.5
Turkmenistan	.8	1.4	2.6	3.1	1.4	2.0	1.9	2.4	2.0	3.1	2.4	2.0	4.0	5.2	6.2	5.7	5.5	8.2
Estonia	—	1.5	3.0	2.9	3.2	3.2	4.2	5.3	6.5	6.6	4.7	5.8	4.6	6.9	7.2	6.8	4.6	6.1

[*]This tax category is comprised of housing not converted to khozraschet, electric power, water supply and sewage, bath, laundering and barbering enterprises, and communal budget-financed enterprises. See D. Gallick, C. Jesina, and S. Rapawy, The Soviet Financial System (U.S. Department of Commerce, Bureau of the Census, International Population Statistics Report Series P-90, No. 23, 1968).

Source: Gosndar stvennyi Biudzet SSSR i Biudzhety Soiuznykh respublik (Moscow: Gosfinizdat, 1962), pp. 98ff; Izdat Finansy, 1966, pp. 101, ff; and 1972, pp. 108 ff.

TABLE 14.8

Taxes on Housing and the Communal Economy, Retained for the Local Budget
by the Republics, Soviet Union, 1950 and 1960-68*

(million rubles)

	1950	1960	1961	1962	1963	1964	1965	1966	1967	1968
Soviet Union	339.7	674.6	729.4	793.7	770.9	802.3	857.2	926.8	197.4	1118.1
RSFSR	249.1	472.1	509.2	537.6	531.0	560.0	605.2	662.6	683.9	781.9
Ukraine	39.4	108.2	119.6	142.1	141.4	146.3	154.4	163.5	165.7	202.1
Belorussia	3.2	8.4	9.8	11.0	10.2	12.1	12.9	12.9	13.2	13.3
Uzbekistan	7.4	10.0	11.2	11.7	8.3	7.7	8.1	8.8	9.8	15.3
Kazakhstan	5.3	11.0	12.0	14.4	17.0	15.5	15.1	18.8	23.3	22.7
Georgia	6.8	11.9	12.8	15.1	11.1	10.1	10.2	11.0	13.8	20.8
Azerbaijan	5.5	12.0	12.0	12.1	11.7	10.6	13.3	9.9	11.6	12.5
Lithuania	2.7	5.6	6.5	8.5	6.1	7.3	3.7	5.0	5.9	3.0
Moldavia	2.3	7.7	7.2	7.3	6.1	5.9	6.9	6.1	7.4	8.2
Latvia	10.3	11.0	11.0	11.8	9.7	9.6	10.0	9.3	10.2	10.5
Kirghizia	.7	2.4	2.4	2.7	2.2	2.2	2.7	3.4	3.8	4.3
Tadjikistan	1.2	3.3	3.7	4.1	3.2	2.8	2.8	2.5	1.7	3.3
Armenia	2.5	5.2	6.1	8.3	7.2	7.7	8.3	8.0	9.8	13.2
Turkmenistan	1.1	2.2	1.9	3.0	2.2	1.0	1.1	1.4	3.2	3.1
Estonia	2.2	3.6	4.0	4.0	3.5	3.5	2.5	3.6	4.1	3.9

* See Table 14.7 for a definition of this category.

Source: Mestnye Biudzhety SSSR (Moscow: Izdat Finansy, 1970), pp. 14ff.

TABLE 14.9

Sources of Revenue, by Shares, by Size of Population Center, Soviet Union, 1968

| | Cities | | | Districts (Raion) | Worker Settlements | Rural Centers |
	Republic Rank	Regional Rank (percent)	District Rank			
Taxes on the population	13	12	39	15	52	46
Agricultural tax	—	—	—	1	1	17
Local taxes	5	4	18	—	15	3
Other (indirect taxes and subsidies)	82	84	43	84	32	34

Source: Mestnye Biudzhety SSSR (Moscow: Izdat Finansy, 1970), pp. 66, 98, 130, 148, 178, 210.

are of lower quality in rural areas than in urban.[25] This is critical
in Soviet society, where mobility comes through education. Soviet
sources note the lower level of cultural facilities in rural areas as
well. Although equity criteria are violated, the benefit criterion is
met. The implicit tax base of rural areas is lower as a result of the
restrictions on property rights, although the tax rates are similar.
This would fulfill a benefit criterion, for the benefits are proportioned
to the tax base. On the other hand, rural areas are more dependent
on land taxes than urban areas (see Table 14.9). They do not have an
industrial tax base from which to retain revenue from profits. This
leads to an analysis on the basis of ability to pay.

The ability-to-pay criterion judges a taxation system by the
size of the tax base. The larger the base, the larger is the tax payment. The range of tax rates is similar between urban and rural land
users: 40-180 rubles per hectare on urban land; 30-130 on rural land.
However, the wealth base is lower in rural areas. Property rights
are truncated and the land is less valuable as an asset. There also
is no industrial tax base. This implies that the tax burden is relatively
greater on rural citizens, particularly collective farmers.

The heavier burden of taxation of the rural community is
rationalized by ideology and social necessity. Vicinich analyzes the
lower status of the collective farmer.[26] The land use and land tax
systems follow a traditional ideological dichotomy of higher and lower
status, of worker-employee, and of collective farmer. Land use and
property rights are defined by status; so are the tax base and tax lia-
bilities. This dichotomy originated with the exigencies of economic
development. Today, even in rural areas, the role of the land tax is
diminishing as indirect taxes on profits and sales (the turnover tax)
rise to fill the fiscal gap. These new taxes are not differentiated by
status, and fiscal development may be a crack in the monolithic wall
separating these groups.

A MODEL OF BEHAVIOR

The grant of public land that is made to individuals for private
use may be analyzed in conventional indifference curve analysis shown
in Figure 14.1 and in a demand curve for land shown in Figure 14.2.
In the former, an individual with indifference curves $u_0 < u_1$ has preferences for land (T) and a numeraire good (M). At B, the individual
has no land and consumes only the composite good M. This consumption corresponds to Q = 0 on the demand curve in Figure 14.2. If
allowed to use state land at a rental charge, the individual acquires
up to T^* units of land at a rental charge represented by the slope of

FIGURE 14.1

Indifference Curve Analysis of the Grant of Public Land That Is
Made to Individuals for Private Use

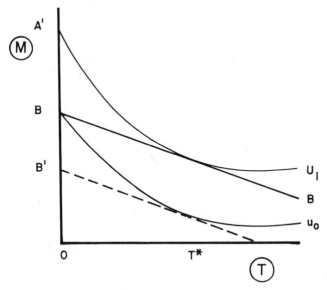

FIGURE 14.2

A Demand Curve for Land

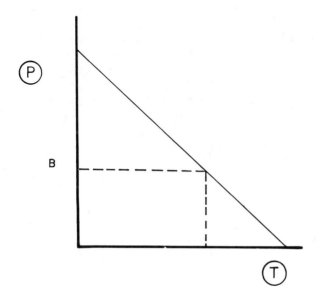

the line BB. Good M is given up to pay the rental charge, but the consumer's welfare has risen from u_0 to u_1. If one measures the value of the grant by the rental charge paid by the individual, the area OBTT* in Figure 14.2, it represents simply the goods given up.

The individual has received more than this value, however. This extra value is represented by the consumer surplus, the triangle above the price line in the demand curve. Consumer surplus also is represented by the increase in utility experienced by the individual when he is allowed to rent the land. This consumer surplus is measured by answering the question: "What would the land user be willing to give up in exchange for the opportunity to rent land?" We assume that the land user would give up good M until he was no worse off than he was before, that is, on indifference curve u_0. This is the equivalent variation measure of consumer surplus. In Figure 14.1, this amount is BB', which is one measure of the consumer surplus triangle (PTB) in Figure 14.2.

Taxes on Soviet land use may be analyzed as either a rental charge or as an extraction of consumer surplus. At first glance, the rental charge seems to be the more appropriate analogy, for taxes are expressed in terms of area under use and we can view the state as a renter to the individual user. Viewing taxes as land rent is not analogous to private rental. First, the consumer may not choose the quantity of land he desires. Second, the land given to him is not freely transferable. Land use maximums are binding constraints, for above-norm usage results in criminal penalties and a 100 percent tax surcharge. Finally, the Soviet legal ideology explicitly states that land is "free."

Soviet taxes on land are more an extraction of consumer surplus than a rental charge, but the two are not unrelated. The level of any rental charge determines the maximum consumer surplus that may be extracted from the user. The lower the rental charge, the greater the potential charge on consumer surplus. When both user charges and rents are extracted from a land user, it can be shown that maximum revenues are obtained by setting the user charge equal to marginal cost (= 0, in this instance) and the economic rent equal to the integral under the demand curve, or

$$P = 0$$

$$CS = \int_{P=0}^{\infty} dP$$

Thus, the revenues of the state are maximized by <u>not</u> setting a price on the use of land. When more than one individual is taxed, the gain

in revenue from any increased user charge must be offset against the
loss of consumer surplus from those forced out of land use.

When is the land user forced out of land use? In Figure 14.1,
it is when the marginal rate of substitution of land for other goods
diminishes, that is, when the consumer no longer is willing to give
up M for T. This occurs when the tax on consumer surplus exceeds
BB' and the consumer is better off without the land than with it. The
consumer remains on indifference curve u_0 and uses no state land.
Note that this result is independent of the user charge.

The abolition of private land use by increasing the extraction of
consumer surplus is not symmetrical to the abolition of land use
through expropriation, or eminent domain. In Figure 14.1, an expropriation occurs when the consumer, renting land (T^*), is allowed to
rent no longer and utility is unchanged. The value of this negative
grant, or taking, is BA'. There is no reason for BA', the value of a
negative grant, to equal BB', the value of a positive grant. There
are thus two valuations of the grant that may be made: the value at a
taking or expropriation and the value at a giving or granting. The
value depends on the initial position that one assumes for the land
user.

Economic rent is identical conceptually to the concept of consumer surplus. This can be demonstrated by Figure 14.3, where the
decision of the consumer to relinquish land is analyzed. The individual

FIGURE 14.3

The Decision of the Consumer to Relinquish Land

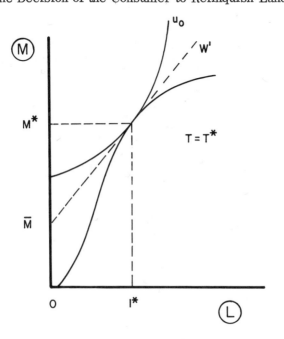

has received the land grant T^* with net opportunities represented by
OT. The opportunities contribute to the acquisition of the numeraire
good M, but require the complementary inputs of L (labor or material
inputs). Supplying these inputs causes disutility to the consumer, as
shown in the indifference curve u_0. The opportunities are subject to
diminishing returns as more of the complementary inputs are applied
to the fixed stock of land (T^*). The supply of complementary inputs
is valued by the alternative opportunities of those inputs, such as a
wage; this is represented by the dotted line $\bar{M}W'$. Facing these
choices, the consumer would add L^* complementary inputs to the
land, with a return of M^*, measured along the vertical axis. M^* may
be divided into the implicit returns due to the alternative opportunity
of the other outputs $(\bar{M}M^*)$ and the implicit returns to land $(O\bar{M})$. The
implicit returns to land may be taxed away as consumer surplus, but
when the returns to the complementary factors are taxed away, the
complementary factors are turned to alternative uses. Labor on the
agricultural plot is withdrawn or material inputs in housing are not
purchased.

If the Soviet land assigned to an individual is unused, the individual loses the rights to the land and it reverts to the state for
reassignment. On agricultural land, a tax liability may fall on a
collective farm worker who has moved from the land, that is, taken
his complementary inputs to another use. The tax then reduces
wages in the alternative occupation and discourages the transfer of
labor from the collective farm sector to alternative uses.

NOTES

1. Constitution of the USSR, translated in H. Berman and
J. Quigley, Basic Laws on the Structure of the Soviet State (Cambridge:
Cambridge University Press, 1969), pp. 1-28.

2. Frederic Pryor, "The Extent and Pattern of Public Ownership in Developed Economies," Weltwirtschaftliches Archiv, Band
104, Heff 2 (1970), pp. 159-88.

3. The concept of a grant is analyzed extensively in K. Boulding,
Economy of Love and Fear (Belmont, Calif.: Wadsworth, 1973);
K. Boulding, M. Pfaff, and J. Horvath, "Grant Economics: A Simple
Introduction," The American Economist, Spring 1972, pp. 19-34.

4. The concept of property under Germanic (or code) law has
rights of possession, use, and disposition. Those of the text are
more appropriate for economic analysis. For the discussion of property rights concepts in more detail, see E. M. Clayton, "Property
Rights Under Socialism," an unpublished paper.

5. G. A. Aksenenok, Zemel'nye pravo-otnosheniia VSSR (Moscow: Gosizdat Iurid-Lit, 1958), p. 114, citing from the decree "O priusadebnykh uchastkakh rabochikh i sluzhashchikh, sel'skikh uchitelei, agronomov i drugikh ne chlenov kolkhozov, prozhivaiushchikh v sel'skoi mestnosti," SP SSSR, July 28, 1939, no. 47, p. 362.

6. In this article the Land Code of the RSFSR is cited; Land Code of the RFSFR is translated in Soviet Statutes and Decisions 9, no. 1 (1972) and in S. A. Fishbein, "A Private Citizen's Access to Land in the USSR," unpublished paper, University of Illinois, 1973, from Vedomosti Verkhovnogo Soveta RSFSR, no. 28 (1970). Land Codes vary between republics primarily in the legal maximums allotted to citizens. Other provisions are virtually identical except where noted. Land use also is regulated by the Fundamentals of Land Law: Osnovye Zemel'noga Prava, Vedomosti Verkhovnogo Soveta USSR, no. 51 (1968), and in Pravda, December 14, 1968, translated in the Current Digest of the Soviet Press 21, no. 1 (1969).

7. A hectare is about 2.5 acres. Thus, the largest urban housing plot would be less than one-fourth of an acre, or about 50' x 200'. Data are from Instruction of the RSFSR Gosstroi of December 19, 1966, cited in D. B. Burmistrov, S. I. Vinokur, and S. V. Svoikin, Spravochnik nalogogo rabotnika (Moscow: Gosfinizdat, 1967).

8. J. Wilczynski, "Towards Rationality in Land Economics under Central Planning," Economic Journal 79, no. 315 (September 1969), pp. 540-59.

9. Soviet legal scholars debate whether land, which cannot be exchanged for money, is property. Houses, which can be sold, are property. Erofeev outlines the arguments on both sides and concludes that the majority of scholars believe that land is a special form of state property. B. V. Erofeev, Osnovy zemel'nogo prava (Moscow: Iurid, Lit, 1971), pp. 11-14.

10. Shared property, such as housing cooperatives, are subject to more complex restrictions on transfer. The transfer of property granted to a collective farmer also is more complex because it belongs to the entire household.

11. Bulleten' Verkhovnogo Suda RSFSR, no. 6 (1974), pp. 5-6.

12. R. W. Davies, The Development of the Soviet Budgetary System (Cambridge: Cambridge University Press, 1958), p. 313.

13. In 1939 rural budgets received only 10-15 percent of their budgets from local sources, whereas urban budgets received 30-35 percent; Davies, op. cit., p. 312. In 1968, rural budgets received only 3 percent from local sources and no unit received more than 18 percent. Tax revenue shares, by size of population center, in 1968, are given in Table 14.6.

14. Agricultural tax, Soviet Union:

	1940	1950	1960	1970
Tax in million rubles	209.5	797.8	396.6	326.9
Percent retained at the local level	78	50	100	100

Source: Mestnye Biudzety SSSR, 1962, 1970.

15. The agricultural tax law is "O sel'skokhoziaistvennom naloge" of August 1953, revised by the Council of Ministers on July 25, 1957 (Instruction No. 235) and on January 7, 1972 (Instruction No. 3). Holzman surveys the extensive history of this tax in F. D. Holzman, Soviet Taxation (Cambridge, Mass.: Harvard University Press, 1962), pp. 180-99. The building and land tax is "O mestnykh nalogakh i sborakh," April 10, 1942. Excerpts used in this paper were published in Burmistrov, Vinokur, and Svoikin, op. cit. and Ia. Stepanov, E. A. Chernysheva, and S. A. Vishniakov, Sostavlenie i ispolnenie Biudzeta Raiona (Moscow: Izdat Finansy, 1972).

16. Provisions of Soviet local taxes were taken from Burmistrov, Vinokur, and Svoikin, op. cit. and G. L. Mariakhun, S. V. Svoikin, S. I. Vinokur, and A. A. Artem'ev, Nalogi i sbory s naseleniia (Moscow: Izdat Finansy, 1964).

17. According to Davies, the Extra Ordinary Revolutionary Tax of 1919 had similar guidelines. That tax was a last major attempt at massive direct taxation. Soon after, the government relied increasingly on indirect taxation. Davies, op. cit., p. 27 n.

18. Burmistrov, Vinokur, and Svoikin, op. cit., p. 130.

19. Taxes on buildings and on land were separate until 1955. After that date, the tax data were combined. In 1954, the last year for which separate data are available, 30-40 percent of the tax was on land and 60-70 percent on buildings. The share of land in the tax was lower in the Caucasus, higher in the Baltic republics, and much higher in the Central Asian republics. Shares for selected years were as follows (percentages):

	1940	1950	1951	1952	1953	1954
Land rent	30	42	40	39	37	36
Building tax	50	58	60	61	63	64

Source: Gosudarstvennyi Biudzet SSSR i Biudzhety soiuznykh respublik (Moscow: Gosfinizdat, 1957), p. 11.

20. Burmistrov, Vinokur, and Svoikin, op. cit., p. 127.

21. There are few alternative assets in the Soviet Union. Savings accounts are the most widely available; the interest rate is low

and often the returns are made by lottery. Pejovich analyzes the concept of assets complementary to employment (labor supply) in the context of the Yugoslav firm. S. Pejovich, "The Firm, Monetary Policy and Property Rights in a Planned Economy," Western Economic Journal 3, no. 3 (1969), pp. 193-200.

22. The Marxian view of economic rent and the tax structure (differentiated by regional differences in fertility and location) indicate that the Soviets themselves view their tax system as extraction of economic rent. Mishan has shown that consumer surplus is the analytical equivalent of economic rent. E. J. Mishan, "Rent as a Measure of Welfare Change," American Economic Review 49, no. 3 (1959).

23. W. Hirsch, The Economics of State and Local Government (New York: McGraw-Hill, 1970), p. 95.

24. The ability to pay principle states that tax burden should be related to the ability to bear the burden. The benefit principle states that tax burden should be related to benefits received. See Hirsch, op. cit., p. 50.

25. A. Vucinich, "The Peasants as a Social Class," in The Soviet Rural Community, ed. James R. Millar (Urbana: University of Illinois Press, 1971), pp. 307-24.

26. Ibid.

15

POST-KHRUSHCHEV REFORMS
AND SOVIET PUBLIC
FINANCIAL GOALS
Gertrude E. Schroeder

This chapter is the last in a series of studies detailing and analyzing the fate of various parts of the broad program of economic reform outlined by Premier Kosygin in September 1965.[1] The chapter concerns the changes in financial arrangements governing relationships of producing enterprises with the banks and state budget. Although focus is on the industrial sector, many aspects of the discussion and conclusions have relevance for the economy as a whole. The study (1) describes the provisions and objectives of the financial reforms; (2) analyzes their impact on macrofinancing of the economy, particularly of investment; (3) assesses their effects on enterprise economic behavior, in terms of the objectives sought; (4) reviews the current controversies over the extent and direction of further "reforms" in financial arrangements.

NATURE AND OBJECTIVES OF THE
FINANCIAL REFORMS

The changes in financial arrangements outlined by Kosygin in 1965 were designed to supplement and implement the general economic reform.[2] They were intended primarily to improve the efficiency of enterprise activity by (1) according the firm more leeway for decision-making in financial matters, particularly with regard to investment and its financing, and (2) increasing the financial autonomy of the enterprise. The expansion of enterprise management's decision-making authority was set forth in a new General Statute on the Socialist State Enterprise promulgated in October 1965.[3] It accorded the firm considerably more freedom with respect to planning, although superior organs still prescribed all key financial indicators: sales, profits and profitability, payments to and from the state budget, the wage fund, and total centralized capital investment. Firms were also given the right to choose among sources of financing for both fixed and working capital and to spend monies from newly created incentive and investment funds, these freedoms to be exercised within parameters set forth in implementing regulations.

The increased financial autonomy given the enterprise was accomplished through several devices, which were viewed as "strengthening khozraschet." They included: (1) making profits and return on capital key success indicators and allowing firms to retain a substantially larger share of their profits; (2) providing for financing all or nearly all enterprise investment from retained profits and amortization deductions, supplemented by bank loans; (3) providing for financing all working capital from similar sources; (4) establishing an enterprise investment fund, the so-called production development fund, formed mainly from retained amortization allowances and profits; (5) charging the firm a fee for state-provided fixed and working capital assigned to it and increasing interest rates on bank credits. The details of these new arrangements were set forth in a series of implementing instructions issued in 1966 and subsequently amended. [4] The new rules and procedures governing enterprise relationships with the banks are spelled out in two government decrees issued in April 1967 and August 1973. [5]

Profits, profitability, bank credit, and the capital charge were viewed as parts of a system of economic "levers" that would automatically induce the enterprise to economize on labor and capital resources and produce what planners and customers wanted. Profits and profitability, along with sales, were established as the key success indicators to which managerial rewards were tied. Moreover, performance with respect to plan targets set for these indicators was made the basis for allocating monies to the new investment and incentive funds. By essentially cutting the enterprise loose from the state budget and allowing it to finance its activities from its own earnings, the reformers evidently hoped to engender a spirit of responsibility that would improve the efficiency with which state resources were used, particularly investment. Thus, a new psychological attitude should replace the long-prevalent, general indifference toward resource use engendered by interest-free capital grants and easy access to budget support. This sense of responsibility would be reinforced, it was thought, by allowing the firm to keep a large share of its "own" profits for self-financing and to have its "own" investment and incentive funds; it would also have easier access to bank credits, in case its "own" resources were insufficient. Under the regime of these economic "levers," the firm would be required to make payments to the state and to the bank out of its "own" profits for the use of fixed and working capital. By the rules of the reform, these payments were charged not to costs, but to profits, on which they had first claim. Their payment thus reduced the amount of profits available for forming the enterprise funds out of which bonuses were paid and new investments could be made. With its "own" profits thus at stake, the enterprise supposedly would be led to economize on the use of existing capital, to choose new investment projects with a view to maximizing returns, and to welcome new technology as a cost-reducer.

The interlocking system of economic levers and altered arrangements with respect to enterprise finance may be viewed as an attempt by the reformers, albeit surely an unconscious one, to simulate a market economy. The state-owned firms were to take on many of the trappings of capitalist firms, with the purpose of eliciting the economizing behavior generally characteristic of firms operating in a competitive market environment. Like capitalist firms, state enterprises would be rewarded for making profits, they would retain a large share of their profits, and they would be responsible for financing their own investment and expansion from these profits or from bank loans. Note, however, that residual profits were the property of the state, not the enterprise. Like capitalist firms, therefore, state enterprises presumably would orient their behavior toward giving customers what they wanted with a minimum expenditure of resources, and a kind of proprietary concern for enterprise assets and financial solvency would be elicited. By establishing accounting arrangements resembling those in market economies the reformers were in effect striving to elicit the desired market-firm behavior from state enterprises without establishing for them, in reality, any of the essentials of a market environment or modifying property rights.

IMPACT OF THE REFORMS ON MACROFINANCING OF THE ECONOMY

As originally outlined, the economic reforms seemed to promise significant decentralization in the financing of economic activity. Since enterprises ultimately were supposed to finance all their activities from internal funds and bank credits, it was thought that budget funds would be used primarily to finance the construction and equipping of new enterprises and to pay for defense, various social-cultural measures, and operations of budget-financed institutions. Thus, the share of total national income that flowed through the budget was expected to decline.[6] This process was to be furthered by the planned gradual establishment of complete self-financing for administrative units above the enterprise level, as these units were transferred from budget-financed units to <u>khozraschet</u> organizations. Also, enterprises themselves were to be grouped into large, financially autonomous associations, which would replace many subdivisions of ministries. The early expectations about the altered role of the budget have not materialized. Instead, state budget expenditures relative to national income increased steadily from 50.9 percent in 1966 to 54.9 percent in 1973. Similarly, expenditures financed under the budget category "Financing the National Economy" rose from 42.8 percent to 49.8 percent of the total during the same period. However, industry's share of these funds was slightly lower in 1970 than in 1960; later data are not available. Although detailed information on Soviet budget expenditures is notably scarce, it seems likely that rapidly growing agricultural subsidies are an important factor in explaining the increasing size of the budget relative to national income. Another hypothesis is that the relationships of banks and state insurance agencies with the budget have been altered in ways that channel a larger share of their receipts and outlays through the budget. Also in contradiction to the spirit of financial decentralization implicit in the reforms, the share of the all-union budget in total budget expenditures has risen sharply—to 52.1 percent in 1970, compared with 42.5 percent in 1965 and 41.2 percent in 1960. Aware that the role of the state budget has increased rather than decreased under the reforms, Soviet economists now explain that such a trend is characteristic of "developed Socialism" and can be expected to continue.[7]

On the other hand, information available with respect to financing state capital investment indicates some success in attaining one of the reform's formal objectives to shift a larger share of the burden of financing investment from the state budget to enterprises and the banks. Before 1965, approximately two-thirds of all investment in the industrial sector was financed through budget grants; the plan was to reduce the share to 40 percent.[8] Simultaneously, the share of "centralized" investment in total investment was supposed to decline at the expense of a rise in the share of "decentralized" investment, financed from retained profits and bank credits. Soviet statistical handbooks do not report data on the sources of financing investment, but some information is given from time to time in articles by Soviet officials and in studies by Soviet economists. Finance Minister Garbuzov reported that in 1973 the budget financed 48 percent of total centralized capital investment; profits supplied 16 percent, amortization deductions accounted for 23 percent, bank credits provided about 3 percent, and the rest came from other sources.[9] The budget financed nearly 68 percent of such investment in 1965, 53.1 percent in 1968, and 48.6 percent in 1969.[10] The share of decentralized investment, in total state investment, was 13.9 percent in 1965 and 23.3 percent in 1973; however, its planned share in 1974 was 13.7 percent. [11] Unfortunately, data for the industrial sector alone are not available. The government has been steadily tightening its control over decentralized investment, particularly after 1971-72, when a large overfulfillment of plans for such investment allegedly contributed to the serious shortfall in the plan for centralized investment. Centralized capital investment is directed mainly toward financing new enterprises and large-scale expansion of existing ones; decentralized investment is supposed to finance mainly smaller projects for new technology, modernization and provision of capacities for making consumer goods (in heavy industry). Both forms of investment are now included in the national economic plan and its key material balances, and both are closely monitored by the financial agencies and the banks. Except for the fact that priority claim on resources is usually accorded centralized investment, there is little difference between the two categories of investment at present.

At first, the workings of the economic reform substantially altered the relative importance of the various sources of revenue for the state budget. As a result of the establishment of profits as a success criterion for enterprises, the imposition of a capital charge paid from profits and a reform of industrial wholesale prices required to effect the first two changes, profit deductions replaced the turnover tax as the most important source of budget revenue for the first time in Soviet history. Whereas in 1965 profits supplied 30.2 percent of total revenue and turnover tax furnished 37.8 percent, in 1968 the respective shares were 36.7 percent and 31.2 percent. Thereafter, the gap began to narrow, in part due to increased turnover tax receipts from sales of alcoholic beverages and consumer durables, on which tax rates are high. In 1973, the shares were nearly equal— 31.9 percent and 31.4 percent, respectively. These trends are also explained in part by the fact that profits taxes and turnover tax are largely substitutes for each other. When industrial wholesale prices are increased, as in 1967, with retail prices unchanged, turnover taxes are automatically reduced on goods for which the tax arises as the difference between wholesale and retail prices (81.4 percent of the total tax in 1973). [12] Profits are highly sensitive to price changes. Thus, industrial profits doubled during 1966-68, when the price reforms were being effected, and they increased only slightly in both 1971 and 1973, when major price reductions were made on machinery products. Finally, a rising share of these profits was retained by enterprises to finance measures formerly charged either to costs or to the state budget.

Before the reforms, profits were paid into the budget in a single form, termed simply "deductions from profits." The state

claimed all profits except for a tiny share used to form an incentive
fund in enterprises and a part left with enterprises, but earmarked
for financing centralized capital investment. Now, profits flow into
the budget through three channels—the capital charge, fixed payments,
and the "free remainder of profits." Originally, it was thought that
the capital charge, levied generally at 6 percent of fixed and working
capital in the industrial sector, would become the most important
channel. This has not occurred, largely because of the small size of
the charge and the exemption of numerous enterprises and a substantial share of fixed assets from the charge. [13] In 1972, the capital
charge accounted for 31.7 percent of total profits taxes, fixed payments accounted for 6.7 percent, and the rest came from deduction
of residual profits into the budget, almost all via the "free remainder"
channel. Fixed payments come almost entirely from the oil and gas
industries, where they arise as explicit rent charges per physical
unit of product, an innovation of the 1967 price reforms. The other
principal source of fixed payments is light industry, where they are
used to siphon off profits from firms whose profitability rates substantially exceed the industry average for reasons not reflecting the
work of the enterprise itself. Together, these three industries
account for over 90 percent of fixed payments. [14] Ministries are given
the right to impose fixed payments in cases where the enterprise earns
high rates of return because of exceptionally favorable location, or
similar reason. The "free remainder of profits" represents residual
profits of enterprises after deduction of the capital charge, fixed payments, interest on bank credit, permissible deductions into incentive
funds, and certain specified payments included in the firm's financial
plan. An elaborate procedure recently has been introduced to regulate
the extraction of this remainder, which must be automatically paid
into the budget in the planned amounts three times each month. [15]

Despite assertions of Soviet financial specialists and economists
that the reforms have had significant effects on state finances, it
would seem that these effects in the main are merely distinctions
without a difference. Contrary to expectations, the government now
channels a larger share of national income through the budget than
before the reforms. Profits and turnover tax continue to provide
about two-thirds of total revenue; that their relative shares have
altered somewhat seems to have little consequence. On the other
hand, the separation of the profits tax into multiple forms of payments
has created much work and many jobs for bank and government bureaucrats, who are required to collect the three kinds of taxes, to audit
payments, to seek out "reserves" for increasing them, and to analyze
the putative consequences of the new tax forms. In particular, the
reforms have enlarged the scope of activities for banks, which must
implement the new credit arrangements and monitor the results of

enterprise financial activities, which have been made much more complex by the reforms. Since the advent of the Brezhnev-Kosygin administration, employment in the state bureaucracy (apparat) has risen by 50 percent. Employment in banking and insurance has increased 55 percent, making it the fastest-growing sector of the economy.

The paucity of published statistics relating to activities of the Soviet banking system makes it difficult to assess statistically the impact of the new arrangements with respect to the relationships of enterprises with the banks. Whereas before the reform, shortages of working capital experienced by enterprises during the year were financed by budget allocations, the new rules require enterprises to obtain bank loans for this purpose. The necessity to pay interest on the loans was supposed to induce firms to avoid such shortages and to economize on the use of working capital in general, particularly with interest payments being raised and charged to profits, rather than to costs as before. The rate of growth of short-term credits (under one year) has not increased appreciably since 1965, and with regard to industrial credits it has slowed somewhat. Bank credits financed 42.6 percent of industrial working capital in 1965 and 44.5 percent in 1972. The press indicates that industrial firms are finding new resources for financing working capital needs, notably temporarily free funds accumulated in the three enterprise incentive funds. In contrast, the volume of long-term bank loans has increased greatly, but from a minuscule base. Total long-term credits outstanding in the state sector rose from 1.5 billion rubles in 1965 to 15.6 billion rubles in 1972.[16] Unfortunately, the published data do not provide a breakdown by branch of the economy. Under the reforms the banks were accorded greater leeway in advancing funds to enterprises for purchase of new technology and plant modernization, as well as for plant expansion and adaptation to produce consumer goods. Nonetheless, the annual volume of credits granted for these specific purposes increased only moderately—from 1.366 billion rubles in 1965 to 2.406 billion rubles in 1972.[17] These sums are quite modest, considering the multiple, many-sided efforts that the government has made to spur introduction of new technology and to increase consumer goods output by plants in heavy industry. Indeed, total loans granted for financing new technology were actually lower in 1972 than in 1965, doubtless because enterprises could use the new production development funds for that purpose. Overall, as already noted, bank credits financed a mere 3 percent of total centralized capital investment in 1973.

IMPACT OF THE REFORMS ON ENTERPRISE
FINANCE AND BEHAVIOR

A basic idea of the reforms was that enterprise performance
would be improved by establishing accounting arrangements that
entailed the self-financing of most or all activities through retained
profits and amortization, with recourse as need be to bank credits.
Prices and bank rules were amended so as to make this possible for
most "normally operating firms." In order to assess the impact of
these changes in the rules on enterprise behavior, it is necessary to
examine the various facets in some detail. First, the term "profits"
has been redefined, so that they now include several items formerly
charged to costs; namely, bonuses for salaried employees, and some
of production worker bonuses, interest on bank credits and losses on
enterprise-managed housing and related facilities.[18] Bonuses are
now paid from the newly created material incentive fund formed out
of profits. A second incentive fund, the social-cultural fund, finances
mainly housing construction and various kinds of employee benefits.
A third fund, the production development fund, finances decentralized
investment specified in the enterprise plan. During 1970-73, when
nearly all firms in industry were operating under the rules of the
reform, the share of profits retained was 38-40 percent. While these
shares are considerably larger than the 29 percent retained in 1965,
the use of these retained profits is rigidly controlled. The rules
direct that total planned profits be allocated in order of priority as
follows:[19] payment to the budget of the capital charge and fixed payments; payment of interest on bank credits; deductions into the three
enterprise incentive funds in amounts required by the rules for their
formation and stipulated in the financial plan; financing of centralized
capital investment provided for by plan; repayment of several kinds
of bank loan; financing increases in working capital and covering
losses incurred with respect to enterprise housing; payments into
centralized funds of associations or ministries. When these specified
payments have been made in amounts planned, the residual profits are
paid into the budget as the "free remainder of profits," which is also
planned. Similar rules apply to the allocation of above-plan profits.
In no way can the enterprise retain residual profits. Indeed, the complaint has often been made that zealous financial agencies, following
the rules and the dictates of their own plans for fulfilling the plan for
profit allocations to the budget, extract the residual before it is
known whether there is one, thereby reducing the firm's own working
capital and violating enterprise rights.[20]

With targets for profits and payments into the budget centrally
determined and the allocation of retained profits specified, the

reforms left little scope for profits to function as an economic lever. At first, however, the enterprises were able to influence considerably the size, growth, and allocation of the three enterprise funds, with consequences that the government did not like. Since 1970, the rules governing formation and uses of these funds have been successively tightened. The size of the funds is now centrally determined for ministries and by them for subordinate enterprises. The enterprises have been discouraged from spending the funds accumulated under the rules, and sizable amounts remain unspent each year. The kinds of payments that can be made from the funds is spelled out in regulations, and expenditures are monitored by the financial organs. When enterprises have used accumulations in these funds to finance current needs for working capital, the financial authorities have sought to curb this practice.[21] Here, too, the severe constraints put on the new funds leave little scope for them to act as "levers," as originally intended, while their complicating effects on enterprise finances have been considerable.

A feature of the reforms on which many hopes were pinned was the establishment of decentralized investment funds in enterprises. It was argued that with its "own" fund the firm would be encouraged to invest in new technology and cost-saving innovations. Aided by the establishment of these funds, the share of decentralized investment in total industrial capital investment increased from 3 percent in 1965 to 20 percent in 1970.[22] Originally, the funds were formed partly from ministry-fixed shares of amortization deductions, partly from sales of surplus equipment and partly from profits. The allocation from profits was related by a complex system of ministry-set coefficients to enterprise performance with respect to plans for sales and profitability. In 1971, 54.9 percent of the funds came from amortization charges, and 34.6 percent came from profits.[23] In 1971, the rules were changed, so that now the amortization allocation increases at the same rate as total amortization charges for capital replacement and the profits allocation is determined as a share of profits fixed by the ministry. The uses to which the funds may be put are specified; unspent amounts remain at the disposal of the enterprise, although a part may now be centralized in ministerial funds. The experience with decentralized investment via this fund has been far from satisfactory to the government. In many cases, funds accumulate, because enterprises cannot obtain the necessary physical resources to carry out desired investments. On the other hand, funds actually spent have increased greatly, reportedly preempting resources that should have been used to complete centralized investment projects. Enterprises are frequently accused of using the funds for unauthorized or unnecessary purposes, and local authorities have imposed levies on the funds to finance road construction. These multiple problems with the

experiment in decentralized investment have for all practical purposes
resulted in its recentralization, as noted earlier.

Another feature of the financial reforms that remains controversial pertains to the introduction of a charge for fixed and working
capital. For most firms the charge is fixed at 6 percent, but for coal
mines it is 3 percent, and firms with low profits and planned losses
pay none. Various kinds of capital assets are exempted from the
charge, for example, bank-credited working capital, capital financed
from the production development fund for two years after commission-
ing, investment financed by bank loans until the loans are repaid, and
others. The many exemptions reportedly total 30 percent of industrial
fixed capital and 50 percent of industrial working capital.[24] Almost
from the outset it has been generally recognized that the capital charge
has not produced the results intended, that is, to induce enterprises
to economize on capital. Although the theorists of "developed Socialism" earnestly argue over the nature and functions of the charge,
most of them agree that its primary purpose is to spur efficiency in
the use of capital. Aside from an initial rush to sell off unneeded
equipment, managers evidently have behaved much as before in regard
to capital stock, if one may judge by press reporting. The reasons
usually cited for the ineffectiveness of the capital charge are its small
size (about one-third of total profit payments into the budget) and the
large share of capital stock exempted from the charge. The press
continues to accuse enterprises of overordering equipment and maintaining excess inventories. Ministries also come in for criticism on
this score. A wide variety of proposals have been aired for remedying
the defects of the capital charge. A frequent suggestion is simply to
increase the charge to 12 percent, the minimum return on new investments that is specified as a general norm in the revised Standard
Methodology for Determining the Efficiency of Capital Investment.[25]
A lively controversy also continues to rage over whether or not the
charge should be differentiated and if so, to what extent and by what
criteria. Other critics recommend removing exemptions and merging
the capital charge along with other profit charges into a single budget
payment fixed as a specified share of profits.[26]

Another financial lever that was supposed to influence enterprise
behavior and increase its independence from the budget was the more
extensive use of bank credits to finance both current operations and
investment. The financial literature repeatedly avers that although
some positive gains have been made, the credit lever has not achieved
the results that were expected. The precise nature of these expected
benefits is obscure. Raising the share of investment financed by
credits seems to be regarded as good per se, and so provisions are
inserted in the annual plans to bring it about. On the other hand, the
higher interest rates for credits introduced as a reform measure in

a 1967 government decree presumably aimed to discourage the use of unnecessary credits. As a result of this measure, the average rate on all credits was increased from 1.7 percent to 2.2 percent.[27] The 1967 decree also expanded the types of projects for which credit could be granted and specified the goal of increasing the credit financing of investment. The share of short-term credits in the financing of working capital has risen somewhat, partly because the enterprise no longer has recourse to budget funds to cover shortages and partly because interest rates are so low as to have little or no influence on enterprise decisions. Although the volume of long-term credits has increased rapidly since 1965, they are a very minor source of financing for investment and much of the increase reflects the liberalized provisions for crediting investments of state and collective farms. As an explanation for the snail's pace at which credit financing of investment has grown, it is asserted that complicated accounting rules, coupled with extraction of the bulk of their profits, leads both enterprises and ministries to try to finance investments through budget funds, either directly or indirectly.[28] Another explanation given is that the existence of the production development fund and the availability of unspent monies in other incentive funds enable enterprises to avoid recourse to bank credit. Still another reason might be the desire on the part of enterprise management to avoid the petty tutelage of banks that accompanies the granting of loans.

Despite general agreement that the new credit levers have had no significant effect on enterprise efficiency in the use of financial resources, financial authorities and economists repeatedly aver that the desired results can still be obtained by "improving the credit mechanism." To this end, a Decree of the Council of Ministers of August 22, 1973 doubled the rates on short-term credits and established a number of differentials depending on the type and purpose of the loan.[29] The new rates, effective January 1, 1974, range from 2 to 8 percent for ordinary loans and are set at 10 percent for overdue loans. Permissible maturities for some types of loans were extended. The decree also appears to give the banks greater powers to monitor enterprise activities and to punish them for a wide variety of undesired practices, in particular, the maintenance of above-norm inventories and the expenditure of funds for unauthorized purposes. The banks are enjoined to see to it that credited investments are carried out in strict accord with plans, time schedules, and technical documentation. Finally, the decree provides for the introduction of a system of credit agreements between banks and enterprises or associations, which fix the amounts of credits to be extended, the purposes and terms of repayment, and explicit measures to be taken to improve the efficiency of enterprise performance.[30] This decree was the culmination of an extensive discussion over the past five years of possible ways to make

the credit mechanism more effective.[31] Recently, financial writers
have been much concerned with devising formulae for measuring the
"effectiveness" of credit, for example, sales per ruble of credit,
profits per ruble of credit, and the like.

EXTENSION OF KHOZRASCHET STATUS

When it became evident that the economic reforms were not
producing the desired results, the statement was often made that these
results would come, when all units of the hierarchy above the enterprise were placed on khozraschet and were operating under the rules
of the reform. This step would establish a common set of success
indicators and financial incentives for all units in the hierarchy from
enterprises to ministries. In 1965, Kosygin explicitly stated that
khozraschet production associations (amalgamations of enterprises)
were to be formed as part of the intended reforms in the industrial
sector. Scarcely any progress was made in extending khozraschet
upward before 1970. As an experiment, the main administrations
(glavki) of the Ministry of Instruments, Automation and Control Systems were converted into autonomous production associations, merging
all enterprises and having their own financial resources. A similar
step was taken with respect to the Main Administration of Auto Transport subordinate to the Moscow City Executive Committee. In 1970,
by special decree of the Council of Ministers, the entire Ministry of
Instruments, Automation and Control Systems was put under a system
of autonomous financing.[32] This experiment, if successful, evidently
was intended to serve as a model for extension to other ministries.
Under the new arrangements the ministry was made fully responsible
for financing all of its activities, including investment and construction
of new plants, from its own resources and normal access to bank
credits. The state continues to establish for the ministry the following
plan indicators: total output, output of key products in physical units,
allocations of materials and equipment, and commissionings of new
fixed capital. The government imposes a constraint on wages by fixing
the wage fund as a percentage of output. Also set for the ministry are
the amount and share of profits that must be paid to the budget. During
1971-75, for example, the share is planned to increase from 41.4 percent of the total in 1970 to 67.4 percent in 1975.[33] The ruble amounts
fixed in the plan for each year must be paid to the budget, regardless
of whether or not the plan for profits is fulfilled. Under the new
arrangements, the associations (former glavki) are directly subordinate
to the ministry, and deputy ministers now direct functional departments, rather than product branches as before. All enterprises belong

to associations, which perform various kinds of services centrally, including centralized accounting with the budget. This ministry evidently was selected for the pilot experiment because its economic situation made success highly probable. The ministry produces mainly high-technology, sophisticated products, 60 percent of which reportedly are new each year, and most of its output is sold at contract prices. Hence, the ministry is highly profitable: The recoupment period for its investment is reported to be a mere two years. While the ministry's experience with self-financing is generally described as successful, some sources cite evidence of the traditional kinds of shortcomings, in particular with respect to the management of investment projects. [34]

At any rate, there has been no move to extend this experiment. Most ministries would be unable to finance all their activities from profits, unless prices were changed. Nonetheless, several small steps have been taken in the direction of extending khozraschet upward. In 1971, a Council of Ministers' decree authorized the formation of reserve funds of various kinds in associations, glavki, and ministries, formed by deductions from profits of subordinate enterprises. [35] The funds may be used for specified purposes, such as bonuses, financial aid to enterprises, social-cultural measures, and investment. An experiment is being conducted to test the efficacy of centralizing all funds for developing and introducing new technology at the ministry level. Finally, impetus has at last been given to Kosygin's plan to establish production associations. This part of the proposed reforms made almost no headway until 1971, when party pressure evidently was exerted to move in this direction. Various kinds of associations were established in the following two years. Finally, in early 1973 a Council of Ministers' decree ordered the ministries to come up within six months with plans to reorganize their administrative apparatus and to group their enterprises into one or another form of association. [36] According to reports, some 1,100 production associations, producing about 12 percent of total industrial output, had been formed as of early 1973. [37] So far as reorganization plans are concerned, footdragging is very evident; as of mid-1974, most of the ministries had not yet submitted plans. [38] Clearly, the upward extension of khozraschet is not popular with the bureaucracy.

SUMMARY AND CONCLUSIONS

The framers of the 1965 economic reforms regarded their financial aspects as critically important for attainment of the reform's main objective of increasing the efficiency of resource use in the

economy. As with other aspects of the reforms, eight years of experience in implementing the new financial arrangements have yielded
little significant improvement. The Soviet press in 1973-74, as in
1963-64, provides ample evidence of the persistence of chronic mal-
functions and wastes of resources typical of the Soviet bureau-
administered economy. It seems correct to conclude once again that
"the more things change, the more they are the same." Thus: (1) the
changes were supposed to reduce the share of national income channeled through the budget; instead, the share has increased; (2) bank
credits were supposed to become a major source of financing investment; in 1974 they provided little more than 3 percent of total centralized investment; (3) decentralized investment was to increase
significantly as a share of total state investment; the share did indeed
increase to nearly one-quarter, only to be cut back by fiat to its pre-
reform level, with tightened control over such investment; (4) financing
of investment through profits and from enterprises' own special investment funds, along with the stress on profits as an incentive, was supposed to alter the traditionally negative stance of firms toward innovation and introduction of new technology; there is no evidence of
significant change in this regard; (5) the capital charge and higher
interest rates on bank credits were supposed to promote the more
efficient use of capital; Soviet sources agree that these levers have
been largely ineffective; (6) the reform's stress on profits was supposed to act as a lever, via new incentive arrangements, for promoting
efficiency; in practice, the retained share of profits has become totally
planned, the profit-related incentives have been increasingly constrained
by a mass of rules and regulations, but most important of all, the state
remains the claimant to residual profits; (7) the reforms were supposed
to be carried out without increasing the size of the bureaucracy; instead, both the state administration and the newly empowered bank
bureaucracy have increased rapidly under the present leadership.

Thus, the financial levers, like other facets of the reforms,
have failed to produce the expected results. What are the reasons?
Probably the most important one is that the management and control
of real flows in the economy has not changed, despite the innovations
in financial flows. In the final analysis, it is the real flows that control enterprise behavior. Real flows are planned, physically directed,
and regulated by the center, as before. The limited initial delegation
of authority over these flows was quickly followed by imposition of
constraints from the center via ceilings, norms, and regulations. In
this cycle of "reforms" we have witnessed not "creeping" but galloping
recentralization. To be specific, ceilings have been put on incentive
funds, limitations have been placed on decentralized investment,
restrictions have been put on expenditures of incentive and investment
funds, the number of obligatory plan targets has been increased, and

bank controls have become more pervasive. Financial "levers" can hardly be effective if the authorities simultaneously restrict both monetary and real incentives. Another explanation for the failure of financial rearrangements to produce the desired results lies in the inherent nature of Soviet value categories. Sales, costs, profits, profitability and capital charges are essentially accounting categories, rather than economic categories. The reason is, of course, that the product prices underlying these categories do not reflect accurately either real resource costs or consumer utilities. Moreover, producers and suppliers are not permitted to respond freely to the prices set; for the most part, they merely conduct accounting on the basis of them. This state of affairs, along with the absence of competition, means that the relationships between enterprises and their customers, suppliers, and banks are essentially administrative connections rather than economic connections. As a consequence, enterprise behavior resembles that of bureaucratic agencies following and manipulating rules, rather than that of economic entities that are answerable for the consequences of their decisions about resource use. The words for the variables to which firms respond are the same in market economies and in the Soviet Union—sales, profits, and profitability— but their essence is different. In the Soviet context, enterprise behavior reflects the manipulation of accounting rules, in efforts to maximize the returns to its position, both tangible and intangible. The behavior of ministries may be viewed similarly. As often as not, the responses to changes in rules is of an accounting nature, rather than an economic nature, that is, in the direction of economizing on resource use or satisfying customers. The ultimate economic goal of the leadership is an output of physical goods and services in the desired quantity, mix, and quality, obtained with a minimum of waste. If the response to a change in financial rules is not the desired one, the solution is sought in another change in the rules, leading to new responses and new rules. This sequence has been the saga of the Soviet reforms, and it has produced a complication of the financial rules and incentive arrangements truly awesome to contemplate.

A third explanation lies in the manifest unwillingness of Soviet officials to accept the consequences of allowing financial levers to operate freely. Simply put, delegation of authority over financial flows widens the opportunity for discretionary behavior and carries the risks that real flows of resource may be altered in undesired ways. Thus, the reforms permitted the accumulation of large bonus and investment funds in enterprise accounts and accorded managers considerable discretion over their expenditure. When the exercise of this discretion produced "wrong" choices, the government responded by curtailing the area of discretion. The consequence was essentially to destroy the efficacy of pecuniary variables as a means for steering enterprises toward more efficient use of resources, the stated purpose of altering financial flows in the first place.

The Soviet press readily admits that although some improvements have resulted, the assorted changes in financial arrangements have left the basic economic problems unsolved. The proposals for further "improving the financial mechanism" range over a wide area—from numerous, largely technical, suggestions for amending one rule or another, to proposals to alter the entire basis for planning and pricing through the mechanism of the "optimally functioning Socialist economy." Most numerous of all are proposals for tinkering with the definitions of output, profits, and profitability, so as to remove the revealed deficiencies of these levers as currently defined. The aim is to devise a set of definitions and rules that will reward enterprises only for that part of profits that results from the firm's own efforts to raise productivity and satisfy customers. While the economists argue, the bureaucrats amend the rules toward the same end. The latest amendments punish enterprises for "intentionally" raising product prices in order to reap profits and redefine fulfillment of the sales plan to include detailed adherence to product mix, quality, and schedules specified in delivery contracts. [39] Various experiments are being conducted to test one or another of the proposals for change.

As of this writing, the field of public finance continues to be in a state of active controversy. Debates rage over essentially the same matters as were argued over a decade ago. In considerable dispute are the theoretical nature and roles of the turnover tax and profits as sources of state income. Some economists propose to abolish the former and to finance state expenditures through one consolidated enterprise payment to the budget out of profits. Others propose to retain the turnover tax but to redistribute the tax over all products so as to reflect the "values" actually created. Thus far, the reforms have left the turnover tax untouched, except for allowing firms to keep a part of it under certain conditions to repay bank loans obtained to finance expansion of products taxed, and except to the extent that price reforms have altered tax rates. Another area of active controversy concerns the "proper" roles of the main sources of investment financing—budget grants, amortization, retained profits, and bank credit. Opinions range from the assertion that state-owned enterprises should be financed for investment purposes by the state to the view that all economic units, both enterprises and ministries in charge of industries, should finance all their activities through bank credits and internal sources, with prices to be changed to facilitate this if need be. With respect to amortization, there is general agreement that the rates are far too low. In some cases, amortization periods are ridiculously long—1,000 years for subway tracks, for example. Rates were scheduled to be raised on January 1, 1975, the first such change since 1963. The new rates reportedly will reduce industrial profits by 4.6 percent.[40] With respect to bank credits, proposals are made to require firms to finance a designated share of investment by this means, the claim being made that bank-credited investment projects are completed sooner and managed more efficiently than those otherwise financed. Even the subject of working capital is a hotbed of discussion, centering around such matters as the degree of latitude that should be allowed to enterprise managers, the optimum proportion of "own" and bank-financed working capital, and the level of interest rates.

Another field of controversy concerns the capital charge and the desirability of introducing charges for other resources, along with the rates to be paid for bank credit and the role of credit in general in the stage of "developed Socialism." The only step taken thus far has been to raise interest rates on some kinds of bank loans. With respect to recommendations to introduce charges for resources other than capital, Finance Minister Garbuzov stated in mid-1972 that such proposals were "worthy of attention."[41] Finally, all of the financial levers—profits, profitability, capital charges, and bank credits— have become subjects for discussion in a voluminous argumentative literature concerning techniques for measuring the efficiency of resource use, seemingly for each and every one in all their myriad aspects. This discussion is more than ivory-tower theorizing among economists. It is aimed at devising and defining technical and financial indicators that will measure the economic effectiveness of expenditures, with a view to incorporating these indicators in plans at all levels and making all or some of them determinants in the system of rewards and punishments. The history of the economic reforms thus far has been one of precisely such proliferation of success indicators and a con- comitant expansion of bureaucratic regulating and monitoring activity, with little payoff in improved performance of the economy up to now. How more of the same medicine can help is hard to see.

NOTES

1. Gertrude E. Schroeder, "Soviet Economic Reforms: A Study in Contradictions," Soviet Studies, July 1968, pp. 1-21; "The 1966-67 Price Reform in Soviet Industry: A Study in Complications," Soviet Studies, April 1969, pp. 462-77; "Soviet Economic Reforms at an Impasse," Problems of Communism, July-August, 1970, pp. 36-46; "The 'Reform' of the Supply System in Soviet Industry," Soviet Studies, July 1972, pp. 97-119; and "Recent Developments in Soviet Economic Planning and Incentives," in Soviet Economic Prospects for the

Seventies, U.S. Congress, Joint Economic Committee, 93rd Cong.,
1st Sess. (Washington, D.C.: U.S. Government Printing Office, 1973),
pp. 11-38.

2. Pravda, September 28, 1965.

3. Gosplan USSR, Ekonomicheskaia reforma v. SSSR (Moscow,
1969), pp. 166-79.

4. Ibid., pp. 235-66.

5. Ekonomicheskaia gazeta, nos. 16 and 20 (1967); Dengi i Kredit,
no. 12 (1973), pp. 3-10.

6. For example, Ya. G. Liberman, Gosudarstvennyy byudzhet
SSSR v. novykh usloviakh khoziaistvovannia (Moscow, 1970), p. 19;
Planovoe khoziaistvo, no. 2 (1967), pp. 37-46.

7. For example, Voprosy ekonomiki, no. 9 (1973), pp. 14-21;
Finansy SSSR, no. 10 (1972), pp. 21-30.

8. Finansy SSSR, no. 6 (1966), pp. 12-20; Planovoe khoziaistvo,
no. 2 (1967), pp. 45-46.

9. Finansy SSSR, no. 1 (1974), p. 12.

10. Finansy SSSR, no. 1 (1966), p. 13; no. 1 (1968), p. 14;
no. 1 (1970), p. 13.

11. Narodnoe khoziaistvo SSSR v 1972 godu (Moscow, 1972),
pp. 474, 477; Finansy SSSR, no. 1 (1974), p. 12.

12. N. G. Sychev, Finansy predpriatiy i otrasley narodnogo
khoziaistva (Moscow, 1973), p. 130.

13. Ibid., p. 148.

14. Ibid., p. 149.

15. Ekonomicheskia gazeta, nos. 3, 4, and 5 (1973), p. 22.

16. Narodnoe khoziaistvo SSSR v 1972 godu, p. 72

17. Ibid., p. 730.

18. Profits data given in the annual statistical handbooks have
not been adjusted for this change in definition; therefore, the series
is not comparable.

19. Gosplan USSR, Khoziaistvennaia reSorma v SSSR (Moscow,
1969), pp. 252-54.

20. Sovetskoe gosudarstvo i pravo, no. 9 (1972), pp. 76-80;
Dengi i kredit, no. 7 (1970), pp. 19-24.

21. Dengi i kredit, no. 2 (1971), pp. 39-43; no. 2 (1972), p. 31;
V. K. Senchagov, ed., Finansy i effektivnost' proizvodstvennykh
fondov (Moscow, 1973), p. 112.

22. Ibid., pp. 117, 125.

23. V. U. Budavay and S. A. Sitarian, eds., Finansy i tekh-
nicheskiy progress (Moscow, 1973), p. 75.

24. Finansy, SSSR, no. 11 (1971), pp. 30-36; Sychev, op. cit.,
p. 148.

25. Ekonomicheskaia gazeta, no. 39 (1969), pp. 11-12.

26. As examples of the literature on the capital charge see, Voprosy ekonomiki, no. 3 (1970), pp. 66-67; no. 9 (1970), pp. 106-11; no. 10 (1968), pp. 53-65; no. 1 (1972), pp. 38-48; Planovoe khoziaistvo, no. 5 (1966), pp. 63-69; no. 12 (1969), pp. 67-77; no. 2 (1967), pp. 37-46; no. 3 (1968), pp. 52-61; Finansy SSSR, no. 8 (1970), pp. 25-33; no. 11 (1971), pp. 30-36; no. 12 (1971), pp. 51-57; Ekonomika i organizatsiia proizvodstva, no. 3 (1973), pp. 24-40; Sovetskoe gosudarstvo i pravo, no. 10 (1972), pp. 111-14; A Z. Seleznev, Stimulirovanie effektivnosti proizvodstva i pribyl' (Moscow, 1973), pp. 125-45; G. G. Kovalevskii and E. A. Lutokhina, Formy chistogo dokhoda pri sotsializme (Minsk, 1973), pp. 182-222; V. N. Ivanchenko, Intensifikatsia proizvodstva i formy ego stimulirovania (Moscow, 1973), pp. 160-81.

27. V. I. Rybin, Kredit: i raschety v. usloviakh reformy (Moscow, 1970), p. 97.

28. I. D. Sher, Finansirovanie i kreditovanie kapitalnykh vlozhennii (Moscow, 1972), p. 121; Dengi i kredit, no. 3 (1974), pp. 38-43; Ekonomika i organizatsia proizvodstva, no. 1 (1971), pp. 46-55; Finansy SSSR, no. 5 (1974), pp. 8-15.

29. Dengi i kredit, no. 12 (1973), pp. 3-10; Finansy SSSR, no. 5 (1974), pp. 32-36; C. V. Borodin, A. N. Demichev, and G. M. Tochilnikov, Finansy i kredit SSSR (Moscow, 1973), pp. 71-72.

30. Dengi i kredit, no. 12 (1973), pp. 3-10; Ekonomicheskaia gazeta, no. 41 (October 1973), p. 8.

31. For example, see, Voprosy ekonomiki, no. 9 (1973), pp. 3-13; no. 6 (1970), pp. 17-38; Dengi i kredit, no. 9 (1973), pp. 36-46; no. 3 (1972), pp. 32-42; no. 8 (1972), pp. 3-12; no. 9 (1972), pp. 52-58; Finansy SSSR, no. 10 (1968), pp. 54-57; Izvestia Akademii Nauk, Seria ekonomicheskaia, no. 5 (1970), pp. 93-105; no. 2 (1972), pp. 65-75; Ye. Stepanova, ed., Vzaimootnoshenia promyshlennosti S byudzhetom i kreditnoy sistemoy v novykh usloviakh (Moscow, 1970), pp. 103-73; Rybin, op. cit., pp. 43-138; Yu. P. Avdiianta, Kredit i povyshenie ekonomicheskoy effektivnosti proizvodstva (Moscow, 1972), pp. 106-38.

32. Izvestia, April 7, 1970.

33. Sotsialisticheskaia industria, December 25, 1973, p. 2.

34. Descriptions and analysis of the various facets of the experiment are to be found in: K. A. Kazankova, V. P. Ignamushkin, and V. I. Ukin, Finansy ministerstv i ob'edinenniy v novykh usloviakh khoziaistvovania (Moscow, 1971), pp. 12-28; Senchagov, op. cit., pp. 141-52; Sotsialisticheskaia industria, December 25, 1973, p. 2; Izvestia, April 8, 1970; Finansy SSSR, no. 12 (1972), pp. 61-67; no. 1 (1971), pp. 44-49; Planovoe khoziaistvo, no. 1 (1974), pp. 78-86.

35. Finansy SSSR, no. 10 (1973), pp. 71-80; Ya. I. Moreynis, Fondy ekonomicheskogo stimulirovania v promyshiennosti (Moscow, 1974), pp. 116-41.

36. Pravda, April 3, 1973.

37. Ekonomicheskaia gazeta, no. 15 (April 1973), p. 3.

38. Pravda, May 31, 1974; July 31, 1974. A statute defining the rights and responsibilities of production associations was issued in May 1974. Ekonomicheskaia gazeta, no. 18 (1974), pp. 9-16.

39. Ekonomicheskaia gazeta, no. 25 (1974), p. 22; Sotsialisticheskiy trud, no. 1 (1973), pp. 155-56.

40. Finansy SSSR, no. 6 (1974), p. 85.

41. Planovoe khoziaistvo, no. 6 (1972), pp. 30-46.

16

ALCOHOLISM AND STATE POLICY
IN THE SOVIET UNION
Vladimir G. Treml

The Soviet government is clearly concerned with the undesirable effects of heavy drinking in the Soviet Union. This concern became particularly evident in the early 1970s with the enactment of a series of decrees dealing with various aspects of the production and consumption of alcoholic beverages and stepped-up antidrinking campaigns.

The issues involved are highly complex and it is virtually impossible to assess fully the direct and indirect costs and benefits of a given policy measure dealing with drinking and alcohol. It would be impossible to understand the difficulties faced by the government without appreciation of the order of magnitude of different aspects of the production and consumption of alcohol in the Soviet Union. Tax receipts, use of agricultural raw materials, consumer expenditures, retail trade sales, and other quantitative aspects of alcohol consumption all constitute significant and often major shares of relevant national totals. It is, therefore, not surprising that the Soviet government is moving cautiously in its antialcohol campaign.

The purpose of this chapter is twofold: (1) to offer a quantitative picture of alcohol production and consumption, and (2) to evaluate the economic aspects of control of drinking and alcoholism in the Soviet Union. Recent excellent studies by Walter Connor, David Powell, and

This is a revised and updated version of a paper originally published in Soviet Studies 25, no. 4 (April 1975). The author gratefully acknowledges the support of the Project on Alcoholism and Alcohol Abuse in the USSR and Eastern Europe of the Russian Research Center, Harvard University. Thanks are also due to Alan Abouchar, Keith Bush, Dimitri Gallik, and Gregory Grossman for their comments and assistance with data.

Peter Solomon have greatly enhanced our understanding of the social and political aspects of heavy drinking in the Soviet Union and of various legal and administrative sanctions used.[1] The focus of this study is primarily on the quantitative aspects of alcohol production and consumption and the commercial and fiscal issues involved.

OVERALL PICTURE

Analysis of Soviet alcohol policy is greatly handicapped by the absence of data, and parts of this study are by necessity rather speculative. Heavy drinking and alcoholism are discussed frequently in Soviet sociological, medical, and legal professional literature and in popular periodicals. However, no matter how voluminous, this literature sheds very little if any light on the overall dimensions of the problem or on its quantitative and economic aspects. Particularly notable by their absence are any data on the total production, sales, and consumption of alcoholic beverages as well as price, tax, and profit data, and statistics on alcoholism, deaths from cirrhosis of the liver, and other health statistics. In fact, in the last ten years we have observed increasing suppression of data that had been regularly published earlier.[2]

And the rather meager amount of statistics concerning alcohol that does appear in the literature is quite often inaccurate. For instance, one series that has been regularly published in national statistical publications is the index of sales of all alcoholic beverages in constant prices.[3] However, because of built-in defects of Soviet price indexes, the published index of sales, in fact, overstates the increases in the consumption of liquor.[4]

Accordingly, the first task of this study was to develop the methodology of estimating the necessary data and then to scan the Soviet literature and, using all available direct and indirect information, to quantify the whole issue of the production and consumption of alcoholic beverages in the Soviet Union. Most of the data were found in technical sources on industry and trade and in regional statistical handbooks. The complete set of collected and estimated series is a part of a larger study being prepared by the author and could not be reproduced here. Selected data relevant to the topic of this study are summarized in Tables 16.1, 16.2, and 16.3.

The most important conclusions of this statistical study are summarized below.

1. <u>Per Capita Consumption: International Comparisons</u>. In the period covered in this study, and probably earlier as well, consumption of alcohol per person of drinking age in the Soviet Union has been one

TABLE 16.1

Output of Alcoholic Beverages in the Soviet Union, 1957-73
(not including illegal production, millions of liters[a])

	Vodka[b]	Wine (grape)	Wine (fruit)	Champagne	Cognac	Beer
1957	1,402	552.0	154	23.8	11.04	1,965
1958	1,454	618.2	169	26.0	12.25	1,991
1959	1,373	669.0	185	28.0	13.64	2,319
1960	1,373	776.8	203	29.9	15.02	2,498
1961	1,457	847.5	222	32.1	17.80	2,667
1962	1,620	1,008.0	243	35.3	20.57	2,818
1963	1,689	1,185.5	265	37.4	23.38	2,807
1964	1,765	1,270.8	291	40.7	25.23	2,830
1965	1,883	1,338.8	318	44.7	26.83	3,169
1966	1,972	1,585.9	328	48.6	29.01	3,437
1967	2,115	1,800.0	350	53.7	30.13	3,613
1968	2,247	1,912.5	410	58.3	32.54	3,830
1969	2,361	2,402.1	453	63.4	35.14	3,970
1970	2,384	2,680.0	505	68.6	37.95	4,190
1971	2,308	2,800.0	562	74.5	40.99	4,410
1972	2,178	2,930.0	626	80.8	44.30	4,690
1973	2,454	2,070.0	697	87.7	47.84	5,080

[a]One liter equals 1.06 quarts.
[b]Including, according to Soviet classification, vodka-based beverages such as various liqueurs, cordials, and flavored vodkas.

Source: Vladimir G. Treml, "Production and Consumption of Alcoholic Beverages in the USSR: A Statistical Study," Journal of Studies on Alcohol 36, no. 3 (1975): 288.

TABLE 16.2

Soviet Supply of Alcoholic Beverages
for Domestic Consumption, 1957–73
(not including illegal production, millions of liters)

	Vodka	Wine (grape)	Wine (fruit)	Champagne	Cognac	Beer
1957	1,401	532.1	154	23.8	11.0	1,967
1958	1,453	588.1	169	26.0	12.3	2,006
1959	1,372	629.3	185	28.0	13.9	2,342
1960	1,383	747.8	203	29.9	15.9	2,521
1961	1,459	809.6	222	32.1	20.2	2,693
1962	1,618	943.0	243	35.3	22.1	2,843
1963	1,688	1,126.1	265	37.4	25.3	2,822
1964	1,769	1,238.6	291	40.7	27.6	2,847
1965	1,893	1,325.5	318	44.7	32.1	3,187
1966	1,976	1,542.4	328	48.6	39.3	3,466
1967	2,120	1,782.4	350	53.7	49.4	3,641
1968	2,256	1,973.7	410	58.3	53.4	3,854
1969	2,370	2,825.5	453	63.4	57.4	3,990
1970	2,392	3,110.3	505	68.6	58.9	4,212
1971	2,316	3,270.8	562	74.5	61.4	4,435
1972	2,191	3,388.3	626	80.8	42.6	4,696
1973	2,458	2,459.6	697	87.7	53.5	5,380

Note: Supply is defined as domestic output, plus imports, less exports. Output of grape wine also adjusted for losses and increases in stock of aging wines.

Source: Vladimir G. Treml, "Production and Consumption of Alcoholic Beverages in the USSR: A Statistical Study," Journal of Studies on Alcohol 36, no. 3 (1975): 291.

TABLE 16.3

Total Soviet Domestic Supply of Alcoholic Beverages
in Value Terms Broken into Types, 1957-73
(millions of rubles)

	Vodka	Wine (grape)	Wine (fruit and berry)	Champagne	Cognac	Beer
1957	5,800	1,308.6	197.1	70.7	86.1	984
1958	7,221	1,537.9	204.5	92.6	115.6	1,003
1959	6,915	1,342.8	190.6	83.2	130.7	1,171
1960	7,067	1,564.4	213.2	88.8	149.5	1,261
1961	7,543	1,594.5	235.3	95.3	189.9	1,347
1962	8,478	1,954.0	272.2	104.8	207.7	1,422
1963	8,963	2,264.7	310.1	111.1	237.8	1,411
1964	9,517	2,618.7	360.8	120.9	259.4	1,424
1965	10,317	2,780.6	391.1	132.8	301.7	1,594
1966	10,908	3,508.1	406.7	144.3	369.4	1,733
1967	11,872	3,952.6	479.5	159.5	464.4	1,821
1968	12,859	4,100.3	586.3	173.2	502.0	1,927
1969	13,675	4,996.6	697.6	188.3	539.6	1,995
1970	15,189	6,080.1	803.0	254.5	848.2	2,106
1971	15,676	6,307.8	904.8	332.2	1,154.3	2,218
1972	16,004	6,507.3	1,020.4	360.4	800.9	2,348
1973[*]						

[*]Not available.

Source: Vladimir G. Treml, "Production and Consumption of Alcoholic Beverages in the USSR: A Statistical Study," Journal of Studies on Alcohol 36, no. 3 (1975): 293.

of the highest in the world. In the late 1960s the Soviet Union ranked
about seventh or eighth among 24 developed nations in per capita consumption of absolute alcohol in all forms (hard liquor, wine, and
beer). However, in terms of absolute alcohol consumed in the form
of hard liquor the Soviet Union ranks first, with 6 liters of alcohol per
person of drinking age, exceeding significantly the second and third
ranking France and the United States, which record about 4.4 liters
each (see Tables 16.4, 16.5, and 16.6). It must also be noted that
while per capita consumption of alcohol has been increasing throughout
most of the world in the last 10 to 15 years, the Soviet Union records
one of the highest rates of increase: 5.1 percent per annum per person
of drinking age compared with an average of 3.1 percent for 14 developed nations.

It will be noted that per capita consumption of absolute alcohol
has been decreasing since 1971. However, an examination of available
statistics shows that the decreases cannot be attributed to the stepped-
up antidrinking campaign. The reduction in 1971 and 1972 was caused
by lower production of vodka caused by poor agricultural harvests of
1971 and 1972. As can be seen from Table 16.1, the output of vodka
in 1973 reached a record high level of 2,454 million liters (13 percent
increase over 1972) as the agricultural output increased in that year.
The increase in consumption of alcohol in 1973 was checked by a
drastic reduction of wine production caused by a disastrous grape
harvest of 1972. We can thus conclude that whatever else the antidrinking campaign calls for it does not include reduction in the production of alcoholic beverages.

2. Regional Differentials. The per capita consumption of alcohol
is high enough to explain the concern of the government, but the national
averages do not tell the entire story. As can be expected in a country
with an ethnically heterogeneous population, the per capita consumption
of alcohol in the Soviet Union is highly differentiated by regions (see
Table 16.7). The southern and eastern republics and republics with
predominantly Muslim population show significantly lower rates of
consumption than the Slavic republics. For instance, in 1967 the
average consumption of alcohol in the form of hard liquor per person
of drinking age was 1.82 liters of absolute alcohol in the three Transcaucasian and the four Mid-Eastern republics as compared with 5.41
liters of absolute alcohol for the rest of the Soviet Union. Comparable
averages of alcohol consumed in all forms (hard liquor, beer, and
wine) were 4.50 liters and 8.31 liters.[5] These statistics reflect
republic averages and there is sufficient evidence showing that similar
Muslim/non-Muslim differentials are observed within the republics.
In all probability, on the average, Slavic nationalities drink three
times as much as Muslims.

TABLE 16.4

Soviet Total and Per Capita Consumption of Absolute Alcohol, 1957–73
(not including illegal production)

| | Total Consumption, Million liters | | | Per Capita Consumption, Liters | | | |
| | Vodka and Cognac | Wines and Beer | Total | Total Population | | Ages 15 and Over | |
				"Hard"*	All	"Hard"	All
1957	551	157	708	2.71	3.48	3.78	4.85
1958	572	168	740	2.77	3.58	3.90	5.05
1959	541	186	727	2.57	3.45	3.60	4.93
1960	546	212	758	2.55	3.54	3.60	5.11
1961	577	225	802	2.65	3.68	3.85	5.35
1962	640	258	898	2.89	4.05	4.21	5.91
1963	669	288	957	2.97	4.25	4.34	6.21
1964	701	311	1,012	3.07	4.44	4.47	6.45
1965	742	337	1,079	3.21	4.67	4.65	6.76
1966	758	382	1,140	3.25	4.88	4.67	7.02
1967	825	431	1,256	3.50	5.32	5.00	7.61
1968	879	473	1,352	3.69	5.67	5.24	8.07
1969	912	624	1,536	3.79	6.38	5.36	9.02
1970	921	682	1,603	3.79	6.60	5.31	9.25
1971	894	719	1,613	3.65	6.58	5.07	9.15
1972	828	754	1,582	3.35	6.39	4.63	8.85
1973	931	623	1,554	3.73	6.22	5.15	8.59

*"Hard" beverages or vodkas and cognacs with alcohol content of 40 percent or more.

Source: Vladimir G. Treml, "Production and Consumption of Alcoholic Beverages in the USSR: A Statistical Study," Journal of Studies on Alcohol 36, no. 3 (1975): 294.

TABLE 16.5

Per Capita Consumption of Absolute Alcohol
in Selected Countries
(liters per person, ages 15 and over)

Country	Year	Hard Beverages	All Beverages
1 France	1966	4.7	24.72
2 Italy	1968	2.08	15.18
3 Switzerland	1966	2.31	12.83
4 West Germany	1968	3.37	12.34
5 Hungary	1970	n.a.	11.00
6 Australia	1966	1.17	10.94
7 Belgium	1967	1.25	10.86
8 United States	1970	4.35	9.88
9 New Zealand	1964	1.70	9.77
10 Czechoslovakia	1968	1.59	9.27
11 Canada	1967	2.84	8.33
12 East Germany	1969	3.35	7.71
13 Denmark	1968	1.29	7.34
14 United Kingdom	1966	1.10	7.19
15 Sweden	1968	3.22	6.59
16 Japan	1968	3.79	5.79
17 The Netherlands	1968	2.61	5.79
18 Ireland	1966	1.51	5.64
19 Poland	1959	3.70	5.58
20 Norway	1968	1.97	4.28
21 Finland	1968	1.97	3.90
22 Iceland	1966	2.76	3.63
23 Israel	1968	1.67	3.10
Soviet Union	1968	5.24 (6.09)	8.07 (10.33)

Note: Figures for the Soviet Union exclude illegal production;
the first figure is the national average and the figure in parentheses
is for urban population only.

Source: Vladimir G. Treml, "Production and Consumption of
Alcoholic Beverages in the USSR: A Statistical Study," Journal of
Studies on Alcohol 36, no. 3 (1975): 297.

TABLE 16.6

Soviet Per Capita Consumption of Absolute Alcohol
in Urban Areas, 1957-73
(without illegal production, liters per person)

	Per Capita of Total Population		Ages 15 and Over	
	Hard Beverages	All Beverages	Hard Beverages	All Beverages
1957	3.89	5.35	5.33	7.33
1958	3.99	5.47	5.46	7.48
1959	3.53	4.96	4.82	6.77
1960	3.40	5.14	4.63	7.00
1961	3.50	5.28	4.75	7.17
1962	3.91	5.91	5.30	8.00
1963	3.99	6.17	5.39	8.34
1964	4.01	6.28	5.41	8.47
1965	4.16	6.59	5.59	8.86
1966	4.08	6.77	5.47	9.08
1967	4.31	7.25	5.77	9.70
1968	4.56	7.74	6.09	10.33
1969	4.61	8.73	6.14	11.63
1970	4.48	8.85	5.96	11.77
1971	4.17	8.66	5.56	11.55
1972	4.12	8.33	5.49	11.11
1973*				

*Not yet available.

Source: Vladimir G. Treml, "Production and Consumption of Alcoholic Beverages in the USSR: A Statistical Study," Journal of Studies on Alcohol 36, no. 3 (1975): 296.

TABLE 16.7

Soviet Per Capita Consumption of Absolute Alcohol
by Republics, 1967
(without illegal production, liters per person of drinking age)

Republic/Regions	Hard Beverages	All Beverages
Soviet Union [*]	5.00	7.89
RSFSR	6.32	9.07
Ukraine	3.12	6.16
Belorussia	4.35	6.71
Moldavia	1.78	7.77
Lithuania	4.88	7.92
Latvia	5.63	8.94
Estonia	6.21	10.23
Georgia	1.14	4.46
Armenia	1.38	4.89
Azarbaidzhan	1.57	4.28
Mid-Eastern region (Uzbek, Kirghiz, Tadzhik, and Turkmen)	2.13	4.53
Kazakh	5.46	8.59

[*] The national averages in this table and Table 16.5 differ
slightly because of different methods of estimation.

Source: Vladimir G. Treml, "Production and Consumption of
Alcoholic Beverages in the USSR: A Statistical Study," Journal of
Studies on Alcohol 36, no. 3 (1975): 298.

The economic, social, and political adverse effects of heavy drinking are thus concentrated mainly in Slavic regions. This, needless to say, adds another dimension to the complex and difficult nationality problem in the Soviet Union.

3. Sex and Age Differentials. There are virtually no data on differentials in consumption of alcohol by sex with the exception of a general observation, which is generally supported by international experience, that the percentage of drinkers is higher among men than women. [6] A recent article on alcoholism in the Soviet Union published in Literaturnaia Rossiia stated that alcoholism was increasing among women faster than among men but no data was provided. [7]

One important factor must be noted with respect to international comparisons of per capita consumption of alcohol. As a result of World War II there are significantly more females than males in the Soviet Union. According to the census data the ratio of females to males (15 years or older) was 1.35 in 1969 and 1.27 in 1970. Since in most countries the female/male ratio is close to one, the per capita consumption of alcohol not corrected for the sex structure of the population would tend to understate the prevalence of drinking in a country with an abnormally high female/male ratio such as the Soviet Union.

No data on age distribution of drinkers are available but, as in the case of male/female drinking, there is some evidence of increasing drinking among minors. [8]

4. Composition of Total Alcohol Consumed. The composition of the absolute alcohol consumed by the Soviet population is changing in a favorable direction, that is, the share of alcohol consumed in the form of hard liquor is gradually declining as wine and beer are becoming more popular. In prerevolutionary Russia, vodka and similar strong beverages constituted 89 percent of total alcohol consumed. [9] In the period of this study the share of alcohol consumed in the form of strong beverages declined from 78 percent in 1957 to 53 percent in 1972 on the basis of state-retail trade statistics; if we would add the illegally home-produced beverages, the shares of hard liquor would be respectively 86 percent and 63 percent (see Tables 16.7 and 16.8).

It must be added, however, that an increasing share of all wine consumed in the Soviet Union is fortified and that the alcohol content of fortified wines is increasing as well. Between 1956 and 1967 the share of fortified wines increased from 77 percent to 85 percent of all wines produced. [10] The beneficial effect of the relative decrease of the share of strong beverages is accordingly somewhat dampened.

5. Illegal Home Production of Alcohol. Illegal home distillation of alcohol from grains, potatoes, sugar beets, and sugar and production of the so-called samogon is widely spread in the Soviet Union, particularly in rural areas. The bulk of samogon is probably produced

TABLE 16.8

Illegal Production and Consumption of Samogon
in Soviet Rural Areas, 1957-72
(40 percent alcohol content,
millions of liters)

	Low Estimate	High Estimate
1957	825	1,076
1958	930	1,024
1959	770	902
1960	783	938
1961	808	933
1962	980	1,075
1963	1,040	1,119
1964	1,013	1,278
1965	1,053	1,153
1966	1,028	1,173
1967	1,055	1,211
1968	1,155	1,303
1969	1,388	1,430
1970	1,348	1,381
1971	1,238	1,305
1972	1,108	1,218

Source: Vladimir G. Treml, "Production and Consumption of Alcoholic Beverages in the USSR: A Statistical
Study," Journal of Studies on Alcohol 36, no. 3 (1975): 306.

for home consumption but some is sold in rural communities and finds
its way into the urban markets (see Table 16.8).

In the five-year period from 1967 to 1972 the population consumed
annually about 1,500 million liters of absolute alcohol in the form of
different state-produced beverages and about 500 million liters of
absolute alcohol distilled illegally.[11]

6. Agricultural Inputs into Alcohol. The cost of producing these
large quantities of alcohol is, needless to say, quite high and places a
heavy burden on Soviet agriculture. In the last five years, the alcoholic beverage industry used about 3 percent of the net output of grain,
6 percent of potatoes, 6 percent of sugar beets, and 60 percent of
molasses. Assuming that most samogon is distilled from potatoes or
sugar, illegal home production preempts an additional 5 percent of
the net output of potatoes and 6 percent of sugar beets.[12]

TABLE 16.9

Soviet Retail Trade and Taxation of
Alcoholic Beverages, 1957–73
(millions of rubles)

	Retail Trade	Changes in Stock	Total Supply	Turnover Tax
1957	8,497	-51	8,446	6,736
1958	9,356	819	10,175	8,171
1959	9,770	63	9,833	7,894
1960	10,737	-393	10,344	8,242
1961	11,237	-232	11,005	8,777
1962	12,349	90	12,439	9,898
1963	13,101	197	13,298	10,542
1964	13,944	357	14,301	11,291
1965	15,213	304	15,517	12,253
1966	16,831	238	17,069	13,342
1967	18,843	-94	18,749	14,614
1968	20,367	-219	20,148	15,733
1969	21,924	168	22,092	17,111
1970	23,850	1,431	25,281	19,425
1971	25,787	809	26,596	20,344
1972	27,372	-331	27,041	20,711
1973	28,924	-534	28,390	n.a.

Source: Vladimir G. Treml, "Production and Consumption of Alcoholic Beverages in the USSR: A Statistical Study," Journal of Studies on Alcohol 36, no. 3 (1975): 292, 302.

7. Tax Revenues and the State Budget. It is difficult to over-estimate the fiscal importance of sales of alcoholic beverages in the Soviet Union. As in prerevolutionary Russia, the tax on alcohol has been one of the mainstays of the Soviet state budget.[13] In the last 10 to 15 years, turnover taxes collected on sales of alcoholic beverages in retail trade and in dining and drinking establishments (see Table 16.9) comprised some 10 to 12 percent of all state revenues and more than 30 percent of all taxes paid by the population. In another parallel with pre-1917 Russia we may note that taxes on alcohol in the last 15 years have just about covered, and in the last few years even exceeded, Soviet defense spending.[14] The financial benefits derived by the state from alcohol are not restricted to tax receipts. Indirect evidence sug-

gests that the production of alcoholic beverages is highly profitable,[15] and so is trade and distribution of these products.

8. Personal Expenditures on Alcoholic Beverages. Alcoholic beverages use up a significant share of the family's budget in the Soviet Union. Since the late 1950s alcoholic beverages comprised between 27 and 29 percent of all food sales in state retail trade and between 15 and 17 percent of all sales.[16]

In the late 1960s expenditures on alcoholic beverages as the share of family budget ranged from some 10 percent for low-income to 15 percent for high-income urban families, and from 7 percent to 8 percent for rural families.[17] In the late 1960s an average urban employee was spending approximately two months' salary on alcoholic beverages. International comparisons would be meaningless, as the Soviet incomes and expenditures are not directly comparable to incomes and expenditures in the West because of different taxation, subsidies, and provisions for free services.

9. General Impact. Measurement of the adverse effects of such phenomena as heavy drinking is always difficult, and the absence of any relevant aggregate statistics makes it impossible in the Soviet case. Scanning of Soviet literature gives the impressionistic picture that could be expected in a country with a high per capita consumption of alcohol: a high degree of correlation between drinking and crime, particularly juvenile crime, traffic and industrial accidents, impaired labor productivity, absenteeism, and a host of medical problems; heavy drinking by one of the spouses is one of the major causes of divorce, and the husband's drinking is given as one of the principal reasons for wives' decisions not to have children. Unfortunately, there are virtually no data describing these phenomena, and it is impossible to say what the overall impact is or how the Soviet Union compares in this respect with other countries.

10. Demographic Impact. There is, however, one adverse demographic trend that can be quantified and that is probably linked to increased consumption of alcohol in the Soviet Union. As we know from published data the crude death rate has been increasing in the Soviet Union since the early 1960s: From 6.9 deaths per 1,000 (the lowest crude rate in Russian history) reported for 1964, the rate has increased to 8.6 deaths per 1,000 in 1973. Some of this increase was expected and is because of the changing age-sex structure of the population, but not all of it can be attributed to these factors. Recently, Soviet demographers have begun referring to other causes of the unfavorable changes in mortality rates. Academician T. Riabushkin, one of the leading Soviet statisticians, noted at a 1973 conference "an adverse trend of rising male mortality among some age cohorts. The factors causing increasing deaths among males are traumatism of all

types, increased consumption of alcoholic beverages, and others."[18]
A similar reference to alcoholism as a cause of increased male mortality was made in connection with analysis of demographic changes
in the Soviet Union and Eastern Europe by another Soviet demographer.[19]
In fact, the available data for both sexes indicate that since the mid-
1960s age-specific death rates have been rising for all cohorts starting
with the age of 30. The change is striking: Examination of available
data shows that between 1939 and 1964 with practically no exceptions,
age-specific mortality was declining. For the ages from 0 to 29 this
trend has continued until the present, but in 1963-64 the mortality
rate for all cohorts in ages 30 and over started to rise and has continued to rise. The available data for a few selected years suggest
that increases in mortality for ages 30 and over is particularly marked
among males, resulting in a widening of male-female life expectancy
differential from 8 years in 1958-59 to 10 years in 1971-72.[20]

FISCAL DILEMMA: POLICY ALTERNATIVES

The most difficult problem facing the Soviet government today
in its genuine effort to combat alcoholism is the issue of taxation and
price.

The Tsarist government relied heavily on revenues from the
spirits monopoly, which in the 1900-13 period provided approximately
three quarters of all indirect taxes and between 25 and 30 percent of
all state revenues. Such a high degree of dependence on a single commodity tax was, of course, fiscal folly as the government painfully
learned in 1914 when in a frenzy of war-produced patriotism the production and sale of spirits were discontinued, plunging the budget into
deep deficit.

Since the early 1930s the Soviet treasury has relied on indirect
taxes, particularly on the tax on alcohol, for the bulk of its revenue.
Today, the turnover tax on alcoholic beverages still yields some 11
to 12 percent of all state revenues. Its importance is so great that
no antialcohol measure can be contemplated without considering its
impact on tax earnings. And, needless to say, the higher the absolute
ruble effect of a planned measure, the more careful the government
must be and the more objections the powerful Ministry of Finance is
likely to raise.[21]

The Soviet government showed little if any concern with the
problem of heavy drinking and alcoholism in the immediate postwar
period. The production of alcoholic beverages, particularly of vodka
and grape wines, was expanding very rapidly. In line with the general
policy of gradual reduction of consumer goods prices, the prices of

alcoholic beverages were cut several times. Between 1947 and 1957 the price of vodka was cut five times for a net decrease of over 60 percent. [22]

The per capita consumption of absolute alcohol for the 1948-50 period was reported as 1.85. That is relatively low by international comparisons—per capita consumption for most developed nations for which the data are available are much higher. [23] These statistics are, however, somewhat misleading. Using the data on sales of alcoholic beverages in rural and urban communities for 1950 we can break the average of 1.85 into an average per capita consumption of 0.8 liters in rural areas and 3.5 liters of absolute alcohol in urban areas. The latter figure is more in line with the prerevolutionary per capita average of 3.4. [24] The very low consumption in rural areas should probably be explained, not by temperance, but by the combination of low money income and high prices of vodka under which the peasants simply could not afford to purchase much state-produced liquor and were relying on illegal home-made samogon.

Since the mid-1950s the consumption of alcoholic beverages started to rise at very rapid rates and the government began to express concern.

With his characteristic penchant for simple and drastic solutions, Khrushchev in 1958 attempted to reduce the consumption of alcohol by increasing the prices of all alcoholic beverages with the exception of beer by 20 percent. [25] However, the resulting decrease in consumption was minimal—a drop of 113 million liters[26] out of total 1957 consumption of 2,100 million liters or a decrease of 5.4 percent. In his memoirs published in the West in 1974 Khrushchev admits the failure of the measure, explaining: "I, too, thought that by raising the price of vodka we could bring the level of consumption down. But it did not work. The only result was that family budgets were hit harder than before, and people had even less money to spend on necessary goods."[27]

In December 1958 the government, apparently dissatisfied with the results of the price increase, followed through with a far-reaching decree directed at more effective control of the consumption of vodka, prohibiting sales of vodka before 10 A.M., prohibiting trade in hard liquor in many categories of stores, and limiting the consumption of vodka in restaurants to 100 grams per person. [28] In January 1959 the increase in the price of wine was rolled back to encourage consumption of beverages of low alcohol content.

Per capita consumption of alcohol continued to increase throughout the 1960s with no serious attempts by the government to check it, possibly because of the fiasco of the 1958-59 measures.

The widespread and relative ease of production of samogon is another major factor that tends to handicap state antialcohol policy. Home distillation of alcohol requires little skill, primitive instruments,

384 ECONOMIC DEVELOPMENT IN THE USSR AND EAST EUROPE

a minimal amount of space, and raw materials that are generally available—potatoes, grain, sugar, sugar beets, or fruits. Samogon-making is primarily a rural phenomenon, but some samogon is apparently also produced or at least sold in cities. This potential supply of a beverage that is readily substitutable for vodka and other liquor has long been used as an argument in favor of state production of alcoholic beverages in sufficient quantities to satisfy the demand, all the possible adverse social and health effects notwithstanding.[29]

We do not have the necessary data to fully quantify the relationship between the prices and quantities of state-produced liquor and the prices and quantities of samogon, but we can speculatively draw some tentative conclusions about the nature of the demand curve for state-produced liquor in the Soviet Union.

The available Soviet data on demand elasticities for alcoholic beverages, all their shortcomings notwithstanding, give some useful insights into the shape of the demand for these products. The data referring to the period from the mid-1950s to the mid-1960s can be summarized as follows:[30]

	Price Elasticity	Income Elasticity
Total state and cooperative retail trade	-0.904	+0.978
Urban trade alone	-0.561	+1.164
Rural trade alone (estimated)	-1.88	+0.45

Most striking is the spread between the urban and rural coefficients of price elasticity of demand. The urban coefficient is reasonable and more or less reflects international experiences: Demand for alcohol is inelastic, indicating that any increase in price would result in a less than proportional decrease in the quantity consumed and in an increase in the total expenditure. The rural coefficient, however, indicates a fairly high degree of elasticity. Any increase in the price of state-produced liquor will be followed by a more than proportional decrease in the quantity consumed. A high degree of elasticity is usually associated with availability of close substitutes and this is, of course, the case in Soviet rural areas where samogon is produced in large quantities.

The income elasticity data are equally instructive. Again, the urban coefficient of income elasticity of demand reflects international experience. The very low rural coefficient, on the other hand, is unusual. Lower income groups, as a rule, have a higher income elasticity of demand for a given commodity than do higher income groups. This is fully borne out by Soviet retail trade data, which show without exception that rural consumers have higher income elasticity of demand for industrial goods than their urban counterparts. State-produced liquor is the only exception and, again, samogon seems to be the answer.

Figure 16.1 shows an approximation of the most probable demand curve for alcoholic beverages in the Soviet Union, reflecting the price elasticities discussed in this section.

FIGURE 16.1

Demand Curve for Alcoholic Beverages in the Soviet Union

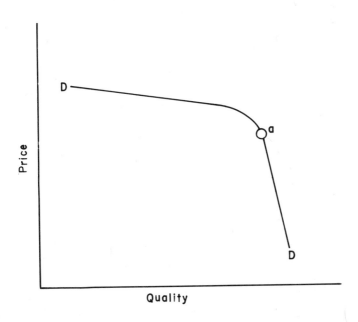

Demand is thus inelastic up to point a̱ which represents the price level in state stores at which production of samogon becomes profitable. Immediately above and to the left of point a̱ the slope of the demand curve changes sharply as samogon enters the market in larger and larger quantities and the demand becomes increasingly elastic. The demand curve does not become completely horizontal because it can be assumed that some citizens will refuse to deal in an illegal market no matter what the price differential might be. However, the demand should be becoming increasingly elastic: Samogon is clearly inferior to vodka because of impurities, but as the state price rises and samogon producers can ask for higher prices they would improve the quality of their product (by using more expensive and better-quality inputs and/or by redistillation), making it a better substitute for factory produced beverages.

The fiscal dilemma faced by Soviet policy makers is illustrated in Figure 16.2, which shows the relationship between the quantity of alcoholic beverages consumed and total state tax revenue with point a' corresponding to point a in Figure 16.1. To the right of the peak of the T-curve, which indicates maximum tax revenues, the curve is quite steep. Any price increase in this segment of the curve would result in decreasing consumption of alcohol but also in more than proportional increases in sales revenues and (assuming constant cost of production) tax collections.

Since alcoholic beverages constitute such a large share of total retail trade sales and consumers' expenditures, any significant decrease in consumption of alcohol resulting from price increases would adversely affect real income and purchases of other commodi-

FIGURE 16.2

The Relationship between the Quantity of Alcoholic Beverages
Consumed and Total State Tax Revenue in the Soviet Union

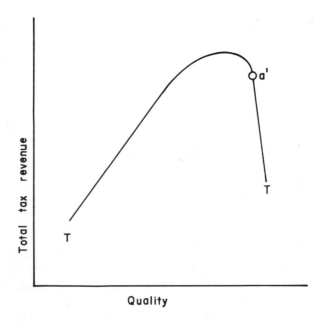

ties, particularly income-elastic commodities. In other words, consumers' rubles would be diverted away from other goods.

It will be noted that the T-curve is much flatter to the left of its highest point. Thus, if the government would continue to combat alcoholism by price increases, samogon would start entering the market in larger and larger quantities, replacing the legal beverages and both the sales revenues in state stores and tax collections would start dropping at a faster and faster rate. In addition to losses in revenues the state would now have to face the problem of increasing liquidity of the population and either begin production of larger quantities of consumer goods other than alcohol or introduce new taxes or other antiinflationary measures.

Of course, it is impossible to derive the curve shown above empirically and select the optimal tax-price point that would avoid these adverse effects. Instead of a single market the Soviet Union has a multitude of different markets with different demand elasticities and different prices of agricultural raw materials that, in turn, control the prices of samogon.

The combined effect of characteristics of the demand for alcoholic beverages, the large absolute magnitude of alcohol tax revenues, and the ready availability of illegal samogon greatly handicap the state's antialcohol policy.

The only possible way of reducing the production of samogon is by effective enforcement of antisamogon statutes, which seems to be rather difficult. It must be pointed out that, in contrast to American moonshine producers, who operate large-scale stills hidden in the woods, illegal distillation of alcohol in Soviet rural areas is small-scale and restricted to homes. [31] This probably makes effective law enforcement more difficult.

Soviet laws against samogon-making have changed over time. According to the 1948 Criminal Code of the RSFSR, which remained in effect until the late 1950s, home distillation for commercial purposes was punishable by prison terms of six to seven years and possible confiscation of personal property; home distillation for personal use was punishable by prison terms of one to two years. [32] Since 1962 the Criminal Code of the RSFSR prescribes one to three year prison terms with or without confiscation of property for commercial distillation, and a prison term up to one year or a fine of up to 300 rubles for noncommercial use. Purchasers of samogon are subject to a 50-ruble fine. [33]

However, all authorities agree that legal and administrative sanctions against samogon-making are not effective, and this problem continues to frustrate the antialcohol policies of the state.

THE CASE OF SUGAR VERSUS ALCOHOL

The economics of alcohol are interrelated with a number of other spheres of the Soviet economy. One such sphere that is influenced to a significant degree by alcohol policies is the production and consumption of sugar. The case of sugar versus alcohol is an involved one but worth exploring for the insights it gives into the conflicting objectives of different policies.

Greater per capita consumption of sugar was a priority goal of Khrushchev's government for the mid-1950s. [34] Genuine concern with the welfare of the consumer was probably reinforced by fiscal considerations as sugar sales yield comfortable turnover tax revenues. At the 21st Party Congress in 1959 Khrushchev announced an upward revision of previously made plans and promised doubling of the output of sugar by 1965 with a projected increase in sugar consumption from 26 to 41-44 kg per person (1 kg equals 2.2 pounds). [35]

Following party directives large tracts of land were transferred to sugar beet production and massive doses of capital investment expanded sugar refinery capacities significantly. Sugar output increased rapidly and Khrushchev's target of 10 million tons was in fact exceeded by 1965. However, the population did not benefit from the larger supply of sugar to the promised extent. The main reason for this was the tie-in between sugar and the distillation of samogon.

Soviet statistical studies indicate that sugar is moderately price elastic and income inelastic, that is, price changes result in more than proportional changes in sales, and increases in income result in less than proportional growth of sales. [36] Thus, since the government could not rely on the effects of slowly rising incomes, the only way of increasing sugar consumption was by cutting retail prices. In fact, the price of sugar was cut by 6 percent in the 1960-63 period and again by 2 percent in 1966. However, both the increase in income and the price cuts were clearly not sufficient to induce the population to buy more sugar. Between 1960 and 1965 the output of sugar increased by 73 percent, while sales in retail trade increased by only 34 percent, resu'ting in a rapid build-up of stocks of unsold sugar. By 1962 the combined inventories of sugar in industry and wholesale and retail trade rose to 4.8 million tons or 60 percent of that year's output.

Thus, while Khrushchev's output target was met in 1965, consumption of sugar reached only 34 kg per person—far short of the projected 41-44 kg. The government was, however, reluctant to engage in drastic price cuts that would have expanded sugar sales because of the tie-in between the prices of sugar and vodka. Home distillation of alcohol from sugar is simple, and even a novice can easily obtain between 0.2 and 0.3 liters of alcohol per kg of sugar. The resulting samogon is of inferior quality, but the price differential makes home distilling attractive.[37] The state thus faced an impasse—to increase the consumption of sugar its price had to be reduced, but at lower prices more sugar would be diverted into samogon making, which, in turn, would reduce sales of state-produced vodka and cut into tax revenues. Cutting the prices of both vodka and sugar was unthinkable from the point of view of both the struggle against drinking and fiscal considerations.

The problems of sugar marketing in the 1960s were compounded by expanding commercial relations with Cuba. The single-crop Cuban economy had only sugar to offer in exchange for badly needed Soviet imports, and large quantities of raw cane sugar began to flow into the Soviet Union's already overcrowded storage facilities. From an average of 200,000 tons in the late 1950s, imports of Cuban sugar jumped to 1.5 million tons in 1960 and continued to grow.[38]

Fiscal and foreign policy considerations took priority over any plans for increasing sugar consumption and keeping down the consumption of alcohol. In 1963 Soviet industry began processing sugar into alcohol—a highly wasteful method of alcohol production. In terms of Soviet state procurement prices, alcohol produced from sugar is twice as expensive as alcohol produced from corn and about 50 percent more expensive than that produced from potatoes or grain. And this is just the cost of materials, to which must be added the costs of labor, capital, power, and other inputs. But apparently all considerations of efficiency had to be discarded in the face of mounting surpluses of sugar, the growing demand for alcoholic beverages, and shortages of agricultural inputs into alcohol-making other than sugar. About 400,000 tons of sugar were used in alcohol-making in 1963; in 1964-65 only small quantities were used, and starting with 1966 the use of sugar for alcohol leveled off at about 400,000 tons per year.[39]

In the meantime, per capita consumption of sugar continued to increase, reaching 40.8 kg in 1973. Since the price of sugar remained stable, the growth in sugar consumption can be attributed mainly to the rising incomes of the population and possibly to an increasing demand for sugar for illegal distillation of alcohol. Prices of alcoholic beverages have been gradually rising and this, of course, makes samogon production more attractive. It must also be noted that other possible raw materials for samogon production, particularly potatoes, have also exhibited significant price increases, making sugar an even more attractive input into illegal distillation.

It is thus possible that the Soviet government will be forced to consider increasing the price of sugar in the near future—a measure that would prove rather unpopular but would be necessary in the overall strategy of antialcoholism policy.

RECENT ANTIALCOHOL MEASURES

Starting in 1970, the Soviet government introduced a variety of measures designed to check the abuse of alcohol in the country. It would take too much space to list and discuss all the measures enacted, and a simple listing should suffice.

In January–February 1970, a number of Soviet newspapers published new regulations limiting trade in vodka to certain shops and restricting the hours of sales to between 11 A.M. and 8 P.M. The price of vodka served in restaurants was almost doubled.[40] In July 1970 retail prices of cognac and champagne were doubled.

In the summer of 1972 a far-reaching decree of the Central Committee of the CPSU and the Soviet Council of Ministers introduced numerous restrictions on the sale of vodka, prohibited the production of vodka of 50 and 56 percent alcohol content, reduced further the hours of sale of strong beverages, and directed Gosplan and various ministries to project a gradual reduction in the production of vodka and an increase in the output of wine and beer. The Ministry of Internal Affairs was directed to expand the system of special institutions for compulsory treatment of alcoholics. Lastly, the decree prohibited free treatment of medical problems related to or caused by heavy drinking (including "traumas") and directed that alcoholic patients be denied sick leave.[41]

In January 1973 the Soviet Supreme Court met in a special session and issued directives concerning the enforcement of antisamogon statutes.[42]

In December 1973 selective price increases for vodka were announced.

And in March 1974, the Supreme Soviet of the RSFSR announced a new decree dealing with compulsory treatment and rehabilitation through labor (trudovoe perevospitanie) of chronic drinkers and the establishment of medical-labor institutions for confinement of such drinkers for periods of one to two years.[43]

It is too early to determine how successful will be the various measures outlined. It will be noted that both output and per capita consumption of vodka declined slightly in 1971-72.[44] It is, however, impossible to say whether the decline in production was a planned measure or resulted from poor harvests in these two years.

It must be noted that these new measures are much better designed than Khrushchev's campaign of 1958-59. They clearly recognize the threat of samogon and are prepared to deal with it. Increases in restaurant prices of vodka, of course, would not have the same effect on illegal home distillation since samogon is not easily substitutable for restaurant-consumed vodka. Increases in

the retail prices of cognac and champagne with no increase in the price
of vodka would also have the same effect since samogon is not a substitute for these two beverages.

Administrative and legal sanctions against samogon are also
being strengthened, and Soviet law-enforcement agencies are repeatedly reminded of their duties.

The antialcohol campaign that started in 1970 is obviously not
completed yet and there are a host of other problems the government
has not faced. The most serious problem, the one least understood
and the one that would be most difficult to correct and remove, is the
cause of heavy drinking.

A NOTE ON STATISTICAL DATA

As was pointed out above, the Soviet official statistical sources
offer virtually no information on production, sales, and consumption
of alcoholic beverages in the Soviet Union. Thus, most of the statistical series have been estimated by the author using fragmentary data
found in such sources as monographs on the food industry, books and
journal articles on production of various alcoholic beverages, and
trade publications. [45]

The estimated series reproduced in this chapter are a part of
a longer study completed by the author earlier and published elsewhere. [46] Space considerations do not allow a fuller explanation and
documentation of the series.

Preparation of some series was relatively simple and straightforward and these series are probably fairly accurate. Thus, while
national statistical handbooks stopped publishing the vodka output data
in 1963, republic handbooks continued the series intermittently,
making possible accurate estimates of national totals. Export and
import of alcoholic data in physical units are also available, albeit
with some gaps.

Other estimates proved to be much more difficult and involved
numerous restrictive and simplifying assumptions. These series are
less reliable and contain some margin of error. Whenever possible
more than one method of estimation was employed and the results
averaged.

As far as possible the estimated series have been verified
against independently available data. The most difficult and the least
reliable series on production of samogon were derived on the basis of
the rural-urban breakdown of sales of state-produced liquor, prices
of different types of alcoholic beverages, and other data. Since certain
assumptions used in the estimation method were too restrictive, two

different sets of estimates—low and high—were provided. The resulting series were checked against a variety of data.[47]

NOTES

1. Walter D. Connor, "Alcohol and Soviet Society," Slavic Review 30, no. 3 (September 1971): 570-89 and Deviance in Soviet Society: Crime, Delinquency, and Alcoholism (New York: Columbia University Press, 1972); David E. Powell, Alcohol Abuse in Eastern Europe, a paper presented at the XII Annual Meeting of Southern Conference on Slavic Studies, University of South Carolina, October 1973; Peter Solomon, "Specialists in Soviet Policy-Making: Criminologists and Criminal Policy in the 1960's," Ph.D. dissertation, Columbia University, 1973, pp. 142-75.

2. The annual Narodnoe khoziaistvo SSSR statistical abstracts ceased publishing statistics on retail sales and changes in inventories of alcoholic beverages in 1963; in the same year publication of output of vodka in physical units was also stopped. In 1970, production data on ethyl alcohol were discontinued, and a price index for all alcoholic beverages replaced the vodka price index. The suppression of data related to drinking is even more surprising when viewed against the background of continuously improving and expanding coverage of Soviet economic statistics observed since 1957.

3. The publication of this index in the short handbook SSSR v tsifrakh v 1973 led a Washington Star-News correspondent to say in his report on increasing alcoholism in the USSR that "for the first time ever there are now official figures to prove it. . . ." John Dornburg, "Russia Won't Sober Up Despite Kremlin's Drys," Washington Star-News, September 8, 1974. In fact, this index has been appearing without interruption since the late 1950s.

4. Soviet price deflators are based on a fixed commodity sample and understate or completely neglect the upward drift of prices resulting from introduction of new products. For instance, in the case of vodka, the official price index did not register at all the withdrawal from the market of the Stolichnaia vodka, priced at 6.14 rubles per liter and the substitution of an identical one in quality and alcohol content, Extra vodka, priced at 6.92 rubles. A price index with a downward bias will, of course, overstate the value of sales index. The extent of this overstatement can be illustrated by the following comparison: The official index of sales of alcoholic beverages for 1972 is 2.83 (1957 = 100), while the index of consumption of alcohol—the next best measure in the absence of accurate sales index—is 2.26

5. Table 16.7. The figures cited exclude Kazakhstan where the aboriginal Kazakhs now constitute a minority (one-third of the total in 1970) and where the per capita consumption of alcohol is understandably closer to Slavic republics than to Muslim regions.

6. Two rather small samples found in the Soviet literature give a ratio of drinking men to drinking women in a rural area as 1.6, F. G. Grigor'ev, "Opyt organizatsii bor'by s p'ianstvom i alkogolizmom v Kanashskom raione," Zdravookhranenie Rossiiskoi Federatsii, no. 11 (1973), pp. 39-40, and as 1.9 in an urban area, A. G. Kharchev and Z. A. Iankova, eds., Sotsialnye issledovaniia: metodologicheskie problemy issledovaniia byta, no. 7 (Moscow, 1971), pp. 167-68.

7. As quoted in Christopher S. Wren, "Alcoholism Seen as Soviet Scourge," New York Times, February 11, 1974.

8. N. Khodakov, "P'ianitsa glazami vracha," Literaturnaia gazeta, July 10, 1974, p. 11.

9. A. Gertsenzon, ed., Alkogolism—put'k prestupleniia (Moscow, 1966), p. 95.

10. V. P. Zotov, Peshchevaia promyshlennost' Sovetskogo Soivza (Moscow, 1958), p. 121; Sh. G. Nazar'ian, Reforma optovykh tsen i problemy dal'neishego sovershenstvovaniia tsenoobrazovaniia v vinodel'cheskoi promyshlennosti SSSR (Erevan, 1972), p. 26.

11. The high-low estimates shown in Table 16.8 averaged and converted to alcohol on the basis of 40 percent alcohol content. There is a great variety of other illegally home-produced alcoholic beverages: "chacha," made out of the residual pressed grapes in wine-making, "tutovaia," or mulberry vodka, and "araka," produced from dates or rice. The share of these regional varieties is probably small and this study will be focused on samogon production. There is probably also significant illegal production of home-brewed beer and wines made from fruits and berries, but these are not considered here.

12. Author's estimates based on output of ethyl alcohol and use of different agricultural commodities in the production of alcohol. New output estimates are from Diamond and Krueger and Whitehouse and Havelka, further adjusted for seed requirements and cattle feed; Douglas B. Diamond and Constance B. Krueger, "Recent Developments in Output and Productivity in Soviet Agriculture," in Soviet Economic Prospects for the Seventies, U.S. Congress, Joint Economic Committee, 93rd Cong., 1st Sess. (Washington, D.C.: U.S. Government Printing Office, 1973), pp. 337-39; Douglas Whitehouse and Joseph Havelka, "Comparison of Farm Output in the U.S. and USSR, 1950-1971," in ibid., pp. 343-50·and 361-63.

13. Since pre- and post-1917 state budgets are not comparable in terms of coverage, national income is a more meaningful base for comparing the burden of alcohol taxes. In 1913 taxes on spirits

amounted to 953 million rubles (Khromov) and comprised about 5.4 percent of the national income of Russia as recalculated in accordance with Soviet principles of national income accounting as 17,725 million rubles (Vainshtein). In the period covered by this study, turnover tax on alcoholic beverages averaged about 5.9 percent of national income, that is, slightly higher than in 1913, as shown in Table 16.9. P. A. Khromov, Ekonomicheskoe razvitie Rossii v 19-20 vekakh (Moscow, 1950), p. 507; A. Vainshtein, Narodnyi dokhod Rossii i SSSR (Moscow, 1969), p. 66.

14. The relationship between defense spending and taxes on liquor is spurious and is reported here as a historical and fiscal curiosity. Most specialists agree that the true military outlays far exceed the published defense budget of the Soviet Union.

15. Soviet standard statistical sources report separate profits for only four major branches of the food industry (sugar, meat, fish, and dairy products) which account for some 60 percent of output, lumping together the remaining branches, which include wine- and vodka-making. This residual group is highly profitable as can be seen from the following: In 1972 the profitability rate (ratio of profits to capital) was 19 percent for all industry, 24 percent for the whole food industry, and 32 percent for the residual food group. Total profits from all branches of the alcohol industry, including vodka, wine, and beer production, may well be around 1-2 billion rubles.

16. The figures shown in Table 16.4 are for sales of alcoholic beverages in retail trade. To obtain expenditure data these figures must be adjusted upward to account for the markup on alcoholic beverages served in restaurants and in public dining facilities. In the late 1960s, these markups ranged from 20 percent of the retail price of wine to 50 percent on vodka (Fridman). These additional expenditures on alcoholic beverages are estimated at some 1.0-1.4 billion rubles in the 1960s. A. M. Fridman, Ekonomika i planirovanie sovetskoi kooperativnoi torgovli (Moscow, 1972), p. 391.

17. V. F. Maier, Dokhody naseleniia i rost blagosostoianiia naroda (Moscow, 1968), p. 174.

18. Voprosy ekonomiki, no. 10 (1973), p. 155.

19. R. Galetskaia, "Demograficheskaia situatsiia v stranakh-chlenakh SEV," Voprosy ekonomiki, no. 4 (1974), pp. 103-113.

20. Writing in 1963, the well-known Soviet demographer B. Urlanis explained the shorter life expectancy of males by their excessive use of tobacco and alcohol. He noted that "without doubt a radical reduction in the consumption of alcohol would lead to a reduction in life expectancy differentials." B. Ts. Urlanis, Rozhdaemost' i prodolzhitel'nost zhizni v SSSR (Moscow, 1963), p. 115.

21. It would be misleading to picture the Central Committee and Council of Ministers as being completely free to manipulate prices,

taxes, revenues, and budget. Of course, there is no serious parliamentary review of the budgetary process in the Soviet Union, but interplay between different agencies, republics, and ministries provides some measure of checks and balances. How little freedom in fiscal matters Khrushchev's government had was illustrated in the early 1960s when a gradual elimination of the personal income tax was announced. This reform was to be completed in five annual steps, but only the first two were put into effect and the reductions were discontinued in 1962 without any official announcement. This embarrassing termination of income tax reduction appears particularly unusual when we consider the fact that the projected loss of state revenue amounted to less than 0.5 percent of the budget. A. Bachurin, "Meropriiatiia krupneishego khoziaistvennogo i politicheskogo znacheniia," Voprosy ekonomiki, no. 7 (1960), p. 9. Brezhnev continued to promise to reinstitute the reform: L. Brezhnev, "Doklad na XXIII S"ezde Partii," Izvestiia, March 30, 1966, p. 6. In fact the interrupted third stage of income tax reduction was not resumed until the mid-1970s.

22. A. N. Malafeev, Istoriia tsenoobrazovaniia v SSSR (Moscow, 1964), pp. 405, 410.

23. Connor, Deviance in Soviet Society, op. cit., p. 36. Falsification of statistical data in the Soviet Union in this period is not unknown, particularly in cases when the accurate statistics would present the Soviet Union in an unfavorable light. However, approximate estimates made by the author of this study indicate that the reported per capita consumption figure of 1.85 liters of pure alcohol is fairly accurate.

24. Gertsenzon, Alkogolism, op. cit., p. 95.

25. Malafeev, op. cit., p. 338.

26. Vneocherednoi XII S'ezd KPSS, Vol. I (Moscow, 1959), p. 31.

27. N. S. Khrushchev, Khrushchev Remembers: The Last Testament (Boston: Little, Brown, 1974), p. 145.

28. Spravochnik partiinogo rabotnika, Vol. 2 (Moscow, 1959), pp. 404-08.

29. As far back as 1927 Stalin argued that "to give up vodka at present would mean to give up revenue; but there are not grounds for believing that alcoholism would be less, because the peasant would begin to produce his own vodka. . . ." E. H. Carr and R. W. Davies, Foundations of the Planned Economy, Vol. 1, part 2 (London: Macmillan, 1969).

30. L. E. Mints and L. S. Kuchaev, eds., Statisticheskoe izuchenie sprosa i potrebleniia (Moscow, 1966), pp. 69, 76; I. K. Beliaevskii et al., eds., Opyt primeneniia matematicheskikh metodov i EVM v ikonomikomatematicheskom modelirovanii potrebleniia (Moscow, 1968), p. 156; L. La Berri, ed., Planirovanie narodnogo

khoziaistva SSSR (Moscow, 1968), p. 503. Income and price elasticities are available for the total trade and for the trade in urban areas. Rural coefficients were estimated on the basis of published urban and total coefficients weighted by the percentage shares of alcoholic beverage sales in rural and urban areas.

31. On the ubiquity of samogon-making and samogon-drinking, see A. Amalrik, Involuntary Journey to Siberia (New York: Harcourt, 1970), pp. 174-75; D. Shumskii, "Samogonnyi probel," Pravda, July 16, 1973, p. 6; A. Gertsenzon, "Mnenie neravnodushnykh," Izvestiia, January 6, 1970, p. 3; and Alkogolism, op. cit., pp. 16-23, 85-89. The latter source reports that in some rural areas during holidays, samogon was being made in all households (p. 88).

32. Ugolovnyi kodeks RSFSR (Moscow, 1957), p. 118.

33. Ugolovnyi kodeks RSFSR (Moscow, 1962), pp. 82-83; Gertsenzon, "Mnenie neravnodushnykh," op. cit., p. 3.

34. In May 1956, the Central Committee and the Council of Ministers issued a directive to expand the production of sugar beets to 50 million tons by 1960 and to increase production of sugar. Ekonomicheskaia zhizn', II, p. 505.

35. Vneocherednoi, op. cit., p. 31.

36. A study of urban trade for the 1948-62 period yielded an income elasticity of demand of +0.651 and price elasticity of demand of -1.221. Mints and Kuchaev, op. cit., p. 69; see also Beliaevskii, op. cit., p. 156, and V. V. Shvyrkov, Zakonomernosti potrebleniia promyshlennykh i prodovol'stvennykh tovarov (Moscow, 1965), p. 72.

37. Responding to Khrushchev's promise of reduced output of vodka and a higher output of sugar at the 21st Party Congress, and after expressing his profuse thanks to the party, a kolkhoznik delegate made pointed reference to the prospects of transforming sugar into vodka by samogon-makers and asked for special legislation to prohibit the use of sugar in illegal alcohol distillation (Vneocherednoi, op. cit., pp. 240-41).

38. Cuba effectively pressed the Soviet Union for higher prices and larger contracted sales and, with the exception of one or two years, the Soviets did pay more than the world market price for Cuban sugar. The world sugar prices prevented the Soviet Union from reducing their sugar surpluses by exports; starting with 1961 (with the exception of 1964) the prices of Soviet exported refined sugar were lower than the prices paid for Cuban raw sugar imported into the Soviet Union. Marshall I. Goldman, Soviet Foreign Aid (New York: Praeger, 1967), pp. 161-67.

39. Both because of the high degree of inefficiency and because of political considerations, reporting of the use of sugar in the production of alcohol would have been embarrassing to the Soviet government and there were some attempts to conceal it in the general

literature. The use of sugar in alcohol production is, however, clearly presented in the technical sources such as V. G. Pykhov, Ekonomika, organizatsiia i planirovanie spirtovogo proizvodstva (Moscow, 1966), p. 27 and 2d ed. (Moscow, 1973), p. 31. See also A. P. Klemenchuk and P. K. Popov, Pishchevaia promyshlennost' RSFSR (Moscow, 1967), p. 67. The estimates given in the text are easily derived from the data presented in these sources.

40. In Moscow the announcement was published in Moskovskaia Pravda on January 30; in Leningrad in Trud on March 13. It is interesting to note that most of the measures introduced are ones that were included in the Postanovlenie of the Central Committee and the Soviet Council of Ministers of December 1958. Thus the Postanovlenie asked Central Committees and Councils of Ministers of the republics "to consider and resolve the question of increasing the price of vodka in restaurants by 50 percent of the retail price level." Spravochnik Partiinogo rabotnika, Vol. 2 (Moscow, 1959), pp. 404-08.

41. Spravochnik partiinogo rabotnika, Vol. 13 (Moscow, 1973), pp. 182-89.

42. Pravda, January 18, 1973.

43. Vedomosti Verkhovnogo Soveta RSFSR, no. 10 (804) (March 7, 1974), pp. 286-88. Incidentally, this new decree is also repetitive of measures enacted in the RSFSR by a decree of the Supreme Soviet in April, 1967, but apparently never enforced.

44. Table 16.1.

45. See such monographs as A. F. Khalaim, Tekhnologiia spirita (Moscow, 1972); Klemenchuk and Popov, op. cit.; Pykhov, op. cit.; A. S. Shakhtan, ed., Razmeshchenie pishchevoi promyshlennosti SSSR (Moscow, 1969); E. M. Tartakovskii, Planirovanie vinodel'cheskoi promyshlennosti (Moscow, 1966); I. N. Zaiats, R. V. Kruzhkova, and I. A. Petrenko, Ekonomika, organizatsiia i planirovanie vinodel'cheskogo proizvodstva (Moscow, 1969); V. P. Zotov et al., eds., Pishchevaia promyshlennost' USSR (Moscow, 1967).

46. Vladimir G. Treml, "Production and Consumption of Alcoholic Beverages in the USSR: A Statistical Study," Journal of Studies on Alcohol 36, no. 3 (1975): 285-320.

47. For example, the estimated series on samogon production (Table 16.8) gives the 1972 per capita production as 11.2 liters. This can be compared with the following estimate. Shumskii, op. cit., p. 6, provides the data that makes it possible to calculate per capita production of samogon in rural areas of the Kharkov region in 1972 as between 7 and 10 liters. It is impossible to say how representative the region is, but the estimates do confirm the series, particularly when we consider that Shumskii refers only to samogon from such inputs as sugar beets and potatoes. In another reference, Gertsenzon,

Alkogolism, op. cit., p. 88, reports that a 1960 study of retail trade in the Dmitrov raion of the Moscow oblast indicated that the quantity of yeast purchased by the population was far in excess of the requirements for home baking. A total of 800,000 liters of samogon could have been produced from the excess yeast in a 15-month period, according to Soviet authors. The Dmitrov raion appears to be representative for at least the Moscow oblast: For instance, per capita liquor sales in 1960 were 83.5 rubles for the oblast and 83.6 for the raion. Using estimates for raion population, we obtain an estimated per capita output of samogon between 4.3 and 5.1 liters. The series shown in Table 16.8 gives the estimated national average as between 3.7 and 4.4 liters. Thus, Gertsenzon's data tends to confirm the accuracy of the estimated samogon series.

NAME INDEX

Balassa, B., 4
Bergson, A., 4, 133, 134, 138
Bognar, J. 135, 137
Brezhnev, Leonid S., 160, 171, 178,
    179, 186, 187, 234, 242, 246, 249
Brubaker, E. R., 4, 43
Burlakov, N., 236
Butz, Earl, 191

Ceausescu, N., 291, 296
Connor, Walter, 368
Csikos-Nagy, B., 136, 137, 307, 316

Desai, P., 4, 5
Dubcek, A., 286

Emelyanov, A. M., 178, 179, 185

Felfoldi, Ianos, 310
Fidler, M., 56

Garbuzov, V. F., 173, 174
Greenslade, Rush, 49, 50

Harrod, Roy, 5, 22, 30, 38, 41, 149
Hicks, John R., 29
Hotelling, Harold, 64

Kadas, Coloman, 63, 64
Kalecki, Michal, 39
Kaplan, Norman N., 4
Khrushchev, Nikita, 44, 157, 158,
    160, 166, 171, 173, 176, 179,
    185, 186, 187, 191, 193, 218,
    249, 279, 280, 383, 388
Kolakov, F.D., 165
Kornai, Janos, 136
Kosygin, A., 348
Krueger, Constance, 173
Kuibyshev, V., 128

Liberman, Yevsei, 181

MacMillan, Carl, 91
Marton, J., 316
Marx, Karl, 336
Melnikov, Academician, 231
Moorsteen, R., 4
Musgrave, R. A., 321

Nesmeyanov, A. M., 193
Noren, James H., 4, 50
Nove, Alex, 187

Palander, T., 63, 69
Patolichev, N., 90
Polyansky, D., 181
Ponomarev, G., 166
Powell, P. R., 4
Pryor, Frederic, 134, 324

Raskin, G. F., 231
Riabushkin, T., 381
Ricardo, David, 336
Robertson, Wade, 49, 50
Rosefielde, S., 91, 127

Solomon, Peter, 368
Stalin, J. V., 218, 306
Strumilin, S., 189
Suslov, I. F., 210

Thunen, J. H. von, 63
Toda, Yasushi, 49
Treml, Vladimir, 50, 56

Vancsa, Jeno, 315
Vicinich, A., 340
Voronov, G. I., 189

Weber, Max, 63, 64, 65, 69
Weitzman, M. L., 4, 5, 6, 20, 21,
    22, 23, 41, 42, 43, 149
Whalley, John, 49
Whitehouse, Douglas, 50
Wilczynski, J., 325

All-Union Congress of Kolkhozniki, 181, 183, 188
All-Union Kolkhoz Council, 188
All-Union Scientific Research Institute on Corn, 232
amelioration (see, land improvement)
amortization, 80, 166, 349, 363
animal husbandry (see, livestock)
armaments industries (see, defense industries)
artificial insemination, 236
associations, 351, 359, 360
Austria, 310
autarky, 90, 104, 137, 172, 190, 196, 238, 311
autonomy of the farm management, 65, 180, 190, 290-92, 293, 296-98, 299, 348, 349 (see also, management in agriculture)
Azerbaijan, 325

Baltic republics, 336 (see also, Latvia)
bank credit (see, credit)
banks, 187, 348, 350, 353, 355
Bashkir ASSR, 233
Belorussian SSR, 218, 262, 265, 268, 272, 273, 274, 276, 277, 278, 279, 281, 282, 283
Benelux Countries, 310
Bialystok wojwodztwo, Poland, 262, 265, 268, 273, 274, 276, 277, 278, 279, 280
bilateral trade, 125-26, 127
bonuses, 80, 177, 291, 293, 294, 298, 360, 362
branch structure of production, 4, 23, 24, 27, 31, 48-49, 148-49
breeding (see, livestock)
Britain (see, United Kingdom)
budget, the state, 48, 173, 348, 349, 350-51, 353, 357, 361, 363
Bulgaria, 284, 286-90, 293-95, 297, 300, 301, 311
bureaucratic methods, 136, 145, 217, 281, 353-54, 360, 364 (see also, direct controls)

"campaigning" methods, 160, 186
Canada, 126, 174, 282
canals, 230-31

capital allocation, 49, 51, 56
capital charges, 52, 80, 349, 350, 357, 361, 362, 363-64
capital flows, 151
capital goods, 51, 208
capital goods sector, 52-53, 54, 59, 60
capital intensity, 48, 49, 52-53, 54, 56, 59, 60, 127, 152, 188, 196
capital/labor ratios, 48, 49, 52-53, 54, 128, 147, 150, 165
capital-labor substitution, 4, 7, 18, 22, 33, 38, 147
capital/output ratios, 7, 22, 29, 30, 43, 48, 52, 148, 149, 164-65
capital, returns to, 52-53, 56, 57, 59, 60, 150, 207, 349
capital share, 4, 21, 39, 149
capital stock, 5, 18, 23-24, 39, 49, 50, 51, 53, 54, 149, 164, 196, 357
catch-up phenomenon, 4, 7, 23, 39
cattle (see, livestock)
Central Asian regions, 171, 230-31
Central Nonblacksoil Region, 180, 215, 226, 227, 228, 234, 237
central planning office (see, planning authorities)
centralization in agriculture, 195, 279, 286-87, 290, 291-93, 297 (see also, agriculture-organizational structure)
centralized planning, 79, 81, 82, 83, 158, 195 (see also, centrally planned economy)
centralized revenue system, 316
centrally determined decisions, 79, 80, 82, 158
centrally planned economy, 63, 64, 75, 79, 96, 158
chemical industry, 164, 165
chemicalization of agriculture, 157, 165, 170, 184, 194
cholesterol, 251
cities' hierarchy, 62-63
climate, effect on agriculture, 162, 165-66, 171, 195, 196, 241, 243, 261
coal export and import, 110, 123, 126, 127

foreign technology, 27, 30, 44, 117
foreign trade, 84-85, 90, 91, 95, 96,
    126-28, 137, 138, 140
foreign trade enterprises, 85-86, 306
France, 310
freedom to change employment, 188
fruit growing, 177, 274, 293

Gdansk, 175
General Consumer and Marketing
    Cooperatives, Hungary, 291
Georgia, 325
German Democratic Republic, 117,
    217, 284, 286, 287, 290, 291,
    294, 297, 298, 299, 300, 311
Germany, Federal Republic of,
    169, 360
"gigantomania," 158, 187
Glavki, 360
Gorkiy Oblast, 233
Gosbank, 187
Gosplan, 162, 229, 390 (see also,
    planning authorities)
grain, export, 191, 192, 311; im-
    port, 115, 124, 126, 172, 191,
    195, 223, 224, 249; prob-
    lems, 195; production, 169, 171,
    172, 176, 177, 178, 205, 225,
    226, 228, 229, 237, 242, 246,
    249, 265; purchasing system (see,
    procurement of agricultural pro-
    duce)
Grodno province, 279
gross agricultural product, 160, 162,
    181, 191, 192-94, 228
gross output indicators, 169
gross revenue, 80

handicraftsmen, 323
harvest failure (see, crop failure)
heavy industry, 60, 83, 91, 96, 109,
    115, 116, 127, 166
Heckscher-Ohlin theory of trade, 91
High Council of Agriculture, Romania,
    291
high priority industries, 48, 49, 54,
    56-57, 59, 60, 128, 150, 151
horses, 277-78, 280, 310
housing, 163, 185, 218 (see also,
    rural housing)
human capital, 215

Hungary, 80, 84, 134, 135, 138, 145,
    218, 284, 286, 287, 289-90, 292,
    298, 299, 300, 301, 306, 317;
    Reform of 1968 (see, New Eco-
    nomic Mechanism); Uprising of
    1956, 306

ideological motivation, 79, 157, 162,
    186, 195, 196
illegal home production of alcohol,
    378, 383, 384, 387-88, 389-90
imperfect competition, 80
import, 90, 91, 104, 109, 116-17,
    118-27
import/consumption ratios, 109
import, dependence on (see, eco-
    nomic dependence)
import of agricultural products, 115,
    125, 191, 195 (see also, import
    of feeds; grain, import)
import of breeding cattle, 236
import of consumer goods, 91, 124-26
import of feeds, 91, 194, 223, 237-38
import of investment goods, 27, 43-
    44, 91, 96, 116-17, 123, 140, 310
import substitutes, 137, 140
incentives, 79-80, 81, 82, 83, 96,
    127, 136, 157, 170, 185, 291-92,
    316, 361
income differentials between rural
    and urban workers, 164, 185,
    186, 194, 214
income distribution, 80, 321
inconvertibility, 145
India, 191
industrial location (see, location of
    economic activity)
industrial output, 3-5, 7, 23, 29,
    31, 36, 39, 43, 44, 48-50
industrial relations, 83, 84, 85
industrial sites, 63, 73
industrial structure (see, branch
    composition of production)
industrialization, 195-96, 212
industries procuring agricultural
    produce, 163-64
industries supplying agriculture,
    163, 165, 166
inflation, 85, 148, 317, 322
infrastructure, 63, 64, 163 (see also,
    agricultural infrastructure)

location theory, 63, 64, 65, 69 (see
    also, socialist theory of location)
low-priority industries, 48, 49, 50,
    54, 56, 59, 60, 123, 127, 150-51
Lublin wojwodztwo, Poland, 262,
    265, 268, 272, 273, 274, 275-
    79, 280

machine-building industry, 83, 117,
    122, 164, 166 (see also, en-
    gineering industry)
machine-tractor stations, 190, 208
machines and equipment, 23, 24, 44,
    51, 53, 116 (see also, agricul-
    tural machinery)
macroeconomic management, 81,
    136, 145, 348, 350
management, 81, 83, 84, 85, 348,
    362, 364
management in agriculture, 180,
    186, 187, 190, 241, 279, 290,
    291, 292-94, 296-97
management, remuneration of, 80,
    83 (see also, bonuses)
man-hours, 6, 7, 29
manpower allocation, 152, 157
market economies, 63, 95, 350, 362
market mechanism, 63, 64, 81, 82,
    84, 87, 307, 324, 350
marketed agricultural output, 162,
    179, 181, 182, 194, 208, 307
material balances, 352
meat, 174, 175-78, 180, 183, 185,
    193, 194, 225, 227, 233, 246,
    249, 251, 272, 313, 315 (see also,
    livestock products)
mechanization of agriculture (see,
    agriculture, mechanization of)
merger of farms (see, farm amal-
    gamation)
metals and minerals, 109, 110, 124
metallurgy, 83, 109, 110, 122, 124
microeconomic considerations, 81,
    136, 317
Mid-Eastern republics, 373
migrating agricultural laborers, 309
migration, 214, 216, 227, 290
milk, 175-77, 180, 182, 185, 225,
    227, 249, 251, 252, 259, 268,
    313 (see also, dairy products)
mining, 110

ministries, 84, 135, 173, 188, 189,
    190, 291, 293, 294, 297, 307,
    334, 351, 353, 356, 358, 359,
    360, 362, 390
modernization, 127, 135
Moldavian SSR, 177, 234, 235
monetary policy, 81
monopoly power, 60, 324
mortality rates, 381-82
Moscow Oblast, 233
MTS (see, machine-tractor stations)
multilateral trade, 126
Muslim population of the Soviet
    Union, 373

nationalization of industry, 323-24
nationalization of land, 324
natural resources, 110, 115, 127,
    157
New Economic Mechanism (NEM),
    Hungary, 80, 84, 86, 87, 133-45,
    306-17
new lands, 169, 171, 180, 192, 205
new products, 148
Ninth Five-Year Plan (1971-75),
    Soviet Union, 158, 163, 164, 166,
    184
Nonchernozem (see, Central Non-
    blacksoil Region)

Ob-Pavlodar Canal, 230
oil export, 110
organizational efficiency, 4, 31 (see
    also, institutional obstacles to ef-
    ficient allocation of resources)
output mix of the farms, 180, 217
overstatement of Soviet output, 148,
    150

packaging, 170, 207
patents, 27
payback periods, 47, 52
peasantry, 181, 225, 280, 282, 283,
    323
pensions, 188
physiocrats, 336
piece-rate system, 292-93
planners' inertia, 116, 117, 127
planning authorities, 64, 79, 81, 83,
    90-91, 136

self-sufficiency (see, autarky)
seller's market, 166
services for agriculture, 163
Seven-Year Plan (1959-65), Soviet
    Union, 160, 163, 193
Shchekino combine, 164
Siberian rivers, 230
size of production units in agricul-
    ture, 158, 165, 187, 188, 189,
    196, 205, 210, 228, 254, 280,
    281, 286, 291, 295, 296, 297-98
slowdown of industrial growth, 3, 5,
    6, 7, 24, 41, 135, 147, 149
social costs, 79
social discontent, 317
social efficiency, 63
social security, 187, 216 (see also,
    pensions)
socialist theory of location, 63, 75
soil differences, 262
sovkhozes (see, state farms)
sown area (see, cultivated area)
soybean, 232
spare parts, 166, 212, 309
specialization of sectors for export,
    96, 104, 110, 115, 127-28
specialized agricultural groups
    (Hungary) (see, agricultural
    associations)
specialized farms, 162, 163, 178,
    180, 186-87, 217, 228, 232, 233,
    286, 294, 295-96, 297, 299, 301,
    315
stabilization, 321
Stalinism, 125, 168, 216, 218
standard of living (see, living condi-
    tions)
State Committee of Procurements,
    Soviet Union, 180
state farms, 162, 166, 173-74, 176-
    77, 179, 181, 183, 185-88, 189,
    205-06, 232-33, 234, 241, 259,
    261-62, 265, 268, 273, 278,
    279, 281, 284, 286, 290, 292-93,
    297, 300, 301, 307, 358
State Farms Economic Concern,
    Bulgaria, 293
Stations for Mechanizing Agriculture,
    Romania, 290, 291, 297
statistics, the quality of Soviet, 95,
    147, 157, 160, 162, 351, 353,
    369, 391

storage, 164, 170, 276, 279, 281
"subjective" policies, 186
subsidization of agriculture, 83, 84,
    172, 173-75, 176, 194, 223, 280
success indicators, 127, 349, 350,
    364
sugar, 251, 388-89
sugar beets, 177, 180, 265
synthetic foods, 193
Szczecin, 175

Tadzhik SSR, 177
Tambov Oblast, 234-35
tariffs, 137, 145
taxes, 48, 60, 63, 80, 83, 85, 86,
    137, 173, 174, 216, 316, 322,
    323, 327, 329, 333-34, 335, 340,
    342-44, 368, 379, 380, 382,
    386-87, 389
tea, 190
technical crops, 169, 170, 171, 180
    (see also, flax; sugar beets)
technological gap, 27, 30, 44
technological levels, 117, 125-27
technological progress, 3-5, 21, 22,
    23, 27, 29, 30, 33, 36, 41, 43,
    44, 91, 117, 126, 147-49, 207
terms of trade of agriculture, 176
trade specialization, 91
trade unions (see, labor unions)
Transcaucasian region, 171, 373
transfers, 186, 322
transportation, 166, 183, 185, 195,
    196, 214, 276, 279, 324
transportation costs, 63, 65, 75, 214
trudoden (see, workday)
TsSU, 162, 174, 193
Turkmen SSR, 177

Ukrainian SSR, 177
undercapitalization of agriculture,
    164
Union of Agricultural Production
    Cooperatives, Romania, 291,
    292, 293
United Kingdom, 169, 172, 174
United States, 27, 30, 44, 52, 164,
    166, 169, 171, 172, 174, 196,
    241, 242, 243, 246, 249, 251,
    252, 261, 310
U.S.-Soviet agreement of 1972,
    192

unsalable goods, 135
Uralsk Oblast, 231
urban population, 162
urbanization, 63, 75
utilities, 324
vegetable growing, 162, 171, 177, 191, 274, 293
vegetable oils, 251
Virgin Lands (see, new lands)
Volga-Ural Canal, 231
Volga Valley, 231
Volgograd Oblast, 231

wages, 80, 82, 83-84, 87, 127, 136, 176, 185, 186, 187, 279, 282, 283, 292, 309, 310, 313, 316, 317, 349, 359
Western countries, 117, 145, 164, 174, 175
Western Europe, 30, 166, 196

wheat, 84, 172, 173, 176, 224, 231
work brigade, 170, 292
workday, 185, 292, 316
work discipline, 82
working capital, 22, 187, 349, 357, 363
working hours, 5, 23, 31, 44, 147-49, 185, 195
world grain market, 192
World War II, impact of, 29-31, 148, 279, 306

yields, agricultural, 169, 170, 172, 223, 226, 227, 228, 229-30, 237, 242, 246, 249, 265, 268, 275, 276, 279, 281, 282, 311, 313
Yugoslavia, 183

Zveno, 189

LIST OF CONTRIBUTORS

ABOUCHAR, ALAN
Department of Political Economy,
University of Toronto,
Toronto, Ontario, Canada

BUSH, KEITH
Radio Liberty,
Munich, Germany

CLAYTON, ELIZABETH
Economics Department,
University of Missouri–St. Louis,
St. Louis, Missouri

COHN, STANLEY H.
Department of Economics,
State University of New York
at Binghamton,
Binghamton, New York

DOHAN, MICHAEL R.
Department of Economics,
Queen's College of the
City of New York,
Flushing, New York

ELEK, PETER S.
College of Commerce and Finance,
Villanova University,
Villanova, Pennsylvania

FALLENBUCHL, ZBIGNIEW M.
Department of Economics,
University of Windsor,
Windsor, Ontario, Canada

FISCHER, LEWIS A.
MacDonald College of
McGill University,
Quebec, Canada

GOMULKA, STANISLAW
London School of Economics and
Political Science,
London, England

JACOBS, EVERETT M.
Department of Economic History,
University of Sheffield,
Sheffield, England

JONAS, PAUL

Department of Economics,
The University of New Mexico,
Albuquerque, New Mexico

KAHAN, ARCADIUS

Department of Economics,
The University of Chicago,
Chicago, Illinois

LAIRD, ROY D.

Department of Political Science,
The University of Kansas,
Lawrence, Kansas

NOVE, ALEC

Institute of Soviet and East European
Studies and Department of International Economic Studies,
University of Glasgow,
Glasgow, Scotland, U.K.

SCHROEDER, GERTRUDE E.

James Wilson Department of
Economics,
University of Virginia,
Charlottesville, Virginia

SCHOONOVER, DAVID M.

Economic Research Service,
U.S. Department of Agriculture,
Washington, D.C.

THORNTON, JUDITH A.

Department of Economics,
University of Washington,
Seattle, Washington

TREML, VLADIMIR G.

Department of Economics,
Duke University,
Durham, North Carolina

ZSOLDOS, LASZLO

Department of Economics,
University of Delaware,
Newark, Delaware

I. Volumes in the Social Sciences, published by Praeger Publishers, Praeger Special Studies, New York:

Economic Development in the Soviet Union and Eastern Europe, Volume 1: Reforms, Technology, and Income Distribution, edited by Zbigniew M. Fallenbuchl, University of Windsor.

Economic Development in the Soviet Union and Eastern Europe, Volume 2: Sectoral Analysis, edited by Zbigniew M. Fallenbuchl, University of Windsor.

Education and the Mass Media in the Soviet Union and Eastern Europe, edited by Bohdan Harasymiw, University of Calgary.

Soviet Economic and Political Relations with the Developing World, edited by Roger E. Kanet and Donna Bahry, University of Illinois, Urbana-Champaign.

Demographic Developments in Eastern Europe, edited by Leszek Kosinski, University of Alberta.

Environmental Misuse in the Soviet Union, edited by Fred Singleton, University of Bradford.

Change and Adaptation in Soviet and European Politics, edited by Jane P. Shapiro, Manhattanville College, and Peter J. Potichnyj, McMaster University.

From the Cold War to Detente, edited by Peter J. Potichnyj, McMaster University, and Jane P. Shapiro, Manhattanville College.

II. Volumes in the Humanities, published by Slavica Publishers, Cambridge, Mass.:

Russian and Slavic Literature to 1917, edited by Richard Freeborn, University of London, and Charles A. Ward, University of Wisconsin, Milwaukee

Russian and Slavic Literature, 1917-1974, edited by Robin Milner-Gulland, University of Sussex, and Charles A. Ward, University of Wisconsin, Milwaukee.

Slavic Linguistics at Banff, edited by Thomas F. Magner, Pennsylvania State University.

Early Russian History, edited by G. Edward Orchard, University of Lethbridge.

Nineteenth and Twentieth Century Slavic History, edited by Don Karl Rowney, Bowling Green State University.

Reconsiderations on the Russian Revolution, edited by Carter Elwood, Carleton University.

III. Additional Volumes:

"Nomads and the Slavic World," a special issue of *AEMAe Archivum Eurasiae Medii Aevi*, 2 (1975), edited by Tibor Halasi-Kun, Columbia University.

Russian Literature in the Age of Catherine the Great: A Collection of Essays. Oxford· Willem A. Meeuws, 1976, edited by Anthony Cross, University of East Anglia.

Commercial and Legal Problems in East-West Trade. Ottawa: Carleton University, Russian and East European Center, 1976, edited by John P. Hardt, U.S. Library of Congress.

Marxism and Religion in Eastern Europe. Dordrecht and Boston: D. Reidel, 1976, edited by Richard T. DeGeorge, University of Kansas, and James P. Scanlan, The Ohio State University.

Detente and the Conference on Security and Cooperation in Europe. Leiden: Sythoff, 1976, edited by Louis J. Mensonides, Virginia Polytechnic Institute and State University.